GREEK RATIONAL MEDICINE

Ratione vero opus est ipsi medicinae
(Celsus, *De medicina*, Proem, 48)

GREEK RATIONAL MEDICINE

Philosophy and medicine from Alcmaeon to the Alexandrians

James Longrigg

Routledge
Taylor & Francis Group

LONDON AND NEW YORK

First published 1993
by Routledge
2 Park Square, Milton Park, Abingdon, Oxfordshire OX14 4RN

Simultaneously published in the USA and Canada
by Routledge
711 Third Avenue, New York, NY 10017

Reprinted 2000

Transferred to Digital Printing 2005

Routledge is an imprint of the Taylor & Francis Group, an informa business

First issued in paperback 2013

Typeset in 10 on 12 point Baskerville by
Witwell Ltd, Southport

British Library Cataloguing in Publication Data
Longrigg, James
Greek Rational Medicine: Philosophy and Medicine from
Alcmaeon to the Alexandrians
I. Title
610.1

Library of Congress Cataloging in Publication Data
Longrigg, James
Greek rational medicine: philosophy and medicine from
Alcmaeon to the Alexandrians/James Longrigg.
p. cm.
Includes bibliographical references and index.
1. Medicine, Greek and Roman. I. Title.
R138.L65   1993
610'.938–dc20   92–28865

ISBN 13: 978-0-415-02594-2 (hbk)
ISBN 13: 978-0-415-6197-7 (pbk)

For Thomas and Elizabeth

Contents

Preface   viii
Introduction   1

1 Pre-rational and irrational medicine in Greece and
  neighbouring cultures   6

2 Ionian natural philosophy and the origins of
  rational medicine   26

3 Philosophy and medicine in the fifth century I:
  Alcmaeon and the pre-Socratic philosophers   47

4 Philosophy and medicine in the fifth century II:
  Pre-Socratic philosophy and the Hippocratic *Corpus*   82

5 Post-Hippocratic medicine I: Medicine and the
  Academy   104

6 Post-Hippocratic medicine II: Medicine from Lyceum
  to Museum   149

7 Early Alexandrian medical science   177

  Appendix: The role of the opposites in
  pre-Aristotelian physics   220

Notes   227
Bibliography   260
Index locorum   278
General index   287

Preface

The Greeks invented rational medicine. In an effort to ensure that this outstanding achievement was accorded proper recognition within our classical curriculum at the University of Newcastle, I set up ten years or so ago a course on the history of Greek medicine. It is, I believe, the only one of its kind offered within classics departments in the United Kingdom. In teaching this course it soon became apparent that my students required some assistance in disentangling the highly complex relationship between philosophy and medicine in the classical period. This book has been written with the modest hope that it might prove to be of some assistance here. Since the majority of my students have little or no knowledge of classical Greek, I have also taken the opportunity to translate and quote at some length a good many passages from our original sources of evidence. Although, in this latter respect, it has been suggested that a choice of less familiar source material would enable me to invest this book with a greater degree of novelty, I decided, however, only selectively to follow this advice. My reasons for doing so are threefold. In the first place, some of the more familiar passages illustrate the points at issue far more effectively than any alternative would do. (This, after all, is largely why these texts *are* familiar.) Again, I thought it would seem rather perverse to seek to illustrate inter-relationships between philosophy and medicine without reference in detail to such texts as *Ancient Medicine* (*De vetere medicina*) and *Sacred Disease* (*De morbo sacro*). And, of course, not all who read this book (it is hoped) will be specialists in this subject.

Papers based upon research in progress for this work have been presented at the Wellcome Institute in London, and at the

PREFACE

universities of Glasgow, Manchester, St Andrews, Newcastle, Oxford, Durham, Warwick and Leiden. In response to editorial invitations certain aspects of this material have been given a preliminary 'airing' in *History of Science* and in *The British Journal for the History of Science*. I am grateful to the editors of these journals for their permission to reproduce this material in the place for which it was originally intended.

I should like to express also my deep gratitude to the Wellcome Trust for twice awarding me a Research Fellowship in the History of Medicine, which enabled me to pursue my researches without distraction; to the University of Newcastle upon Tyne for granting me study leave on both occasions, and to the Small Grants Research Committee for subventions which enabled me to work at the Wellcome Library in London.

I am grateful to Professor Drachmann and to the Editor of Artemis Verlag for their kind permission to reproduce (with slight modifications) figure 7b on p. 209.

I am most grateful to Nancy Longrigg for preparing the indices.

Last, but by no means least, I should like to acknowledge the great kindness of Dr Vivian Nutton of the Wellcome Institute, who read the whole of an early draft of this work, and of Dr Hans Gottschalk of the university of Leeds, who read the penultimate chapter. Their comments have proved invaluable.

Hamsterley Mill, Durham
April 1992

Introduction

Die Philosophie ist die Mutter der Medizin in wissenschaftlichen Rücksicht, und das Wachstum der einen steht
mit der Zunahme der anderen Wissenschaft in ungetrenn-
licher Verbindung.
(K. Sprengel, *Versuch einer pragmatischen Geschichte der
Arzneikunde*, 1846, p. 2)

One of the most impressive contributions of the ancient Greeks
to Western culture was their invention of rational medicine. It
was the Greeks who first evolved rational systems of medicine for
the most part free from magical and religious elements and based
upon natural causes. The importance of this revolutionary
innovation for the subsequent history of medicine can hardly be
overstressed. Here for the first time in the history of medicine was
displayed a strikingly rational attitude which resulted in a
radically new conception of disease whose causes and symptoms
were now accounted for in purely natural terms.

This emancipation of medicine from superstition was the
outcome of precisely the same attitude of mind which the Milesian
natural philosophers had been the first to apply to the world about
them. The natural philosophers' attempts to explain the world
without recourse to supernatural intervention brought about a
transition from mythological conjecture to rational explanation.
Just as the natural philosophers had sought to explain in purely
natural terms such frightening phenomena as earthquakes, thunder and lightning, and eclipses, which had previously been
regarded as manifestations of supernatural powers, so the same
outlook was applied by the medical authors of Hippocratic treatises
to explain such frightening diseases as epilepsy (the 'Sacred

1

Disease'), apoplexy, delusions, madness and even impotence. The clearest evidence of this relationship may be seen in the adoption of the Ionic dialect by these medical authors, although Cos and Cnidus, whence the bulk of the treatises in the Hippocratic *Corpus* seem to have emanated, were both Dorian settlements.[1]

Without this background of Ionian Rationalism, Hippocratic medicine could never have been conceived. Virtually all that sets it apart and above earlier and contemporary medicine, whether Greek, Egyptian or Oriental, has been derived from this philosophical background, that is, its rational attitudes, procedures and modes of explanation; its conviction that human beings should be regarded as products of their environment, made of the same substances and subject to the same physical laws as the cosmos at large; its belief that diseases possessed their individual *physeis* (natures) – that is, they were definable strictly in accordance with natural processes and ran their course within a set period of time, totally independent of any arbitrary, supernatural interference.

Greek rational medicine was transported to Egypt and reached its most impressive climax in third-century Alexandria. Here superstitious beliefs inhibiting the dissection of the human corpse, still deeply entrenched in mainland Greece, were for a brief period abandoned by expatriate Greek doctors. (There is some evidence, too, which asserts that they even vivisected human beings.) Given support and provision by the first Ptolemies, these medical researchers achieved levels of accuracy and sophistication in anatomy which were largely unsurpassed within Western culture until the sixteenth century. Greek medicine, generally, formed the basis of Western medical theory until the nineteenth century and Greek medical deontology still exercises a powerful influence upon medical ethics to the present day.

Philosophy, however, was not only directly responsible for the rise of rational medicine, it also, for good and ill, played a continuous and important role in the development of medicine to Galen and beyond. A factor of the utmost importance in the development of rational medicine was the incorporation of biological and medical inquiries within the framework of early Greek systems of natural philosophy in the sixth and fifth centuries BC. In ancient Greece philosophers and medical men shared a common intellectual background. They subscribed largely to the same general assumptions and, to a considerable extent, adopted the same concepts, categories and modes of reasoning. Thus there developed a close and complex correlation between medicine and philosophy. Aristotle clearly recognises this intricate relationship when he remarks at *De respiratione* 480b24ff.:

> Concerning health and disease it is the business not only of the physician but also of the natural philosopher to discuss their causes up to a point. But the way in which these two classes of inquirers differ and consider different problems must not escape us, since the facts prove that up to a point their activities have the same scope; for those physicians who have subtle and inquiring minds have something to say about natural science and claim to derive their principles thence, and the most accomplished of those who deal with natural science tend to end up investigating medical principles.[2]

Such is the nature of this relationship that one distinguished student of ancient philosophy was prompted to remark that 'it is impossible to understand the history of philosophy . . . without keeping the history of medicine constantly in view.'[3] But the converse of this statement is equally true - notwithstanding Celsus' puzzling assertion that it was Hippocrates himself who 'separated medicine from philosophy'.[4] A primary focus of this book, therefore, will be upon this inter-relationship between philosophy and medicine and attempts will be made to show that it is, at times, of a greater complexity than has hitherto been generally envisaged.

Although rational aspects of Greek medicine will accordingly be emphasised in this study, it should not be assumed that irrational elements were completely eradicated from Greek medical thinking. This is patently not the case. Then, as indeed is still the case at the present day, superstitious beliefs and irrational practices were rife in medicine. It is noteworthy, for example, that it was actually during the fifth-century Enlightenment that the healing cult of Asclepius experienced a dramatic acceleration in its expansion in Greece. It seems likely that the outbreak of the plague in Athens in 430 BC played a significant role in this expansion. Again, many irrational beliefs and practices had become firmly entrenched as part of the folk-medicine of ancient Greece - especially in drug-lore and gynaecology - and were frequently unconsciously adopted even by doctors, who were otherwise fiercely opposed to superstition and irrational practices.

In employing the terms 'rational' and 'irrational' in this Introduction and elsewhere, I am well aware that I may appear to have left myself vulnerable to the criticisms of those anthropologists, sociologists and philosophers who believe that to apply modern concepts to describe earlier and/or more primitive societies results in seriously distorted conceptions of those societies. (In recent times a vigorous debate has arisen concerning this issue.) Every effort, of course, must be made to avoid misrepresentations of this nature. The interpretation of Greek medicine itself has to a certain extent suffered in this way - most especially at the hands of those scholars who persistently speak of it as 'scientific' where the investigations of the Greeks in some fields - impressively rational though they were - hardly fulfilled the strict criteria required by modern empirical science. Nevertheless, I am certainly not unique in my belief that, with all due caution, we are capable of making progress in our understanding of earlier societies. Furthermore, there seems to be no good reason why the terms 'rational' and 'irrational' should not be employed to describe the achievements of that society which was itself the first to define the distinction between them. Celsus, we may note, actually applies the Latin term *rationalis*[5] (his translation of the Greek *logistikos*) to describe a particular medical sect - the Logistici or Dogmatists[6] who, in distinction from the Empiricists, held that medicine required a knowledge of 'hidden causes' - most especially of the constitution of human beings and of the causes of disease - and believed that such knowledge could only be attained through a process of reasoning and subjecting conjecture to the test of experience. His use of this term, however, is more restricted in its application than the more comprehensive usage adopted in this book which certainly embraces Celsus' application of it, but transcends it to embrace more widely those general attempts, ultimately derived from philosophy, to account for phenomena in terms of purely natural causes without recourse to any supernatural agency.

Finally, having extolled the Greeks for their invention of rational medicine, it now behoves me to justify this praise. Doubt has recently been raised as to whether this innovation was entirely a good thing. In his book *Alexander to Actium*, Peter Green has written as follows (p. 486):

> We often hear that the most important advance the Greeks made in medicine was to slough off the incubus of religious or magical superstition, especially as regards the assignation of antecedent causes. There is, obviously, some truth in this assumption, but it can be very misleading. A perverse rational hypothesis is no improvement on a religious one: what is the point of breaking away from superstition if you promptly become a slave to some arbitrary philosophical system? Besides, the religious hypothesis often possesses psychological value, and on occasion may have physical benefits too.

It may be accepted, as Parker has recently perceptively pointed out,[7] that 'a materialist medicine, in a world where science is powerless to prove its postulates, has no more claim to popular support than the psychologically more satisfying arts of the diviner' and that 'without such proof, its theories can only be a kind of dogma, even for the physician himself.' It may also be agreed that upon an individual basis, at any rate, invocation of a religious hypothesis may, indeed, due to the placebo effect, prove more beneficial than any recourse to a rational hypothesis, perverse or otherwise. Yet it is difficult to see how continued appeal to a religious hypothesis could in itself result in significant medical advance. Nor would the replacement of one religious hypothesis, if found unsuitable, by another be likely to result in any appreciable improvement. A rational hypothesis, by contrast, if demonstrably unsuccessful and unsupported by the phenomena, could readily be replaced by another such, which would itself, in its turn, also be kept, modified or abandoned by the support afforded by the phenomena. Thus the rational hypothesis, however 'perverse', is superior to the religious hypothesis in that it is capable of being checked in the light of subsequent phenomena and, if found wanting, is then open to modification or even replacement by a further hypothesis more firmly supported by the phenomena.

1

Pre-rational and irrational medicine in Greece and neighbouring cultures

Morbos tum ad iram deorum relatos esse.
(Celsus, *De medicina*, Proem, 4)

Some records of early medicine in Babylon and Egypt have survived. Although our evidence is in an incomplete and fragmentary state, it is possible to derive some general impressions from it. There is no clear indication that these ancient physicians arrived at any rational conception of disease. Diseases were considered by them to be manifestations of the displeasure of the gods or were held to be caused by the intrusion of some demon or other. The prime purpose of the physician was to appease the god or drive out the demon which had 'possessed' the sick person's body. In order to do so he employed prayers, supplications, sacrifices, spells and incantations.

The ancient Babylonians lived in a world haunted by evil spirits. Whenever they fell ill, they believed that they had been seized by one of these spirits. In their suffering and impurity they sought medical aid and a return to their previous condition. The function of the healer was to help them achieve this end by removing the cause of their illness. Patients were required to atone for their sins and the angry god had to be placated. The treatment involved the employment of ritual involving sacrifice and incantations. In the following text, which conforms to the general pattern, Marduk, the city god of Babylon, is here instructed to make a clay figure in the image of the sick man and perform a ritual incantation to drive out the evil plague demon which had possessed him:

Go, my son [Marduk],
Pull off a piece of clay from the deep,

6

Fashion an image of his bodily form [therefrom] and
Place it upon the loins of the sick man by night.
At dawn make the 'atonement' for his body,
Perform the incantation of Eridu,
Turn his face to the west,
That the evil Plague-demon which hath seized upon him
May vanish away from him.

> (Translated in R. Campbell Thompson,
> 1903-4, vol. II, p. 101)

The usual practice was for the clay model then to be carried out of the house and destroyed, carrying away with it the demon which had been transferred into it by the magical formulae.

Epilepsy is a disease which, because of its sudden, dramatic onset and the frightening symptoms manifested during a *grand mal* attack, has been (and still is) regarded with superstitious awe. Two recently translated, duplicate cuneiform tablets,[1] which together provide the almost complete text of the twenty-fifth and twenty-sixth tablets of a medical diagnostic series known as the *Sakikku* or 'All disease', preserve invaluable evidence of Babylonian views regarding the nature of this disease. As is clearly evident from the extract quoted below, we are presented with an accurate and comprehensive description of many features of an epileptic seizure, which provokes comparison with the later and better known account in the Hippocratic treatise, *De morbo sacro* (see Chapter 2, pp. 35ff.).

12. [If at the time] of his fit [the patient] loses consciousness and foam comes from his mouth, it is *miqtu* [diurnal epilepsy].
13. [If at the time] of his fit he loses consciousness and his arms and legs bend round to the same side as his neck, it is *miqtu*.
14. If at the time of his fit . . . takes hold of him and foam comes from his mouth, an [unfulfilled] vow made by his father has seized him. He [the child] will die.
15. If at the time of his fit after it has taken hold of him foam comes from his mouth, - hand of *Lilû*.
16. If at the end of his fit when his limbs become relaxed again his bowels are sometimes seized and he has a motion, it is 'hand of ghost' [nocturnal epilepsy].
17-18. If at the end of his fit his limbs become paralysed, he

7

is dazed [or dizzy], his abdomen is 'wasted' [sc. as of one in need of food] and he returns everything which is put into his mouth . . . , - hand of a ghost who has died in a mass killing. He will die.

19-22. If at the end of his fit his limbs become paralysed, [the demon] 'pouring out' upon him so much that he loses control [of his functions]; if when he thus 'pours out' upon him his eyes are red and his face expressionless; if his *sĕr'ānu*-vessels pulsate at a quickened rate and he cries although the tips of his fingers and toes remain cold; if when the exorcist asks the sick person to repeat [a prayer] he repeats what he says to him, but after [the demon] has let him go he does not know what he said, - hand of *Lilû-la'bi*.

23. If before his fit a half of his body is 'heavy' for him and pricks him, and afterwards he has a fit with loss of consciousness and he loses control [of his functions], it is *miqtu*. At midday it will be most serious for him.

24-25. If before his fit he suffers from frontal headaches and is emotionally upset, and afterwards he . . . [. .] his hands and feet, [and] rolls from side to side [on the ground] without deviation [of the eyes] or foam[ing at the mouth], it is a fall due to emotional shock, or 'hand of Ishtar'. He will recover.

26. If when he has his fit [the fallen person] is looking sideways or the whites of his eyes deviate to the side, and blood flows from his mouth, for female [patients] it is *Lilû*, and for male, *Lilītu*.

Unlike the Hippocratic author, however, who, as shall be seen below, rejects superstitious and supernatural causation and gives an entirely natural explanation of the disease, our unknown Babylonian unequivocally maintains: 'if epilepsy falls once upon a person [or falls many] times, [it is (as a result of) possession] by a demon or a departed spirit'.

The outlook of the more prestigious and influential[2] Egyptian medicine is not dissimilar. The ancient Egyptian, too, believed that sickness was caused by evil spirits or by the anger of the gods. The surviving Egyptian medical papyri[3] consist largely of pre-scriptions of drugs interspersed with magical spells which were believed to impart efficacy to the prescriptions which follow. Many of these remedies contain noxious or offensive ingredients which were, presumably, intended to make them as unpalatable as possible to the possessing spirit. Coprotherapy is much in evidence. A good example of this nauseating practice may be seen in the *Hearst Papyrus* (85):

> O ghost, male or female, thou hidden one, thou concealed one, who dwellest in this my flesh, in these my limbs. Lo, I brought thee excrements to devour! Beware, hidden one, be on your guard, concealed one, escape!

In ancient Egypt and Mesopotamia, then, the views of the physician on the causes of disease and the operation of remedies were so linked with belief in supernatural forces that a rational understanding of the organs and functions of the body or of the operation of the remedies applied to it was impossible.

There is, however, one medical treatise, dating from early antiquity, which makes one hesitate before dismissing Egyptian medicine, at least, as being completely dominated by magic. This is the famous *Edwin Smith Surgical Papyrus*, named after its purchaser, which was copied in the seventeenth century BC from a work written in the third millennium. This treatise is organised in a systematic manner and seems, at first sight, to be free from the magical elements which pervade other Egyptian medical papyri such as the *Hearst* and the *Ebers Papyrus*. J. H. Breasted, the best modern editor and translator of the papyrus, has claimed that the work is in the true sense scientific.[4] His contention, however, has by no means been universally accepted and it has been claimed that there are magical elements contained within the treatise.[5] It is maintained that the use of such formulae as: 'it is a malady which I will contend with' or 'wrestle with' implies a belief in magic and entails that the author was still a magician at heart. This conclusion, however, does not necessarily follow since the author could be merely expressing himself figuratively or, more probably, adopting a familiar and traditional mode of expression. The surgeon would be dealing with observable physical causes. It is hardly likely, therefore, that he would regard their effect as due to possession by a demon with whom he would have to 'wrestle'. Moreover, two cases in the papyrus deal with a similar complaint: Case 18 describes a wound in the temple; Case 21 is that of a split in the temple. The surgeon 'contends' with the latter, yet merely 'treats' the former. Are we then to believe that the surgeon would consider the one to be of a mysterious magical origin, the other the result of an observable physical cause?

While this controversy cannot be definitely settled upon the available evidence, Breasted's claim is not, in my view, persuasive. It derives its plausibility from the fact that, unlike the physician, the surgeon had to deal with afflictions which were the result of observable physical causes and had little or no connection with the malignant demons of disease. (It has been suggested on the basis of the wounds described in the papyrus that its author was a surgeon in the army.) A wound caused by a weapon, tool or fall would be well understood and treated accordingly, whereas the causes of a stroke, or epilepsy, for example, would be quite mysterious and their effect regarded as due to the patient's being possessed by some demon or other. Since belief in magic is prevalent throughout the rest of the Egyptian medical papyri and pervades our earliest surviving medical literature generally, there seems to be no good reason to doubt that this particular surgeon, too, was a true child of his times and also believed in the powers of the supernatural.

H. E. Sigerist, however, influenced by Breasted's evaluation of the *Edwin Smith Papyrus*, finds in ancient Egyptian medicine 'the beginning of medical science, a science . . . which endeavoured to explain the phenomena of life and death, rationally without having recourse to the gods' and believes that 'the Egyptians anticipated views and methods of the pre-Socratic philosophers in Greece.'[6] It is true that the Greeks were well acquainted with and admirers of Egyptian medicine.[7] And, if Diodorus can be trusted, the practice of incubation, a striking feature of the healing cult of Asclepius and other cthonic cults, had its origin in Egypt.[8] It seems likely, too, that the Greeks owed a good part of their pharmacopoeia, and some of their gynaecological and (possibly) surgical techniques and practices to the Egyptians. The miraculous, tranquillising drug dispensed by Helen of Troy to soothe her guests in *Odyssey* IV. 220-32, for example, is described as a gift from a woman of Egypt. In his comedy *Peace* (*Pax* 1253), Aristophanes refers to the fame of healing drugs from that country and ingredients carrying the label 'Egyptian' appear in several Hippocratic drug prescriptions.[9] Egyptian ingredients also figure frequently in Hippocratic gynaecological treatises[10] and may reflect in addition the influence of Egyptian gynaecology generally, since both the medical papyri and the Hippocratic *Corpus* display parallel interests in 'birth prognoses'[11] and in both disorders are held to be caused by displacements of the womb.[12] In surgery, too, it has been claimed that there are similarities in the respective Egyptian and Hippocratic descriptions of wounds in the head.[13] But notwithstanding these parallels,[14] there is no firm evidence to suggest that the rational attitude manifested so strikingly in the Hippocratic *Corpus* was itself derived from Egypt along with particular borrowings.[15] It is, perhaps, worth observing here that the Greeks themselves, who are generous, indeed, over-generous, in acknowledging their intellectual debts to cultures more ancient than their own, in their views upon the origin of medicine[16] nowhere recognise any debt to Egypt.[17] Furthermore, throughout its long recorded history, Egyptian medicine reveals itself as extraordinarily static – perhaps, as has recently been suggested, because its support and sanction by ritual, by belief in magic, and by the priesthood had rendered it 'immune to revisionary processes that tend to be associated with scientific growth' and perhaps because codification and legal sanctions had further militated against change.[18] Given its petrified nature, it would, to say the least, have been exceedingly curious if Egyptian medicine should then have exercised totally disparate kinds of influence in the Heroic Age of Greece and, again, two or three centuries later.

From the Homeric poems, our earliest literary source of evidence for Greek medicine, it is patently clear that the attitudes towards sickness and disease in the Heroic Age were not sub-stantially different from those manifest in ancient Egypt and Mesopotamia, where the views of the physician on the causes of diseases and the operation of remedies are linked with belief in the supernatural. As Celsus says, 'morbos . . . ad iram deorum immortalium relatos esse', diseases were attributed to the wrath of the gods – although here the gods, for the most part, act directly and not through the intermediary of demons or evil spirits. For example, in the first book of the *Iliad* the plague which attacks the Greek army besieging Troy is represented as supernatural in origin, sent by Apollo as punishment for Agamemnon's arrogant treatment of his priest Chryses, who had come to the Greek camp to try to ransom his captured daughter:

The arrows rattled on the shoulders of the angry god when

he moved and his coming was like the night. Then he sat down apart from the ships and let fly a shaft. Terrible was the twang of the silver bow. He attacked the mules first and the swift dogs, but then he loosed his piercing shafts upon the men themselves and shot them down and continually the pyres of the dead thickly burned. For nine days the missiles of the god ranged throughout the host.

(Homer, *Iliad* I. 46-52)

Eventually, the Greeks, at the suggestion of Achilles, consulted the soothsayer Calchas. He revealed to them that Apollo had sent the disease to avenge his priest and that the god would not lift the pestilence until the girl had been returned to her father, without a ransom and with a hecatomb of oxen for sacrifice. The Greeks complied, purified themselves, cast the 'defilements' into the sea and sacrificed to Apollo. The god was placated and the plague ceased. Here we have a fairly typical example of religious medicine. A god angered at some offence sends disease; the cause of this anger is divined through augury; the god is placated by prayer and sacrifice and the sickness abates.

On a more individual level, too, the arrows of Apollo and those of his sister Artemis are held to be the cause of the sudden onslaught of disease, with Apollo responsible for killing men and Artemis women. Together they killed the six sons and six daughters of the unfortunate Niobe, who had boasted that she was superior to their mother Leto, who had produced only two children. Phrontis, Menelaus' helmsman, Rhexenor, son of Nausithous, king of Phaeacia, and many others also fell to Apollo's silver bow, while Artemis slew Laodamia, daughter of Bellerophon, and Coronis, daughter of the Lapith Phlegyas (see p. 17). Elsewhere in Greek epic other gods are held to be the cause of disease and death. In *Odyssey* IX. 411ff. the Cyclops Polyphemus, deluded by Odysseus' strategem, is told by his kinsmen that his blinding is a malady sent by almighty Zeus, and in Hesiod's *Works and Days* (238-45) it is Zeus again who sends famine and plague which kills men and renders women barren:

But for those whose hearts are set on violence and cruel deeds far-sounding Zeus, the son of Cronos, ordains punishment. Often even a whole city suffers for a bad man who sins and devises wicked deeds. The son of Cronos from heaven inflicts upon the people great misery, famine and plague together. The men perish, the women are barren and their homes become few through the cunning of Olympian Zeus.

Earlier in the *Works and Days* (100-4), however, according to some scholars, Hesiod puts forward a rather different conception of disease from that found elsewhere in Greek epic. Here Hesiod is describing how Zeus, angered by Prometheus' theft of fire on behalf of mortals, sought vengeance. To exact retribution he created the woman Pandora, so called because all the Olympians each gave her a gift, as a 'bane to men who eat bread'. When this insurmountable snare (δόλον . . . ἀμήχανον) was completed, she was sent with Hermes as a gift to Epimetheus. He, unmindful of his brother's warning, accepted her. Previously the tribes of men had lived on earth free from ills and grievous diseases. But Pandora took the lid from the jar which contained the gifts from the gods and scattered these evils. (Only Hope remained within the jar.) And, in consequence, as we learn from vv. 100-4:

> Countless plagues wander among men; for the earth is full of evils and the sea is full. Diseases spontaneously (αὐτόμαται) come upon men continually by day and by night silently bringing mischief to mortals; for wise Zeus took away speech from them.

On the basis of the verses quoted above, it has been maintained that these diseases come upon men in the natural order of things and the word αὐτόμαται emphasises that they are not despatched according to divine whim, but come of their own accord.[19] But even though the diseases are described here as having the power to act spontaneously, it should not be overlooked that initially they were the (deadly) gifts of the gods. It should also be borne in mind that the object of the Olympians' combined wrath is mankind as a whole and not any particular group or individual; the form of the myth, then, explains the lack of specificity here. In any event, it should not be assumed that in Homeric epic all diseases alike are regarded as sent by the gods. While diseases with a dramatic onset and/or frightening symptoms, like plague, are described as being of supernatural agency, it seems very doubtful that less severe and more common maladies would have been so regarded. Minor and, indeed, inglorious ailments are hardly suitable ingredients for inclusion

13

in the heroic world of Greek epic. The *Odyssey*, too, preserves a distinction drawn between severe and dramatic diseases sent by the gods and other ailments apparently not directly attributed to divine agency. In Book XI. 172ff., in a scene of great pathos in which Odysseus meets his dead mother in the Underworld, he seeks to learn the cause of her death and asks her whether it was due to the arrows of Artemis or a 'long sickness'.

> But come now, tell me this and give me an accurate answer.
> What doom of death that lays men low has been your undoing?
> Was it a long sickness, or did Artemis, shooter of arrows come upon you with her grievous shafts and destroy you?
>
> (*Odyssey* XI. 171-3)

Hesiod's conception, then, is not fundamentally different from that found elsewhere in Greek epic. Like Homer, he remains committed to an ontological conception of disease, regarding it as an entity possessing a separate existence of its own. Fränkel's further claim,[20] however, that 'from Hesiod's realisation that diseases and other pains afflict mankind according to their own impulse and nature, a straight line leads to the theory and empirical methods of a Hippocrates' is quite untenable. Even though the diseases described here by Hesiod have the capacity to act spontaneously, their origin is ultimately divine. By contrast, in the Hippocratic writings the belief that diseases could have a supernatural cause or that they were capable of a separate existence of their own is firmly rejected; in these treatises disease is regarded as a natural process, a disturbance of the equilibrium of the constituents of the body, and physiology replaces divine nosology. Furthermore, as G. E. R. Lloyd points out,[21] rightly castigating Fränkel for drastically underestimating the difference between Hesiod and the Hippocratics here, the possibility of understanding and controlling disease through the art of medicine is not even hinted at by Hesiod.

However, in addition to causing death and disease, the gods also cured diseases and healed wounds. When, for instance, in the *Iliad* (V. 99ff.), Diomedes is hit by an arrow and bleeding profusely, Pallas Athena answers his prayer by healing him immediately and restoring him to the battle. Aeneas, when his hip is crushed by a stone hurled by Diomedes in his turn, is rescued first by Aphrodite (V. 305ff.), then by Apollo, and

14

finally nursed back to health by Artemis and Leto (V. 447ff.).
Glaucus' haemorrhaging arrow wound is also healed by Apollo,
who staunched the black blood (XVI. 528). We find the same
belief in divine cure in the *Odyssey*. In a metaphor employed to
illustrate the shipwrecked and storm-tossed Odysseus' relief at
the sight of land (*Od*. V. 394ff.) his feelings are compared to the
reaction of children who see their father, at death's door, relieved
of his sickness by the gods:

> As welcome as is the glimpse of returning life in a father
> to his children, when he has lain sick, suffering strong
>   pains,
> and wasting long away, and the loathsome daimon has
>   assailed him,
> but then, and it is welcome, the gods delivered him from his
> sickness, so welcome appeared land and forest to Odysseus.

The *Odyssey* also provides evidence of the use of magic in the
treatment of wounds. In the nineteenth book (vv. 455–8), where
Odysseus is wounded at a boar hunt, the sons of Autolycus
bandage the wound skilfully and stop the bleeding with an
incantation (ἐπαοιδή), evidently employed to constrain the deity
to perform his healing function:

> Then . . . the wound of the noble, god-like Odysseus
>   they bound
> skilfully and checked the dark blood with an incantation.[22]

In ancient Greece, as in Egypt and Babylon, religious medicine
became firmly established. Priests in their temples and sanctuaries catered to an eternal human need. Even long after the advent
of rational medicine in Greece some, when stricken by illness, as
we see from Thucydides' account of the plague,[23] were more
strongly motivated to seek aid from a priest than a physician.
Others, too, turned as a last resort to religion to seek a cure for
their illness. Those patients who sought their healing in religion
could turn in ancient Greece to a wide range of gods and demi-
gods. The earliest Greek god of healing was probably Paeon,
who appears in Homeric epic as the physician of the gods.
Subsequently his name became an attribute of other gods and
was used to denote their healing function – for example, of Zeus
at Dodona and Rhodes, of Apollo, of Dionysus, of Asclepius and
of Helios. Goddesses came to be regarded as the tutelary deities of

women. Hera, for example, was held to be the patroness of marriage and of female sexual life generally. She assisted women in childbirth. Eileithyia, the divine midwife, was identified with her but on other occasions regarded as her daughter. Artemis performed a similar role as a birth goddess and served as the protector of young girls. Healing functions were also attributed to Athena. In Oropus she was worshipped as Athena Paeonia and in Athens as Athena Hygieina.

Among demi-gods skilled in the art of healing, the seer Melampus, grandson of Aeolus, is especially notable. His most memorable feat was his cure of the daughters of Proteus, King of the Argolid, who had been driven mad and were wandering the countryside fancying themselves to be cows. According to Apollodorus, his method of treatment was to increase their madness by means of shouting and orgiastic dancing and then to purify it, when at its peak, with a cathartic remedy containing black hellebore (Christmas rose, a Ranunculus), a drastic, indeed potentially lethal potion, that fully earned its description in antiquity as the 'Great Concitator'. (Herophilus subsequently called it 'the bravest of captains' since 'after stirring up all within, it sallies forth itself in the van.'[24]) According to Theophrastus, this remedy was thereafter called 'Melampodium'. A sanctuary was built for Melampus at Aegosthena in Attica and an annual festival instituted in his honour.

A descendant of Melampus, Amphiaraus, also became famous as a seer and divine physician. Amphiaraus was one of the Seven against Thebes. Legend has it that as he was fleeing from that city in defeat he was saved from his pursuers by Zeus who engulfed him, chariot, horses and all, in a cleft in the ground made by his thunderbolt. Important centres of his worship were established at Thebes, Oropus and Athens. His procedure at these sanctuaries was to cure by giving advice to suppliants during their incubation upon the earth in which he resided. According to one late source, these suppliants had to abstain from wine for three days and from food for one day, then sacrifice a ram and sleep upon its fleece. During that sleep the god would advise them how their affliction might be cured. Pausanias records (I, 34, 4) that it was the practice in the Amphiareion at Oropus for the cured to throw gold and silver coins into the spring near the temple to express their gratitude.

Another demi-god who achieved a considerable reputation in

medical mythology, both as a healer and as a teacher, is the Centaur Chiron, who is credited with the discovery of the medicinal properties of many herbs. According to Pliny, the panacea *Centaurion,* was discovered by him and another, *Chironium,* was attributed to him. Pliny credits him in addition with the discovery of the medical properties of white bryony, *ampelos Chironia.* He is also said, after instruction by Artemis in their properties, to have given the plants of the genus Artemisiae their name and introduced them into the *materia medica.* Galen informs us that his name was also attached to certain types of chronic ulcer and Paul of Aegina explains that old ulcers, difficult to heal, were called 'chironian', as if they required Chiron himself to come and cure them. According to legend, Chiron had numerous disciples including Melampus, Jason, Aristaeus, Achilles and Asclepius himself.

Of all the gods and demi-gods who are depicted in Greek mythology practising the art of healing, Apollo became the god of healing *par excellence.* But he was subsequently eclipsed by his own son Asclepius. Doubtless, the latter's ascendancy was only possible because legend had already invented the family relationship. Ovid's tale in the *Metamorphoses* (XV.622ff.) well illustrates Asclepius' greater subsequent importance as a healing god. In 292 BC Rome was harrowed by pestilence. The senate, after all human efforts had proved to be of no avail, sought divine aid in desperation, and sent a delegation to Delphi to supplicate Apollo's assistance. Apollo advised them to seek help from his son Asclepius at Epidaurus. This deity accompanied them on their return journey in the form of a huge snake which swam ashore on to an island in the Tiber (later named the island of San Bartolemmeo), where a temple was subsequently established in honour of the god.[25] There Asclepius resumed his heavenly form and put an end to the plague.

Hesiod is the first to preserve details of the legend of the birth of Asclepius. He tells us that Coronis, the beautiful daughter of the Lapith Phlegyas, was bathing in the Boebian Lake, when Apollo saw her and desired her. She became pregnant by the god. Her father, however, had promised her in marriage to her cousin Ischys. The wedding preparations were in progress when Apollo was informed by a white raven. In his anger the god punished this messenger of evil tidings which, thereafter, wore black plumage and was feared as a herald of disaster. He then shot down Ischys. Artemis slew Coronis and her innocent companions. However, when Apollo saw the body of Coronis upon her funeral pyre, he felt pity for his unborn son. Removing him from his mother's womb, he took him to the cave of Chiron on Mt Pelion. There Asclepius grew up and was instructed in the art of healing by the Centaur. He became a famous physician and was consulted from far and wide. But when he presumed to restore the dead Hippolytus to life, he was slain by the thunderbolt of Zeus. This legend is also related by Pindar, with some modifications, in his beautiful ode addressed to Hiero, tyrant of Syracuse, during the latter's illness. In the same ode, which he seems to have composed *c.* 473 BC, Pindar also enumerates the various types of patients resorting to Asclepius in the hope of a cure:

> And whosoever came suffering from the sores of nature, with limbs wounded by grey bronze or far-hurled stones, or with bodies wasted by summer's heat or winter's cold, he delivered them, different ones from different pains, tending some with kindly incantations, while he set others on their feet again with the knife.
>
> (Pythian III, 46-55)

In the last third of the fifth century Asclepius was transformed from a minor cult hero into a major god. The terrible impact of the great plague of Athens in 430-427 BC seems to have considerably increased his influence. Although, as Thucydides records, that dreadful epidemic led to some disillusionment with conventional religion, since it was thought to make no difference whether one worshipped the gods or not, as believer and nonbeliever perished alike, others were clearly driven to seek for a more powerful magic. In 420 BC, during the Peace of Nicias, Asclepius was solemnly inducted into Athens in the form of his sacred snake and lodged at the house of Sophocles until a shrine could be built for him.[26] This cult's widening popularity can be seen in Aristophanes' decision to single it out as a suitable subject for comedy when he burlesqued its rites in his comedy the *Plutus* (performed in 388 BC) and presented there a farcical account of the practice of incubation in the temple of Asclepius. In the following short extract from the play, the slave Carion describes the trickery of the priests and the miraculous cure by Asclepius of the blindness of Plutus, god of wealth:

CARION: Then we went to the precinct of the god. When the cakes and offerings were dedicated as food to Hephaestus' flame, we laid Plutus down in the customary manner. And each of us arranged a pallet for himself . . . the attendant of the god extinguished the lamps and ordered us to sleep, saying that if anyone should hear a noise, he should keep quiet. We all lay down in an orderly fashion. I was unable to sleep. A pot of porridge, which stood a small distance from an old crone's head aroused my desire. I had a wondrous urge to creep towards it. Then, looking up, I catch sight of the priest stealing the cakes and figs. After this he went circling round all the altars in the hope that a cake might have been left behind. Then he consecrated these into a kind of sack. I considered that the deed had full sanction and got up after the pot of porridge.

WIFE: Most wretched of men, did you not fear the god?

CARION: Yes, by god, I did – lest he might get to the pot first, garlands and all. For the priest warned me of him beforehand. When the old crone heard the noise I made, she put out a stealthy hand. Then I hissed and took it between my teeth like a sacred snake and she immediately drew it back. She wrapped herself up in her bedding and lay quiet, farting through fear more pungently than a polecat. I, by that time, was gobbling up a lot of the porridge . . .

CARION: The god visited every patient in a very orderly manner, examining their diseases on his round. Then a servant placed beside him a stone mortar and pestle and a little medicine chest . . . . The god sat down beside Plutus. He first took hold of his head and then took a clean napkin and wiped all round his eyes. Panacea covered his head and the whole of his face with a scarlet cloth. Then the god clucked. There then darted out from the temple two serpents of monstrous size.

WIFE: O dear god.

CARION: The two of them slipped quietly under the scarlet cloth and licked his eyes, as it appeared to me. . . . . Plutus arose his sight restored.

(Aristophanes, *Plutus* 659ff.)

19

Another account of these procedures, no less humorous in its own way, is preserved by Aelian, taken, he tells us, from the Sicilian historian Hippys of Rhegium:

> A woman had a worm and the cleverest of the physicians despaired of curing her. So she went to Epidaurus and begged the god to free her from the parasite. The god was not there, but the attendants made her lie down where the god was in the habit of healing the suppliants and she lay quiet as she was enjoined. But the servants of the god began to treat her and removed her head from her neck. Then one of them inserted his hand and drew out the worm, a great brute of a beast. But they were no longer able to fit the head in place and restore it to its usual fitting. Then the god arrived and was angry with them for undertaking a task beyond their wisdom and he himself with the irresistible power of a god restored the head to the body and raised up the suppliant.
>
> (Aelian, *De natura animalium* IX. 33)

Hippys is said to have lived 'at the time of the Persian Wars'. If this assessment is correct, we would then have early evidence of the practice of this healing cult.

Details of many other equally miraculous cures have survived. Pausanias records that on his visit to Epidaurus he saw six votive columns upon which were engraved 'the names of men and women healed by Asclepius, together with the disease from which each suffered and how he was cured'. Similar steles could be seen at the sanctuary at Cos and at other sanctuaries as well. Archaeological excavations at Epidaurus have disinterred three of the columns seen by Pausanias together with fragments of a fourth. They contain seventy case histories, 'cures (*iamata*) of Apollo and Asclepius', inscribed in the fourth century BC. They provide valuable information of the different types of patients who sought healing within the temple and the kinds of cures achieved. The following is not untypical:

> A man had his toe healed by a snake. The man, in a terrible state because of a malignant ulcer on his toe, was carried outside in the daytime by the attendants and he sat down upon a seat. When sleep overcame him, a serpent came out of the Sanctuary and healed his toe with its tongue. When

the patient awoke, he was healed. He had seen a vision: it seemed that a beautiful youth was spreading a potion upon his toe.

(*Inscriptiones Graecae*, IV^2.1, nos 121-2, pp. 70-3, ll.113-19 (E. J. and L. Edelstein, *Asclepius*, vol. I, no. 423 A XVII))

Once firmly established at Athens the cult of Asclepius spread swiftly. Another sanctuary was built in the Piraeus. Then the cult spread to the Aegean islands and to Asia Minor. It became established at Pergamum by the mid-fourth century BC and its sanctuary there became as famous as those at Cos and Epidaurus. In 292 BC, as was seen above, Asclepius was brought to Rome, as he had been brought to Athens over 130 years earlier. The cult then spread to Africa. In Egypt, Asclepius was identified with Imhotep. More than 400 temples and shrines were dedicated to him all over the western ancient world. Some of them were still actively engaged in his worship as late as the sixth century AD.[27]

Until not so very long ago, it was widely assumed that the temple of Asclepius at Cos was the cradle of Greek medicine. It was argued that, just as Egypt and Mesopotamia had priest-physicians so, in similar fashion, the priests of Asclepius were physicians; that his temples were centres of research and training, where medical experience was accumulated and transmitted to subsequent generations; that Hippocrates was himself an Asclepiad, a member of its hereditary priesthood (Plato, *Protagoras* 311b); and, finally, that Hippocrates was said to have been the first to separate medicine from philosophy, thereby creating rational medicine at Cos. By the early Roman imperial period the story had become widespread that Hippocrates had learned medicine from studying the *iamata* on display in the Asclepeion at Cos. Strabo (*Geographia* XIV, 2, 19) informs us that 'Hippocrates was trained in the knowledge of dietetics by the cures dedicated there' and, according to the version recorded in Pliny (*N.H.* XXIX, 2), who cites Varro as his source, Hippocrates is said to have copied out the cures inscribed on the walls of the temple. Subsequently the temple burned down and Hippocrates employed the information he had acquired from the *iamata* to invent rational medicine:

The subsequent history of medicine lay hidden in darkest night until the Peloponnesian War. Then Hippocrates, who was born on the island of Cos, among the foremost in fame and power and sacred to Aesculapius, restored it to the light. It had been customary for patients recovered from illness to inscribe in the temple of that god an account of the help that they had received, so that afterwards similar treatment might prove beneficial. Hippocrates is said to have written out these inscriptions, and, as Varro among us believes, after the temple had been burned, founded that branch of medicine called 'clinical'.[28]

Upon the basis of this evidence, then, it has been frequently claimed in the past that Hippocratic medicine had its origin in temple practice. Littré even went so far as to claim, at least for a time, that the Hippocratic treatise *Coan Prenotions* was a collection of temple records.[29] Prima facie, however, it seems paradoxical that rational medicine should have developed from such an environment. The *iamata* inscribed upon the votive offerings and displayed upon the temple walls were clearly intended to have the psychological effect of encouraging future suppliants as well as displaying the gratitude of the cured and publicising the healing powers of the deity. These temple cures are in most cases immediate miracles and are instantaneously successful. In marked contrast, however, the Hippocratic treatments present detailed observations of the course of diseases over a period of several days, weeks even, and in a very high proportion of instances end fatally. Furthermore, the circumstantial evidence presented by Pliny is highly dubious.[30] Archaeological investigation has revealed no traces of any structure belonging to an earlier temple on the site and, moreover, seems to indicate that the Asclepeion was not itself built until relatively late in the fourth century BC by which time, of course, the island was already famous for its secular healers. It may be noted, however, that Herzog, the excavator of the temple, nevertheless believed that the Asclepeion was different from its counterparts elsewhere in Greece and that Coan physicians came to practise there medicine of a rational nature.[31] Herzog argued that the use of the Asclepeion by Coan physicians is paralleled in the organisation of the Academy, the Lyceum and the Museum at Alexandria, all of which centred their intellectual activities around cult practice. As evidence for the different nature of the Coan Asclepeion he pointed not only to the absence of *iamata* on the site but also to the presence of decrees appertaining to doctors found there.[32] But as the sanctuary was one of the sites in Cos where public documents were regularly displayed, the presence there of decrees honouring physicians should cause no surprise. The absence of *iamata*, too, could be explained in a variety of ways: earthquakes are not uncommon in that area and the site itself reveals evidence of having been plundered in antiquity. Furthermore Strabo's testimony (VIII, 6, 15) seems to indicate quite clearly that the practice at Cos was not fundamentally different from that evidenced elsewhere. Here Strabo informs us:

> Epidaurus is famous for the manifestation of Asclepius and he is relied upon to heal all kinds of disease, and has a temple there which is always full of patients and dedicated tablets on which the cures are inscribed just as at *Cos* and Tricca. (my italics)

The view, then, that Hippocratic medicine had its origin in temple practice at the Asclepeion at Cos is untenable. The general attitude of contemporary Greek authors themselves also supports its rejection. Thucydides, for example, in his account of the Athenian plague draws a clear distinction between the initial treatment of the disease and the subsequent recourse to prayers in the temples and consultation of oracles by those afflicted by it (II, 47). In the famous choral ode to man in the *Antigone* (361-2) the avoidance of irremediable disease is included as one of his remarkable achievements. (In the *Prometheus Bound* (446-83), however, while medicine is classed along with agriculture and navigation as a natural art, its institution is assigned to a demi-god. But significantly, its founder here is not Asclepius, but Prometheus.) The author of the Hippocratic treatise *De vetere medicina*, Chap. 2, depicts medicine as an established art which had developed by a process of trial and error over a long period of time.

However, notwithstanding this widespread attitude amongst the Greeks patently at a variance with the view that Greek rational medicine developed from the healing cult of Asclepius, it has in the past frequently been maintained that the Asclepiadae were priest-physicians who practised their healing skills in the temples of Asclepius and that, since Hippocrates himself (and other Coan physicians) is explicitly designated as an Asclepiad, then by implication Hippocratic medicine must have developed from temple practice.[33] This line of argument is rightly rejected by most modern scholars and the Asclepiadae are widely held to be not temple-physicians, but doctors who were members of a *koinon* or guild which was initially a clan of hereditary physicians who worshipped Asclepius as the patron of their art and claimed descent from the god in much the same manner as the Homeridae traced their descent from Homer. This medical clan, it has been suggested, developed into something like a guild by the further admission or adoption of new members from outside the clan and ultimately the term Asclepiad acquired the connotation of medical practitioner. However, this belief itself, that the Asclepiadae at Cos were originally an exclusive group, linked by ties of blood, which provided an institutional framework for Coan physicians and controlled access to the medical profession[34] is not supported by firm contemporary evidence and has recently been attacked by W. D. Smith,[35] who maintains that this view is largely the result of a backward projection of the situation in the second century BC. The further claim that the introduction at Cos of payment for teaching ultimately contributed to the demise of a professional *koinon* whose membership originally depended exclusively upon descent[36] is, as Smith points out,[37] doubtful in the extreme. For, when Plato tells us in the *Protagoras* that Hippocrates taught for a fee, there is no suggestion that in doing so Hippocrates himself established this precedent. Furthermore, the impression of medical practice presented by the Hippocratic treatises themselves is that of a wide and open calling without restriction as to who might or might not set himself up as a practitioner. To practise medicine at Cos, then, it was necessary neither to be a priest nor a member of an exclusive guild. The cult of Asclepius and its temple healing in any case, as has already been seen, appears to have reached Cos relatively late. The initial development of the Asclepeion there does not seem to have actually taken place until about the middle of the fourth century BC by which time the island was already famous for its secular medicine.

However, some striking affinities can be found between Hippocratic medicine and the healing practised within the temples of Asclepius. In certain of the Epidaurian inscriptions the god is depicted as employing drugs in his treatment of the sick, recommending diets and even administering an emetic. In others, he is said to have appeared to his patients in their dreams as a surgeon who effected miraculous cures. At a later date, according to Aelius Aristides,[38] he is even said to have resorted to phlebotomy. But although the divine healer does not disdain the use of magical drugs and the use of supernatural powers, the actual conception here of the aetiology of disease is secular rather than religious. The god is represented as behaving in a manner similar to that in which contemporary Hippocratic doctors behaved. Evidently, as several scholars have pointed out,[39] the healing dispensed within the precincts of the temples of Asclepius was conceived with the human doctor's practice as its model. It was, as Parker says, essentially 'a secular medicine . . . but with an injection of supernatural power'.[40]

Thus, far from it being the case that Hippocrates derived his medical knowledge from the temple walls of the Asclepeion at Cos and established rational medicine upon the basis of this knowledge, as Pliny records, the converse seems to be true: temple healing was itself strongly influenced by Hippocratic practice. Although there does not seem to be any evidence to support co-operation between the priests of Asclepius and Hippocratic doctors, neither is there any strong evidence of marked hostility between them.[41] The Edelsteins' suggestion that many sought treatment at the temples of Asclepius not as an alternative to treatment at the hands of their doctors, but once such treatment had failed,[42] is both psychologically convincing and seemingly supported by implication at Thucydides II, 47, where, as we saw, the sick are said to have sought divine help when all human skills proved unavailing when faced with the plague.[43] Thus, it seems more likely that religious medicine was itself influenced by its secular counterpart than vice versa. Accordingly, the origins of Greek rational medicine must be sought elsewhere.

2

Ionian natural philosophy and the origins of rational medicine

Primoque medendi scientia sapientiae pars habebatur.
(Celsus, *De medicina*, Proem, 6)

Our earliest evidence of Greek medicine reveals, then, that, as in ancient Egypt and Mesopotamia, the causation of disease and the operation of the remedies applied to the sick were so linked with superstitious beliefs in magic and supernatural causation that a rational understanding of disease, its effect upon the body, or of the operation of remedies applied to it was impossible. The sixty-odd works of the Hippocratic *Corpus*, however, provide a striking contrast and are virtually free from magic and supernatural intervention.[1] Here, in this collection, for the first time in the history of medicine complete treatises have survived which display an entirely rational outlook towards disease, whose causes and symptoms are now accounted for in purely natural terms. The importance of this revolutionary innovation for the subsequent development of medicine can hardly be overstressed. This emancipation of (some) medicine from magic and superstition, was the outcome of precisely the same attitude of mind which the Milesian natural philosophers were the first to apply to the world about them. For it was their attempts to explain the world in terms of its visible constituents without recourse to supernatural intervention which ultimately paved the way for the transition to rational explanation in medicine, too.

Like their poetical predecessors in ancient Greece, these Ionian thinkers firmly believed that there was an orderliness inherent in the world about them; they believed in a universe regulated by causal laws. The alternation of day and night, the regularities of springtime and harvest, the regular procession of the heavenly

26

bodies through the night sky, would all, doubtless, have contributed to bring about this conviction. Again like their predecessors, the natural philosophers attempted to explain the world by showing how it had come to be what it is.[2] As the basis for their evolutionary cosmogonies they sought for a unifying hypothesis to account for this order and proceeded, to a greater or lesser extent, to deduce natural explanations of the various phenomena from it, making no attempt to invoke, as their predecessors had done, the agency of supernatural powers. They themselves called their search 'inquiry into nature' (*historia peri physeōs*) or later 'philosophy' (*philosophia*).[3]

When I claim that there came into being in the sixth century BC an outlook unhampered by any religious belief in divine, arbitrary intervention, my intention is not to maintain that all religious beliefs were subsequently completely eradicated from the minds of the pre-Socratic philosophers or that they all sought to explain the world about them in the cold light of pure reason. This is patently not the case. For philosophy was turned by the Pythagoreans, for example, into a religious way of life, and the strong religious elements in their thought greatly influenced the development of the exact sciences in particular. In Empedocles' thought, too, his religious beliefs seem to have exercised a considerable influence upon his physics. However, it is important to note that, even where religion and philosophy are most closely intertwined, nowhere[4] can there be found any recourse to supernatural agency to account for the origin of the world or the operation of cause and effect within it. Although, it may be noticed, Empedocles makes extravagant claims to be able to influence the natural course of events (see Frag. 111 cited in Chapter 3, p. 69), his account of the origin and continued working of the world, though based upon the authority of a god (see Frag. 23.11), makes no appeal to divine intervention. Like his Ionian predecessors he seeks to explain the world about him in terms of purely natural causes. By an appeal to divine authority, he gives an account of the origin and operation of the world which cuts out divine intervention.

Two elements, then, characterise early Greek philosophy, the search for a unifying hypothesis and the search for natural as opposed to supernatural and mystical explanations. On turning to the Pythagoreans, however, it is immediately seen that although they satisfy the first of our criteria for a definition of philosophy at this date, they clearly do not seek natural

27

GREEK RATIONAL MEDICINE

explanations in quite the same manner as their Ionian predecessors had done. It might, therefore, be objected that their outlook should not be regarded, strictly speaking, as philosophical. This objection, I believe, cannot be sustained. For the Pythagorean attempt to explain the phenomena upon the basis of their own unifying hypothesis itself presupposes the pioneering work of the Ionian natural philosophers and could not have been propounded before the work of these thinkers. Notwithstanding their deeply religious beliefs, the Pythagoreans, like the Ionians, were not hampered in outlook by any belief in divine intervention in their attempts to explain the phenomena of the world about them. Aristotle, it may be noticed, clearly recognises that the Pythagoreans follow closely in the footsteps of the Ionians. For, at *Metaphysics* A8, 989b29ff. (*D.K.*58B22), after commenting upon the point of difference between them, he writes:

> the so-called Pythagoreans employ stranger principles and elements than the natural philosophers; the reason is that they took them from non-sensible things . . . [and adds] they still discuss and busy themselves wholly with nature; they generate the universe and watch what happens to its various parts, affections and activities. They use up their first principles and causes upon these things, as though agreeing with the other physicists that Being is just so much as is sensible and is embraced within what they call the universe. But, as I said, they maintain causes and first principles that are adequate to lead up to even the higher kinds of reality and are better fitted to them than to discussions about nature.

It appears that a variety of factors coalesced in the sixth century BC to initiate this intellectual revolution.[5] Its place of origin, the Ionian Greek city of Miletus on the west coast of Asia Minor, was possessed of tremendous energy. A colony herself, according to ancient tradition she had founded on her own account no less than ninety new colonies. Through these offshoots - one of which was the settlement at Naucratis in Egypt - she came into contact with older neighbouring cultures. As a result of her trade in materials and manufactured goods brought to the coast from Inner Anatolia and by the export of her own manufactures she became extremely wealthy. Shipping, trade and industry, then, brought Miletus great prosperity and a wide range of contacts with other lands and cultures. The standard of living of her citizens was too obviously the product of human energy and initiative for there to be any need to acknowledge an indebtedness to the gods, more familiar in agrarian economies. This secular spirit, which relegated the gods to the background, was doubtless fostered by the fact that the Milesians were not inhibited by any demands of a theocratic form of society. There was at Miletus no professional priesthood jealous to preserve a dogmatic religious orthodoxy. There was no one true religion expounded from a common sacred book by universally recognised spokesmen and supported by an organised religious authority. Unlike their Oriental neighbours, the Milesians were not constrained to adhere to any inviolable dogmatic code and they shared with their counterparts in other Greek city-states a common experience of regular participation in political debate and a characteristically irreverent attitude towards traditional authority, coupled with the tolerant belief that any citizen was entitled to voice his opinion on any subject. Moreover, the affluent environment of commercial Miletus provided both the leisure and the stimulus for disinterested intellectual inquiry. The claim of both Plato[6] and Aristotle[7] that the source and spring of philosophy is wonder or curiosity is justified. After making this point, the latter adds that history supports this conclusion; for it was after the provision of the chief necessities, not only for life, but for an easy life, that the search for intellectual satisfaction began.

In pre-philosophical Greek poetry one finds a firm belief in supernatural causation. In the *Iliad*, for example, Zeus is the cause of thunder and lightning and earthquakes are attributed to the activity of the sea god Poseidon:

> The Father of the Gods thundered terribly from on high and from below Poseidon caused the boundless earth to quake and shook the lofty mountain peaks.
>
> (Homer, *Iliad* XX. 56-8)

> even Okeanos fears the lightning of great Zeus and his terrible thunder when it crashes from heaven.
>
> (Homer, *Iliad* XXI. 198-9)

Each of these deities is accorded a traditional epithet denoting these activities. Zeus is elsewhere depicted as 'Lord of the

Thunder and Lightning' (*Keraunobrontēs*)[8] and Poseidon as the 'Earthshaker' (*Ennosigaios*).[9] In similar fashion, as was seen above, the plague which decimated the Greek army investing Troy is held to have been sent by Apollo, the archer god.[10] Even a less dramatic and a much more mundane phenomenon like rainfall is attributed to supernatural agency. The sixth-century lyric poet, Alcaeus of Lesbos, declares: 'Zeus rains upon us, and from the sky comes down enormous winter', and later, in the fifth, Aristophanes exploits the comic potential of this traditional belief in the *Clouds* (*Nubes*, 367ff.), when the old peasant Strepsiades describes his earlier belief that the rain was caused by Zeus urinating through his 'chamber-pot sieve'.

When we turn to the Milesian thinkers, however, we see immediately that their intellectual outlook is totally different. With them rational causation supplants supernatural explanation. Thales, who is described by Aristotle as the 'originator' (ἀρχηγός) of Ionian natural philosophy, for example, puts forward as his unifying hypothesis the belief that all things come from water.[11] In accordance with this hypothesis he maintains that the earth floats on water[12] and this idea allows him not only to dispense with Atlas, but also enables him to give a natural explanation of earthquakes without having recourse to Poseidon:

[Thales] said that the Earth is held up by water and rides like a ship and when it is said to 'quake' it is then rocking because of the movement of the water.

(Seneca, *Quaestiones naturales* III, 14 *D.K.*11A15)

In similar fashion, Thales' successors, Anaximander and Anaximenes, put forward a natural explanation of earthquakes without reference to Poseidon:

Anaximenes said that when the earth becomes soaked or parched it breaks and is shaken by the high ground that is broken off and falls. It is for this reason, too, that earthquakes occur both in times of drought and during heavy rains; for in droughts, as has been said, the earth becomes dried up and breaks, and when it becomes excessively wet by the rains, it falls apart.

(Aristotle, *Meteorologica* B7, 365b6 *D.K.*13A21)

(A similar theory is attributed to Anaximander by Ammianus (XVII 7, 12 *D.K.*12A28).)

Both these thinkers hold that thunder and lightning, far from being symptoms of Jovian displeasure, are caused by wind:

> With regard to thunder, lightning, thunderbolts, waterspouts and whirlwinds: Anaximander says that all these are caused by wind. When it is enclosed in thick cloud and forces its way out by reason of its fine texture and lightness, then the tearing makes the noise and the rent, in contrast to the blackness of the cloud, produces the flash. Anaximenes is of the same opinion.
> (Aëtius, III 3, 1 *D.K.*12A23 and III 3, 2 *D.K.*13A17; *Dox.* 367–8)

Eclipses, too, had previously been superstitiously held to be caused by Zeus. Archilochus, for example, tells us (74, 3), 'the Father of the Olympians, made night at noon, when he concealed the light of the shining sun.' Now, in similar fashion, these phenomena are given purely natural explanations by the Milesians. Anaximander, for example, believed that the sun and moon were really wheels of fire rotating around the earth, enshrouded in concealing mist. Out of a single aperture in each of them fire emerges, 'like air from the nozzle of a pair of bellows'. Eclipses are due to a total or partial blocking of these apertures.[13] Anaximenes, who was even less sophisticated in his astronomy than Anaximander, seems to have believed that the heavenly bodies were fiery leaves.[14] He also postulated invisible, earthy celestial bodies,[15] which were carried round with the fiery heavenly bodies and it is generally assumed that he did so in order to explain eclipses. The manifest naïvety of these particular explanations should not be allowed to obscure the intellectual revolution which they in fact represent.

In rejecting supernatural causation the Milesians also rejected by implication Homeric theology. They nevertheless seem deliberately to have retained and applied to their own first principles epithets which had traditionally been applied to the anthropomorphic deities which figure so largely in Homeric epic. Aristotle, for example, tells us that Anaximander, like most natural philosophers, considered his *archē* to be divine because it was 'deathless'[16] and 'indestructible'. (According to Hippolytus he described it as 'eternal and ageless'.[17]) We similarly learn that

Anaximenes held that his first principle, *aēr*, was a god.[18] In addition, the latter seems to have believed that such gods as there were in the world themselves arose from this divine, all-encompassing air.[19]

It is clearly apparent that these Milesian attitudes persisted during the fifth century. Empedocles' four elements are not only invested with the actual names of divinities,[20] but they also usurp the privileges and powers that were previously the prerogatives of the Olympian gods, who are thus deliberately diminished in status. Although Empedocles describes the Olympians as 'long-lived' and 'richest in honour',[21] he none the less claims that they, too, are temporary combinations of the elements.[22] For Empedocles the elements are the new immortal gods.[23] The same outlook is also apparent in the views of Diogenes of Apollonia, another philosopher who, like Empedocles, strongly influenced contemporary medicine in the fifth century. Diogenes, who had revived Anaximenes' monistic hypothesis (see Chapter 3, p. 76), not only describes his first principle as 'eternal' and 'deathless'[24] – epithets which, as was seen above, had previously been applied in Homer to the Olympian gods – but he also explicitly declares air to be a god:

For this very thing [i.e. *aēr*] I hold to be a god, and to reach everywhere, and to dispose everything and to be in everything.

(Simplicius, *In physica* 152.22 D.K.64B5)

The pre-Socratics, then, as Vlastos has perceptively observed,[25] dared to 'transpose the name and function of divinity into a realm conceived as a rigorously natural order' and to take 'a word (sc. θεῖον), which in common speech was the hallmark of the irrational, unnatural and unaccountable, and made it the name of a power which manifests itself in the operation, not the disturbance, of intelligible law'.

Just as the Milesian natural philosophers had sought to explain in purely natural terms such frightening phenomena as thunder and lightning, earthquakes and eclipses, which had previously in mythology been superstitiously attributed to the activity of anthropomorphic gods, so the same outlook was applied by medical authors to the causation of disease – especially those diseases which manifested themselves with dramatic and frightening symptoms. As Werner Jaeger has perceptively pointed out,[26] the clearest evidence of this relationship between philosophy and medicine may be seen in the fact that the medical literature of the fifth and fourth centuries BC is written in Ionic. Although Cos and Cnidus, whence the treatises in the Hippocratic *Corpus* seem to have emanated, were both Dorian settlements,[27] the *Corpus* itself is written throughout in the Ionic dialect, which became initially the literary medium not only for philosophy but also for history.[28] Furthermore, the enrolment of medicine within this intellectual movement, which expounded its beliefs in writing, would, given the development of literacy within classical Greece, have resulted in a wider dissemination of rational explanations of medical phenomena amongst the literate.

As Pliny has complained (*N.H.* XXIX, 2), the early history of Greek medicine is shrouded in darkness. Consequently, in order to illustrate the influence of Ionian rationalism upon medicine, it is necessary to resort to examples chosen from a period over a century later than the lifetimes of the Milesian founding fathers. Let us take first the more dramatic case of epidemic[29] disease. It was seen in the preceding chapter that Homer attributed the disease which decimated the Greek army investing Troy to the anger of Apollo. The Hippocratic writings, in marked contrast, as we shall see shortly, explain the onset of such diseases, i.e. 'diseases, which arise whenever men are attacked by one disease at the same time' ([Hippocrates] *De natura hominis* 9, 14), in purely natural terms without recourse to supernatural agency and, in general, hold them to be caused by a corruption of air.[30]

Thucydides, too, it may be observed here, reveals the same rational attitude in his account of the great plague of Athens.[31] While there seems no good reason to doubt that he was familiar with contemporary medical literature and influenced by the spirit of Hippocratic medicine, it would be unwise to conclude that his rationality of approach was itself derived exclusively from contemporary medicine. Thucydides is manifestly a child of the Enlightenment and the writing of history itself had, in any case, been influenced earlier by Ionian natural philosophy, when Herodotus enrolled himself within this tradition and adopted Ionian rational attitudes to describe an earlier war. Although many of his Athenian contemporaries clearly believed that the plague was of divine origin,[32] and frequent and diverse attempts were made to propitiate Apollo in particular,[33] Thucydides does not suggest that it was due in any way to supernatural causes. While he does not himself explicitly connect the outbreak of this disease with climatic conditions prevailing at the time, Diodorus, who closely models himself upon Thucydides in his own account of the plague, initially attributes it to the breathing of corrupted air caused by the overcrowded conditions within the city[34] and in his later description of the renewed outbreak in 426 BC ascribes it to the heavy rains of the previous winter, to the poor crops affected by the rains, and to the failure of the Etesian winds.[35] Elsewhere, however, Diodorus reveals himself ambivalent upon this matter of causation, when he explains the later epidemic which affected Carthaginian troops besieging Syracuse in 397 BC as due to divine retribution for the pillage of the temple of Demeter and Core.[36]

Herodotus also reveals a similar ambivalence regarding the causation of disease. Despite the manifest influence upon him of Ionian rationalism evident in his frequent doubts or outright disbelief in stories invoking the supernatural, on several occasions he remains committed to the Homeric belief that diseases are caused by divine displeasure.[37] For example, in his discussion of the madness and suicide of Cleomenes, King of Sparta (VI, 75), he records initially three different stories, each attributing the king's fate to retribution for some offence against the gods. He later mentions (VI, 84) that the Spartans denied that Cleomenes' madness was heaven-sent; it was attributed by them to his adoption of the Scythian practice of drinking unmixed wine. At the end of his account, however, he supports what he considers to be the popular belief that Cleomenes was punished for corrupting the Pythian priestess so that she declared that Demaratus was not the true son of Ariston. Again, he considers that the illness and death of Pheretime, whose body was infested with worms, was due to divine retribution for the excessive vengeance she had exacted upon the people of Barce (IV, 202). Finally, he records, and apparently accepts, the Scythian belief that the Enareis were impotent as the result of Aphrodite's anger at their sacking of her temple at Ascalon (I, 105).[38]

The Hippocratic *Corpus*, however, is largely free from such ambivalence and one of the most striking manifestations of this new rational attitude in medicine can be seen in *De morbo sacro* – a work generally held to have been written either at the end of the fifth or at the beginning of the fourth century. The primary aim of this treatise is to demonstrate that epilepsy – an affliction which has particularly striking and frightening symptoms (especially during a *grand mal* attack) and has consequently throughout history been widely regarded with superstitious dread – is no more divine or sacred than any other disease and that it has a natural cause like all other diseases. Its author emphatically rejects the traditional religious belief familiar to us from Homer and elsewhere, that diseases are sent by the gods, and contends that one is more likely to be cleansed of such pollution by a god than to be polluted by him.[39]

In the opening chapter of this treatise our author contends that people think this disease is of divine origin because of their inexperience and their wonder at the peculiar symptoms which characterise it:

> I do not believe that the so-called 'Sacred Disease' is any more divine or sacred than any other disease. It has its own specific nature and cause; but because it is completely different from other diseases men through their inexperience and wonder at its peculiar symptoms have believed it to be of divine origin. This theory of divine origin is kept alive by the difficulty of understanding the malady, but is really destroyed by the facile method of healing which they adopt, consisting as it does of purifications and incantations [καθαρμοῖσί τε . . . καί ἐπαοιδῆσιν]. But, if it is to be considered divine on account of its remarkable nature, there will be many sacred diseases, not one.
>
> ([Hippocrates] *De morbo sacro*, Chapter 1, VI.352L.)

In the same chapter he attributes the origin of this belief that epilepsy is of divine origin to 'magicians, faith-healers, charlatans and quacks' who held this condition to be sacred in order to conceal their own ignorance:

> In my opinion those who first attributed a sacred character to this disease were the sort of people we nowadays call magicians, faith-healers, charlatans and quacks. These people also pretend to be very pious and to have superior knowledge. Shielding themselves by citing the divine as an excuse for their own perplexity in not knowing what beneficial treatment to apply, they held this condition to be sacred so that their ignorance might not be manifest. By choosing suitable terms they established a mode of treat-

ment that safeguarded their own positions. They prescribed purifications and incantations.

([Hippocrates] *De morbo sacro*, Chapter 1, VI.354L.)

The author points out that these imposters exploited this allegedly divine nature of the disease as safeguard for themselves by blaming the gods should the patient die: 'if the patient were cured, they would obtain a reputation for cleverness; but if he were to die, they would have safe and established excuses and the defence that the gods, and not themselves in any way, were responsible.' He is critical of such people for their ignorance, deceit and impiety as well as the methods of healing employed by them.

In Chapter 2 of this text he similarly stresses that epilepsy is no more divine than other diseases; that, like them, it arises from natural causes and is curable - provided that it has not become too deeply ingrained by long lapse of time:

I believe that this disease is no more divine than any other disease; it has the same nature as other diseases and a similar cause. It is also no less curable than other diseases unless by long lapse of time it is so ingrained that it is more powerful than the drugs that are applied. Like other diseases it is hereditary.

([Hippocrates] *De morbo sacro*, Chapter 2, VI.364L.)

Finally, in Chapter 18 he includes epilepsy within his general aetiology of disease:

This so-called 'Sacred Disease' is due to the same causes as other diseases, to the things that come to and go from the body, to cold and sun and changing restless winds. These things are divine so that there is no need to put the disease in a special class and to consider it more divine than the others; they are all divine and all human. Each has its own nature and character; none is irremediable or unsusceptible to treatment.

([Hippocrates] *De morbo sacro*, Chapter 18, VI.394L.)

The author's own explanation of the 'Sacred Disease' is recorded in Chapter 3, VI.366L. of the treatise, where he sets out to explain the manner in which it comes about and to identify its precipitating cause. He maintains that 'the brain is responsible for this disease, as it is for the other most serious diseases' and believes that there are 'veins' leading to the brain from all over the body. These vessels normally carry air (which, under the influence of Diogenes of Apollonia, he considers to be responsible for sensation and consciousness). This air is drawn in by them and spread throughout the body. If, however, it should be cut off anywhere and trapped in any part of the body that part becomes paralysed. Various symptoms are then described which arise when the flow of air is blocked by discharges especially of phlegm. This general theory of disease is then applied to epilepsy, which, we learn, comes about 'when the routes for the passage of phlegm [from the brain] are blocked and the discharge enters the "veins"' (Chap. 7, VI.372L.). An epileptic seizure is then described with accurate clinical detail: 'the patient then becomes speechless and chokes; he foams at the mouth. He clenches his teeth and his fists, rolls his eyes, loses consciousness and, in some cases, passes excrement.' The immediate cause of each of these symptoms is then given in turn.

This general explanation of the 'Sacred Disease' as the result of the flooding of the brain by phlegm, a condition, we are told, which is especially prevalent when the wind is southerly, is, of course, highly speculative.[40] What is important, however, is our author's conviction that this disease is due not to any supernatural agency, but entirely to natural causes. It is interesting and, at first sight, not a little surprising, to note that, although any idea of divine intervention is firmly ruled out, the notion of the divine is not excluded entirely. Instead of simply denying that the 'Sacred Disease' is divine, he asserts that all diseases are divine – all alike are divine and all natural. For him the whole of nature is divine, but this belief does not allow any exception to the rule that natural effects are the result of natural causes. Here, again, may be discerned the continuing influence of Ionian natural philosophy. The Milesians, as we saw, in rejecting supernatural causation, had not rejected the notion of divinity altogether, but had regarded their own first principles as divine and had even invested them with the epithets previously applied to the anthropomorphic deities of Homeric epic. Jaeger has acutely pointed out that:

> the predicate, ... the Divine, is transferred from the traditional deities to the first principle of Being (at which

37

they arrived by rational investigation), on the ground that the predicates usually attributed to the gods of Homer and Hesiod are inherent in that principle to a higher degree or can be assigned to it with greater certainty.[41]

According to our medical author, diseases, too, share in this divinity in the sense that, as parts of the cosmos, they also possess their own individual *physeis*, which display in the regular pattern of their origin, development and operation the same intelligible laws inherent in the world about them.[42]

An identical attitude towards epilepsy in particular and diseases generally is displayed in the treatise *De aere aquis locis* – a work which some scholars have thought to have been written by the same author as that of *De morbo sacro*.[43] In Chapter 3 of the former work an attempt is made to account for certain diseases as due to the effect of particular climatic and topographical factors. It is maintained, for example, that in cities 'exposed to hot winds and sheltered from the north' the following diseases are endemic:

> The women are unhealthy and prone to fluxes. Again, many of them are barren through disease and not naturally so, and frequently miscarry. The children are liable to convulsions and attacks of asthma and to what is thought to cause the disease of childhood and to be a sacred disease. The men suffer from dysentery, diarrhoea, ague, chronic fevers in winter, pustules and haemorrhoids.
>
> ([Hippocrates] *De aere aquis locis*, Chapter 3)

It is noteworthy that there is no suggestion here of supernatural causation. The women, for instance, are held to be barren as a result of environmental factors and not because of retribution exacted by a vengeful deity as was previously suggested elsewhere. The supernatural origin ascribed to epilepsy is briefly mentioned and summarily dismissed in the same sentence.

Later in the work (Chapter 22) our author turns to discuss the impotence which afflicted certain Scythians, the so-called 'Anarieis', which was superstitiously regarded as a divine affliction. Such men, he tells us, were held in awe and reverence by their fellows who feared for themselves:

> The rich Scythians become impotent, do women's work, live like women and talk in the same way. . . . The Scythians themselves lay the blame upon a god and revere

and worship such men, each fearing for himself. I myself hold that these and all other afflictions are divine and so are all others, none being more divine or more human than another; all are alike and all divine. Each of them has its own nature and none happens without its natural cause. I will explain how, in my own opinion, this condition arises. As a result of riding, they develop arthritis because their feet are always hanging down from their horses. Then those who are severely afflicted become quite lame and drag their hips. They treat themselves in the following way. At the onset of the disease they cut the vein behind each ear. In their weakness caused by loss of blood they become drowsy and fall asleep. Then, when they wake up, some are cured and some not. In my opinion the semen is destroyed by this treatment. For there are vessels beside the ears which, if cut, cause impotence. After this, when they come to women and are unable to have intercourse, they do not take it seriously at first but keep it quiet. But when, after the second, third and even more attempts, the same thing happens, they consider that they have offended in some way against the deity whom they hold to be the cause of their affliction. Then, judging themselves unmanly, they put on female attire, act as women and join with women in their work.

([Hippocrates] *De aere aquis locis*, Chapter 22)

According to Herodotus' apparently near contemporary account (*Histories* I, 105, above p. 34), however, the Scythians themselves explained their 'female disease' as a consequence of their sacking the ancient temple of Aphrodite Ourania at Askalon.[14] Herodotus himself appears to accept this explanation. But, as we see here, the medical author's explanation of this disease, though speculative and highly conjectural, in sharp contrast makes no recourse to the supernatural and is entirely consistent with his naturalistic outlook. He believes that, as a result of horse-riding, the Scythians become prone to varicose veins which they then seek to treat by cutting the vein that runs behind each ear. This treatment, he claims, causes impotence because it 'destroys the semen' – evidently he believed that cutting this vein disrupted the link between the source of the semen (presumably the brain here) and the genitals.

A further affinity with *De morbo sacro* may be seen[45] in the fact that the author of *De aere aquis locis* also seeks to refute the idea of supernatural intervention by an implied *Modus Tollens* form of argument.[16] Just as in the former treatise it is argued that if epilepsy were of divine origin, all types would be affected alike, but since the bilious escape, all types are not alike affected and thus this disease cannot be divine; so, in similar fashion, it is here maintained that the impotence which afflicts rich Scythians cannot be of supernatural origin since, if it were, it should affect everyone alike. But it does not, for the poor suffer less from this complaint because they do not ride; the affliction, therefore, cannot be divine. Both of these medical treatises reveal here not only a rational attitude but also the influence of modes of argument developed outside medicine by their philosophical contemporaries, who may themselves have been influenced by political and/or legal practice. As Lloyd further suggests (op. cit. p. 89), the doctors' particular need to explain their procedures, persuade their patients to adopt their treatment or defend themselves when confronted by others may well have led to this characteristic emphasis in the Hippocratic *Corpus* on logic and consistency of argument.

The treatise *De genitura* also considers impotence and in Chapter 2 several explanations are put forward to account for the plight of eunuchs, including this belief in the impairment of the spermatic vessels beside the ears:

> Eunuchs do not have intercourse because their seminal passage is destroyed. This passage goes right through the testicles themselves. From the testicles to the penis extend numerous fine ligaments by which it is raised and lowered. These are severed in the operation for castration. In consequence eunuchs are impotent. In the case of those whose ligaments are destroyed, the seminal passage is obstructed, for the testicles become calloused; and the ligaments, having become hard and insensitive, because of the callus, are unable to stretch and relax. Those who have had an incision made beside the ear are capable of intercourse and emitting sperm, but the amount is small, weak and sterile. For the greater part of the sperm goes from the head past the ears into the spinal marrow; but this passage becomes obstructed when the incision has formed a scar.[47]

Here again the disability is regarded as due to purely natural causes and there is absolutely no suggestion of any supernatural origin of the affliction.

Another disease, whose onset can be no less dramatic and terrifying than that of epilepsy is apoplexy. The very Greek word used to denote this sudden affliction, *apoplēxiē*, carries the connotation of being struck with violence. To the Greeks there was the added implication of being struck by lightning or by a thunderbolt together with the terror aroused by such a calamity. Anchises, the father of Aeneas, is a well known victim of this disease. He was struck down by a bolt of lightning for having boasted of his sexual relationship with Aphrodite. A passage in Celsus makes this connection between the heavens and the disease abundantly clear:

> We also see on rare occasions some who have been struck [*attonitos*], stupefied in mind and body. It comes about sometimes by lightning stroke, sometimes by disease: the Greeks call the latter *apoplexia*.
>
> (*De medicina* III.26)

As Edwin Clarke has pointed out,[48] the Latin terms for apoplexy, *attonitus* and *sideratio*, more obviously preserve this association. There are several scattered references to apoplexy, its symptoms and aetiology in the Hippocratic *Corpus*. *De morbis* II, for example, contains the following succinct description:

> A healthy subject is taken by a sudden pain in the head; he suffers immediate loss of speech, breathes stertorously and his mouth gapes open. If someone calls him or shakes him, he only groans and understands nothing. He urinates copiously without being aware of it. If fever does not supervene, death ensues within seven days, but if fever does supervene, he usually recovers.
>
> ([Hippocrates] *De morbis* II.21)

Other clinical features are mentioned elsewhere in the *Corpus*: elderly men are most susceptible to apoplexy; it occurs most frequently between the ages of 40 and 60 and is more prevalent during wet weather.

Notwithstanding its sudden and alarming manifestations, however, nowhere in the Hippocratic writings is there any trace of a suggestion that it is due to a supernatural cause. Although a

41

variety of particular causes are put forward, there is universal agreement that apoplexy is a disease of the brain.

Identical attitudes towards these afflictions are also apparent in the short work *De virginum morbis*. Here the author promises to deal with the so-called 'Sacred Disease', with apoplexy and with 'terrors', which cause those affected by them to imagine that they see evil demons. The first two of these complaints are passed over and the author devotes himself to the third. He tells us that young women who do not marry when of marriageable age are particularly liable to such complaints. Their cause, he maintains, is due to the retention of blood. Some young women, when afflicted in this way as a result of the corruption of their blood, suffer delusions in which they feel themselves bidden to jump from heights or to throw themselves into wells and hang themselves. (The wells would conveniently afford both the rope and the drop.) When reason returns, these women are often tricked by diviners into dedicating their costliest garments and other valuables to Artemis, although their recovery was due merely to the evacuation of blood. Our author recommends that such women should marry as soon as possible and points out that when they become pregnant they are completely cured of these irrational delusions:

First of all I shall deal with the so-called 'Sacred Disease' and with apoplexy and with terrors which people fear exceedingly – to the extent that they become deranged and imagine that they see hostile demons, sometimes at night, sometimes in the daytime, sometimes both. Because of such visions many already have hanged themselves: more women than men; for the female is more fearful and weaker by nature. Young girls, who remain unmarried when ripe for marriage, suffer this affliction more at the descent of the menses. Before this time they are not much distressed by these matters. For later on the blood streams into the womb to flow away outside the body. Thus when the orifice of the exit is not open and more blood keeps on flowing in . . . then, having no outlet, the blood, because of its quantity, wells up into the heart and diaphragm. When these parts were filled, the heart became stupefied. Then, from this sluggishness came numbness and from numbness delirium took hold . . . shivering coupled with fever starts up . . . the patient is driven mad by a violent inflammation; she becomes murderously inclined because of the putrefaction; fears and terrors are aroused by the dark; the compression around the heart causes these girls to hang themselves; their spirit, being distraught and in anguish by the corruption of the blood, brings an evil in its train. It is an evil of a different sort and it specifies fearful things. These delusions bid the girls to leap and fall into wells and hang themselves on the grounds that these actions are better and offer all kinds of advantage. When the girl is not affected by visions, she experiences a certain pleasure, which makes her fall in love with death as though it were something good. When she has come to her senses, the women dedicate to Artemis, among many other objects, the costliest garments. They are ordered to do so by diviners; but they are thoroughly deceived. Release from this malady comes about when there is nothing hampering the outflow of blood. I order young girls, when suffering such an affliction, to marry as soon as possible. For, if they become pregnant, they regain their health. If a girl does not marry, then immediately at puberty, or a little later, she will be afflicted by this or by another disease. Among married women, the sterile are more prone to suffer from these conditions.

([Hippocrates] *De virginum morbis*)[19]

There is abundant literary evidence, particularly in Greek tragedy, that madness and mental diseases generally were regularly attributed to the agency of the gods.[50] Herakles, for example, is afflicted by Hera's malevolence with a delusional rage which culminates in the murder of his own family; Ajax is driven mad by Athena to prevent him from killing Odysseus and the sons of Atreus; Orestes is hounded to madness by the Furies after the murder of his mother and, in the *Bacchae*, both Pentheus and Agave are driven mad by Dionysus. However, in the Hippocratic *Corpus* madness and mental diseases are regarded as not essentially different from diseases of the body and the same kinds of purely natural causes are put forward to account for them. Afflictions of this type, no less than their physical counterparts, are here regarded as investigable and treatable. There is no suggestion that their origin is in any way supernatural. (It should not be overlooked here that Empedocles

43

seems to have explained pathological madness upon the basis of physical causation (see Chapter 3, p. 71, n. 71).)

The treatise *De morbo sacro* again provides our most important evidence upon this matter.[51] In the opening chapter, to support his contention that other diseases are no less 'wonderful and portentous [than epilepsy], yet no one considers them sacred', this medical author cites by way of example the parallel of:

> men . . . who are mad and deranged from no obvious cause and do many strange things . . . groaning and shouting and choking in their sleep; while others, jumping up out of their beds and fleeing outside, are out of their minds until they wake up, when they are as healthy and sane as they were before.

Later in the treatise he puts forward his own views regarding the causes of mental disturbances; all of which, including his major concern, epilepsy, he attributes to afflictions of the brain. 'All of these afflictions', he declares, 'come from an unhealthy brain.' Madness, he maintains, ensues when the brain is abnormally moist, for then it necessarily becomes agitated and, as a result, varying visual and acoustic sensations are engendered which, as they appear and sound, are described by the tongue. Our author expands upon this theory in the next section. Here it is learned that the brain may be corrupted both by phlegm and by bile, producing two different manifestations of madness. Whereas those whose madness is due to phlegm are 'quiet and neither shout nor cause a disturbance', those who are maddened by bile are 'noisy, restless, evil-doers, always up to mischief'. Cases of continued madness, he believes, may, like the majority of such maladies, be cured by one who knows how to produce by means of regimen dryness and moisture, cold and heat in the human body, and can distinguish the right moment for the application of remedies hostile to the disease, without recourse to purifications and magic.

This explanation of the causes of madness, epilepsy and other mental disturbances by purely natural causes stands in marked contrast with the belief in the supernatural causation of these afflictions found in contemporary works of Greek tragedy as well as with the diagnoses of those charlatans who, as our author himself points out, attribute one type of epilepsy to Poseidon, another to Apollo, a third to Ares, a fourth to Hecate and still another to the Mother of the Gods. Yet it might be objected, and not without some justification, that this is hardly less speculative than the theories under attack. Although in the opening chapter of the treatise our author criticises his opponents for 'pretending to have superior knowledge about what causes and what cures disease', he is himself susceptible to this same charge since the particular treatment recommended by him, dietetic control of temperature and humidity, in reality affords no greater possibility of cure. While his establishment of a naturalistic basis for the understanding of madness and his rejection of any reference to the divine or demonic marks a release from one sort of mystification, he achieves this at the cost of the substitution of another.[52] His manifest confidence that salutary effects are to be derived from the anti-bilious or anti-phlegmatic diet he recommends is itself clearly a matter of faith. Our author is patently over-confident in his assessment of the procedures he advocates. Although they are, in principle, capable of being subjected to further tests with a view to their verification, in practice, they remain speculative and untested. However, although one may justifiably entertain the gravest reservations regarding the particular theory propounded here, the importance, for the subsequent development of medicine, of the general intellectual framework within which it was evolved can hardly be overstressed.

The rejection of belief in the supernatural causation of disease and in the efficacy of spells, incantations and purifications, as evidenced above, represents, then, medicine's greatest and most enduring debt to philosophy. Although, as can clearly be seen, the particular explanations put forward were at times highly speculative and naïve, nevertheless this innovation whereby people now sought to account for sickness, both physical and mental, upon a rational, natural basis paved the way for medicine's future development as a science. For this great advance, however, the burgeoning science had a very heavy price to pay. For, as we shall see, the continued subordination of medicine to philosophy was to pose a grave threat to the former's most advantageous development. Essentially, the procedure of the natural philosophers was a priori and deductive. To account for the order which they believed underlay the changing phenomena of the world about them, they sought for a unifying hypothesis upon which to base their evolutionary cosmogonies and, rejecting

ing any invocation of supernatural powers, proceeded to deduce their purely natural explanations of the phenomena from that hypothesis. To take an early and convenient example to illustrate their procedure: Anaximenes, traditionally considered the third of the Milesian philosophers, is recorded as having deduced his explanations of certain meteorological phenomena from his unifying hypothesis that air is the first principle of all things. The doxographer Aëtius tells us:

> Anaximenes said that clouds are formed when the air is thickened further; when it is compressed further still, rain is squeezed out; hail occurs when the descending water condenses, and snow, whenever some portion of the air is included within the moisture.

> (III 4, 1 *D.K.*13A17)

Here Anaximenes implicitly rejects the traditional belief that Zeus sends the rain and deduces instead from his first principle the natural explanation that it is 'squeezed out' from the clouds.

The earliest natural philosophers seem to have been primarily - though by no means exclusively - concerned with meteorological phenomena. In the fifth century, however, as we shall see in the following chapter, the philosophers increasingly sought to extend their views about the world at large to man himself, and, as a corollary to this, began to base their medical theories upon their philosophical postulates. This idea that man and the outside world are made of similar materials and behave according to similar rules, which is already implicit in Anaximenes' thought,[53] can be clearly discerned in Heraclitus, who believes that man's very life is bound up with his surroundings.[54] But it was not until the fifth century, as a direct result of an increased interest in medicine itself, that the implications of this idea were fully drawn out by later philosophers. The impulse, then, to turn from macrocosm to microcosm was considerably quickened by the influence of medicine. Philosophical thinking was thus, in its turn, coloured by a widening interest in medicine. Burnet is correct in his contention that 'it is impossible to understand the history of philosophy from this point onwards without keeping the history of medicine constantly in view.'[55] However, as shall be seen in the following chapter, for its influence upon philosophy here medicine itself had a very heavy price to pay.

3

Philosophy and medicine in the fifth century I

Alcmaeon and the pre-Socratic philosophers

et morborum curatio et rerum naturae contemplatio sub iisdem auctoribus nata sit.

(Celsus, *De medicina*, Proem, 6).

It is unfortunate that no Greek medical literature written earlier than the treatises of the Hippocratic *Corpus* has survived. Our evidence for Greek medical theory prior to the fifth century BC is frustratingly sparse. Herodotus tells us (III, 125) that Croton in southern Italy had a reputation for medicine which was enhanced by Democedes, the son of Calliphon, 'the best physician of his day'. According to Herodotus, Democedes practised medicine first at Aegina and at Athens. He was then employed in the service of Polycrates, tyrant of Samos, until the latter met his death at the hands of the Persian, Oroites, in 522 BC. Democedes was subsequently brought as a prisoner to Sardis where he won the favour of King Darius by curing him of a dislocated ankle. He also, according to Herodotus, successfully treated Darius' wife Atossa, who had an abscess (φῦμα[1]) on her breast that had burst and was spreading. In gratitude for a complete cure without mutilation the queen helped him to escape from Persia and return to his native Croton, where he married the daughter of the athlete Milo.[2]

If we can trust Herodotus here, it appears that Croton had a well established reputation for medical practice that went back until the sixth century. Another of its sons who achieved distinction in this field is Alcmaeon, the son of Peirithous. Alcmaeon is the only pre-Hippocratic doctor whose medical theories have survived in any form. That they survived at all, as Heidel has suggested,[3] may have been pure accident. Alcmaeon's interests seem to have been primarily medical and physiological, but, like so many of his Greek contemporaries, his interests were wide. Some of the problems which aroused his curiosity either had engaged or were subsequently to engage the interest of the natural philosophers. Aristotle, therefore, took note of his opinions and he was later dutifully included by Theophrastus in his *Physical Opinions*, his work on the history of philosophy (rather than by Meno in his history of medicine). The assessment of the doxographical writer Diogenes Laërtius (VIII, 83 *D.K.*24A1), that 'most of what he says concerns medicine, though he sometimes treats of natural philosophy' may in this particular instance be accepted.

Alcmaeon has been variously described by modern scholars as the 'Father of Anatomy'; the 'Father of Physiology'; the 'Father of Embryology'; the 'Father of Psychology'; the 'Creator of Psychiatry'; the 'Founder of Gynaecology'; and, indeed, more comprehensively, as the 'Father of Medicine' itself.[4] Given the scanty nature of our surviving evidence, it would be prudent to avoid such extravagant assessments. But it is, nevertheless, apparent that Alcmaeon is a figure of great importance in inter-relations between medicine and philosophy.[5] Alcmaeon's influence both upon later philosophical and medical thought was considerable. Owing to our lack of pre-Hippocratic Greek medical literature, it is impossible, notwithstanding the confident assessments cited above, to say whether or not he was the actual originator of the medical theories attributed to him. Our evidence, however, suggests that he was an original and independent thinker. Whether he himself actually originated the theories attributed to him is of subsidiary importance. What is important is that his medical beliefs reveal precisely the same rational outlook characteristic of the Ionian natural philosophers before him and the pre-Socratic philosophers after him.

It is unfortunate that our evidence is so deficient that it is impossible even to determine his dates with a high degree of accuracy. It is also a matter of some controversy whether or not he was a member of the Pythagorean Brotherhood. In one source he is listed as one of the Pythagoreans,[6] while another specifically tells us that he 'heard Pythagoras'.[7] Until quite recently it was the generally accepted view amongst modern scholars that he was a Pythagorean.[8] They based this claim upon the following evidence: Alcmaeon lived at Croton, where Pythagoras first established his Order; Diogenes Laërtius tells us that he 'heard

Pythagoras' and that he addressed himself in the opening words of his book to Brotinus, Leon and Bathyllus - who seem to have been Pythagoreans;[9] both Iamblichus and Philoponus list him among the contemporaries of Pythagoras 'young in his old age'; he believed in the immortality of the soul, and made great use of opposites. With one or two exceptions, who speak of him unreservedly as a Pythagorean,[10] later writers, however, have been more guarded or even hostile to the view that he was a Pythagorean.[11] References to master-pupil relationships in the doxographical writers are notoriously unreliable and Diogenes' remark that Alcmaeon 'heard Pythagoras' may have no more significance than that someone (Sotion, perhaps?) fitted him into a line of succession. Again, Burnet's assumption that Alcmaeon dedicated his treatise to the Pythagoreans[12] (though accepted by Ross and, with some reservation, by Heidel[13]) has been shown to be misguided.[14] There are no parallels for dedications at this period, and a discourse which takes the form of a personal address, like that of Empedocles to Pausanias, does not necessarily imply agreement with the views held by the person to whom it is addressed. Since Iamblichus' list of Pythagoreans (*V.P.* 267) also includes, in addition to that of Alcmaeon, the names of Parmenides, Melissus and Empedocles, who were not Pythagoreans, it is of dubious value as evidence. At *Metaphysics* A5, 986a22ff. (*D.K.*24A3) Aristotle compares Alcmaeon's theory of opposites with that of the Pythagoreans and asserts that either he derived his theory from them or they derived theirs from him:

> Others of the same group [the Pythagoreans] say that there are ten principles, set out in a co-ordinated series, viz. limit and unlimited; odd and even; unity and plurality; right and left; male and female; resting and moving; straight and crooked; light and darkness; good and bad; square and oblong. Alcmaeon of Croton appears to have had the same idea and either he borrowed it from them, or they from him. For Alcmaeon † was [young] in the old age of Pythagoras † and gave a similar exposition to theirs. For he says that most of the things which affect humans go in pairs, but he speaks of opposites not, as the Pythagoreans do, as specific, but haphazard, e.g. white and black; sweet and bitter; good and bad; large and small. He threw out vague suggestions about the rest, but the Pythagoreans specified how many

and what the opposites were. From both we may understand that the opposites are principles of existing things.

Why Aristotle should consider that such a natural point of view must have been borrowed by either from the other – especially as he himself had just emphasised the importance of the role of certain contrarieties in Ionian thought – is difficult to comprehend. In any case, as Vlastos has pointed out,[15] two pairs of opposites which, on any view, are characteristic of Pythagoreanism, namely Peras-Apeiron and Odd-Even, are conspicuously absent from those of Alcmaeon and, furthermore, are alien to all that is known of Alcmaeon's thought. Aristotle himself, we may note, actually remarks that Alcmaeon did not conceive of the opposites in the same way as the Pythagoreans did. So, then, far from providing evidence that Alcmaeon was a Pythagorean, our evidence here surely implies that Aristotle did not regard him as such.

The same passage in the *Metaphysics* (986a29ff.) provides our only direct testimony for Alcmaeon's date. Unfortunately the MSS and the ancient commentators are divided about Aristotle's precise wording here. The text of the crucial sentence here: καὶ γὰρ ἐγένετο τὴν ἡλικίαν 'Αλκμαίων ἐπὶ γέροντι Πυθαγόραι, ἀπεφήνατο δὲ παραπλησίως τούτοις is obviously corrupt. The words ἐγένετο τὴν ἡλικίαν and ἐπὶ γέροντι Πυθαγόραι are omitted by the Laurentian MS (A^b) and do not occur in Alexander. They do, however, appear in E and Γ and are included by Asclepius in his commentary (39.21 Hayduck). Although these words have been long suspected as being a later interpolation, they were admitted by editors until Ross bracketed them as later additions in his edition of the *Metaphysics*. Ross believes, however, that the statement is likely enough to be true and appeals to Iamblichus *V.P.* 104 (*D.K.*67A5), where Alcmaeon is included among the contemporaries of Pythagoras 'young in his old age'. But, as this same list also contains the names of much later philosophers like Philolaus, Eurytus and Leucippus, it is of little or no value as evidence here. Ross further argues that the suspiciousness of these words is further increased since Aristotle only once mentions Pythagoras elsewhere and nowhere claims any knowledge of his date. Although this argument is repeated by Jaeger, it is hardly cogent. Aristotle is known to have written treatises on the Pythagoreans, now unfortunately lost, in which he certainly mentioned Pythagoras himself. Moreover, this is the obvious context where Aristotle would have assigned a date to Alcmaeon; only here, for example, does he 'date' Anaxagoras and Empedocles. It is a curious argument, in any case, to claim that Aristotle only once mentions Pythagoras elsewhere and nowhere claims any knowledge of his date and, on the basis of this single context, to reject the passage where he is named and apparently dated. Even if this dating does represent the opinion of an interpolator and does not stem from Aristotle himself, there is no reason why it should not be approximately correct. Accordingly, Diels' conjectured addition of νέος (young) before ἐπὶ γέροντι Πυθαγόραι has much to recommend it; while a precise dating is impossible upon the available evidence, a period of activity around the second quarter of the fifth century BC would pose no insurmountable chronological problem with regard to the theories and views attributed to Alcmaeon.[16]

We learn from Galen[17] that Alcmaeon was the author of a book entitled *On Nature*. Aristotle wrote a polemic against Alcmaeon[18] and presumably had direct access to this work. It seems likely that Theophrastus also used the work at first hand for his lengthy summary of its author's views on sensation. The doxographical writer Diogenes Laërtius has preserved the opening words of this book:

> Alcmaeon of Croton, son of Peirithous, spoke these words to Brotinus,[19] and Leon and Bathyllus. 'Concerning things unseen the gods possess clear understanding, but in so far as men can proceed by inference [τεκμαίρεσθαι] . . . I say as follows.'[20]

The theory of knowledge, propounded here by Alcmaeon at the very beginning of his work, stands in marked contrast to the dogmatic certitude prevalent elsewhere amongst the pre-Socratic philosophers (for Xenophanes, however, see p. 101). Alcmaeon here displays a much more modest attitude when he contrasts the certainty attainable (only) by the gods with the inferential procedures which mortals are forced to employ. The gods know the truth directly, but human beings, he contends, can only feel their way by interpreting such evidence as is afforded in the visible world. Alcmaeon, then, has renounced the dogmatic belief of his philosophical contemporaries in a single *archē* and their confident, a priori deductions from it and advocates instead a humbler but more empirical approach.

Yet, despite his rejection of the extended philosophical approach here, his medical theory reveals a continued willingness to draw upon philosophy when it suits his purpose and when it is compatible with his theory of knowledge. Aëtius preserves for us the following brief description of his theory of health:

> Alcmaeon holds that what preserves health is the equality [*isonomia*] of the powers – moist and dry, cold and hot, bitter and sweet and the rest[21] – and the supremacy [*monarchia*] of any one of them causes disease; for the supremacy of either is destructive. The cause of disease is an excess of heat or cold; the occasion of it surfeit or deficiency of nourishment; the location of it blood, marrow or the brain. Disease may come about from external causes, from the quality of water, local environment or toil or torture. Health, on the other hand, is a harmonious blending of the qualities.
>
> (Aëtius, V 30, 1 *D.K.*24B4)

Here is revealed a totally different conception of disease from that encountered previously in Greek epic. In Homer the more dramatic diseases, at any rate, are represented as being outside nature and subject to the whim of the gods. Although Hesiod took a step away from this belief and held that diseases were not invariably subject to individual divine decision, but were capable of attacking people of their own accord, he nevertheless shares with Homer the belief that they possessed a separate existence of their own. Alcmaeon, however, rejects this ontological conception of disease and holds it to be due to disturbances of the body's natural equilibrium. He thus regards disease as a part of nature and, in consequence, subject to the same rules that operate in the world at large.

Just as Alcmaeon's Milesian predecessor Anaximander had viewed the cosmos in terms of a balance or even a legal contract between equal opposed forces,[22] so now in the human body health is regarded as being due to the equilibrium (*isonomia*) of the powers composing it, while the supremacy (*monarchia*) of any one of them causes disease. The terms 'isonomia' and 'monarchia', if actually employed by Alcmaeon, mark the application of politico-social concepts to the physical sphere in a manner paralleled in both Anaximander and Heraclitus.

The subsequent influence of this medical theory was great. It is not only adopted within the Hippocratic *Corpus* and employed, for example, by the author of *De vetere medicina* as the basis for his own dietetic theory, but it is also combined with the four element theory and given a physiological application when Empedocles maintains that a man's flesh and blood are made up of particles of the four world components on the pattern of *isomoiria*, and, where this gives way to inequalities, deviations from perfect health and wisdom occur.[23] Its subsequent influence can be traced through the physician Philistion of Locri[24] and thence to Plato.[25] Under the influence of the Empedoclean theory the constituent humours of the human body were limited to four, blood, phlegm, black bile and yellow bile (see Chapter 4, p. 91). The theory of the four humours has exercised a powerful influence throughout the history of medicine and, like its philosophical counterpart, was subsequently linked with this view of disease as the result of a disequilibrium within the body. Health, so it was believed, returned when the imbalance was restored. As a consequence of this conception, dietetics, in its widest sense, was accorded a role of primary importance within Greek medicine. The doctor, to restore health and redress the imbalance, would prescribe for the patient not only a specific diet (in the modern sense), but also a comprehensive regimen of life, recommending, according to the patient's individual requirements, baths, massages, gymnastic exercises and even changes of climate.

Alcmaeon's physiological interests and, in particular, his investigations into the nature of the sense organs, seem to have had an even greater influence upon subsequent philosophical thought. For his preoccupation with these matters stimulated the interest of later philosophers in them to such an extent that after him psycho-physiological inquiries become almost a standard topic of investigation (see Table 1). Most of our information regarding Alcmaeon's views upon this subject is preserved in Theophrastus' *Fragment on Sensation*, Chapters 25 and 26 (*D.K.24A5*):

Among those who explain sensation by what it is unlike, Alcmaeon begins by defining the difference between man

Table 1 Alcmaeon and his pre-Socratic successors

The following physiological queries, which Alcmaeon seems to have been the first to raise, subsequently became stock questions.

Topic	Alcmaeon	Hippon	Empedocles	Anaxagoras	Diogenes	Atomists
Nature of the semen	Semen considered to be brain substance. Aëtius, V 3, 3 (*D.K.* 24A13).	Semen held to be moist and to flow from the marrow. Censorinus, 5, 2 (*D.K.* 38A12), Aristotle, *De anima* 405b1 (*D.K.* 31A4), Hipp. *Ref.* 1, 16 (*D.K.* 38A3).	A form of blood. See Longrigg, 1985a, pp. 277ff.	It seems likely that Anaxagoras, like Democritus, subscribed to a preformationist theory (pangenesis) and held that all the parts of the body are present in the seed. See Lonie's useful remarks (1981, p. 66, n. 84).	Semen is the 'foam of the blood'. Clement, *Paedagogus* I 6, 48 (*D.K.* 64A24), Vindicianus, Fragmentum para 1, Aristotle, *H.A.* 511b30 and Simplicius, *In phys.* 153.13 (*D.K.* 64B6). See Longrigg, 1985a, pp. 278ff.	According to Democritus semen is derived from the whole body including its principal parts such as bone, flesh and sinews. Aëtius, V 3, 6 (*D.K.* 68A141). According to Leucippus it is a portion of the soul (Aëtius, V 4, 1 *D.K.* 67A35).
Reproduction and sex differentiation	Both parents contribute seed. Sex of embryo is determined according to which contributes the most. Censorinus, 5, 2ff. (*D.K.* 24A13) and 6, 4 (*D.K.* 24A14).	Both parents contribute seed (Aëtius, V 5, 3 *D.K.* 38A13) and the sex of the embryo is determined by the quality of the semen (i.e. whether it is concentrated and strong or	Both parents contribute seed (Aristotle, *De. gen. an.* 722b10 *D.K.* 31B63). Sex of embryo is determined by whether the seed enters the womb when the latter is hot or cold (Aristotle, *De. gen. an.* 723a23 *D.K.*	Only males produce seed. Females provide the place for it to develop. Males come from the right testicle, females from the left (or from the right or left hand side of the body respectively?). Males develop in	Only the male produces seed. Censorinus, 5, 4 (*D.K.* 64A27).	According to Democritus both male and female produce seed (Aëtius, V 5, 1 *D.K.* 68A142). Sex is determined in the womb according to whether the mother's or father's seed prevails (Arist., *De. gen. an.* 764a6 *D.K.* 68A143).

Part of body first to develop	The head according to Aëtius, V 17, 3. But see too Censorinus, 5, 2 (*D.K.* 24A13).	The head according to Censorinus, 6, 1 (*D.K.* 38A15).	fluid and weak). Aëtius, V 7, 3 and Censorinus, 6, 4 (*D.K.* 38A14).	31B65). See Longrigg, 1965a, pp. 314-15.	The heart. Censorinus, 6, 1 (*D.K.* 31A84).	the right of the womb, females in the left (Aristotle. *De. gen. an.* 763b30 *D.K.* 59A107).	The brain. Censorinus, 6, 1 (*D.K.* 59A108).	Flesh then bones, sinews and other parts. Censorinus, 5, 4 (*D.K.* 64A27).	According to Plutarch (*An. prol.* 3 p.495E *D.K.* 68B148). Democritus held it was the navel. According to Aristotle (*De. gen. an.* 740a13 *D.K.* 68A145) he held the external parts were the first to be differentiated. Censorinus (6, 1 *D.K.* 68A145) claims that the head and belly were first.

Table 1 Continued

Topic	Alcmaeon	Hippon	Empedocles	Anaxagoras	Diogenes	Atomists
Mode of nourishment of embryo	Through the whole body (Aëtius, V 16, 3 D.K. 24A17). See Rufus in Oribas. III 156 C.M.G. VI, 2 2 136 (D.K. 24A17) and p. 61 below.	By certain protuberances within the womb. Censorinus, 6, 3 (D.K. 38A17).	According to Soranus via four vessels (two venous and two arterial) through the navel (Gynaec. I 57 p. 42, 12 Ilb. D.K. 31A79) — but see Longrigg. 1985a, p. 282 n. 23.	Through the navel. Censorinus, 6, 3 (D.K. 59A110).	By certain protuberances within the womb. Censorinus, 6, 3 (D.K. 64A25) By 'cotyledons'. Aristophanes, Epit. hist. anim. I 78 (D.K. 64A25).	By sucking upon a bit of flesh within the womb. Aristotle, De gen. an. 746a19. See 740a33 and Aëtius, V 16, 1 (D.K. 68A144).
Seat of the intellect	The head according to Aëtius, V 17, 3 (D.K. 24A13).	The head according to Censorinus, 6, 1 (D.K. 38A15).	The blood around the heart. Porphyr., De Styge ap. Stob. Ecl. I 49, 53 p. 424, 14W (D.K. 31B105). Theophrastus, De sens. 10 (D.K. 31A86).	Brain. Censorinus, 6, 1 (D.K. 59A108).	The air around the brain. Theophrastus, De sens. 39ff. (D.K. 64A19). (For Aëtius' statement that Diogenes held the heart to be the seat of the intellect, see below, Chapter 6, n. 67.)	According to Aëtius, IV 5, 1, Democritus held the seat of the intellect to be in the brain but at IV 4, 6 he claims the latter held that the reasoning part of the soul was in the thorax (D.K. 68A105).

56

Cause of sleep	Due to the withdrawal of the blood into the 'blood-flowing'(?) veins. Aëtius, V 24, 1 (*D.K.* 24A18). See below, p. 62.	NO EVIDENCE	Due to a proportionate cooling of the heat within the blood. Aëtius, V 24, 2 (*D.K.* 31A85).	Due to weariness as a result of bodily activity. Aëtius, V 25, 2 (*D.K.* 59A103).	Due to the blood filling the veins and driving the air into the chest and stomach. Aëtius, V 24, 33 (*D.K.* 64A29).	According to Aëtius (V 25, 3 *D.K.* 67A34) Leucippus held that sleep was caused by the separating off of the finer particles to a degree which exceeds the accession of psychic heat.
Sterility of mules	That of males due to the fineness and coldness of the semen; that of females due to failure of the womb to open wide. Aëtius, V 14, 1 (*D.K.* 24B3).	NO EVIDENCE	Due to the hardening of the mixture of the semen from male and female (akin to the alloying of metals). Aristotle, *De. gen. an.* 747a34 (*D.K.* 31B92). Aëtius, V 14, 2 (*D.K.* 31A82) is corrupt.	NO EVIDENCE	NO EVIDENCE	Due to the malformation of their genital passages (*poroi*) resulting from their artificial creation. Aristotle, *De. gen. an.* 747a29 (*D.K.* 68A149).
Physiological psychology of perception	See Theophrastus, *De sens.* 25ff. (*D.K.* 24A5).	NO EVIDENCE	See especially Theophrastus, *De sens.* 1–2 and 7–24 (*D.K.* 31A86).	See Theophrastus, *De sens.* 27–37 and 59 (*D.K.* 59A92).	See Theophrastus, *De sens.* 39–48 (*D.K.* 64A19).	See especially Theophrastus, *De sens.* 49–58, 60–83 (*D.K.* 68A135).

and the lower animals. Man, he says, differs from the other creatures because he alone has understanding, whereas they have sensation, but not understanding; thought and sensation are different, not, as Empedocles holds, the same. He next speaks of each sense separately. Hearing, he says, takes place through the ears because they contain a void, which resounds. Sound is produced in the cavity and the air echoes it. Smelling is effected by means of the nostrils along with respiration when air is drawn up into the brain. Tastes are distinguished by the tongue. Since it is warm and soft it dissolves substances by its heat and, owing to its porous and delicate structure, it receives and transmits the flavour.

[26] Eyes see through the water surrounding them. That the eye contains fire is evident, for the fire flashes forth when it is struck. Vision is due to the gleaming element and the transparent when it gives back a reflection; the purer this element is, the better the eye sees. All the senses are connected in some way to the brain. Consequently they are incapacitated if it is moved or shifts its position. For it obstructs the passages through which the sensations take place. Concerning touch he tells us neither the manner nor the means whereby it is effected. This, then, is the extent of his explanation.

As is clear from the above, Alcmaeon has conducted empirical investigations of some, at least, of the sense organs in accordance with the methodological principles he set out at the beginning of his book. In the course of these investigations he appears to have discovered certain passages or 'pores' which he inferred led to the brain. In the case of the nose and the ears these passages are obvious and evidently included the nostrils, Eustachian tubes and the external auditory meatus. (It is extremely unlikely that Alcmaeon had discovered the olfactory and auditory nerves.) In the case of the eyes, however, a more detailed examination of the internal structure is required before any connection with the brain becomes apparent. A late source, Chalcidius, who translated the *Timaeus* into Latin in the fourth century AD, actually provides the information (*Commentary on Plato's 'Timaeus'* (pp. 279ff. Wrobel *D.K*.24A10)) that Alcmaeon was the 'first to dare to approach the excision of the eye' (primus exsectionem [oculi] adgredi est ausus). Chalcidius' statement

58

here is unfortunately terse and ambiguous: it is not clear whether *exsectio* indicates dissection pursued as part of an investigative process; and, if so, whether it was performed upon a human or upon an animal subject; whether that subject was alive or dead; or whether it suggests a surgical operation carried out by Alcmaeon.

It has been claimed on the basis of Chalcidius' report that Alcmaeon was the first to employ human dissection as a general method of investigation. In the sentence preceding the mention of Alcmaeon, Chalcidius, it is true, expressly refers to human dissection when he mentions certain illustrious men who 'artus humani corporis facta membrorum exsectione rimati sunt'. However, most scholars have rightly rejected this suggestion on the grounds that Chalcidius does not confine his reference solely to Alcmaeon, but includes Callisthenes and Herophilus, and that there is no evidence of human dissection before the third century BC when, for a brief period, human dissection and even vivisection were practised at Alexandria (see Chapter 7). Chalcidius' comment here must be restricted solely to Herophilus. (Many of the features of the detailed description of the eye given by Chalcidius below must also be similarly restricted to the Hellenistic period. For example, it was only after Herophilus' work that the view that the eye contained four membranes became canonical (see Chapter 7)). It is most unlikely, then, that Alcmaeon dissected or vivisected human beings.

G. E. R. Lloyd believes[26] that Chalcidius' reference is to an anatomical investigation performed upon an animal and argues that, in the light of Aristotle's comment at *De partibus animalium* 645a26ff., where he urges his readers to overcome their natural squeamishness regarding the investigation of the parts of the body (see Chapter 6, p. 159), 'there is nothing surprising in Chalcidius considering the first person to cut open an animal for an anatomical inquiry an adventurous man.' Viewed against the background of a culture, however, wherein animals were regularly sacrificed and slaughtered for the purpose of divination, Lloyd's claim is far from convincing. Chalcidius' Latin - *ausus est* ('dared') - seems strongly to suggest a human subject. But was that subject alive or dead? Since the latter alternative has just been ruled out on the grounds that there exists no evidence for the dissection of the human corpse at this time, we are left with the remaining possibility of a surgical operation upon a human subject for a therapeutic purpose.[27] Lloyd rejected this proposal on the grounds that 'so far as the text of Chalcidius goes, *exsectio* relates not to any surgical procedure, but to the problem of 'demonstrating the nature of the eye'.[28] But a surgical operation like this could very well have been regarded by Chalcidius as an important first step towards a later 'demonstration of the nature of the eye' – particularly if, as a result of that operation, discoveries were made concerning the eye's nature. Once the diseased or damaged eyeball had been excised, the structures leading from the back of the eye and passing through the optic foramen towards the intra-cranial cavity would have been revealed. The most prominent and distinct of these is the optic nerve. Although Alcmaeon, of course, had no clear conception of the function of the optic nerve *qua* nerve, it is very likely that he found here his passage connecting eye to brain.

Having discovered, then, that the eyes, no less than the nose and ears, were linked to the brain, Alcmaeon seems to have inferred that all the senses were similarly connected and that the brain, therefore, must be the seat of the intelligence. He declared that if the brain moved or shifted its position sensation was impaired since the passages through which the sensations pass were blocked (*De sensibus* 26). Although Alcmaeon's discovery of connections between eyes and brain may have involved the use of a knife or scalpel to excise the eye, in the case of the nose and ears a probe would have been sufficient to demonstrate the passages leading from these organs to the brain. Thus, the empirical investigations Alcmaeon conducted may well have been quite limited in scope and may not have involved any proper dissection at all.[29] Consequently it would be mistaken to regard him as the inventor of systematic dissection.

As a result of his investigations into the physiology of the sense organs Alcmaeon concluded, then, that the brain was the seat of intellectual activity. He thus became one of the earliest protagonists in the debate as to whether the heart or the brain was the centre of the intelligence. This debate rumbled on down through the centuries until the sixteenth century at least, when it is echoed, for example, in Bassanio's query in the *Merchant of Venice*: 'Tell me where is fancie bred, or in the heart or in the head?'

Alcmaeon was followed in his decision to award primacy to the brain by the natural philosopher Diogenes of Apollonia, the author of the Hippocratic treatise *De morbo sacro*, by Plato in the *Timaeus* and by the two great Alexandrian anatomists Herophilus and Erasistratus. Those who, on the contrary, favoured the heart as the seat of the intellect included Empedocles,[30] Philistion, Aristotle, Diocles, Praxagoras and the Stoics. One might have expected that the discovery of the nerves by the Alexandrians and their demonstration of their origin in the brain would have settled this issue once and for all. But even after it had been demonstrated by dissection that the brain must be the seat of the intellect, the Stoic philosopher Chrysippus sought doggedly to defend his school's dogma by appealing to Praxagoras, a medical authority of about half a century earlier.[31]

Our remaining evidence of Alcmaeon's physiological interests is scanty and, at times, inconsistent. He seems to have been particularly concerned with reproduction, sex differentiation and embryology. Aëtius tells us that he believed the semen to be a part of the brain (V 3, 3 *D.K.*24A13) – a theory at least compatible with the importance he assigns to the brain generally. Censorinus, however, maintains that he was opposed to this view (*De die natali* 5, 2 *D.K.*24A13). Censorinus also informs us in the same passage that, unlike those who believed that offspring came solely from the father's seed, Alcmaeon believed that both sexes produced seed and adds elsewhere (6, 4 *D.K.*24A14) that he held that the offspring became the same sex as that parent which had produced the most seed.

We learn from Aristotle at *De generatione et corruptione* 752b25ff. (*D.K.*24A16) that Alcmaeon considered that the white of the egg served as the 'milk' or nourishment for the developing embryo. It has been claimed upon the basis of this report that Alcmaeon had undertaken a detailed study, employing vivisection, of the development of the chicken embryo;[32] but such an assumption goes far beyond the actual evidence. According to Aëtius (V 16, 3 *D.K.*24A17), Alcmaeon believed that the embryo absorbed nutriment through its whole body 'like a sponge'. Rufus, however, tells us[33] that he believed that the embryo took in food through its mouth (στόματι) while still in the womb. Olivieri's clever emendation[34] of στόματι to σώματι (body) renders these two reports consistent and should be adopted. Aëtius further informs us that Alcmaeon held that the head was the first part of the embryo to be formed in the womb (V 17, 3 *D.K.*24A13). Again, it seems more likely that he arrived at this belief (if he did) by inference from his theory that the brain is the seat of the intellect than as the result of dissection. Censorinus, it may be noted, declares that Alcmaeon admitted that he had no definite views on the subject since no one could observe which part was the first to be formed (*De die natali* 5, 3 *D.K.*24A13).

Another piece of evidence concerning Alcmaeon's physiological beliefs which has been overpressed by scholars is Aëtius' report that he believed that sleep ensued when the blood withdrew into the 'blood-flowing (?) veins' (εἰς τὰς αἱμόρρους[35] φλέβας); that waking resulted from its diffusion again through these vessels and that a complete withdrawal resulted in death (V 24, 1 *D.K.*24A18). As was seen above, it has been claimed that Alcmaeon dissected animals. In the course of these dissections, it is further argued, he observed that in a dead animal certain vessels, i.e. the principal arteries, were either bloodless or contained very little blood. Having wrongly concluded that this was also the case in a living body, it is maintained, he then drew a distinction between two types of blood vessel and distinguished arteries from veins (the 'blood-flowing vessels').[36] If this reconstruction were correct, it would appear, then, that Alcmaeon was also the originator of a theory which, developed by Praxagoras and adopted by Erasistratus, thereafter exercised a dominant role as a 'deadly heritage'[37] in Greek medicine – the theory that the arteries contained not blood, but *pneuma*. Several scholars, however, have wisely enjoined caution here.[38] It is stressed that this interpretation rests upon a far from certain textual emendation and it is pointed out that even if the term αἱμόρρους was actually used by Alcmaeon, the implied contrast could be between the major blood vessels on the one hand and any other vessels on the other, which were imagined to hold little or no blood. Furthermore, as Lloyd again points out (op. cit.), since the belief that sleep is due to a reflux of the blood into the interior of the body becomes a common one and is adopted both in the Hippocratic *Corpus* and by Aristotle, it seems more likely that Alcmaeon may have had some such theory in mind here, rather than that he made erroneous inferences from observations of bloodless arteries in dead animals.

Alcmaeon's physiological interests, and, in particular, his researches into the nature of the sense organs seem to have had important influences upon later philosophical thought. His preoccupation with these matters seems to have stimulated the interest of later philosophers in them. After Alcmaeon, as we shall see, such physiological questions as the nature of the semen, sex differentiation, the cause of sleep, the mode of nourishment of the embryo and even the reason for the sterility of mules, become almost standard topics of inquiry among the natural philosophers and their biological interests, in their turn, had important repercussions upon their general philosophical standpoints. Even Parmenides' interest in these matters in his *Way of Opinion* may be significant. For, if he could show in a work which he himself described as containing 'no true belief'[39] how equally or even more plausible explanations could be given for the old problems first mooted by the cosmologists, and also how even the most 'modern' biological and physiological queries could be answered upon the simple but explicitly erroneous basis of the widely accepted opposition of fire and night,[40] he would have considerably reinforced the subversive conclusions he had deduced in his *Way of Truth*.

Parmenides' arguments in the *Way of Truth* mark a watershed in the history of pre-Socratic philosophy. By the exercise of his rigid, deductive logic he had denied all motion and change in the physical world. He was supported in these conclusions by his disciples Zeno of Elea and Melissus of Samos. Other philosophers, however, were unable to accept his uncompromising declaration that the natural world was sheer illusion and, each in his different way, sought to circumvent Parmenides' arguments and rehabilitate empirical reality. Broadly, their attempts to evade the Eleatic *elenchus* fell into two categories. The Pluralists sought to evade Parmenides' denial of coming-into-being and passing-away by postulating a plurality of eternal and immutable entities which were able by their combination and separation to account for the great diversity of the phenomena of everyday experience. The main protagonists of pluralism were Empedocles, Anaxagoras and the Atomists. The Monists, by contrast, found their answer to Parmenides by reviving and modifying earlier monistic theories. Diogenes, for example, following Anaximenes, adopted air as his *archē*, while Hippon revived the theory of Thales and maintained that water was his first principle.

It is significant that each and every one of these philosophers reveals a marked interest not only in medicine and biology generally, but also in the particular biological queries raised by

Alcmaeon.[11] It is clearly evident in almost every instance that their biological interests exercised considerable influence upon their physics. In the case of the Monists, for example, it is noteworthy that both Diogenes and Hippon adduce physiological arguments in support of their revised monistic hypotheses. Diogenes supports his revival of Anaximenes' theory that air is the basic substance[12] by pointing to the fact that human beings and all other animals live by breathing air; that air is their soul and intelligence since, when it is taken away, their intelligence fails and they die; that the semen is aeriform and, since it produces new life, its aerated nature is an important indication that air is the vital substance.[13] Hippon's arguments in support of water or 'the moist'[14] as his first principle are similarly of a physiological nature. He associates youth and suppleness with moisture, old age and death with dryness.[15] He points out that the soles of the feet are insensitive because they lack moisture,[16] and he appeals, like Diogenes, to the nature of the semen, eliciting support this time from its liquid nature.[17]

The same trend is apparent in the Pluralists. Empedocles, it may be noted, subsequently takes up each and every one of the physiological inquiries mooted by Alcmaeon. He also, like the latter, adopts a pore theory to explain sense perception, respiration and even the sterility of mules. He does not, however, confine this idea to the explanation of purely physiological phenomena but employs it generally within his physics. In order to circumvent the impasse caused by the Parmenidean *elenchus* Empedocles postulated his theory of the four elements, earth, air, fire and water, each of which bears a close resemblance to the Parmenidean One-Being in that it was uncreated and could not be destroyed. All things in the physical world, he maintained, come into being through the mixture and interchange of these four eternal elements. According to Aristotle, he held that mixture is only possible between things whose pores are of the same size and shape.[18] Since Alcmaeon had employed a pore theory to explain perception and Empedocles makes elaborate use of pores for the same purpose, it is likely that he has extended this theory from the sphere of sense perception to the world at large rather than vice versa. It should also be noted that Love (one of his two motor causes introduced to counter the Parmenidean denial of motion and change), which plays so important a role in his physics in bringing unlike element particles together, is regarded by him as the self-same impulse towards union that is found within human bodies. He looks upon his motor cause from a physiological viewpoint and declares that no mortal has yet realised that the same Love which people recognise in their own bodies performs an identical function in the world at large.[49]

These physiological interests are even more clearly apparent in Anaxagoras' thinking and exercise even more comprehensive an influence upon his physics generally than was the case with Empedocles. Anaxagoras seems to have been especially interested in nutrition. The scholiast in Gregorius Nazianzenus preserves the problem which beset him. 'How', he asks 'can hair come to be from what is not hair, and flesh from what is not flesh?'[50] The answer he sought had to satisfy the canons of Eleatic logic. His solution was to claim that everything is pre-existent in our nourishment:

> it seemed to him quite impossible that anything should come into being from the non-existent or be dissolved into it. At any rate, we take in nourishment that is simple and homogeneous, such as bread or water, and by this are nourished hair, veins, arteries, flesh, sinews, bones and all other parts of the body. Which being so, we must agree that everything that exists is in the nourishment we take in, and that everything derives its growth from things that exist. There must be in that nourishment some parts that are productive of blood, some of sinews, some of bones, and so on.
>
> (Aëtius, I 3, 5 *D.K.*59A46)

Simplicius provides some further evidence of Anaxagoras' concern with the problem of nutrition and growth.[51] It seems likely that he arrived at his general physical theory as a result of his preoccupation with these very problems.[52] This view that Anaxagoras' physiological interests influenced his physics is also supported by his use of *sperma* as a new technical term[53] and by Simplicius' comment[54] that he 'passed from the mixture in the individual to the mixture of all things'. It therefore seems very likely that Anaxagoras found in physiology his way to circumvent the Eleatic impasse.

Although, as has been seen above, this heightened interest in biology and medicine in the fifth century had important influences upon the formation of physical systems at that time, the interest of the philosophers in these matters, conversely, exercised a still greater influence upon medicine itself. For the philosophers, in extending their views upon the world at large to human beings themselves, began in consequence to subordinate medical theory to their general philosophical standpoint. (Anaxagoras, however, as has just been seen, is an exception in that he largely argues from microcosm to macrocosm.[55] While it could be maintained that Diogenes and Hippon follow an identical procedure, it should not be overlooked that both these thinkers employ physiological arguments in support of their respective attempts to revive a *previously propounded* monistic hypothesis.)

It is clear, for example, from the following passage in the *Anonymus Londinensis* XI, 13 (*D.K.*38A11) that Hippon sought to account for the origin of disease upon the basis of his single philosophical first principle:

> Hippon . . . believes that there is in us a natural moisture by which we are sentient and by which we live. When such moisture is in its normal condition, the living creature is healthy, but when it dries up, the animal loses consciousness and dies. For this reason old men are dry and insensitive, because they lack moisture. Similarly the soles of the feet, because they have no share of moisture, are insensitive. * but in another book the same author says that the aforementioned moisture changes through excess of heat and excess of cold, and thus brings on diseases.* He says it changes to become moister or drier or coarser or finer or into other substances. Thus he defines the cause of disease, but he gives no indication of the individual diseases that arise.

Hippon, however, is a relatively minor figure,[56] whose subsequent influence upon medicine was slight.[57] Of greater importance in the history of medicine are the Atomists, who also formulated their philosophical theory to circumvent the Eleatic impasse. Our knowledge of the founder of the atomic theory Leucippus of Miletus is unfortunately sketchy.[58] More information has survived regarding his successor Democritus of Abdera. It will be convenient, therefore, to concentrate upon the latter's more developed version of the atomic theory. Democritus subsequently became a legendary figure and, in consequence, not only medical, but magical and alchemical writings were ascribed to him. Great caution must, therefore, be exercised in assessing the authenticity of this evidence. In the twelfth tetralogy of the Alexandrian catalogue of his works, several medical titles are attributed to him (*D.K.*68A33), namely *Prognosis, On regimen* (or *Dietetics*) and *Medical Opinion*. None of these treatises has survived and they may have existed only as figments of some biographer's imagination. Equally dubious is the claim that Hippocrates studied under him (*D.K.*68A10).[59] Other sources present highly circumstantial accounts of meetings between the two men.[60] According to one story Democritus became mentally deranged and the citizens of Abdera sent a delegation to Cos to beg Hippocrates to come and cure the philosopher. According to another, Hippocrates found him sitting under a plane tree surrounded by the bodies of animals he had been dissecting.[61] These anecdotes are highly dubious. However, more trustworthy evidence has survived attesting to Democritus' medical interests and the manner in which he sought to base his theories upon his atomic theory.

It is evident from one fragment (Frag. 234) that, like the majority of Greeks, Democritus attached the greatest importance to a sound regimen, to prevention rather than cure, and maintained that although their health lies in their own hands, people frequently destroy it in their ignorance, through intemperance. In another fragment (Frag. 159) Democritus imagines the body impeaching the soul on the grounds that it is responsible for its pains and troubles. He declares that the body should win its case, for it is the soul that ruins it by its neglect, drunkenness and love of pleasure. Neither of the above fragments is explicitly based upon the atomic theory, yet they are both totally in accord with a theory which held that the soul is material and all experience, both bodily and psychic, results from the beneficial or disturbing effects of the entry of atomic complexes into the organism.

This connection, however, is more apparent in his biological writings. Sufficient evidence has survived of his biological interests to reveal a detailed and comprehensive study which must have rivalled that of Aristotle himself. It is noteworthy that each of the particular biological queries raised by Alcmaeon is taken up by Democritus. His answers in response to these problems reveal, in certain instances at least, that his theories were formulated in accordance with his general philosophical theory.

The atomic theory clearly underlies his explanation of the mechanism of life and death, for example. The soul, he believes, is formed of tiny spherical atoms, which, under pressure from the external atmosphere, are constantly being extruded from the body. Respiration, however, restores the balance since the inspired air contains other minute spherical atomic particles which are able to make good this loss. However, whenever outflow greatly exceeds inflow, death ensues.[62] A milder and reversible preponderance of outflow over inflow, according to Leucippus at any rate, induces sleep.[63]

Democritus' account of sensation is similarly based upon his atomic theory. Theophrastus provides us with a full account of his detailed explanation of the various senses upon this basis at *De sensibus* 49-83 (*D.K.*68A135). All sensation is explained as a form of contact or touch. But whereas the other senses are accounted for upon the basis of the different sizes and shapes of the atomic particles, vision is given a rather more elaborate explanation. According to Theophrastus, Democritus held that vision is effected by fine films of atomic particles given off in the image of the object seen (*eidōlon*) which meet with effluences from the observer to form a solid impression in the air (*entypōsis*), which then enters the pupil of the eye.

The atomic theory also clearly underlies Democritus' views upon reproduction and embryology. Like his somewhat older contemporary Diogenes (see pp. 77-80), he believed that the vehicle of life was *pneuma* (*D.K.*68A140), which was transmitted via the semen and drawn from every part of the body (*D.K.*68A141). He thus agreed with Alcmaeon and Empedocles in holding that both parents contributed seed (*D.K.*68A142), that sexual differentiation took place in the womb and that it was dependent on whether the male or female seed prevailed (*D.K.*68A143). He rejected, however, the determining role in this function that Empedocles ascribed to heat and cold.[64] This postulate, which maintained that seed was derived from all parts of the body, has been called the 'pangenesis theory'[65] because Darwin himself in his work *Variations of Animals and Plants under Domestication* (London, 1868) drew attention to the close similarities between it and his own 'Provisional Hypothesis of Pangenesis'. It subsequently exercised a considerable influence upon later Greek biological thought and is apparent not only in several works of the Hippocratic *Corpus*,[66] but also in the doctrines of the Methodist sect. Aristotle himself describes and criticises this theory at *De generatione et corruptione* 721b6-724b31.

The influence in the history of medicine, however, of Democritus' two older contemporaries, Empedocles of Acragas and Diogenes of Apollonia, was even greater still. Both of these men, who may actually have been practising doctors themselves, exercised, for good and ill, an enormous impact upon contemporary and subsequent Greek medicine. Empedocles, the more important of the two, affords the clearest illustration of this new development, which resulted in the subordination of medical theory to philosophy. In the light of his pronounced medical interests this was a natural development. These interests are attested by his own words: for example, in one fragment he makes Pausanias, to whom he addresses his poem, the extravagant promise that he will 'learn all the drugs that are a defence against ills and old age' and that he will 'bring back from Hades the strength of a man who has died'.[67] Elsewhere he boasts of his fame as a doctor in the following words:

> When I come to flourishing towns I am honoured by men and women. They follow me in their thousands, asking me where is the road to profit, some desiring oracles, while others long pierced by grievous pains, ask to hear the word of healing for all kinds of illness.
>
> (Diogenes Laërtius, VIII, 62 *D.K.*31B112)

We also have some secondary evidence, which purports to supply details of Empedocles' medical activity together with his exploits in what might be described as public health engineering. However, tales of a similar nature are regularly linked with the names of other pre-Socratic philosophers and are in some cases clearly biographical inventions based upon some saying or other of the philosopher concerned.[68] It would be most unwise, therefore, to take these stories too seriously.

In addition to his physical poem *On nature* and his religious work *Purifications* (*Katharmoi*), Empedocles is credited on two occasions in the tradition with the authorship of a medical treatise. Diogenes Laërtius tells us (VIII, 77 *D.K.*31A1) that he wrote an Ἰατρικὸς λόγος - a medical treatise comprising some 600 lines, and the Suda attributes to him Ἰατρικὰ καταλογάδην - medical writings in prose (*s.v.* Empedocles *D.K.*31A2).

Unfortunately no definite quotation from this work has been preserved in any of our sources (although some scholars have claimed that Fragment 111 is derived from this medical work).[69] It has also been suggested[70] that there is a reference to an Ἰατρικόν by Aristotle at *Poetics* 1447b16-20, where he cites Empedocles as an example of a poet who 'treats a medical or scientific topic in verse'. Pliny's comment, too, that both Hippocrates and Empedocles pointed out at different places in their writings the power of fire to alleviate pestilence (*N.H.* XXXVI, 69, 202) could conceivably entail reference to a medical work by Empedocles. But in neither case is the evidence certain and there remains the distinct possibility that the tradition of a separate medical work by Empedocles stems simply from the wide interest he displays in medical matters in his physical poem. The polemic explicitly directed against him in *Ancient Medicine*, Chapter 20, too, could be accounted for upon this basis. If, however, Empedocles did actually write a medical treatise, its loss would then mark another occasion for deep regret that our knowledge of the early history of rational medicine is so severely truncated and that so vital a document for our understanding of the complexity of the relationship between philosophy and medicine has failed to survive.

We are fortunate, however, that a sufficient number of the fragments of the physical work has survived to enable us to formulate a general impression of what must have been a comprehensive and tightly integrated system of biology. The sustained manner in which Empedocles is able both to put forward a theory of health and to explain a very wide range of biological phenomena upon the basis of his philosophical postulate is impressive for its economy. Indeed, because Empedocles was so successful in explaining a great diversity of biological matters in this way, his views became highly influential in this field and thus provided a major contributory factor to the dominance of the four element theory for over two millennia. Any rejection of this theory would have required a total reformulation of the biological sciences which had developed so rapidly upon this basis.

We have already seen above how Empedocles combined his four element theory with Alcmaeon's theory of health. He maintained that the flesh and blood of human beings are made up of particles of these four world components in more or less equal proportions:

> And the earth anchored in the perfect harbours of Kypris and met with these in almost equal proportions with Hephaestus, with Water and with gleaming Aither – either a little more of it or less of it with more of the others. From these did blood arise and different forms of flesh.
>
> (Simplicius, *In physica* 32. 3 *D.K.*31B98)

The predominance of any one of these elements, he believed, resulted in deviations from perfect health or wisdom or even sanity.[71] The composition of the other parts of the human body is also explained by him in accordance with his four element theory. Bone, for example, we learn from a fragment containing a clever parody of a line of Homer (*Iliad* XXIV. 793), is composed of the elements mixed according to the following formula: 25 per cent water; 50 per cent fire; 25 per cent earth. Or, as he puts it more poetically himself, using a metaphor derived from the smelting of metals:

> The kindly earth received in her broad melting-pots two parts of gleaming Nestis [water] out of the eight, and four of Hephaestus [fire]; and there arose white bones divinely fitted together by the cementing of Harmony.
>
> (Simplicius, *In physica* 300. 19 *D.K.*31B96)

The large proportion of fire in this mixture seems to have been required to account not only for the whiteness[72] of bone, but also for its hardness. Elsewhere in Empedocles' physics fire plays an active role and acts as a solidifying agent.[73] According to Simplicius, however, the preponderance of fire was required to account for the whiteness *and the dryness* of bone,[74] but the latter quality seems rather to have been derived from the earth in its composition, as Philoponus suggests.[75] It should not be assumed that Empedocles believed that all four elements were present in every substance. It may be noted that the formula for bone cited above does not include air (although Theophrastus mistakenly assumes all four elements to be present,[76] and both Simplicius and Philoponus make an unconvincing attempt to interpret this fragment so as to include air).[77] We might notice that this element is also missing from the make-up of sinews.[78]

The composition and operation of the organs of the body are

also cleverly explained by Empedocles in accordance with his element theory. The eye, for example, is composed of all four elements.[79] Two of these, fire and water, play a predominant role in vision, which he seeks to elucidate by employing the analogy of a lantern. This simile, which is rich with Homeric overtones and *double entendres*, is preserved by Aristotle:

> Even as when a man, intending to make a journey through the wintry night, makes ready a light, a flame of blazing fire, fastens to it linen screens against all manner of winds and they scatter the blast of the ever-blowing winds, but the light leaping out through them, shines across the threshold with unfailing beams, as much as it is finer; even so did she [Love] give birth to the round-eyed pupil,[80] the primeval fire, enclosed in membranes and fine tissues.[81] These keep out the deep water that surrounds the pupil, but they let through the fire, as much of it as is finer.
>
> (*De sensu* 437b23ff. *D.K.*31B84)

Aristotle complains later in this treatise (at 438a4ff.) that there is an inconsistency in Empedocles' theory of vision. At one time, he alleges, the latter appears to explain vision upon the basis of a visual ray theory, at another, by means of effluences from the objects seen. Since Aristotle made his complaint, much ink has been spent by scholars trying to reconcile these two standpoints.[82] However, it should be noted that Theophrastus' description and criticism of Empedocles' theory of vision (at *De sensibus* 7ff. and 59ff.) is in complete harmony with the fragments and with Plato's evidence at *Meno* 76c (*D.K.*31A92), where it is held that Empedocles explained perception on the basis of pores and effluences. Nowhere does Theophrastus attribute a visual ray theory to Empedocles and, although he submits the latter's views on perception generally to searching criticisms, he makes no mention at all of what would have been a fundamental inconsistency in the latter's theory of vision. His own criticisms are based entirely upon the pore and effluence theory. He totally ignores Aristotle's criticisms in the *De sensu* and evidently, realising that Aristotle has interpreted the lantern simile too literally, passes over his master's attack in silence and makes his own criticisms from a better attested standpoint.

Empedocles also exploits the four element theory with similar skill to account for physiological processes like digestion and nutrition. Fortunately sufficient evidence has survived to enable his views here to be reconstructed with reasonable confidence. Simplicius tells us that he held that food was first cut and ground up in the mouth by the teeth (*In phys.* 371. 33 *D.K.*31B61); it was then digested in the stomach, i.e. it was broken down into its constituent elements by a process of putrefaction (*sēpsis*),[83] presumably under the action of the innate heat of the body.[84] Once this digestive process had been completed, the nutriment was then carried to the liver, where it was turned into blood,[85] itself a compound of all the elements in (more or less) equal proportions (*In phys.* 32-3 *D.K.*31B98) and thence distributed through the blood vessels (Soranus, *Gynaec.* I 57, 42. 12 IIb. *D.K.*31A79) and assimilated by the body by a process of 'like to like' (Aëtius, V 27, 1 *D.K.*31A77). Empedocles apparently considered flesh to be a thickening and secondary formation of the blood since both are composed essentially according to the same formula (cf. B98 last line and Aëtius, V 22, 1 *D.K.*31A78) – although, presumably, blood would contain a somewhat larger proportion of water than flesh.[86]

From the above account it can be seen how remarkably economical Empedocles is in his use of his hypothesis and how successfully he is able to exploit it to explain a wide range of biological phenomena. Several ideas of considerable importance for the subsequent history of medicine are discernible in the above account. The concept of innate heat, for example, which promoted the process of putrefaction described above and subsequently (after modification of nomenclature) played an extremely influential role in later Greek biology and medicine, seems to have been developed by Empedocles, who gave a wider physiological significance to Parmenides' correlation of cold with death and warmth with life.[87] It also played an important role throughout the whole of Empedocles' biology and is employed by him in his theory of sex differentiation (*D.K.*31A81), embryology (*D.K.*31A74), and in his explanation of sleep (*D.K.*31A85). This theory of the innate heat not only became widely prevalent amongst pre-Socratic philosophers who were contemporaries or immediately subsequent to Empedocles,[88] but it was also widely adopted by the Hippocratic writers and subsequently taken up by Philistion, Plato and Aristotle.[89] Empedocles seems also to have believed that the purpose of respiration was to cool the innate heat.[90] This theory, too, became

73

highly influential and was adopted by Plato,[91] who probably himself derived it from Philistion.[92] Aristotle,[93] also adopts this theory which he, too, probably derived from the 'Sicilian tradition'. Although he expressly criticises Empedocles for not having explained the purpose of respiration (*De resp.* 473a15ff.) his criticism is of doubtful validity. For it seems likely that Philistion derived from Empedocles not only his four element theory and the doctrine of innate heat, but also this view of the purpose of respiration. Furthermore, several pre-Socratic philosophers immediately subsequent to Empedocles, who have clearly taken into account certain of his biological theories, also subscribe to the belief that the purpose of respiration is to moderate the innate heat.[94] While it is possible that this theory represents a later development upon the basis of Empedoclean biology, each of these thinkers is directly influenced by Empedocles and they are not all obviously inter-related.

The innate heat, as was seen, acts upon nutriment and breaks it down by the process of putrefaction (*sēpsis*). Aristotle is very critical of Empedocles for his use of this term and claims that he is either wrong or has used a bad metaphor when he describes the formation of mother's milk as decomposed blood (*De gen. an.* 777a7 *D.K.*31B68). Resorting to etymology, Empedocles had claimed that blood was turned by *sēpsis* into a 'white putrefaction', i.e. he exploited the similarity between πύον (pus) and πύος ('beestings', colostrum or the first milk secreted towards the end of pregnancy). Aristotle objects that milk is not a putrefaction, but rather a 'concoction' (πέψις) (*De gen. an.* 777a9ff.) of the blood-like liquid. But, although he is severely critical of Empedocles' view of the *process* whereby milk is formed, their respective *standpoints* are very similar indeed. From the above account it can be seen that Empedocles believes that blood is the agent of nutrition and that milk itself is a surplus residue of blood.

This belief in blood as the agent of nutrition has been correctly described by Solmsen as 'one of the fundamental discoveries of ancient physiology',[95] but he goes on to maintain that 'we may never be able to identify the first proponent of this idea, yet we can say with confidence that it was formulated in the first third of the fourth century' by '*physicians who kept up the tradition of Empedocles*' (my italics). He categorically denies this theory to Empedocles himself. 'Nothing', he says (p. 454), 'indicates that

74

he regards it as the agent of nutrition: it is hard to believe that so significant a doctrine should have remained unrecorded. . . . Empedocles is not likely to have known it.' But Solmsen has overlooked Simplicius' evidence here where just such a doctrine is attributed to Empedocles. Although Simplicius has to some extent reformulated his account in Peripatetic terms, he is usually a most reliable source. He is, moreover, in the present instance supported by evidence (again overlooked by Solmsen) which shows that this belief in the blood as the agent of nutrition was also unequivocally held by a contemporary of Empedocles and one who is demonstrably influenced by his biological theories. In the *Historia animalium* 511b30ff. Aristotle preserves Diogenes' own description of the blood vessels. In the penultimate sentence Diogenes states that 'the thickest blood is consumed by the fleshy parts': τὸ αἷμα τὸ μὲν παχύτατον ὑπὸ τῶν σαρκωδῶν ἐκπίνεται. (Or as Vindicianus, whose testimony is a close paraphrase of the *Historia animalium* here, expresses it: *alia pars [sanguinis] carne bibitur (D.K.*64B6).)

Simplicius also informs us in the above account that once the digestive process in the stomach had been completed, the nutriment was then carried to the liver where it was turned into blood (*In phys.* 371. 33). Again, if we can trust Simplicius, as I believe we can, we have adumbrated a theory of digestion/nutrition which assigns a haematopoeic function to the liver and which subsequently became the most widely accepted theory of digestion in European medicine until the seventeenth century AD. Solmsen, however, accuses Simplicius of downright invention here;[96] but this is hardly in character and certainly there are no grounds for distortion. Some support for Simplicius here might be found in Plutarch's comment at *Quaest. conv.* V, 8, 2, 683e (*D.K.*31B150) that Empedocles (who, it may be observed, rarely uses his epithets merely for purely decorative purposes and is especially fond of *double entendres*) applied the adjective 'polyhaematon' (πολυαίματον) 'rich in blood' to the liver.[97]

It was seen above that Empedocles considered milk to be a surplus residue of the blood. It seems likely that he considered the semen, too, to belong to this category and to be a 'putrefaction' of the blood. Unfortunately no direct evidence of Empedocles' views on the nature of the semen has survived; but there can be no doubt that he, no less than other contemporary pre-Socratic writers, was deeply interested in this matter (see *De gen. an.* 747a34

*D.K.*31B92). In the *De anima* Aristotle represents Hippon deliver-
ing a polemic against the view that the soul is blood and seeking
to refute this view by pointing out that the seed is not blood,
apparently assuming that the soul or life principle is transmitted
with the semen. The theory under attack here is almost certainly
that of Empedocles,[98] although the Sophist Critias is the sole
person actually named by Aristotle as identifying the soul with
blood. However, Aristotle tells us (*De an.* 405b5ff. *D.K.*88A23)
that these thinkers hold that sensation is the most essential
characteristic of the soul and believe that it arises from the nature
of the blood. Again, in his Commentary upon this passage (*In de
an.* prooem. 9. 19 *D.K.*88A23) Philoponus, having identified
Critias as 'one of the Thirty [tyrants]' then, significantly, attributes to him the line of Empedocles which states that 'thought is
blood around the heart' (B105.3). Thus it is probable that Critias
has followed Empedocles here and may even, as Guthrie has
suggested,[99] have learned of the Empedoclean theory from the
Sophist Gorgias. In any case, it should be noted that later
authorities do not share Aristotle's puzzling reluctance to cite
Empedocles by name here.[100] Since, as we saw, Empedocles
believed that mothers' milk was formed by the putrefaction of
surplus blood and he evidently believed that tears and sweat were
similarly formed (Aëtius, V 22, 1 and Plutarch, *Quaest. nat.* 20, 2
p.917A *D.K.*31A78), it seems likely that he held a similar view of
the nature and formation of the semen. This theory, as shall be
seen below, when further elaborated by Diogenes in accordance
with his own first principle, subsequently became the dominant
belief in later Greek biology.

There is some evidence that Diogenes, like Empedocles, may
have actually been a physician. He may even have written a
medical treatise.[101] Again like Empedocles, he seems to have
sought to base his medical theory upon his first principle
ἀήρ, which he adopted from Anaximenes. According to
Theophrastus, Diogenes held that health was the result when a
large amount of air in its normal condition mingled with the
blood and lightened it, penetrating throughout the whole of the
body. Whenever the condition of the air was not normal,
however, and failed to mix with the blood, the latter coagulated,
became weaker and denser and sickness ensued:

Pleasure and pain come about in this way. Whenever a

large amount of air mixes with the blood and lightens it, in accordance with nature, and permeates throughout the whole body, pleasure ensues; but whenever the air is present contrary to nature and does not mix, then the blood sinks down, becomes weaker and denser, and pain ensues. It is similarly the case with confidence, *health* and their opposites.

(Theophrastus, *De sensibus* 43 *D.K.*64A19)

Again like Empedocles, Diogenes sought to explain biological phenomena and physiological processes by deduction from his first principle. He believed, for example, that the soul was air and that air was the agent of thought. He also attempted to account for the different levels of intelligence encountered within the animate world upon this basis. Although according to his monistic hypothesis all things are composed of air, he endeavoured to discriminate in the first place between the animate and inanimate by claiming that living creatures differ in that they have within them air that is warmer than that outside, but much cooler than that near the sun (Simplicius, *In phys.* 152. 22 *D.K.*64B5). He then stressed that this warm air was capable of many differentiations, both among the different species of living creatures and among the individuals which make up any given species. Theophrastus has preserved in the *De sensibus* several instances of the manner in which Diogenes differentiated between levels of intelligence possessed by various living creatures. Although all creatures derive their intelligence from this same air, variations in intelligence may be caused by such factors as moisture or even physical structure. As thinking depends upon pure, dry air and moisture hampers intellect, thought is consequently at a low ebb when one is either asleep, drunk,[102] or in a state of surfeit. The intellectual immaturity of children is also explained upon this basis: since they have more moisture in their bodies than adults, the drier air is prevented from permeating the whole body. Diogenes also believed that other creatures were inferior in intellect to man because they breathe air that comes from the earth and also take a moister nourishment. (It seems to be this theory of Diogenes that is parodied by Aristophanes at *Nubes*, 227ff.) At this point, it seems to have occurred to Diogenes that, according to his theory, birds would be the most intelligent of all creatures since they breathe the purest air. This thought, however, did not shake his faith in his general theory. His immediate reaction was to introduce a saving clause to the effect that this was not so since the flesh of birds was solid and prevented the air from permeating completely throughout their bodies by checking it in the vicinity of the stomach (*De sensibus* 44 *D.K.*64A19) where it was all used up in the digestion of food. (Hence the rapidity of the digestive process in birds!) This reaction illustrates well the harmful effect of the deductive approach to an empirical study. It also enables one to see why Aristophanes chose Diogenes as a fruitful subject for parody here.

Diogenes' explanation of the cause of sleep – another of the topics raised by Alcmaeon – is also clearly based upon his first principle. According to Aëtius (V 24, 3 *D.K.*64A29) he held that sleep ensued when the air in the veins was driven towards the chest and stomach. Should the air leave the blood altogether, death was the result. His account of sense perception, too, is heavily based upon his general hypothesis as can be clearly seen from the details preserved by Theophrastus:

> Diogenes attributes thinking and the senses, as he does life, to air. . . . The sense of smell is produced by the air round the brain. The air is massed there and is commensurate with the odour . . .*
>
> 40. Hearing is produced whenever the air within the ears is moved by the air outside and spreads towards the brain. Vision occurs when things are reflected in the pupil, and this, being mixed with the air within, produces sensation. Proof: if there is inflammation of the veins, there is no mixture with the air within, nor is there vision, although reflexion takes place exactly as before. Taste occurs to the tongue by what is rare and gentle. As for touch, he did not define either how it was effected or its objects.
>
> (*De sensibus* 39ff. *D.K.*64A19)

As can be seen here, his theory of vision required objects to be reflected in the pupil. They are only actually seen, however, if the 'pupil is mingled with the internal air' which is mind. The mind is pure, dry air. When the vessels of the eye are inflamed, sight is impaired because the passage of air is interrupted, although the image appears in the pupil just the same. Keenness of vision depends upon the purity of the air and the fineness of the vessels and also upon a lustre in the eyes which promotes reflection (*De sensibus* 42). Hearing takes place when air within the ear is stirred by that outside and transmits this motion to the brain. The sense of smell is produced by the air round the brain. It is massed there and blended to be 'commensurate' with the odour. Keenness of scent is associated with a small amount of air in the head (because it and the odour are then mixed most quickly (*De sensibus* 41), and also with the length and narrowness of the passages through which the odour is drawn (which give a better opportunity for discrimination). It is for this reason that some animals have keener scent than human beings; though the human sense of smell is keen when the odour and the air in the brain are compatible and mix easily. Acuteness of hearing is explained on similar principles.

Although Diogenes seems to follow Alcmaeon in regarding the brain as the central organ of sensation and thought, rather than the heart, as Empedocles and his Sicilian followers believed,[103] he is eclectic in his borrowings and elsewhere in his biological theories he clearly reveals his debts to Empedocles. Like the latter, for example, he adopts the theory of the innate heat together with the belief that the purpose of respiration is to cool that heat. His debts to Empedocles are especially apparent in his account of the semen, preserved as part of his detailed description of the blood vessels by Aristotle in the *Historia animalium* (III. 2 511b30 D.K.31B6). Here, towards the end of this long fragment, Diogenes describes the spermatic veins and then, after declaring that the thickest blood is consumed by the fleshy parts, maintains that the surplus blood passes into these veins and becomes fine and warm and foam-like. We learn in addition from Clement of Alexandria that Diogenes described the semen as the 'foam of the blood' (*Paedagogus* I, 6, 48 D.K.64A24). (In similar vein Vindicianus speaks of Diogenes' description of the semen as 'spumam sanguinis' (D.K.64B6).) Clement further tells us that when the blood is warmed by the innate heat and then agitated and stirred up, it becomes 'like foam' through an admixture of air. From the above evidence it can be seen that Diogenes not only shares with Empedocles the theory of the innate heat but also, like him, believes that blood is the agent of nutrition and that the semen is surplus nutriment, i.e. blood – but blood which has become 'like foam' through an admixture of air. It seems that Diogenes here has modified the Empedoclean theory that the soul is blood in order to meet Hippon's criticism that the soul cannot be blood because the semen, which transmits the soul or life principle, is not blood.[104] This view that the semen served as the vehicle of the soul and was a modification of surplus nutriment, i.e. blood which, when 'concocted' by the superior innate heat of the male and mixed with *pneuma*, took on its characteristic white foam-like appearance, was to prove highly influential in the history of biology. It was adopted by Aristotle,[105] who even made the same appeal to etymology as Diogenes had done.[106] It was later adopted by the Alexandrian doctors Herophilus and Erasistratus.[107] It was also taken over by the Stoics[108] and Galen subsequently subscribed to it.[109]

Aristotle links this theory of the semen with the doctrine of the *pneuma*. He, like Diogenes, explains the foamy nature of the semen as the result of an admixture of air. Several scholars have claimed that Diogenes was the actual originator of the subsequently highly influential *pneuma* doctrine.[110] As can be seen here, there is strong evidence to support this claim. Jaeger, however, has adduced persuasive reasons for believing that antecedents of the *pneuma* theory can be traced back ultimately to Empedocles. He believes that Aristotle derived this theory of *pneuma* with other related doctrines from the (so-called) 'Sicilian' school of physicians.[111] Although Jaeger himself has removed support from this theory by his subsequent argument that Diocles of Carystus was not a pupil of Philistion of Locri as was initially widely believed (see Chapter 6, pp. 162ff.) but rather a younger contemporary of Aristotle, nevertheless, as Solmsen points out,[112] the idea of 'Sicilian' influence here cannot be dismissed altogether, since from Empedocles onwards through the *Timaeus* to Aristotle's biology, air is one of the four elements from which all living creatures are formed and is an integral part of their make-up. However, if our assessment that Diogenes was much influenced by Empedoclean biology is correct, then these two apparently conflicting standpoints are easily reconciled.[113]

The above examination of the biological theories of the pre-Socratic philosophers clearly shows how philosophy came to exert a powerful influence upon medicine. From its connection with philosophy, medicine derived certain important benefits. It now became incorporated within self-consistent and tightly integrated systems. Rational modes of explanation, based upon formal, deductive reasoning and sustained by logical argument, were now sought to account for the phenomena in an ordered world whose laws were discoverable. Man himself was regarded as part and parcel of that world, a product of his environment, made of the same substances and subject to the same laws of cause and effect that operate within the cosmos at large. Furthermore, the diseases to which he is prone were themselves defined strictly in accordance with the same natural processes and ran their course within a set period of time totally independent of any arbitrary, supernatural interference. But the debit side was almost equally great for, along with these benefits, medicine took over the pernicious legacy of a priori reasoning, the tendency to deduce explanations from a preconceived position, which resulted in the propensity to accommodate observed facts to pre-established convictions. This had an adverse effect upon the development of a more empirical method manifestly more appropriate for the advance of medicine. Experimentation was seriously inhibited and such 'experiments' that were carried out were, almost invariably, employed to confirm preconceived standpoints. The dangers inherent in this subordination of medical theory to philosophy did not pass unrecognised and, as shall be seen in the next chapter, a vigorous, but unavailing, opposition was mounted against this intrusion of philosophical theory and methodology into the sphere of medicine.

4

Philosophy and medicine in the fifth century II

Pre-Socratic philosophy and the Hippocratic *Corpus*

multos ex sapientiae professoribus peritos [medicinae]
fuisse.

(Celsus, *De medicina*, Proem, 7)

The danger to medicine inherent in these attempts made by the
natural philosophers to account for the composition of human
body and explain its physiological processes upon the basis of
their unifying hypotheses is clearly recognised by the author of
the Hippocratic treatise *De vetere medicina*. He vigorously rejects
the intrusion of philosophical postulates into medicine. In this
remarkable work there is apparent for the first time some
recognition of the distinction that should be drawn between
philosophy and medicine, whose autonomy here is firmly
defended. Our author is clearly conscious of the opposition
between the dogmatic, a priori methodology of the natural
philosopher and the more empirical approach required of the
physician. The treatise opens with a polemic against those who
adopt a philosophical postulate as the basis for their discussion.
It is maintained that medicine, unlike 'the mysteries of heaven
and the regions below the earth', has no need of any such 'new
fangled' postulates; that 'medicine has long had everything to
hand, with a principle and method already discovered by which
many good discoveries have been made over a long period; while
what remains will be discovered, if the inquirer is competent and
is familiar with discoveries already made and conducts his
inquiry with these as his starting-point'.

All those who have attempted to speak or write about
medicine, have assumed for themselves a hypothesis as the
basis for their discussion – heat, cold, moisture, dryness, or

anything else they wish, narrowing down the causal principle of diseases and death for men and making it the same in all cases. They are manifestly in error in many of their novelties. They are especially blameworthy because they are dealing with an art that really exists, one employed upon the weightiest of considerations by all men, who hold in especial honour its good practitioners and craftsmen. This would not be so if there were no medical art at all, or no research were carried out in it and no discovery made; but all would be equally inexperienced and unlearned in it and the treatment of the sick would be managed entirely by chance. As it is, however, this is not so; but, just as in the case of all the other arts, their practitioners differ greatly from one another in respect of their manual skill and intellect, so, too, is it the case in medicine. Consequently, I considered that it has no need of a new fangled hypothesis, as do obscure problems, which necessarily require the use of a hypothesis if one attempts to discuss them, for example those of the heavens and the regions below the earth. If anyone were to express a judgment about these matters, it would not be clear either to the speaker himself or to his audience whether his statements were true or not. For there is no test whose application brings certain knowledge.

But medicine has long had everything to hand, with a principle and method already discovered by which many good discoveries have been made over a long period; while what remains will be discovered, if the inquirer is competent and is familiar with discoveries already made and conducts his inquiry with these as his starting-point. But whoever rejects and spurns all these and attempts to carry out his inquiry by a different method and by a different fashion and then declares that he has made some discovery, deceives and is deceived. For it is impossible.

([Hippocrates] *De vetere medicina*, Chapters 1 and 2)

Again, in Chapter 12 he proudly declares that medicine has been able to rise by the power of reasoning from deep ignorance to approximate exactness and, therefore, its discoveries should be admired as being the result of excellent and correct research, not of chance:

I say that we must not for this reason reject the ancient art of medicine as being non-existent or as ill-founded in its research if it does not attain exactitude in every respect: but we ought far rather, since (I believe) it has the power to have risen by reasoning from great ignorance to approximate exactness, to admire its discoveries as being the result of good and correct research, not of chance.

In Chapter 20[1] Empedocles is expressly singled out as representative of the objectionable influence of this 'philosophical' approach to medicine. The medical author even goes so far as to claim here that, far from medicine's being a subordinate study to 'physics', the converse really applies and clear knowledge about the nature of man[2] can only be acquired through a study of medicine:

> Certain physicians and sophists assert that it is impossible for anyone to know medicine who does not know what man is and that to treat patients correctly it is necessary to learn this. Their doctrine, however, tends towards philosophy in the manner of Empedocles and others who have written about nature, what man is originally, how he first came into being and from what elements he was constructed. . . . I believe that clear knowledge about nature can be acquired from no other source than medicine. One can attain this knowledge when one has a proper comprehension of medicine itself, but until then it seems to me to be far from possible.

The author of this remarkable little work, then, firmly rejects any attempt to resort to untestable hypotheses to account for the causation of disease. In stressing the importance of empirical observation in medicine he reveals his awareness of methodological issues and the distinctions that should be drawn between different intellectual disciplines. Yet, notwithstanding his castigation of this use of arbitrary postulates generally and his scathing criticisms of theories based upon the hot, cold, wet and dry (see especially Chapters 15 and 16), he himself appears vulnerable to the very criticisms he levels at his philosophical opponents in adopting as a basis for his own theories postulates which appear to be hardly less arbitrary. However, this apparent discrepancy between our author's declared policy and his actual practice does not in any way invalidate his important recommendation that unverifiable a priori postulates should be excluded from an empirical science like medicine. Although, admittedly, his own medical theory concerning the components of the human body is not without certain similarities to that which he especially singles out for attack, it is important to realise that he is deeply convinced that the particular theory which he adopts has been confirmed by lengthy experience and its employment has led to many excellent discoveries over a long period of time (see Chapter 2 quoted above).

He outlines this theory in Chapter 14:

> there exists in man the salt, bitter, sweet, acid, astringent, insipid, and countless other things, possessing powers of all kinds in number and in strength. These, when mixed and blended, are neither manifest nor cause the man pain; but, whenever one of them is separated off and becomes isolated, then it is both manifest and causes a man pain.

Basically his standpoint is the same as that previously propounded by Alcmaeon, who, as was seen above (Chapter 3, pp. 52ff.), held that when the various powers are mixed and blended there is *isonomia*, but when one of them has been 'separated off' and 'stands alone', it then gains predominance (*monarchia*) over the others and causes a man pain. An origin as early as this, or even earlier, is consistent with the author's claim that medicine is an established *technē* based upon long practical experience.

Another Hippocratic work which attacks philosophical intrusion into medicine is the treatise *De natura hominis*. Like *De vetere medicina*, this work stresses the autonomy of medicine and it, too, cites a fifth-century philosopher explicitly by name – a very rare occurrence in the Hippocratic *Corpus*. On this occasion the philosopher mentioned by name (Chapter 1) is Melissus, the Samian general who defeated the Athenian fleet in 441/440 BC[3] and a disciple of Parmenides.[4] Unlike *De vetere medicina*, however, this treatise does not attack philosophy in general. Its author confines his polemic specifically to those philosophers who hold that man, like the world at large, is composed of a single basic substance. It is clear that this polemic is levelled at contemporary philosophers and doctors and is not intended as a retrospective attack upon the Milesian Monists of the sixth century such as Thales or Anaximenes; but rather upon their latter-day successors, who had revived Ionian monism in the fifth - men like Hippon of Samos, who had adopted Thales' first principle, water,[5] as his *archē*, or Diogenes of Apollonia, whose revival of Anaximenes' hypothesis that air is the source and basic substance of all things[6] - including man himself - had become very widely known and influential in the last third of the fifth century.[7] To render his attack more effective against these unitarians he cleverly exploits the arguments and methodology of contemporary philosophy. His reasoning is sophisticated and requires close attention.

Although our author attacks generally all those who hold that man is constituted of a single substance, it seems that he has especially in mind Diogenes here. Despite the opposition of their respective standpoints, there exists between *De natura hominis* and Diogenes' work *On Nature* some striking similarities in composition and argument.[8] For example, in Chapter 2 of the medical treatise its author contends:

> I hold that if man were basically of one substance, he would never feel pain, since, being one, there would be nothing to hurt. Moreover, if he should feel pain, the remedy would likewise have to be single. But, in fact, there are many remedies because there are many things in the body, which when abnormally heated, cooled, dried or moistened by interaction, engender disease.
>
> ([Hippocrates] *De natura hominis*, Chap. 2, (VI.34L., 17ff.)

In the second fragment of Diogenes' work the philosopher argues as follows:

> if the things that exist at present in this world - earth and water and fire and air and all the other things apparent in this world - if any of those were different from the other (different, that is, in its own proper nature), and did not retain an essential identity while undergoing many changes and differentiations, it would be in no way possible for them to mix with each other, or for one to help or harm the other . . . unless they were so composed as to be the same thing. But all these things, being differentiated from the same thing, become of different kinds at different times and return into the same thing.
>
> (Simplicius, *In phys.* 151. 28 D.K.64B2)

The composition of these two arguments is identical in form. First the opposing theses are presented hypothetically; then there follows their individual refutations; and, finally, we have a statement of each author's personal belief. But, whereas Diogenes attacks pluralism, the author of *De natura hominis* rejects monism. Again, each argument turns upon a similar point: whereas Diogenes contends that, if there were a plurality, harm (*blabē*) would be impossible, the medical author maintains, conversely, that if there were a unity, there would be nothing to cause pain. For the latter, then, pain is inexplicable upon a monistic hypothesis for it entails an interaction of different substances, which is impossible on the hypothesis that the human body is formed of a single substance. Conversely, for Diogenes, harm is inexplicable in accordance with a pluralist hypothesis because, in this case, the mixture and interaction of different substances is impossible. Thus the two arguments, identical in form, are diametrically opposed in contention.[9] In the light of these similarities[10] it is hard to resist the conclusion that the author of *De natura hominis* is here cleverly exploiting the very form of argument Diogenes had himself employed to refute pluralism (and, especially, as we see from Fragment 2, that particular brand of pluralism advocated by Empedocles) in order to attack the revised monistic doctrine adopted by Diogenes.

However, as we have seen, the author of *De natura hominis* cites the Eleatic philosopher Melissus explicitly by name when he ridicules the protagonists of monism. Using a metaphor derived from wrestling (Chapter 1), he caustically points out that these people, through their lack of understanding, overthrow their own theories by the very terms they use to describe the One-Being, which they identify each with one of a variety of different entities:

> one of them asserts that the one and all is air, another fire, another, water, and another, earth . . . adopting the same concept, they do not give the same account of it, which shows that their knowledge is at fault.

Thus they 'set up on its feet again the theory of Melissus'. This citation of the Eleatic philosopher is no mere passing reference, since there are several other allusions to Melissus in *De natura hominis*. In Fragment 7, for example, Melissus argues:

the One-Being . . . (2) . . . does not feel pain . . . for, if it should suffer any such thing, it would not still be one . . . (4) nor does it feel pain; for, if it were in pain, it would not be entire. For a thing in pain could not be for ever, nor has it the same power as what is healthy. Nor would it be all alike if it were in pain. For it would feel pain by the addition or subtraction of something, and would no longer be the same. (5) Nor could what is healthy feel pain, for then what is and is healthy would perish, and what is not would come to be.

In this fragment the Eleatic, after having declared that 'what is' is everlasting, infinite, one and homogeneous, and that it neither perishes, nor grows, nor changes, makes the additional point that it feels neither pain nor grief. Pain is incompatible with completeness and with the rule that reality must not undergo addition, subtraction or destruction.

The affinity between this argument in Fragment 7 of Melissus and that employed in Chapter 2 of *De natura hominis* is striking. Whereas Melissus argues that if 'what is' felt pain, it would not remain the same; but it does remain the same, so it does not feel pain: the medical author argues, conversely, that if man was a unity, he would not feel pain; but, since he evidently does feel pain, he cannot be one.

Like Diogenes, Melissus seems in his attack on plurality to have in mind especially the Empedoclean version. His contention at Fragment 7.4, quoted above, that Being feels no pain, since pain is incompatible with completeness and with the rule that Being cannot undergo addition, subtraction or destruction, seems to be directed against Empedocles, who appears to have held that pain is caused when the sense organs encounter objects dissimilar to the mixture of the elements in their own composition.[11] Again, Fragment 8, although clearly intended as a general polemic against plurality, also seems to carry a specific reference to the four element theory in the following words:

If there were a plurality, things would have to be of the same kind as I say the One is. For, if there is earth and water and air and fire . . . each of these must be such as we first decided and they cannot be changed or altered, but each must be always just as it is.

In Fragment 7.2 Melissus maintains that his conception of One-Being excludes the possibility of alteration on the grounds that it would not in that case remain the same:

> for if it is altered, what is would of necessity not be the same, but what was formerly must perish and what is not must come to be.

Conversely, as has already been seen, Diogenes maintains that change is only possible on the hypothesis of a single identical substance:

> My opinion, in sum, is that all existing things are differentiated from the same thing, and are the same thing.

Both of these thinkers, then, in attacking pluralism seem to have in mind especially the Empedoclean concept of it. Yet their respective arguments have taken opposite routes. Indeed, the one argument is the converse of the other. Notwithstanding their doctrinal difference, there exists between Melissus and Diogenes some striking resemblances in expression. Diller has argued that Melissus wrote later and criticised Diogenes.[12] The chronology, however, is loose and both thinkers are clearly contemporaries. Granted the affinities between them, it is chronologically the more likely that Diogenes, the younger of the two, is reacting against the Eleatic.[13]

If this is the case, then the citation of Melissus by name in the *De natura hominis*, together with the metaphor from wrestling employed here, falls into perspective. The medical author, cleverly exploiting his intellectual background, employs against Diogenes an argument of Melissus which the former evidently believed he had successfully managed to evade. The medical author uses to support pluralism an argument which had actually been used to attack it and employs, in a reversal of chronology, a Melissan argument against Diogenes, i.e. an Eleatic argument against plurality is used to attack the revived monistic hypothesis.[14] Of course, in the last resort, the author of *De natura hominis* is no more likely to accept the Eleatic conception of unity than the revived monism advocated by Diogenes for he is a convinced pluralist subscribing to the theory of the four humours.

Notwithstanding these vigorous and, at times, quite sophisticated attacks upon the continued intrusion of philosophy, the Hippocratic *Corpus* clearly reveals much evidence of philosophical influences. Whereas some treatises reveal the thoroughgoing influence of a single philosopher, others are eclectic and select from different philosophers theories which suit their particular needs: others, again, while adopting no particular philosophical theory, reveal themselves none the less deeply influenced by the concepts and categories of pre-Socratic philosophy generally: some even, while unequivocally condemning the intrusion of philosophical postulates into medicine, are at the same time guilty of a fundamental ambiguity when defining their own particular standpoint.

The treatises *De vetere medicina* and *De natura hominis* both afford clear illustrations of this last category. As has been seen, the author of the former work, although forthright in his denunciation of the attempt to base medical theory upon a newfangled philosophical hypothesis, subscribes himself to a postulate which seems hardly less speculative when he adopts as the basis for his theory of health a conception which can be traced back to Alcmaeon and ultimately to Anaximander. His hostility towards the encroachment of philosophy into the sphere of medicine is shared by the author of *De natura hominis*. This writer, however, has a more restricted target and specifically levels his attack against attempts to base medicine upon the unitarian hypothesis that man is composed of a single substance. But, notwithstanding his polemical purpose, this author, too, enrols himself within the intellectual tradition created by the Ionian Rationalists when he sets out to answer the question of the constitution of man. He emphatically declares that he is not going to assert that man is composed of air, or fire, or water, or earth, or anything which is not manifest in man, on the ground that such beliefs go far beyond the strict domain of medicine (Chapter 1). His own theory, which he believes to be empirically justified, is that the human body is composed of the four humours, blood, phlegm, yellow bile and black bile:

> The body of man has in itself blood, phlegm, yellow bile and black bile. These constitute the nature of his body, and through these he feels pain or enjoys health. Now he is particularly healthy when these constituents are in due proportion to one another with regard to blending, power,

and quantity, and when they are perfectly mixed. Pain is experienced whenever one of these constituents is deficient or in excess or is isolated in the body and is not blended with all the others. For, whenever any one of these is isolated and stands by itself, of necessity not only does the place which it left become diseased, but also the place where it stands and floods causes pain and distress through being over-full.

([Hippocrates] De natura hominis, Chapter 4)

But this theory itself patently reveals philosophical influences and is, in fact, an analogue of the Empedoclean theory of the four elements. Although the philosophical theory is here modified and brought into conformity with what our author believes to be the facts of medical experience, his own hypothesis is the counterpart of Empedocles' theory[15] in that he not only limits the basic constituents of the body to four, but also, like that philosopher, attempts to explain man as a product of his environment, conforming to the same laws operating within the cosmos at large. Furthermore, his doctrine that health ensues when these four humours stand in equal proportions to each other and that pain is the result when any one of them is in a state of deficiency or excess is a variation on a familiar theme and affords additional testimony to the immediate influence of philosophy in general and of Empedocles in particular.[16]

It is highly ironical that a treatise which is so concerned to attack a particular form of philosophical intrusion into medicine should itself not only manifest strong philosophical influences in this way, but also, as a result of these influences, should formulate a theory which, more than any other, was to contribute to the dominance of philosophy over medicine for the next two millennia and beyond. For the first clear statement of the classic and influential doctrine of the four humours appears here in *De natura hominis*. In fact, this treatise is the only Hippocratic work which expounds this theory.

De natura hominis presents a highly schematic and comprehensive system. Elaborate correlations are drawn between the four basic humours, the four primary opposites and the four seasons.[17] Each of the humours is associated with a particular season and with two of the primary opposites. Blood, yellow bile, black bile and phlegm are each held to predominate in turn according to the appropriate season. Blood, the dominant humour in spring, is, like that season, characterised by the qualities hot and moist. In similar fashion, yellow bile, like summer, is hot and dry; black bile, like autumn, is cold and dry, and phlegm, like winter, is cold and moist. The symmetry and all-embracing nature of this theory, together with the support it could derive from broad appeals to empirical phenomena, ensured its subsequent dominance. Its fourfold symmetry was later to embrace the four tastes, the four main organs of the body, the four ages of man, the four winds, and, ultimately, after the advent of Christianity, even the four Evangelists.[18]

Humours, in the sense of obvious and basic bodily fluids, most probably go back to the very dawn of Greek medicine and even beyond into Egyptian medicine. Phlegm, for example is mentioned in both the *Ebers* and the *Edwin Smith Papyrus*, while bile is mentioned in fragments of Archilochus (Frag. 96 Diehl) and Hipponax (Frag. 51 Diehl). It would be a mistake, however, simply to assume that the canonical four humours grew by accretion and differentiation from an original two (bile and phlegm), with the subsequent addition of blood and the differentiation of bile into yellow bile and black bile. This theory of the four humours, as Lonie says,[19] marks a 'revolution in medical science, a new way of looking at the human body, which was the result of philosophic development in the fifth century'. It was the prior conception of Empedocles which made possible the identification of these four humours as the constituent elements of the human body. The classic medical theory of the four humours arises immediately out of the pre-Socratic philosophical background and is a direct corollary of the Empedoclean four element theory in that these four humours play a role in the human body analogous to that played by the elements in the world at large.

In spite of these vigorous – though not entirely self-consistent – attacks upon what was recognised as a dangerous intrusion of philosophy into medicine, the temptation to formulate axiomatic systems based upon first principles from which explanations of particular phenomena could be deductively derived proved hardly less strong in medicine than in Greek science generally. Several treatises in the Hippocratic *Corpus* manifest this tendency to a degree which would have incurred the stern

disapproval of the author of *De vetere medicina*. But, notwithstanding the specific rejection in *De natura hominis* of any
attempt to base medicine upon a monistic hypothesis in general,
and the hostility displayed there towards Diogenes of Apollonia
in particular, two works in the Hippocratic *Corpus*, *De flatibus*
and *De morbo sacro*, are patently strongly influenced by this
philosopher. The author of the former, which is perhaps more of
a sophistic essay than a serious medical treatise,[20] follows Diogenes' lead in holding air to be of fundamental importance in the
world generally and instrumental in causing disease. *De morbo
sacro*, by contrast, is a much more serious work, written, as has
been seen, to explain on rational grounds the nature and causes
of epilepsy and, at the same time, to combat superstitious beliefs
held about this disease. Upon the basis of two theories, both held
by Diogenes, the belief that the brain is the seat of the intelligence
and air is the source and principle of intelligence in the living
organism, the medical author elaborates a comprehensive explanation of disease based upon purely natural causes. Epilepsy, the
most important disease for his immediate purpose, he maintains
(see Chapter 2, pp.34ff.), is caused by the stoppage of air in the
'veins'[21] by a flow of phlegm from the brain.

The influence of the atomic theory may also be detected within
the Hippocratic *Corpus*. Caution, however, must be enjoined
since nowhere is this influence explicit. Just as it has proved
difficult to determine in some instances whether or not
Democritus' biological theories were firmly derived from his
unifying hypothesis, so in certain of these medical treatises it is
hard to say for certain whether use has been made of atomistic or
mechanistic principles originally evolved by the atomic philosophers. Furthermore, the pre-Socratic philosophers shared many
common assumptions, which were adopted and freely adapted by
the medical authors to serve their own particular purposes. Thus
we must be careful to heed Lonie's warning that:

whenever there is a clear similarity between a doctrine expressed
by the [medical] author, and a doctrine known to have been held
by one or other pre-Socratic philosopher, we cannot certainly
establish the influence of that philosopher, if there is no reason
why the view should not have been held by another, and perhaps
earlier, philosopher as well.[22]

Wellmann has maintained that the influence of Democritean

atomism can be detected in the treatises *De natura pueri* and *De morbis* IV.[23] In the manuscript tradition the *De natura pueri* is a continuation of the *De genitura* and, since the opening words of *De morbis* IV seem to carry a clear back-reference to *De natura pueri*, Littré, after some initial hesitation, was persuaded to print all three works as a single continuous treatise (VII.470–614L.). And this viewpoint is still widely accepted.[24] The description of the growth of hair presented at *De natura pueri*, Chapter 20, has been cited as evidence of the influence of the atomic theory upon the medical author since it closely parallels the explanation of the growth of horn attributed to Democritus by Aelian.[25] According-ing to this account, the growth of horn results from a flow of moisture to the spot through a network of veins and channels penetrating the bone covering the head, which is thin, membra-nous and of loose texture (ἀραιόν, i.e. the interstices of void between the atoms are presumably comparatively large). The horn is subsequently hardened by contact with the cold air outside. Its successful growth is dependent upon the suitability of the channels, the right porosity of the top of the skull, together with such accidental features as the breadth of the forehead. Aelian then goes on to describe how this theory could account for the difference between the horns of castrated and non-castrated bulls and explain why some cattle are hornless. The similarity with the medical author's explanation of the growth of hair is immediately apparent (Chap. 20, VII.506–8L.):

> Hair grows in the following manner: it grows longest and most luxuriant where the epidermis is most loose in texture [ἀραιοτάτη] and where it has an appropriate amount of moisture for its nourishment. Where the epidermis subsequently becomes porous [ἀραιή], there, too, hair subsequently grows – on the chin, the pubes, and elsewhere. (2) Both the flesh and the epidermis become porous at the same time as when the sperm comes into being; the veins, too, become more dilated than previously. For in childhood, the veins are narrow and the semen does not pass through them. The same is true of menstruation in young girls. The way is opened at the same time for menstruation and the semen. When the epidermis has become porous, the pubic hair of boy and girl begins to

grow. At the same time the hair has an appropriate amount of moisture for its nourishment, not less.

It is noteworthy that just as Aelian's account contains a discussion of castrated and hornless cattle, so the medical author concludes his own description with a parallel discussion of eunuchs and baldness. In consequence, although Lonie very properly counsels caution and reminds us (p. 63) of the similarity with Empedocles' account of the growth of nails,[26] it is difficult not to believe that Democritean influence is at play here.

Similarly, our author's use of the doctrine of pangenesis as the basis of his theory of reproduction has been seen as another instance where Democritus' influence can be established. Wellmann,[27] pointing to the fact that pangenesis is explicitly attributed to Democritus in the doxographical tradition,[28] concluded that the atomist was the source of the doctrine expounded at *De genitura*, Chapters 6–8. (Lesky, too, has argued[29] that the theory makes most sense in an atomic context and believes that Democritus was its originator.) Lonie, however, again dissents and is unwilling to accept that adoption of the pangenesis theory entails Democritus' influence. He points to the possibility that this theory might have been propounded earlier by Anaxagoras (see Chapter 3, n. 65); to its occurrence in other Hippocratic treatises; and to the impression given by Aristotle in the *De generatione animalium* (721a30ff.) that he is arguing not against an individual opponent, but rather against a well known and frequently canvassed view supported by a variety of premises in a more or less public debate.

However, be that as it may, even Lonie is prepared to accept with Wellmann[30] that Democritean influence does underlie the explanation of twins outlined at *De natura pueri*, Chapter 31 (VII.540L.):

Twins are born from a single act of intercourse in the following way: wombs have multiple cavities, curved in shape, at varying distances from the pudenda. Animals which produce large numbers of offspring have more of these cavities than those which produce fewer. This is true of domestic and wild animals and of birds. Whenever the semen happens to be divided into two cavities on its arrival in the womb, and neither of the cavities releases it into the other, then each of these separate portions in each cavity envelops itself within a membrane and becomes alive in the same way as I have said the single embryo does. That twins are born from a single act of intercourse is illustrated by the bitch, sow and those other animals which produce two or even more young from one copulation; each of the embryos in their wombs occupies its own cavity and membrane. We ourselves see these things happening and these animals for the most part produce all their offspring on the same day. In the same way, twins are born to the woman, too, as a result of a single copulation, each in its own cavity and membrane. She bears both of them on the same day, one emerging first with its membrane, then the other. Because twins are born with one of either sex, I maintain that in man and woman - indeed, in every animal - there exists both weaker and stronger varieties of sperm. The sperm does not come all at once, but spurts out in two or three spasms. It is not possible that all the sperm, both the first and the last to be ejaculated, should always be of equal strength. The cavity, then, which happens to be entered by the thicker and stronger sperm develops a male. Conversely, a female develops in that entered by the moister and weaker sperm. If strong sperm enters both, both twins become male; if the sperm that enters both is weak, both become female.

It is clearly apparent here that a theory of multiple birth in animals has been borrowed and adapted in order to account for the birth of human twins. The above account, as Lonie points out,[31] reads oddly - unless one supposes that the medical author is referring in his opening sentence to animals, not humans. For if the human uterus had several cavities, instead of just two, multiple births would then be as common in humans as in animals. The medical author, therefore, has borrowed a theory about multiple birth in animals to account for the birth of human twins and reveals this debt in his opening words. Although no evidence has survived of any explanation by Democritus of the production of twins, Aelian records that he held the following theory regarding prolific birth in animals such as the sow and bitch:

Democritus says that the sow and the bitch are multiparous and adds the explanation that they have many uteri and

places receptive of seed. Moreover, the semen does not fill
up all of these at one encounter; but these animals copulate
two or three times so that the parts receptive of the semen
may be filled by continuity.[32]

There are close similarities both in language and in detail
between these two accounts. The two essential features of
Democritus' theory, namely the multipartite structure of the
womb and the successive ejaculation of semen, both appear in
the medical work. Here, however, these features are taken over
from the animal kingdom and adapted to explain the birth of
human twins: the human female has only two such 'cavities'
(κόλπους) within the womb and the successive ejaculations of
semen are employed also upon a qualitative basis to explain
sexual differentiation. Whereas Democritus believed that both
parents contributed seed and that sexual differentiation depended
upon whether the mother's or father's seed, derived from the
sexual parts, 'prevailed',[33] the medical author subscribed to a
more comprehensive modification of the pangenesis theory
(Chaps 6–8)[34] and held that both male and female produced seed
of 'sexual bi-potence' (Lesky's term, i.e. each parent can produce
both male and female sperm) and thus could give a systematic
account not only of sexual differentiation but also of features
inherited from both parents.

It seems safe, therefore, to accept that our author has been
influenced by Democritus in his genetic and embryological
theories. These treatises, however, present an eclectic combination of hypotheses and influences of other pre-Socratic philosophers, viz. the Pythagoreans, Cleidemus and Anaxagoras –
whose work has also been detected in them, albeit to a lesser
extent than that of Democritus. But, whatever the degree of
eclecticism manifested here, as Lonie correctly points out (p. 70),
our author displays a quite remarkable ability to integrate
disparate borrowings into a consistent whole. He also reveals
considerable originality in his systematic adaptation of a philosophically derived hypothesis to serve as the basis for his own
theories of genetics and embryology.

The influence of Heraclitus, by contrast, is rather more clearly
marked in the *Corpus*. In the treatise *De alimento*, for example, a
later Heraclitean, reproducing with some skill his master's
aphoristic style, applies his theory of perpetual change to the

assimilation of food by a living organism. *De victu* I is also written in Heraclitean style and reminiscences of Anaxagoras, and, possibly, Empedocles and Archelaus, can be found in this treatise.[35] The influence of Pythagorean numerology may be detected in the treatises *De hebdomadibus*, *De carnibus* and *De natura pueri* and, perhaps, even in the importance assigned to 'critical days' generally since Celsus actually describes them as 'Pythagorici numeri'.[36]

Philosophical influence, however, was not limited to the adoption by medical writers of unifying philosophical postulates. Many of the pre-Socratic philosophers, as has been seen, had themselves developed a keen interest in medicine and biology and certain of the particular theories which they put forward in these fields, whether derived directly from their general hypotheses or, at least, formulated in accordance with them, exercised a very considerable influence upon contemporary and subsequent medical theory. The two most influential philosophers in this respect, as has been seen, are Empedocles and Diogenes. Although philosophically poles apart, with Empedocles advocating a pluralist and Diogenes a monistic hypothesis, there nevertheless exists in their biological thinking a high degree of unanimity between these two. It is clear that Diogenes is considerably influenced by Empedocles' comprehensive biological system and has successfully adapted certain of the latter's theories to bring them into conformity with his own philosophical hypothesis.[37] Certain of the physiological doctrines initially propounded or, at least, developed in part by these two pre-Socratic philosophers, as has already been seen, exercised a lasting influence – particularly through the so-called 'Sicilian' tradition in medicine – which can be traced within the Hippocratic *Corpus* to Plato, Aristotle, the Alexandrians, Galen and beyond. Among these doctrines might be mentioned the theory of *pneuma*; the concept of innate heat as the prime agent of embryological, digestive and other physiological processes; the belief that respiration served to cool the innate heat; the idea that blood was manufactured in the liver and served as the agent of nutrition; and the notion that the semen, like milk, was a form of surplus nutriment.

The Hippocratic *Corpus*, then, reveals abundant evidence of the influence of philosophy upon medicine. As Heidel has remarked, 'Hippocratic medicine . . . reflects and shares the virtues and limitations of contemporary science.'[38] Without its background of Ionian Rationalism Hippocratic medicine is inconceivable. Although the continued subordination of medical theory to philosophical postulate can be seen in several treatises to have brought about the very situation that the author of *De vetere medicina* is so concerned to reject, and the logical satisfaction of an axiomatic system was frequently purchased at the cost of a diminution of empirical observation, nevertheless, on balance, philosophy did far more good than harm. For from its philosophical background medicine derived its rational attitudes and modes of explanation, its conviction that human beings were a product of and influenced by their environment, made of the same substances and subject to the same physical laws as the world at large, together with the belief that diseases were the result of strictly natural causes and ran their individual courses within a set period of time totally independent of any arbitrary, supernatural interference. Philosophy, in short, as Lonie rightly points out,[39] provided the categories within which the physician ordered his experience.

However, another impressive feature of Hippocratic medicine is the empirical outlook which permeates certain of the treatises and is manifested to a high degree in *Epidemics* I and III, which have come to be looked upon as the very model of clinical observation. The following case study is not untypical:

In Meliboea a youth, who had been feverish for a long time as a result of drunkenness and much sexual indulgence, took to his bed. His symptoms were shivering, nausea, insomnia and lack of thirst.

On the first day, there passed from his bowels a large quantity of solid stools with much fluid. During the following days he passed a large quantity of watery, greenish excrement. His urine was thin, sparse and of bad colour. His respiration was at long intervals and deep after a time. There was a rather flabby tension of the upper part of the abdomen extending laterally to both sides. Cardiac palpitation was continuous throughout. The urine was oily.

Tenth day: he was delirious, but calm, well-behaved and silent. Skin dry and taut; stools either copious and thin or bilious and greasy.

Fourteenth day: all symptoms exacerbated. Delirious with much rambling speech.

Twentieth day: out of his mind; much tossing about. No urine passed; small amounts of fluid retained.

Twenty-fourth day: died.

(*Epidemics* III, Case 16, III.146–8L.)[40]

(Here it is immediately apparent that the doctor, who carefully records this unfortunate youth's case history makes no appeal to supernatural causation, but attributes his patient's death to his own drunkenness and sexual indulgence.)

This empirical approach has come to be commonly regarded as an original characteristic of Greek medicine – a spontaneous growth engendered by the treatment of wounds, perhaps, or even the result of the development of dietetics for the training of athletes. Scholars have consequently found in *De vetere medicina* a stark antithesis drawn between the original, more sceptical and empirical approach of these doctors and the confident, dogmatic, a priori methodology of the pre-Socratic philosophers. But this assessment, though widely prevalent, is surely too simplistic and the relationship between philosophy and medicine in the fifth century is, in reality, of a far greater complexity than has generally been recognised. For, in the first place, the Hippocratic empiricism, exemplified so impressively in the *Epidemics* and elsewhere in the Hippocratic *Corpus*, is manifested within a rational framework which is itself derived from philosophy.[41] And even the author of *De vetere medicina* himself, while vigorously denouncing the encroachment of the unverifiable philosophical postulate into medicine and advocating a return to a more empirical methodology, has nevertheless adopted as the basis of his own theory of health a concept which, as was seen above, can be traced back not only to Alcmaeon, but ultimately to Anaximander.

In contrast to the dogmatic certitude of the philosophers, the author of *De vetere medicina* adopts a more sceptical attitude towards the possibility of the attainment of knowledge and advocates a more empirical procedure. In Chapter 1 (above, p. 83) he concedes that postulates are required by those studies of 'unseen and doubtful matters' (*ta aphanea te kai aporeomena*) such as 'what goes on up in the sky and below the earth' (*ta meteōra, ta hypo gēn*) – both main areas of scientific interest.[42]

But he criticises those philosophers who engage in such speculations and claim to have discovered the truth, on the grounds that
they are relying upon baseless suppositions, adding that the truth
of these is not plain either to the speaker or to his audience for
there is no test of verification which can be applied. He makes the
same point again in Chapter 9 when he contends, perhaps as
Festugière has suggested[43] in reaction to Empedocles, who had
sought to introduce the notion of measure into the composition
of the bodily parts, that in medicine there are no exact standards,
reference to which would give exact knowledge other than
sensation; that 'no measure, neither number nor weight, can be
found by reference to which you will attain accurate knowledge
other than bodily sensation'.[44]

This same sceptical empirical attitude, however, can be traced
to an earlier stage in the history of Greek medical thought. As has
been seen (Chapter 3, p. 51), Alcmaeon in the opening words of
his treatise draws a sharp distinction between human inference
and divine certainty, holding that only the gods can attain clear
understanding concerning things unseen; mortals can only feel
their way by interpreting the signs afforded them in the visible
world. It would, however, be unwise to find in this fragment
confirmation of the widespread assumption that this humbler
attitude towards knowledge was 'inculcated by the nascent
science of medicine with its detailed observation of particular
cases and its awareness of fallibility in diagnosis'.[45] For this
outlook, shared by Alcmaeon and the author of *De vetere
medicina*, makes an even earlier appearance in the history of
Greek thought and is unequivocally expounded in the fragments
of the wandering poet/philosopher Xenophanes of Colophon,
who had so devastatingly exploited the implications of Ionian
natural philosophy in order to attack traditional Homeric
theology and had even employed particular natural explanations
in the manner of the Milesian philosophers to foster this attack.

In Fragment 34 - four lines of quite seminal importance for the
subsequent development of Greek thought - Xenophanes is
recorded as maintaining:

> Certain truth [*to saphes*] no man has seen, nor will anyone
> know about the gods and about everything of which I
> speak; for even if he should fully succeed in saying what is

the case, nevertheless he himself does not know, but in all
things there is opinion.

(Sextus, *Adversus mathematicos* VII, 49ff. *D.K.*21B34)[46]

Although the Sceptics later seized upon these lines as an anticipation of their own view that knowledge is unattainable,[47] Sextus
adds elsewhere[48] that others interpret Xenophanes differently and
claim that he is not abolishing comprehension of every criterion,
but rather substituting opinion for knowledge as a criterion for
judgement. One suspects that this latter, unbiased opinion is
likely to approximate more closely to the truth. The fragment
seems prefatory in character[49] and, if it formed part of the preface
of a physical poem following the Milesian tradition,[50] its import
would then be that clear knowledge about things divine and
about natural science lies beyond human attainment. In this
event the fragment would then display, in both sentiment and in
wording, quite remarkable affinities with the criticism which, as
we have just seen (p. 101), the author of *De vetere medicina*
levelled at the pretentiousness of his philosophical opponents.
The connections between these two passages, as Barnes
maintains, 'are close . . . too close to be coincidental'.[51]

Xenophanes' more cautious attitude regarding the possibility
of attaining certain knowledge of these matters by humans is also
coupled with the belief that such knowledge that can be acquired
by mortals can only be attained by a process of protracted
investigation. In Fragment 18 he declares:

The gods did not reveal to men all things in the beginning,
but in the course of time by searching they find out better.

(Stobaeus, *Ecl.* I 8, 2 *D.K.*21B18)

This emphasis upon personal search over a protracted period of
time marks the first statement in extant Greek literature of the
idea of progress – an idea which was rapidly to gain ground on
the earlier and antithetical theory of a degeneration from a
golden age in the distant past. The effect of this conception of
knowledge as a steady, gradual progression resulting from man's
own efforts and powers of invention is clearly apparent in many
fifth-century authors. We find this idea of progress expounded
in, for example, the *Prometheus Vinctus*,[52] Sophocles' *Antigone*[53]
and Euripides' *Supplices*.[54] It also appears in the *Sisyphus*[55] of
Critias and, most significantly, in *De vetere medicina*

itself (Chapter 3), where the medical author argues that *medicine* came into existence by 'sheer necessity' which compelled men to seek relief from their sufferings, caused by a strong and brutish regimen, by developing cultivated foodstuffs and cooking their meals – processes which required a lengthy period of time to develop. 'The coincidences of thought and also of vocabulary, between these various authors', as Guthrie perceptively remarks,[56] 'strongly suggest a common source which may possibly have been Xenophanes.'

This parallelism of outlook and methodology between Xenophanes and Alcmaeon on the one hand, and the particularly close affinities in thought and wording between the fragments of Xenophanes and *De vetere medicina*, on the other, strongly suggest the following scenario: although deeply influend by the Ionian natural philosophers (many of whose beliefs he exploits to serve his own particular purposes in attacking Homeric theology), Xenophanes rejected the over-confident, a priori dogmatism of these philosophers and advocated in its stead a more empirical approach, which was subsequently adopted by the developing practical art of medicine to serve as a secure methodological basis for its future growth. It may well be the case that Alcmaeon had an important role to play in this development. Cornford's contention, however, that 'the empirical theory of knowledge was a medical theory first formulated by Alcmaeon'[57] is, as has been seen, demonstrably wrong. 'First formulated as a medical theory by Alcmaeon' might be nearer the truth. Later, when in the fifth century philosophy began increasingly to encroach into the realm of medicine and attempts were made to subordinate this hitherto more empirical study to a philosophical postulate, the author of *De vetere medicina*, vigorously resisting what he regarded as a dangerous intrusion, turned back to Xenophanes and reaffirmed against his own fifth-century philosophical opponents the attitude which the former had previously displayed in his reaction against the dogmatic certitude of the Milesians.

Thus, even when philosophy and medicine seem to be in diametrical opposition to one another, their inter-relationship is very much more complex than appears upon the surface, since the more empirical outlook confronting the dogmatic approach of the philosophers is itself no less a direct outcome of earlier pre-Socratic philosophical debate.

5

Post-Hippocratic medicine I
Medicine and the Academy

Nam quae demum causae vel secundam valetudinem praes-
tant, vel morbos excitent . . . ne sapientiae quidem professores
scientia comprehendunt, sed coniectura persecuntur.

(Celsus, De medicina, Proem, 46)

The author of the Hippocratic treatise *De vetere medicina*, as was
seen above (Chapter 4), clearly recognised the dangers to the
development of medicine inherent in the attempt to base medical
theory upon philosophical hypotheses. Notwithstanding his
vigorous polemic against this intrusion, however, the practice
continued unabated and philosophy continued, for good and ill,
to exercise a dominant influence upon medicine. The
Hippocratic author presciently singled out Empedocles for
especial condemnation as a representative of this reprehensible
procedure, and, as we shall now see, it was the medical and
biological theories based directly upon or, at least, formulated in
accordance with the latter's philosophical postulate that
exercised the greatest influence upon the subsequent history of
rational Greek medicine.

While Wellmann describes Empedocles as the 'founder of the
Sicilian school of medicine',[1] Burnet goes even further and claims
that Galen actually made Empedocles the 'founder of the Italian
school of medicine' and speaks of it as 'still living in the days of
Plato'.[2] But neither Galen, nor any other ancient authority
specifically states this. The passage of Galen cited by Burnet does
not, as he believes, support his claim either that such a 'school'
existed or that Empedocles was its founder. Galen merely tells us
here (*De methodo medendi* 1, 1 X5K.):

In former times there was great rivalry between the doctors

in Cos and at Cnidus as they strained to prevail in the number of their discoveries. For these were the two surviving branches of the Asclepiads in Asia, after the decline of the Rhodian branch. They were joined in that 'noble strife', which Hesiod praised, by the doctors from Italy, Philistion, Empedocles, Pausanias and their disciples. There were these three wonderful bands of doctors competing with each other. The Coan group was fortunate in having the most and the best performers, but the Cnidian ran it close. The Italian, too, was of no small merit.

Wellmann also made an unsuccessful attempt to identify members of this so-called 'Sicilian school' of medicine. For example, he claims that Acron, a contemporary and fellow citizen of Empedocles and, reputedly, the author of a medical work in the Doric dialect,[3] reveals the latter's influence in the method he allegedly adopted to rid Athens of the plague.[4] According to Oribasius (V, 300) Acron kindled a huge bonfire in order to make cold, moist air warm and dry. But this is poor evidence to support the thesis that Acron adopted Empedocles' four element theory. Empedocles' correlation of opposites and elements seems to have been rather different from this (see below, p.107) and, if one were to think of the four element theory here, one would be more naturally inclined to think of the Aristotelian version. Furthermore, although, according to Pliny, Empedocles is said to have had recourse to an identical procedure to eradicate the plague, the same is said of Hippocrates himself. Thus it seems more likely that these stories are all the result of assumptions that, *qua* leading doctors, they would have been able to deal with the major epidemic which occurred in their lifetime. Nor, it might be added, does Pliny's explicit statement at *N.H.* XXIX, 1, 5 (*D.K.*31A3) that

> another group [of doctors], which men called 'empirical' from their reliance on experience, began in Sicily, with Acron of Acragas, who was recommended by the authority of the physicist Empedocles

offer any worthwhile support to Wellmann's claim here, since the methodology adopted by Empedocles could in no manner of means be called 'empirical'; quite the contrary. In any case, this tradition results from a deliberate 'archaisation' on the part of Empiricists attempting to prove that their persuasion was older than that of their dogmatic rivals.[5] Under the circumstances, then, a wiser policy would be to speak of the 'Sicilian tradition' in medicine instead of a 'Sicilian school' of medicine, since, undeniably, some doctors subsequently adopted certain of Empedocles' theories as the basis of their own medical and biological beliefs.

The most important of these doctors is Philistion, who wrote on medicine in the fourth century BC (see below, p.110) and was a native of Locri in southern Italy. He was, however, called 'the Sicilian' because of the medical views he adopted.[6] The *Anonymus Londinensis* preserves the following account of his views:

> Philistion of Locri thinks that we are composed of four 'forms', that is of four elements – fire, air, water, earth. Each of these, too, has its own power; of fire the power is the hot, of air it is the cold, of water the moist, and of earth the dry. * * According to him diseases come into being in many ways, but speaking more generally and in outline it is possible to speak of a threefold causation: (1) because of the elements; (2) because of the condition of our bodies; (3) because of external causes. * Diseases are caused by the elements when the hot and moist are in excess, or when the hot becomes less and weak. * * They arise through three types of external causes: (1) by wounds and sores; (2) by excess of heat, cold and the like, or change from heat to cold or cold to heat; (3) by change of nutriment to what is unsuitable or destructive. * Diseases are caused by the condition of the body in the following way. When, he says, the whole body breathes well and the breath passes through without hindrance, health ensues. For breathing takes place not only through the mouth and nostrils, but also throughout the whole body. When the body does not breathe well, diseases ensue, and in different ways. For when breathing is checked throughout the whole body a disease * * *
>
> (*Anonymus Londinensis* XX, 25ff.)

Empedoclean influence is plainly apparent here in Philistion's adoption of the four element theory. It should be noted, however, that, in adopting the four elements, Philistion attributes to each element a single opposite, hot to fire, cold to air, wet to water and dry to earth. Some scholars have assumed[7] that Empedocles' procedure in developing his element theory was simply to take over four of the traditional opposites of Ionian natural philosophy and turn them into the substances of the four elements. In the Hippocratic treatise *De vetere medicina,* as was seen above, he is actually singled out as representative of those guilty of the reprehensible practice of applying newfangled philosophical postulates to medicine and the hypothesis that there are four powers active in the human body, the hot, cold, wet and dry, is given as an example of such a postulate.[8] That Empedocles should be directly named and this particular example chosen might seem to offer support to the view that he arrived at his element theory by identifying these opposites each with the appropriate cosmic mass. However, it seems doubtful that Empedocles' actual procedure was to make this simple identification. A close examination of his fragments reveals that he did not exclusively identify these four opposites with his elements. His correlation of opposites and elements is much more complex. In Fragment 21, for example, the sun (i.e. fire) is described as bright and hot, water as cold and dark and earth as compact and solid:[9]

Come, look at the things that bear witness to my earlier discourse in case there was any deficiency in their form in my previous account. First the sun, bright to behold and everywhere hot and all the Immortal Ones which are bathed in heat and bright radiance: and rain, dark and chill in all things; and from the earth stream things that are compact and solid.

(Simplicius, *In phys.* 159.13 *D.K.*31B21)

And it is possible to catch a glimpse elsewhere of the roles assigned to the hot and the cold, the rare and the dense, the bitter and the sweet, and so forth.[10]

Philistion subsequently adopted the Empedoclean four elements as the basis for his own medical theory. But in identifying each element with one of the four opposites, hot, cold, wet or dry, he evolves a more effective correlation of elements and opposites and parts company in this respect, at any rate, with the element theory as it is revealed in the surviving fragments of Empedocles' poem *On Nature.* In other respects, however, he reveals a closer allegiance to the latter: for example, in his belief that diseases are caused whenever one or other of the elements becomes predominant; in his belief in the concept of the innate heat and his view

that the purpose of respiration is to cool that innate heat.[11] His
theory that breathing 'takes place not only by way of the mouth
and nostrils, but also over all the body' has also been widely
believed to be a borrowing from Empedocles.[12] But recently this
traditional interpretation of Empedocles' famous fragment
(B100), where he seeks to illustrate the mechanics of respiration
by drawing an analogy with a young girl playing with a
clepsydra – in this case a domestic utensil used for transferring
liquids from one container to another – has been challenged and
the belief that Empedocles is here committed to a theory of
breathing through pores in the skin has been rejected.[13] Both
Philistion and Plato, who are in other respects demonstrably
influenced by Empedocles, believe that respiration occurs
through the skin and thus offer some support to the traditional
interpretation. But it is hard to accept that Aristotle, who
otherwise makes no mention of skin breathing in his discussion
of Empedocles' theory, could have been mistaken in translating
the ambiguous ῥινῶν as 'nostrils' rather than 'skin' and that
Empedocles could have failed to mention the nostrils in an
account of mammalian respiration. If one is prepared to allow
that Philistion was capable of innovation in the element theory
itself, then perhaps one should be equally indulgent and grant
that he may also have developed on his own account the idea of
skin breathing upon the basis of Empedoclean theory.

It is unfortunate that no unimpeachable testimony as to the
time of Philistion's medical activity has survived. However, we
learn from Diogenes Laërtius, on the authority of Callimachus,[14]
that Eudoxus of Cnidus learned medicine from 'Philistion the
Sicilian' and in the Second Letter, which purports to have been
written by Plato to Dionysius II, tyrant of Syracuse, Plato makes
the following appeal:

> Do you still need Philistion? If so, by all means keep him;
> but if not, send him here and let Speusippus have his
> services. Speusippus joins me in this request; and Philistion
> also promised me that if you release him he would be eager
> to come to Athens.
>
> (314d. Frag. 2 Wellmann)

This letter is of very dubious authenticity, yet its implication that
Philistion served as a medical adviser to Dionysius II might be
true notwithstanding, and would thereby establish Plato's

acquaintance with him. (At the very least it entails that its author thought that Philistion was alive at this time.) Furthermore, in a celebrated fragment the comic poet Epicrates, while poking fun at the Platonic method of diairesis, mentions 'a certain doctor from the land of Sicily' taking part in the process[15] which makes one wonder whether Philistion fulfilled the desire ascribed to him in the Second Letter and visited Athens.

We learn from the Seventh Letter[16] (p. 324a) that Plato's first visit to Magna Graecia took place when he was 'almost forty' (i.e. c.387BC). He subsequently visited Sicily on two further occasions, in 367 and again in 362, in the hope of converting the younger Dionysius, who had succeeded his father on the throne, to the true philosophical principles of government. It seems likely, then, that it was through his direct acquaintance with Philistion that Plato became so deeply influenced by 'Sicilian' medicine. This influence is clearly apparent in Plato's great cosmological dialogue, the *Timaeus*. Towards the end of this work, for example, Plato expounds a tripartite classification of diseases. According to the first of these classes, diseases are held to be due to the excess, deficiency, varietal unsuitability[17] or displacement of the four primary bodies, earth, air, fire and water:

> The origin of diseases is, I suppose, plain to all. There are four forms from which the body is composed, earth, fire, water, air and disorders and diseases arise from the unnatural excess or deficiency of these, or from their displacement from their proper place to an alien one; and, furthermore, since there happen to be more than one variety of fire and the other elements, the reception by the body of an inappropriate variety of one of them and all similar irregularities produces disorders and diseases.
>
> (*Timaeus* 81eff.)

This theory is basically a blend of the view that disease is due to an excess of a bodily constituent and the Empedoclean four element theory.[18]

Plato's third class contains diseases primarily caused by the blockage of respiration:

> A third class of diseases must be conceived as occurring in three ways; from breath, from phlegm or from bile: whenever the lung which serves to distribute the breath to the

body, is blocked by rheums and does not afford clear passages, the breath, being unable to pass one way but entering by another in more than its proper volume, causes on the one hand the parts deprived of respiration to rot, but in the other parts, by forcing its way through the veins and distorting them, it dissolves the body, and is cut off at its centre which contains the diaphragm. Thus are caused countless painful disorders, often accompanied by much sweating.

(*Timaeus* 84cff.)

The correspondences between these two classes of disease and the first and third of the three classes attributed to Philistion in the *Anonymus Londinensis* XX, 25 (quoted above) are striking and strongly suggest that Plato is here dependent upon Philistion as an intermediary for many of his theories regarding the aetiology of diseases. He also shares with the latter the belief that the purpose of respiration is to cool the innate heat (cf. *Timaeus* 70c) and the view that breathing takes place through pores in the flesh (*Timaeus* 79c).[19]

The second class of diseases described by Plato at *Timaeus* 82b are the diseases of the tissues. It seems to have been overlooked by scholars that here, too, we have a further development upon the basis of Empedoclean biology. These diseases, we learn, come about as a result of a reversal of the normal course of nutrition. This process is based upon the assumption that blood is the ultimate nutriment of the body. Blood is itself held to be formed directly out of 'digested' food (80d) and contains substances suitable for the nourishment of all the tissues. Sinews are formed from the fibrin and flesh from the coagulated blood from which the fibrin has been removed. Sinews and flesh, in their turn, produce a viscous fluid, which glues flesh to bone and nourishes both the bones and the marrow. In this way, the appropriate substances in the blood are built up to form and restore the various tissues. When the tissues are formed in this order, health is generally the result.

Again, as there are secondary formations in nature, there is a second category of diseases to be noted by one who is minded to understand them. Since marrow, bone, flesh, and sinew are composed of the elements – and blood also is formed of these same bodies, though in a different way –

most of the other diseases arise in the same manner as those previously described; but the most severe of them have dangerous results in this way: whenever the process of formation of these secondary substances is reversed, then they are corrupted. In the natural course of events, flesh and sinews arise from blood - sinew from the fibrin to which it is akin, flesh from the coagulation of what is left when the fibrin is removed. Furthermore, the viscous, oily substance that comes from the sinews and the flesh, not only glues the flesh to the structure of the bones, but also nourishes the growth of the bone itself around the marrow; while at the same time the purest part, consisting of triangles of the smoothest and oiliest sort, filtering through the close texture of the bones, from which it distils in drops, waters the marrow. When the process takes place in this order, the normal result is health.

(*Timaeus* 82b-e)

A reversal of this process, however, causes disease. When the flesh decomposes, it discharges corruptions into the blood vessels. The blood itself becomes discoloured and bitter, acid and saline, and produces bile, serum, and phlegm of all sorts. These products of corruption ultimately destroy the blood and, denying the body nourishment, are carried throughout the veins spreading corruption and dissolution.

Diseases occur when the order is reversed. For, whenever the flesh decomposes and discharges its decomposed matter back into the veins, then the blood in the veins, which is extensive and of every sort, mixing with the air, takes on a variety of colours and bitternesses, as well as acid and saline qualities. It develops bile, serum and phlegm of all sorts. All these products of reversal and corruption first destroy the blood itself, and themselves providing the body with no further nourishment, are carried everywhere through the veins, no longer maintaining the order of their natural courses. They are in mutual conflict because they can derive no benefit from one another and they make war upon any constituent of the body that stands firm and stays at its post, spreading destruction and decay.

(*Timaeus* 82e-83a)

In his commentary upon this passage Cornford remarks[20] that he is unable to find evidence that any medical writer had formulated this notion of a reversal of nutrition as the cause of a special class of diseases. Solmsen endorses Cornford's comment and adds that as far as he knows there is no evidence that any medical writer had built up a comparable theory of nutrition or had established such a scheme of the interdependence of tissues.[21] But, as was seen in Chapter 3, p. 74, our sources attribute just such a theory of nutrition entailing a similar interdependence of the tissues to Empedocles. According to this evidence, it will be recalled, Empedocles held that nutriment was first cut and ground up in the mouth by the teeth, then digested in the stomach, i.e. broken up into its constituent elements by a process of 'putrefaction'. The nutriment was then carried to the liver, where it was turned into blood, itself a compound of all the elements in (more or less) equal proportions, which was then distributed through the blood vessels and assimilated by the body on the basis of 'like to like'. Empedocles, as was seen, apparently considered flesh to be a thickening and secondary formation of the blood since both are composed essentially according to the same formula. Although Solmsen maintains that Plato evidently 'felt that the Empedoclean theory [of the four elements] was not essential to an understanding of the mechanics of digestion and nutrition',[22] the close parallels between these two accounts reveal that Plato's views upon the secondary tissues were ultimately based upon Empedoclean biology. In both accounts blood is the ultimate nutrient of the body; blood is composed directly from digested food; blood is composed of the four elements, and flesh is a secondary formation of blood. Since there is no clear evidence to suggest that this notion of disease as a reversal of the normal process had been formulated by any previous medical writer, and Empedocles himself had pre-empted the idea of 'putrefaction' in order to explain other physiological processes (see Chapter 3, p. 74) the actual theory of disease described here may well be Plato's own innovation.[23]

Plato's adoption of the four element theory, as Solmsen has correctly remarked,[24] was a decisive event in the history of science. In the *Timaeus* the elements are firmly established as the four exclusive physical principles and it must be due in part, at least, to his adoption of them that these four entities play a similar role in Aristotelian and Stoic physics. Given the allegiance of three of the four most influential schools of philosophy in antiquity, the four element theory exercised a dominant role in Western natural science for over two millennia. The influence of 'Sicilian' medicine transmitted via Philistion, as has been seen, must have played an important role in enhancing in Plato's eyes the appeal of the four element theory. Unlike Empedocles, however, he does not regard the elements as deities whose divinity is manifested in their eternal and immutable natures. Like his pre-Socratic predecessors, he modifies the original theory to bring it more into accord with empirical phenomena and maintains that the elements undergo a continuous process of intermutation. Like Anaxagoras, Diogenes and the Atomists before him, Plato associates eternity and indestructibility with principles more ultimate than the four elements.[25]

On his first visit to Magna Graecia Plato was not only strongly influenced by 'Sicilian' medicine, but he also acquired a detailed knowledge of Pythagorean mathematics. Indeed, so markedly does Plato reveal the influence of these two bodies of knowledge in the *Timaeus* that one might be inclined to sympathise with Taylor's description of this dialogue as an amalgamation of Pythagorean religion and mathematics and Empedoclean biology – though not, of course, with his discredited thesis that 'it is a mistake to look in the *Timaeus* for any revelation of distinctly Platonic doctrines'.[26]

We learn from the Seventh Letter (p. 326b) that Plato visited Italy before travelling to Sicily. It seems likely that it was during this visit that Plato made the acquaintance of a man with whom he was to enjoy a long and close friendship and who many years later intervened on his behalf at a critical period. This man was the Pythagorean statesman and general, Archytas of Tarentum. He was of such great ability, we are told,[27] that the Tarentines elected him general for seven consecutive years, although under their constitution this office could normally be held only for a single year. In addition to his political and military abilities, Archytas was a very gifted mathematician. His most striking achievement was his brilliant solution of the 'Delian' problem, upon the lines previously laid down by Hippocrates of Chios, by an extremely elegant three-dimensional construction that enabled him to find two mean proportionals in continued proportion between two given straight lines.[28]

Archytas, however, was not only a brilliant mathematician, he was also a Pythagorean and there is evidence to show that he firmly subscribed to the major tenet of the Brotherhood that the key to all nature lies in mathematics. This article of Pythagorean faith is expressed by him in a long fragment preserved by Porphyry,[29] where he declares that it is not surprising that mathematicians can give true judgement on all natural phenomena, both generally and in detail. His deep faith in Pythagoreanism is manifested most strikingly in a passage quoted by Stobaeus in the *Florilegium*,[30] where he expresses his belief that calculation is the ruling force in the sphere of human relations and morality, and that due regard to this principle promotes harmony.

While there is no explicit mention in the Seventh Letter of any ideological exchange between Archytas and Plato, later writers, used by Cicero,[31] inform us that Plato visited Western centres of Pythagoreanism with the express purpose of learning about that philosophy. These reports most probably contain at least a kernel of truth. However that may be, the Pythagorean conviction that the world is an orderly unit (a *kosmos*), whose laws are discoverable and to be found in mathematics,[32] and their consequent belief that by contemplating the order revealed in the universe and by assimilating himself to it, man himself can become progressively purified until he ultimately escapes the cycle of birth and attains immortality is an outlook patently most acceptable to Plato.[33] If, as seems likely, the Pythagoreans, with whose thinking Plato was so much in sympathy, had already attempted to incorporate the four elements within their own philosophical system,[34] then this factor, too, must have contributed considerably towards Plato's decision to adopt this theory. (It is, perhaps, worth recalling that the one Pythagorean whose name is explicitly connected with the four element theory, Philolaus (Frag. 2), is also held to have been the teacher of Archytas.[35])

The influence of the Pythagoreans upon Plato is manifested most strikingly in the *Timaeus*. Plato's aim in this dialogue is to establish firmly upon metaphysical foundations the ethical teachings of Socrates. He employs the regularities of the heavenly bodies in order to demonstrate that the universe works in accordance with reason and moral law. By showing that the universe reveals within itself clear evidence of rational purpose, Plato could then maintain that, if men displayed in their own lives the same reason and moral law they would not be acting contrary to nature, as the Sophists had maintained, but rather fulfilling their own being as parts of nature. Cornford has aptly described this Platonic standpoint in a manner which renders its affinity with the Pythagoreans self-evident: 'The kernel of Plato's ethics', he writes, 'is the doctrine that man's reason is divine and that his business is to become like the divine by reproducing in his own nature the beauty and harmony revealed in the cosmos' (*Plato's Cosmology*, 1937, p. 34). True morality for Plato, then, is not a product of human evolution, but rather based upon an everlasting cosmic order instituted by reason. It is an order and harmony of the human soul which is itself a microcosm of the soul of the world.

The Sophists, whose teachings Plato is here concerned to refute, had exploited in a most destructive manner the implications of pre-Socratic natural philosophy. By drawing the corollary that if nature is a blind and irrational force, then law, morality and justice are merely later products of purely human origin, they thereupon maintained that, being the creations of convention, law and morality could be altered at will. The more extremist among them, represented by Thrasymachus in the *Republic* and Callicles in the *Gorgias*, even went so far as to claim that life wherein one satisfied all one's personal desires in a manner completely uninhibited by law or convention was truly life in accordance with nature.

In the tenth book of the *Laws* (888e–890b) Plato draws a picture of the type of pre-Socratic evolutionary system which resulted in this materialist atheism. This passage has been conveniently summarised as follows:[36]

some, says the Athenian, assert that all things come into being partly by nature [*physei*], partly by chance [*tychē*], and partly by design [*technē*]. Fire and water, earth and air, they say, all exist by nature and chance, not by design; and these inanimate things then bring into existence the Sun and Moon, the Stars, and the Earth. They all move 'by the *chance* of their several powers . . ., and according as they clash and fit together with some sort of affinity – hot with cold, dry with moist, soft with hard, and in other mixtures that result, by *chance, of necessity* . . ., from the combination of opposites – in that way they have generated the whole Heaven, animals and plants, and the seasons, not owing to intelligence or design or some divinity, but by *nature and chance'*. Art . . . is a later product, mortal and of mortal origin. There are the fine and useful arts, and the art of statesmanship. All law is artificial, not natural; so religion and morality are matters of convention, which vary from place to place and can be altered at human pleasure. This leads to the belief that might is right, to impiety and faction.

Although Plato's concern here is to draw a generalised picture embracing the materialist cosmogonies of Empedocles, the Atomists and even Anaxagoras, whose concept of Mind is elsewhere severely criticised for not working with conscious design but merely as the initiator of the cosmic whirl in which the world comes into being mechanically,[37] it nevertheless seems safe to say that he has Empedocles' system particularly in mind here.[38] Aristotle, too, with like purpose, employs Empedocles' conception of mechanical evolution in biology as a paradigm of the view which he, no less than Plato, wholeheartedly condemned, the view that the order of the world was the result not of intelligent purpose, but of the undirected play of necessity.[39]

In the *Philebus* (28d) these two opposing viewpoints are directly contrasted. Here Socrates asks the young Protarchus whether the universe is 'at the disposal of a force that works without plan, at random, and just as it may chance' or, on the contrary, whether it is 'an ordered system, guided by some admirable reason or intelligence'. To this Protarchus replies that it seems impious to doubt that all things are directed by a mind which is manifest in the appearance of the cosmos and in the revolutions of the heavenly bodies. Socrates thereupon concludes that we shall not agree when some clever person tells us that all things are in a disorderly condition. And similarly in the *Sophist* (265c) Plato contrasts divine craftsmanship with the commonly expressed belief that nature gives birth to things as a result of some spontaneous cause that generates without intelligence.

To counter these materialist tendencies and their pernicious effects upon traditional morality, Plato sets out in the *Timaeus* to meet the cosmogonists upon their own ground by putting forward a cosmogony of his own. In this cosmogony he makes use of all the resources of contemporary science, but reinterprets this material in order to show that the universe has an everlasting order and harmony, which is revealed most manifestly in the architecture of the heavens, so that the young may be persuaded, not by law, but by an appeal to reason, that there is no contrast between nature and the world of law and order and that these are one and the same.

Plato's primary aim, then, in the *Timaeus* is to convince his readers that the universe, far from being the fortuitous outcome of blind and aimless mechanical forces, operates in accordance with reason. This teleological purpose clearly underlies his discussion of the elements. Since he conceives of the world as the result of a divine plan, it is necessary for him to represent the elements, too, as endowed with the quality of orderliness. They must have a rational structure. So Plato bases their structure upon geometrical shapes.

Earlier thinkers, Plato argues, had simply assumed the existence of the four elements as the original principles of all things and taken them as the starting point in their cosmogonies. No one, he maintains, had been concerned to explain their generation or give an account of their properties. But, far from being original principles, elements (*stoicheia*, i.e. 'letters', as it were, of the universe), he urges, should not be ranked even so low as syllables (48b). Having denied them their status as elements, Plato promises to give a detailed account of them starting from the very beginning. He is careful to add that his account can be no more than a probable story since in his opinion there is no possibility of an exact science of nature. As the objects of physical science are constantly changing and can be apprehended only by the senses, exact truth as to their nature can never be attained. Plato presents, then, in the *Timaeus* the best account possible of the physical world (see 44c, 48d, 57d).

We come across the elements for the first time at *Timaeus* 31b–32c. They are conceived in this mythical account of creation as the materials which the Demiurge or Divine Craftsman, who represents divine reason working for ends that are good, puts together to form the body of the world. Here Plato deduces the existence of the four elements by maintaining that fire and earth are necessary - the one to render the earth's body visible, the other to make it tangible. But these two elements, being extremes, cannot hold together without a third to serve as a bond. The most perfect bond is that which makes itself and the terms it connects a unity in the fullest sense. The most perfect type of proportion, continuous geometrical progression, effects this most perfectly.

Three terms, however, are insufficient since the primary bodies are not planes, but solids. Two geometrical means, therefore, have to be inserted between fire and earth. Accordingly, water and air are introduced and the final result is the sequence of the four elements determined by the double equation: fire/air = air/water = water/earth.

It would be naïve to believe that Plato arrived at the four elements by means of this a priori play of mathematical fantasy. Their existence is arbitrarily assumed and their disposition based upon a false arithmetical analogy. Plato's aim here is to demonstrate that the world has been formed in accordance with rational design and he himself elsewhere in the *Timaeus* regards the four elements as an established belief. His use here of geometrical progression to determine the proportions existing between the elements provides a further link with the Pythagorean Order. The discovery of the different mathematical progressions certainly belongs to the Brotherhood and Plato may well have acquired this particular piece of mathematical knowledge from Archytas with whose name the arithmetical, geometrical and harmonic progressions are explicitly connected.[40]

Plato's aim to show that the world is orderly and constructed in accordance with a divine plan is even more apparent in his later discussion of the elements in the second part of the dialogue. At 47eff. Timaeus proposes to begin his story of creation again, but this time with a change of emphasis. The preceding part of the dialogue has dealt, in the main, with the rational or final cause of the world. But rational design came into conflict with factors in the physical world which, being 'destitute of reason', produce their various effects 'at random and without order'. It now becomes necessary to consider these irrational factors which limit the purposive activity of the Demiurge.

In his previous discourse Timaeus had drawn a distinction between two orders of existence, the intelligible and unchanging model, the world of the Forms, and its changing and visible copy, the physical world. This distinction is a familiar one from the *Republic* and other dialogues. We are now told that a third factor is necessary since the other two by themselves are insufficient. This new entity is described at its first appearance as the 'Receptacle' or as the 'Nurse of all Becoming' and is finally identified as 'Space' (51eff.). The sensible copies of the Forms, we learn, are not self-subsistent, but require the support of a medium. This medium is Space and, being eternally existent, it provides the copies of the Forms, which appear in it like images in a mirror, place wherein they can achieve the limited degree of reality which they are capable of attaining. To illustrate this relationship between Form, Copy and Receptacle, Plato employs the simile of the father, mother and child, comparing the Form to the father, the Receptacle to the mother and the 'nature that arises between them' to their offspring. In drawing this simile Plato probably had in mind that embryological belief held by Anaxagoras, among others, that the female contributed nothing to generation but only provided the place in which the embryo developed.[41] According to this theory, the mother contributes no part of the embryo's substance and her own features do not reappear in the child. Similarly, the Receptacle is itself characterless; it has no features which might intrude upon the copies that are mirrored in it. (At 50eff. Timaeus compares the Receptacle to a base used by a scentmaker which must itself be odourless in order that it might serve as a base for any perfume whatsoever.) Although Plato's analysis of physical bodies is not without influence upon Aristotle, it should not be assumed that the Receptacle is introduced to account for their material nature.

The Receptacle, then, has no visible appearance and is described as 'a nature invisible and characterless, all-receiving, participating in some very puzzling way of the intelligible and very hard to apprehend' (51aff.). It is apprehended, we learn later (52b), not by rational understanding like the Forms, but by 'a sort of bastard reasoning'. It is an independent and eternally existing factor necessary in every process of becoming since it provides a situation for all things that come into being and thereby enables each of them to 'cling to some sort of existence on pain of being nothing at all'.[42] As the Receptacle is utterly devoid of all characteristics, it can receive throughout its entire extent all the likenesses of intelligible and eternal things. Among these entities which temporarily arise in Space Plato expressly mentions the empirical instances of the four elements and is thereupon stimulated to raise the question whether there are models to serve as originals for these copies. He concludes that there do, indeed, exist independently real Forms of earth, air, fire and water, which serve as eternal models for their sensible copies in the physical world.

By representing these vestigial traces of the elements as the closest approximation to cosmic order that can possibly result from undirected mechanical activity, Plato brilliantly exploits his choice of the cosmogonic myth as the vehicle for his exposition. Having chosen to expound what is essentially a conceptual analysis in the form of a fictitious genesis, it is possible for him to use his imaginary creation of the universe in time to represent symbolically aspects of the cosmos as it exists at all times and so vividly to make the point that undirected, chaotic movements could not possibly result in the formation of a cosmos, a world system characterised by the prevalence of stable and periodic rhythmical movement. Plato's account of pre-cosmic chaos, broadly speaking, has its analogues in Empedocles' Sphairos, Anaxagoras' conception of a pre-cosmic condition of 'all things together' and the random and aimless motion postulated by the Atomists. Like his pre-Socratic predecessors, Plato describes an initial period of mechanical activity which leads to the aggregation of like to like; but according to Plato, this process cannot itself form a cosmos. A cosmos cannot simply come into being 'by nature and chance' (see *Laws* 889bff.); on the contrary, order and design are its prerequisites. Evolution without guidance is insufficient to explain the formation of an orderly world.

According to Plato's metaphysical account, then, the elements have now lost the proud position they formerly enjoyed in Empedoclean physics. They are reduced to transitory impressions in the Receptacle, mere fleeting images of their own eternal Forms. The fire in this world, for example, is merely a transient reflection in the Receptacle of the Form of fire. However, since Plato conceives of the world as the result of a divine plan, it is necessary for him to represent the elements, too, which have come into being as reflections of their Forms in the Receptacle, as being of rational structure. This structure, he maintains, must be based upon geometrical shapes. So, in addition to giving a metaphysical account of the elements, Plato later in the *Timaeus* describes at length their mathematical derivation. His geometrical construction of the elements should be regarded as supplementary to his metaphysical account of them rather than as an alternative to it. Having decided to expound his views upon the world in the form of a fictitious cosmogony, he can consistently regard genesis as such as prior to cosmic genesis. As Solmsen perceptively remarks,[43] 'cosmic genesis presupposes physical genesis and is a refinement of it.'

The Demiurge, or Divine Craftsman, sets to work upon the elements in their disorderly condition in order to make them as fair and good as possible. His first step in the process of reducing them to order is to give them a distinct configuration by means of shapes and numbers (53bff.). It is immediately apparent that his procedure is completely in accordance with a priori assumptions. Since the universe is a three-dimensional object, it is assumed that its contents must be three-dimensional solids. Since the cosmos is to be the result of a divine plan and the god desires to make it as perfect and as beautiful as possible (see 30dff.), if these three-dimensional solids are to be part of a beautiful and perfect cosmos, they must themselves be as beautiful as possible. The most beautiful of all three-dimensional solids are the regular solids whose theoretical construction had been completed by Theaetetus at the Academy. Therefore, if the universe is to be composed of elements (and it is), the particles of each element must be a regular solid. Furthermore, since it is necessary to account for change in what is to be primarily an orderly physical world, it is requisite that these bodies should be able to change into and interact with one another according to natural laws. It seems likely, as Cornford has suggested,[44] that Plato's elaborate account of the structure of the primary bodies was intended by him as a deliberate correction of the Atomists, who had given their particles all varieties of shape. Plato with his teleological outlook is not willing to leave this matter to chance (compare his attitude at *Laws* 888e–890b). The basic elements of his universe are to be shaped by reason into definite mathematical forms so that even the lowest recognisable level of nature exhibits order. Plato, then, restricts the 'unlimited polymorphism' of the Atomists and bases his physical science upon more economical principles.[45]

It is important to realise that the choice of the regular solids is the premiss which determines the Craftsman's procedures. It is simply not true that every volume is enclosed by planes, although this is not made immediately apparent. Plato's aim is to build up four of the regular solids, namely the pyramid (tetrahedron), octahedron, icosahedron and the cube in such a manner that they are capable of changing and interacting with each other. The first three of these solids, however, have equilateral faces, whereas the cube has square faces. Since the Craftsman is depicted as constructing these four three-dimensional solids out of two-dimensional planes, he might have been expected to have taken the equilateral triangle and the square as his elementary plane figures and constructed these solids out of them. It is not immediately clear why he did not adopt this course since his theory of breaking down these solids into their plane faces and then recombining these planes into other solids would have worked just as easily upon this simple basis. His actual procedure, however, is much more complicated.

We are told that every rectilinear plane surface is composed of triangles (53c), i.e. it can be divided into these figures. The triangle, of course, represents the surface contained by the minimum number of straight lines and, for this reason, is adopted here by Plato as his irreducible element. It should be noted, however, that Plato suggests at 53d that there might be 'principles yet more remote than these known to Heaven and to such men as Heaven favours'. And we have already had the hint at 53b that these more ultimate principles are lines and numbers. There, it will be recalled, the Craftsman began his task by giving the vestigial occurrences of the four elements distinct configurations by means of shapes and numbers. Plato's reasoning, then, seems to be that just as planes can be constructed out of triangles, so triangles, in their turn, can be constructed from lines and lines themselves represented by numbers. This mode of thinking is purely Pythagorean and is paralleled in Alexander Polyhistor's account of Pythagorean doctrine preserved by Diogenes Laërtius.[46] According to Alexander, the Pythagoreans identified the four elements with certain solids which were constituted of lines which, in their turn, could be equated with arithmetical points. These elements could change into one another. This evidence is highly controversial, however, and scholars have differed widely in their attitudes towards it. Whereas some believe that this material is incontestably influenced by the *Timaeus*, others are prepared to believe that we have here elements of genuinely early Pythagorean doctrine.[47] All triangles, Plato points out, are derived from two, i.e. any triangle can be divided into (or composed out of) two right-angled triangles formed by dropping a perpendicular from any angle to the opposite side. Each triangle so formed must be one of two types: either right-angled isosceles (that which has on either side the half of a right-

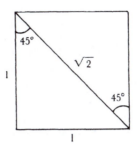

Figure 1 The right-angled isosceles triangle – the basic triangle of the cube.

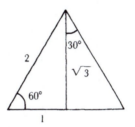

Figure 2 The right-angled scalene triangle (half-equilateral) – the basic triangle of the other regular solids.

angle (see Figure 1), or right-angled scalene (that which has unequal parts of a right-angle allotted to unequal sides (see Figure 2). Whereas the former is a unique type, the latter has a large variety of shapes. It is necessary, therefore, to choose the best of these shapes and this is confidently asserted to be the half-equilateral.

The reason why Plato adopted these two basic triangular units is highly controversial. The most imaginative and persuasive explanation is that of Popper,[48] who suggests that Plato has adopted these two units in order to get round the difficulties caused by the discovery that the side and diagonal of a square are incommensurable. This discovery had caused a major crisis not only in mathematics but in Pythagorean philosophy generally. How could it be confidently claimed by them that 'all things are number', if it could actually be proved that no whole number could express the ratio between the side and diagonal of a square? However, although $\sqrt{2}$ cannot be expressed arithmetically, it can be represented geometrically. It may be significant, then, that Plato incorporates $\sqrt{2}$ in one of his basic triangular units. But the same difficulty reappears with the case of other irrational numbers, e.g. $\sqrt{3}$. By using the half-equilateral triangle as his other basic shape, Plato finds a place in his world system for multiples of $\sqrt{3}$ also, since the sides of this triangle are in the ratio of $1:2:\sqrt{3}$. Perhaps, as Popper suggests, he believed that all irrational numbers could be explained as multiples of $\sqrt{2}$ and $\sqrt{3}$.

Upon the basis of these two irreducible triangles Plato constructs four of the five regular solids.[49] His procedure is to build up the three regular solids whose common surface is an equilateral triangle from the right-angled scalene, and the fourth solid, the cube, from the right-angled isosceles triangle. His constructions seem unnecessarily complicated. Instead of constructing the equilateral triangular face from two half-equilateral triangles, he in fact employs six of these elements (Figure 3) and, instead of building the square out of two isosceles triangles, he uses four (Figure 4). Having constructed in this way these two surfaces, he then sets them together to form the four regular solids, building the pyramid, the octahedron and the icosahedron out of 24, 48 and 120 elementary half-equilateral triangular units respectively and the cube out of 24 isosceles units. Each of these regular solids is then identified with one of the four elements in a manner which enables him to account for their characteristic qualities and specific behaviour (55dff.):

> We must distribute the figures whose origin we have just described between fire, water, earth, and air.
>
> Let us assign the cube to earth; for it is the most immobile and most plastic of the four bodies. The figure that has the most stable faces must especially have this character. Of the triangles we assumed at the outset, the isosceles has naturally a more stable base than the scalene, and of the equilateral figures composed of them, the square is, in whole and in part, a more stable base than the equilateral triangle.
>
> Accordingly, we maintain the probability of our account

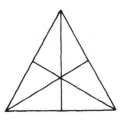

Figure 3 Construction of the equilateral triangular surfaces of pyramid octahedron and icosahedron.

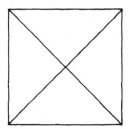

Figure 4 Construction of the square surfaces of the cube.

by assigning this figure to earth; and the least mobile of the remainder to water, the most mobile to fire, and the intermediate to air. Again, we assign the smallest body to fire, the largest to water, and the intermediate to air; the sharpest to fire, the next sharpest to air, and the least sharp to water. Taking all these figures, the one which has the fewest faces [the pyramid] must necessarily be the most mobile as well as in every way the most penetrating and sharpest of all, and, moreover, being composed of the fewest identical parts, the lightest; and the second figure [the octahedron] comes second in these respects, the third [the icosahedron] third. Thus, in accordance with logic and likelihood, let us regard the solid which has taken the form of the pyramid as the element and seed of fire; let us regard the second of the figures we constructed as that of air and the third water.[50]

125

Since the cube, which has been assigned to earth, is composed of a different basic triangle from that of the other three solids, it is necessary for Plato to deny that the earth can be transformed into fire or air or water (56d). Only these three 'elements', being composed of the same basic triangle, can be transformed into each other. Although Plato follows his pre-Socratic predecessors in their attempt to bring the four element theory into greater accord with empirical phenomena and agrees with them that these bodies are transformed one into the other,[51] his general theory, unfortunately, does not allow him to account for the intermutation of all four of these primary bodies. His failure to incorporate earth within the cycle of intermutation leads him to suggest that its transformation is purely illusory. The misgivings he voices at 54a may stem from this failure to account for the phenomena in this particular respect. Aristotle, we may note, criticises Plato severely on this very issue and points out that the exclusion of earth is unreasonable, contrary to observed facts, and based upon a priori principles:

> It is absurd not to allow all the elements to be generated from each other. This they must and do uphold. But for one element alone to have no part in the change appears neither reasonable nor in accordance with sensation; but all alike change into one another. It turns out that these philosophers in discussing the phenomenon make statements which are in conflict with the phenomena. The reason is that they have a wrong conception of primary principles and want to bring everything into line with certain hard and fast opinions.
>
> (*De caelo* 306a1ff.)

Having assigned the regular solids to the four primary bodies, Plato at 56c-57c describes their various transformations. The intermutation of the elements rests upon certain presuppositions, namely, transformation is based upon surface; during this process there is always conservation of surfaces; the molecules of earth, air, fire and water can be broken down into their basic triangles; like particles cannot act upon like; and, since the earth's basic triangles are of a different pattern from those of the other three regular solids, they can only combine to form cubes. Timaeus describes first the upward transformation from earth to fire. The tetrahedron, being the most active, mobile and penetrating of the solids, is held to be the principal agent of change. It acts upon the other three solids and breaks them down. Since earth has been assigned the cubical figure, it cannot undergo transformation. Transformation occurs in the other two cases. Fire breaks down water to form two particles of air and one of fire. This transformation may be represented as follows:

> One icosahedron (water) is broken down into 2 octahedra (air) and 1 tetrahedron (fire), i.e. 20 faces of the icosahedron (120 basic triangles) = 2×8 faces of the octahedron (48 basic triangles) + 1×4 faces of the tetrahedron (24 basic triangles).

This description fits the facts of experience: when water is boiled, it changes into steam and vapour. If the fire continues its action, the newly formed octahedra are broken up to form two tetrahedra, two pyramids of fire. Thus water can be transformed upwards wholly into fire.

The downward transformation of fire into air and air into water is next described (56e). In this account the most mobile and active body is depicted as being outnumbered by its more unwieldy opponent. Should it fail to force its way through, it is overcome and shattered. In that event, the faces of two fire particles are re-formed as a single particle of air, i.e. 2 tetrahedra of fire = 1 octahedron of air, i.e. 2×4 (24 basic triangles) = 1×8 (48 basic triangles). The process continues with the transformation of the resulting air particle into water. Its parallel in nature is the formation of mist and cloud and rain. In the latter case 2½ octahedra of air combine to provide the 20 faces (120 basic triangles) required for a single icosahedron of water.

Thus Timaeus accounts for the transformation of the elements upwards from water to fire and downwards from fire to water. No further change, we learn,[52] can occur beyond these limits in either direction: 'for no kind that is homogeneous and identical can either cause or suffer any change from what is similar to and identical in character to itself.' It is an arbitrary assumption on the part of Plato that, during change, the particles of one element can break up those of another, but are not permitted to break up each other. It is quite unreasonable that he should maintain, for example, that while the sharp corners of the pyramid can slice cubes, octahedra and icosahedra into their component triangles, each pyramid is itself unaffected by its own kind.

Having demonstrated that the world at large is both

constructed and operates in accordance with rational purpose, Timaeus turns, towards the end of the dialogue, from macrocosm to microcosm and describes the structure and functions of the human body together with the diseases to which it is prone. The same teleological, axiological and physical principles are clearly applied in this sphere, too, superimposed upon a basis of Empedoclean theory. The creation of human beings, since they are to be mortal, is entrusted by the Demiurge to younger gods, his own offspring. Having received from him the immortal principle of the soul, they proceeded to fashion a mortal body round it to serve as the vehicle of the soul (42e-43a):

> In imitation of their own maker [i.e. the Demiurge who had constructed the Cosmos in the same manner], they borrowed portions of fire and earth and air and water from the world – on condition that these loans should be repaid – and welded them together, making each separate body out of all four of the elements.

Copying the spherical shape of the universe – the 'most perfect and most like itself of all figures' (33b) – these gods first formed the head and confined within it the circuits of the immortal soul. They then provided the head with a body for its support and to serve as its means of locomotion. They located sense organs in the fore-part of the head, as instruments, to enable the soul to find its way about.

In spite of the strong influence of Empedoclean physics and biology generally throughout the *Timaeus*, Plato here follows the lead of Alcmaeon, who had located the seat of the intellect in the brain rather than in the vicinity of the heart as Empedocles had maintained (see p. 60). Diogenes' decision to adopt this view of the brain as the central organ of sensation and thought most probably also influenced Plato here. It should not be overlooked that Diogenes had successfully accommodated the four element theory to his own theory of matter;[53] had adopted along with it much Empedoclean biology; and, in propounding a teleological theory of nature, had advocated a standpoint highly congenial to Plato.

Having constructed the body, the younger gods also incorporated within it 'a soul of another nature', mortal this time and subject to terrible and irresistible affections – pleasure, pain, rashness, fear, anger and hope, which they mingled with 'irratio-

128

nal sense and all-daring love'. To protect the immortal soul as far as possible from pollution, they placed the neck between the two kinds of soul to keep them apart. Then they encased the mortal soul within the thorax, which they divided into two parts since the mortal soul was itself bipartite. The part endowed with 'courage and passion and a love of contention' they housed nearer the head, midway between the midriff and the neck, in order that, being obedient to reason, it might join with the immortal element in controlling and restraining the appetitive part of the soul. This latter part they located between the midriff and the navel, placing it as far away as possible from the 'seat of council', so that it might cause the least possible disturbance and allow the highest part of the soul to take thought in peace for the common good.

It is clear that the procedure of the gods is deliberately made consonant with the tripartite psychology of the *Republic* and elsewhere. The only differences are that here each part of the soul is provided with a specific location in the body and its two lower elements are expressly stated to be mortal. The same philosophical principles also underlie the description of the bodily organs whose position, structure and functions are determined from a teleological rather than from a physiological standpoint. The internal organs are taken in two groups separated by the diaphragm and made to correspond to the higher and lower portions of the mortal soul. The heart and lungs, which are located above the diaphragm, are considered first. The heart, which is regarded as the centre of the blood vessels and the 'wellspring' of the blood, is at the same time held to be the seat of the spirited element of the soul (*to thymoeides*), which corresponds to the guardian class within the *Republic*. This class serves as its garrison or standing army and is subordinate to the philosopher-rulers. It embodies the virtue of manly courage. When the rational part of the soul, situated in the head, the citadel and headquarters of sense perception, realises that a wrongful act is taking place in some region of the body, it sends down a message to the spirited element in the guardhouse. The blood in the heart then begins to boil with rage and surges through the blood vessels to quell the disturbance. To cool and calm the heart whenever it is unduly heated by the action of the *thymos* or spirited element in this way, and to act as a buffer when it is agitated, the lungs were created 'soft and bloodless and perforated within by cavities like a sponge' and located next to the heart. (Here, it will be noted, having departed earlier from the Empedoclean belief in the heart as the seat of the intellect, Timaeus returns to 'Sicilian' theory in holding that the lungs act (partly) in a cooling capacity.)

Below the diaphragm the gods set the stomach which is likened to a manger. To it they tethered the appetitive soul 'like an untamed beast', placing it as far away as possible from the seat of counsel. The liver and spleen were also located by them in the lower part of the trunk. They are assigned no specific physiological functions. The liver's role is to keep the appetites under the influence of reason (71a-e). Although the appetitive soul is totally incapable of reason, it can be influenced by visions and dreams. These, we are told, are reflected in the liver 'as in a mirror' and are themselves dependent upon the state of that organ. The spleen is given the role of keeping the liver bright (72c) which it does by absorbing the impurities that form within it from time to time.

The same teleological and psychological principles also underlie the formation of the rest of the body. The 'authors of the human race', aware of its likely intemperance in food and drink, made provision against this danger in order that it should not quickly be destroyed by disease and perish without fulfilling its end. They created the so-called lower belly to serve as a receptacle for superfluous food and drink, and made the bowels 'convoluted so that the food should be prevented from passing quickly through and compelling the body to require more, thus producing insatiable gluttony and making the whole race hostile to philosophy and culture and rebellious against the most divine part of our nature'.[54] Here again, psychological motivation is pre-eminent over physiological function.

At this point in the dialogue Timaeus turns to describe the various tissues of the body. Creation is now back again in the hands of the Demiurge and explicitly based upon the geometrical theory of matter described earlier. The Craftsman begins with the creation of the marrow. To form this tissue the god selected the smoothest and most accurately formed of the basic triangles of all four elements and mixed them together in due proportion. (Up to now we have heard of no differences in the two basic types of triangle other than difference in size. Here we learn that some of these triangles are very far from perfect. Being copies of the perfect triangles of mathematics they are incapable of attaining complete perfection of form.) Part of the marrow is then moulded by the Demiurge into a spherical shape to contain the divine seed, i.e. the semen (see 91b) and is called by him the 'brain' (*enkephalon*) to signify that the vessel containing it would be the head, i.e. that it would be 'in the head' (*en kephalō*). Other parts of the marrow are divided into elongated shapes to be enclosed in the vertebrae of the spine and other bones. The marrow is clearly regarded as the most important of all the tissues, whose functions are explained by reference to it.

Bone is formed next. It is, we learn, a composite of marrow and carefully sifted and refined earth which has been hardened by repeated immersions into fire and then water. It is impossible to read this account of the formation of bone with its evocation of the two human techniques of baking and the smelting of metal without being reminded of Empedocles. The latter's own description of the formation of bone in Fragment 96 employs the same metallurgical simile[55] and in both accounts the capacity of fire to act as a hardening agent is recognised.[56] There are, however, some significant differences in the two accounts. According to the *Timaeus*, earth, not fire, is the predominant constituent of bone and the agency of both fire and water is invoked in the hardening process.

Having made the bone, the Craftsman fashioned it in the form of a sphere to surround the brain, but left a narrow opening to provide a means of continuity between the brain and spinal marrow. To surround the marrow of the neck and back, he then formed the vertebrae, which he placed under one another like 'pivots', starting at the head and extending throughout the whole of the trunk. (The spine is made up of many vertebrae to ensure its flexibility.) To protect all the seed, he fenced it in a stony enclosure. In this description of the construction of the backbone, as Taylor points out,[57] we seem to have yet another deliberate correction of Empedoclean belief. According to Empedocles the spine was originally single and continuous until broken by the animal turning round (presumably within the womb). This variation proved useful and contributed to the animal's chances of survival.[58] Thus while according to Empedocles the articulate structure of the spine of vertebrates is the result of an accident, in the *Timaeus*, by contrast, the spinal column is carefully constructed in accordance with the purposive activity of the Demiurge.

After completing the skeleton, the Craftsman's next task was to clothe it with flesh. By itself the bony skeleton was too brittle, too inflexible, and, being prone to decay due to variations in temperature, would not have been able to protect the seed within it. The Craftsman, therefore, created the sinews and the flesh to overcome these deficiencies. 'By binding all the limbs with sinew contracting and relaxing about their sockets', he enabled the body to bend and stretch and he devised the flesh to serve as a defence against heat and cold and protect the body in a fall. The flesh was also provided with a 'warm moisture' which cools the body in summer 'by moistening it outside', and warms it in winter.[59] Flesh is composed of water and fire and earth,[60] suffused with a 'ferment' composed of acid and saline (74c). Doubtless this ferment or leaven is introduced to take into account the secretions from the skin. (Plato's language here indicates another allusion to the simile of the baker.) Air is not expressly listed among the components of flesh here and it might seem that we have a departure from Empedocles' belief that all four elements are ingredients of flesh (see Frag. B98). But flesh is produced from defibrinated blood (82d) and blood is nutriment cut up small by the action of fire and is thus an amalgam of all four roots. Furthermore, the marrow, which is described as the *archē* of all the tissues (73b), itself contains all four elements. Consequently, any departure from Empedocles here can only lie in the relative proportions of the four elements in the composition of flesh. In describing the composition of the sinews Plato does not provide an analysis of their constituent elements, but contents himself merely with the remark that sinew is an intermediate substance, more tense and consistent than flesh but softer and more pliable than bone.[61] The god, then, enveloped the bones and marrow with these, binding the bones to one another with sinews before burying them all under a covering of flesh. The flesh, it may be noted, is unevenly distributed. Those bones containing the greatest amount of the life substance, marrow, namely the skull and the spine, are given virtually no flesh to protect them, whereas others, like the thighs, are more thickly covered. This seems a paradoxical arrangement since one might have expected that the brain, for example, housing, as it does, the immortal parts of the soul, would have been surrounded by solid bone and thick flesh to protect it against injury. But while Plato acknowledges that if the human race had been so equipped it would have been able to enjoy a life span at least twice as long and at the same time healthier and freer from pain, since solidity of bone and thickness of flesh inhibit sensitivity and apprehension, it was decided that a nobler but less long-lived race should be created. Accordingly, the bones of the skull were made thin, without flesh or sinews. The head, however, could not be left totally unprotected. So it was provided with a covering of hair, 'light and sufficient to provide shade in summer and shelter in winter, without being an obstacle to perception'. The creation of hair, it will be noticed, is described in terms totally consistent with Plato's elementary physics.

Plato has been applauded for this decision radically to part company here with 'Sicilian' medicine and locate the seat of the intellect in the brain rather than in the region of the heart. But any praise should be tempered by the reflection that this conclusion was not arrived at upon any scientific basis. It was not, in fact, until the third century BC that it was scientifically established that the brain was the seat of the intellect, when the Alexandrians discovered the nerves in the course of their careful, systematic dissections of the human body and traced them to within the brain (see Chapter 7).

Given the scale of the influence of 'Sicilian' medicine upon the *Timaeus*, Plato must have had very compelling reasons for departing here from the belief in the primacy of the heart. At *Timaeus* 73c, as we have seen, the immortal part of the soul was located in the brain marrow in the head, which was then, to avoid pollution, physically separated from the mortal elements of the soul by the neck, deliberately interposed to keep them apart. Having provided for the physical separation of the highest part of the soul, Plato evidently felt no less constrained to separate it from the lower functions on physiological grounds as well. Here, too, he seems anxious to avoid 'polluting the divine beyond what was absolutely unavoidable'. This motivation, it now becomes apparent, was primarily responsible not only for Plato's innovation in introducing the marrow and assigning it a role of fundamental importance in the formation of the tissues, but also for his departure from the belief in the primacy of the heart. There is no evidence to suggest that Empedocles, notwithstanding his interest in the composition of other tissues, had

133

previously concerned himself with the formation of marrow and, assuredly, in stressing the prime importance of the marrow and claiming that the other tissues were formed for its protection, Plato has gone beyond Empedoclean theory. But, in doing so, it should be noted, he has, in the final analysis, nevertheless again proceeded in accordance with Empedoclean principles, since marrow is itself a composition (of the most perfect triangles) of the four elements.

However, in making the brain and the semen from marrow and in locating the seat of the intellect in the head, Plato does part company with Empedocles. As was shown in Chapter 3, the latter held the soul to be blood. It will be recalled that Hippon, who believed that the semen flowed from the spinal marrow,[62] attacked this view and sought to refute it by pointing out that the semen is not blood, apparently assuming that the soul or life principle is transmitted via the semen. Blood in Empedocles' system also serves as the seat and agent of thought (Frag. 105) and a human's sensitivity, intelligence and general ability is dependent upon the blending of the elements in its make-up.[63] But in addition to believing the soul to be blood and blood to be the seat of intellectual activity, Empedocles also believed that the blood served as the agent of nutrition. This latter belief, as we have seen, was subsequently adopted by Plato. Having done so, however, he evidently could not then accept that the one substance (blood) could serve as the agent for two very diverse functions – that of transmitting (via the semen – itself a residue of the blood) the immortal element of the soul and, at the same time, of catering to the appetites by serving as the agent of nutrition. Accordingly, Plato distanced himself from this view that the semen is blood and adopted instead the theory of Alcmaeon and others that the semen is brain substance.[64] Like Alcmaeon, too, Plato locates the seat of the intellect in the head, thus departing radically from 'Sicilian' medicine in this respect. Plato, then, is unwilling to accept that the blood, which serves for him, no less than for Empedocles, as the vehicle of nutrition, could also serve as the carrier of the immortal element of the soul.[65] It is interesting to observe that Diogenes of Apollonia, who, as we saw above, had successfully accommodated Empedocles' seminal theory to take into account Hippon's criticism of it, by claiming that the seed is a modification of blood, had previously arrived at a very similar position to Plato's here in that both philosophers adopt a teleological approach to biology; both maintain that the seat of the intellect is located in the brain; both believe that blood is the agent of nutrition; and both believe that the soul is transmitted with the semen. The crucial respect in which they differ, however, clearly reveals Plato's psychological motivation in distancing himself from 'Sicilian' (derived) theory. Diogenes' belief that the semen is (aerated) blood is replaced in the *Timaeus* by the view that the semen is marrow or brain substance.

Having described the construction of the human body, Timaeus now proceeds to give an account of certain of its physiological processes, namely digestion, the movement of blood and respiration. Some of these processes are only perfunctorily treated and anatomical connections between the various organs are only vaguely described. The influence of 'Sicilian' medicine is again very much in evidence, especially in the theories of digestion and respiration described here. Plato's knowledge of internal anatomy is of a very low order and is patently not based upon any human, or even animal, dissection. Like his contemporaries, he does not distinguish between veins and arteries and has no conception of the heart's role in the movement of the blood; nor, indeed, of the chambers of the heart. The lungs, as we have seen, are given a dual function, that of cooling the innate heat in the heart and moderating the passions that arise within it. The liver is given no physiological function at all.

Timaeus first gives a rudimentary description of the 'irrigation system' which carries nutriment throughout the body. Two main channels (i.e. presumably the aorta and vena cava) run along the back on the left and right hand sides. (From Plato's sketchy description of the heart at 70b as 'the knot of the veins and the fountain of the blood' it may be inferred that these two veins have their origin in the heart.) These dorsal vessels are then split in the region of the head and their ends are plaited so as to cross each other in opposite directions, those from the right being slanted towards the left side of the body and those from the left towards the right. (The intention here is twofold - to secure the head to the body, and to enable the body as a whole to be informed of the effect of sense perceptions coming from the members on either side.) The underlying aim of this account is to explain how the blood (the nutrient) is distributed throughout the body. Plato's general scheme - although much less complete - has affinities with Diogenes of Apollonia's account of the vascular system (see Aristotle, *Historia animalium* 511b30ff. *D.K.*64B6) and may have been derived from this source.

Having described the main channels of the irrigation system, Timaeus then explains how the blood is driven through them by the agency of respiration. (Plato, it should be stressed, has no conception either of the heart as a pump or of the circulation of the blood. For the former discovery we have to wait until Erasistratus' impressive anatomical investigations had led him to this conclusion. And for the latter - notwithstanding several unsuccessful attempts to pre-empt it for the Greeks - we have to wait nearly two millennia.) The blood is driven through the irrigation channels by the force engendered by the natural motion of the internal fire striving to reach its own kind. This, in turn, imparts to the surrounding air a 'circular thrust' (*periōsis*) (79a–e). The mechanism of respiration is essentially currents of air and fire. The lungs, it may be noted, actually play as little a part in the respiratory process as the heart does in the distribution of blood. Their function is here the mechanical one of sustaining the movement of the internal fire which, as shall be seen, 'digests' the food in the belly and raises the blood so formed from the belly to the veins.

The entire process is based upon his geometrical physics. The principle that bodies composed of smaller particles are impervious to larger particles, while those consisting of the larger particles are not impervious to the smaller, Timaeus declares, must be accepted if the process is to be understood. Fire, for example, being composed of the smallest particles can, in consequence, penetrate water, earth and air and anything composed of these elements. And so, in the body, fire and air have the capacity to penetrate skin and flesh because their finer particles can pass through these coarser materials. The belly can retain food and drink, but is permeable to fire and water, whose particles are smaller than those of its own structure. These two elements can pass in and out through its walls. This penetrating capacity of fire and air is utilised by the Demiurge to provide a mechanism to drive the blood upwards into the veins from the belly.

The process is illustrated by a somewhat obscure analogy with a weel or fish-trap (see Figure 5).[66] The currents of air pass in and

out of the body by certain routes conceived by Plato to form a
pattern resembling a fish-trap – a woven basket of reeds with a
wide opening at the top, but containing, immediately below this
opening, a cone which stretches downwards inside to form a
narrow internal entrance and render escape difficult for any
trapped fish. The Craftsman weaves first a network of fire and air
on the model of a trap, but in the present instance he inserts not
one, but a pair of funnels at the entrance, making one of them
bifurcated. The whole of the interior of the vessel is made of fire,
while the funnels and the main vessel itself are of air. The
Craftsman then applies this structure to the living creature (see
Figure 6). The funnels are let into the mouth and nose and
elongated at their lower ends to form the trachea and gullet. At its
upper end the breath funnel is divided into two outlets, the nose
and the mouth. (This is so that we may breathe while the mouth
is full.) Having fitted the funnels, the main vessel is made to
'grow all round the hollow part of the body' and the whole is
given an alternating movement, a flow into the funnels which is
followed by a backward flow. The network correspondingly
sinks in and out throughout the body and 'rays' of fire which
stretch through the interior follow the movement of the air in
either direction, i.e. when we inhale through the mouth the
currents of air converging along the body on all sides flow
together into the 'funnels' (i.e. the columns of air defined by the
mouth and nose, gullet and trachea); upon exhalation, the
columns of air flow back again and out through the nose and
mouth. The pressure of the breath thus reverses the motion of the
currents of air from outside and the external air displaced in
consequence then sinks into the body through pores in the skin
to fill the space inside that would otherwise have been left empty,
since the 'rays' of fire follow the movements of the air in either
direction. (This internal fire is described as being separated into
'rays' because it passes along the same channels or pores as the
air.) The whole process is then reversed. The air which has
entered through the pores in the skin passes out again via the
same route by which it entered and sets the external air moving
again towards the funnels of the mouth and nose. For his theory
of respiration Plato has adopted from Philistion this belief in
transpiration through pores in the skin. As was seen above
(p.108), there has been considerable controversy as to whether
Empedocles himself subscribed to such a belief in cutaneous

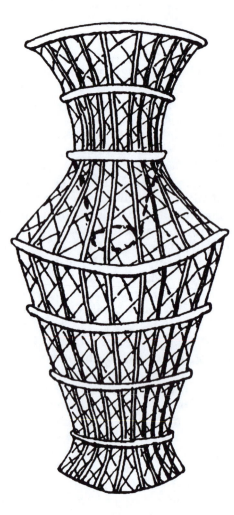

Figure 5 The weel or fish-trap (constructed on the principle employed for the common lobster-pot, but here the narrow entrance is constructed by inserting a separate funnel into the main body of the trap). Drawn by Elizabeth Lazenby after Cornford, 1937, p. 311.

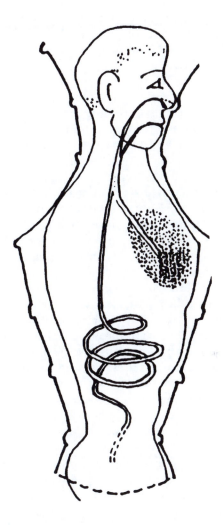

Figure 6 The trap transferred to the human body (the internal funnel leads to the lungs and belly and has a double exit through the mouth and nose). Drawn by Elizabeth Lazenby after Cornford, 1937, p. 311.

respiration over the whole body. Unfortunately our source, *Anonymus Londinensis* XX, 25, says only that this was the belief of Philistion. It is therefore impossible to say how fully developed this theory was prior to its adoption by Plato. It might be not unreasonable to suspect that here, as elsewhere in the *Timaeus*, an original borrowing has been considerably elaborated upon by Plato.

It remains for the respiratory process to be linked with digestion and the distribution of blood as nourishment through the irrigation system. By providing the force to keep the internal fire constantly in oscillation, respiration enables it to penetrate and cut up the food and drink in the belly with its sharp particles and then to carry the blood so formed along with its own movement through the veins. The rhythmical movement of respiration is itself maintained mechanically by the principle of 'circular thrust' (*periōsis* or *antiperistasis*, as it is called by Aristotle and others later). Since there is no empty space, on exhalation the expelled breath dislodges the neighbouring air, which successively displaces its own neighbours, and under this transmitted compulsion, a current of air is driven round and enters the body through the pores in the flesh. The initial cause of this impulse is the internal fire, which has its own tendency to move towards its like. (Here, again, physiology is based upon general physics.) The warm breath exhaled by us contains fire which carries the air along with it outwards through the nose and the mouth as it makes its way to join the fire surrounding the universe. When this breath emerges from the body, it then loses its accompanying fire and is cooled. At the same time, the dislodged air is driven round by the circular thrust. Entering the body through the pores, it approaches the internal fire and is itself heated.

This newly heated air, however, does not continue to traverse the body to emerge by the mouth and nose. Instead, it is tacitly assumed that the air which has entered through the pores must also make its exit by the same way. Having been heated by the internal fire it then passes out again through the pores. In so doing, it reverses the circular thrust and drives the cooled air in the vicinity of the mouth and nose back into the body in inhalation. Thus instead of revolving full circle, the process, as Galen remarks,[67] comprises a series of half-turns in contrary directions, corresponding to the rhythmical reversal of the currents of air. Plato is evidently seeking in his theory to account for the fact that, when we inflate our lungs with a deep breath, this air does not subsequently escape through the skin, but has to be expelled again through the nose and the mouth.

This mechanical, oscillating process of respiration is employed, as was seen above, to effect digestion. At 80d–e Timaeus turns to provide a fuller account of the manner in which it gives rise to the formation of blood and hence brings about the nourishment and growth of the whole body. The internal fire, as it accompanies the breath, parallels the latter's oscillating motion and, in doing so, its sharp and highly mobile pyramids penetrate the food in the belly and cut it up into minute fragments. These particles of nutriment are then driven into the veins from the belly and are thence distributed throughout the whole body. The particles themselves are suffused with a red colour caused by the action of the fire upon a moist material.[68] This stream of red nutriment flowing through the veins is, of course, the blood and from it are derived all the substances needed to replenish the wastage in our tissues and so ensure that the regular constitution of the body is preserved. This wastage is caused by the assault of the elements outside the body, which results in a constant dissolution of its substance, allowing particles to escape and fly off to join their own kind.[69] This conception also underlies the formation of the macrocosm described at *Timaeus* 32c–33b.

Plato has adopted here the theory that blood is the agent of nutrition. This theory, as was shown above, can be traced back directly to Empedocles. Again, we can clearly see not only the extent to which Plato is influenced by 'Sicilian' medicine, but also the manner in which he takes over a theory and adapts it to bring it into accord with his general physical theory. The same is true of his account of growth and decay. Young creatures, it is maintained, grow because, although they are soft, being formed from their parents' seed (i.e. marrow) and nourished on milk, the basic triangles of their constituent elements are, as it were, 'fresh from the slips' with their joints 'firmly locked together'. (The metaphor is from ship-building.) Thus their triangles, which are younger and stronger than those composing food and drink, prevail over the latter and cut them up.[70] The young animal then grows, nourished by a process of 'like to like'.[71] However, when the 'roots' (i.e. the basic components, the sides[72]) of the triangles

141

are loosened as a result of many conflicts, they become incapable of cutting up nourishment and are themselves easily divided. Eventually the animal is overcome and succumbs to the condition called 'old age'. When, finally, the bonds of the triangles of the marrow no longer hold out under the stress, they part asunder and release the bonds of the soul, which then flies away. When death comes about contrary to nature, it is painful and distressing. But when it comes about naturally it is pleasant. The least distressing of all deaths is that which comes to close the natural course of old age.

Having accounted for the physiological processes of the body and for natural death upon the basis of his physics, Plato now describes the various ways these processes may become disordered. The threefold classification of disease which he now presents is, as has already been shown (p. 110), heavily dependent upon 'Sicilian' medicine. But it is also apparent that here, too, the material he adopts has been considerably elaborated upon and adapted to make it consonant with his general physical theory. The first class of diseases comprises those due to the excess or deficiency, varietal unsuitability or displacement of the four elements. Here Plato presents his basic conception of the causation of disease, one which underlies his explanation of the second and third classes. Its priority is underlined here by his emphasising (82b) that health can only be preserved by a uniform and proportionate replacement of the wastage that constantly occurs. This class of diseases corresponds generally to the first of Philistion's own three classes and it seems likely that Plato is influenced by the Locrian here, although the latter's explanation seems much simpler. Fevers especially, we learn at 86aff., are caused by the excess of one or other of the elements, while their periodicity is dependent upon the relative mobility of that element. Thus an excess of fire produces a continuous fever, whereas excesses of each of the other elements produce intermittent fevers: excess of air causes a quotidian, which has an intermission of less than a day; excess of water, which is more sluggish than air or fire, a tertian, with a full day's intermission, and excess of earth, the most sluggish element of all, a quartan, which has two full days of intermission.

The second class is of diseases that are the result of the development of disordered conditions of the tissues. The original generation of these tissues was described at *Timaeus* 73bff. There it was learned that marrow and bone and flesh and sinew are all composed of the four elements. Blood, too, has a similar composition, though formed in a different way from the rest.[73] Although the majority of diseases affecting these tissues are caused in the manner just described, worse disorders are caused by an unnatural reversal of the processes by which the tissues were initially formed.

In the ordinary course of nature flesh and sinew are formed from blood, sinew from the fibrin of the blood and flesh from defibrinated, coagulated blood. A viscous, oily substance arising from flesh and sinew glues flesh to bone as well as feeding the growth of bone round the marrow. The purest part of this viscous substance, consisting of the smoothest and slipperiest triangles, filters through the close texture of the bones and waters the marrow. When these tissues are formed in this order, health is the result; but when the order is reversed, disease ensues. (The brief allusion to the basic triangles here reveals that Plato's account of the diseases of the tissues is firmly grounded upon his geometrical atomism.)

As a result of the reversal of this ordered composition of the tissues and their nourishment by the blood, flesh is first decomposed[74] and the products of its decomposition are discharged back into the veins. The blood in the veins is extensively mixed with air. It then takes on a variety of colours and bitter properties, as well as acid and saline qualities, and develops bile, serum and phlegm of all sorts. These morbid secretions destroy the blood and, providing themselves no nourishment for the body, are carried everywhere through the veins, spreading destruction and decay.

The decomposition back into blood in this way is less serious, since the roots of the tissue remain firm and recovery is easy. However, whenever the fluid (?) (nama) that binds flesh and bone together degenerates as a result of an unhealthy way of life, it becomes rough, saline and dried out, instead of being oily, smooth and viscous. It ceases to provide nourishment to the bone and to bind flesh and bone together. Then the corrupted substance crumbles back into the flesh and sinews and separates from the bone. The flesh, falling away from its roots, leaves the sinews bare and full of brine. It then falls back into the blood stream and aggravates the disorders already described.

Grievous though these afflictions are, the situation becomes still worse when the cause of the trouble is more deep-seated. When, for example, the thickness of the flesh does not allow the bone to obtain sufficient air, it becomes overheated and decays. No longer able to absorb the fluid that sustains it, it dissolves back into that fluid. The fluid then dissolves into flesh and the flesh into blood. Thus the diseases of the parts previously mentioned are made much more virulent. The worst case of all, however, occurs when the marrow itself becomes diseased because of some deficiency or excess (84c4ff.). The whole of the normal functioning of the body is then reversed and the most serious and deadly diseases ensue. In all the above cases of disease the general character of the malady is the same, but the deeper its seat, the more serious it is and the less hope there is of recovery.

In his analysis of the diseases of the tissues Plato described the origin and nature of the humours, phlegm and bile, but discussed them only in so far as these products of corruption affected the normal functioning of the blood. He now proceeds, as part of his analysis of a third class of diseases, to describe the ailments caused by these morbid humours. However, he introduces his account with a description of those diseases caused by *pneuma*. This third class of disease is primarily concerned with afflictions of the various organs or parts or with the body as a whole, as distinct from those involving the elements or the tissues. It includes pulmonary complaints like consumption, bronchial affections, pleurisy and tetanus (*opisthotonos*), which are caused by *pneuma*; epilepsy, which is due to phlegm and black bile; psoriasis, eczema and other skin diseases, which are caused by phlegm; and diarrhoea, dysentery and other disorders, which are due to bile. Taylor sees in the roles assigned here to bile and phlegm evidence to support his thesis that the views expounded in the *Timaeus* do not contain the doctrines of its author but are 'exactly what we should expect in a fifth-century Italian Pythagorean who was also a medical man'.[75] Bile and phlegm, however, are commonly mentioned throughout the Hippocratic *Corpus* and also in the *Anonymus Londinensis* as causes of disease and there seems to be no good reason for assuming a specific Pythagorean influence here – particularly when it is recalled that Philolaus held that phlegm was hot,[76] whereas Plato seems to adopt the more common belief that it is cold.[77]

Those diseases due to lung congestion closely parallel Philistion's third class of diseases, which are also due to a blockage of respiration. The second group here is attributed to the formation of air inside the body as a product of decomposing flesh. This explanation is similar to a theory which Diocles seems subsequently to have adopted.[78] Thus, in both instances, it seems likely that the influence of 'Sicilian' medicine is at play. Despite the frightening symptoms manifested by two of the diseases mentioned here, tetanus and epilepsy, Plato attributes them to purely natural causes in a manner similar to that of the Hippocratics. He even humorously rationalises the name 'Sacred Disease' – so called because of the popular belief that those afflicted were possessed by some supernatural power – by suggesting that the name is appropriate since it is the 'sacred' part (i.e. the brain marrow) that is affected.

Finally, Plato turns to disease in the soul and traces its origin to a defective inherited constitution or to bad upbringing. Both nature and nurture can be responsible here. As the immortal soul is housed within a mortal body, certain psychic disorders are liable to arise. This belief that certain disorders of the soul are due to purely physical causes is not, of course, entirely new and can be discerned in several earlier pre-Socratic and Hippocratic writers.[79] Like his predecessors Plato rejects the view that mental disorders are supernatural in origin and treats them as essentially no different from diseases of the body. His analysis, however, is more elaborate and is firmly based upon his theory of the tripartite soul. The three seats of the soul are explicitly mentioned at *Timaeus* 87a3-4, where psychic disorders induced by vapours arising from the morbid humours, bile and phlegm, when pent up within the body, are described as making a person ill-tempered and moody if they collect in the region of the *epithymētikon*, rash or cowardly if they affect the *thymoeides*, and dull and forgetful if the *logistikon* is invaded.

Plato identifies two main disorders of the soul, both of which are considered to be a form of 'folly' (*anoia* – which denotes the state when reason is failing to exercise due control over the rest of the soul), namely madness (*mania* – passionate excitability) and stupidity (*amathia* – dull, lethargic ignorance). These conditions, as was seen, arise from a defective constitution inherited from parents or from a bad upbringing. Persons so afflicted, however, since they have not chosen their bodily disposition, should not be blamed for it (although they are not absolved from the responsibility of making every effort 'to escape from badness'). When, for example, people are unable to control their desire for sensual pleasures, it should be recognised that this desire has a physical source and that in many individuals inherited defects or faulty upbringing make it especially difficult for their reason to gain control. The remedy for such disorders, Plato contends, lies not in violent intervention with drugs, which should only be employed as a last resort, but in careful, remedial training, both physical and mental, from the earliest years; in providing the appropriate regimen and gymnastic exercises to remove the prevailing imbalance between soul and body.

Plato's medical exegesis at *Timaeus* 81e-86a has aroused widespread disapproval among scholars,[80] and their criticisms are comprehensively reiterated by Rivaud in his Budé edition of the *Timaeus*,[81] where he describes Plato's medical theory as rudimentary, incoherent in comparison with the treatments contained in the Hippocratic *Corpus*, eclectic, derivative and lacking in originality: a truly damning indictment! But surely this is less than half the truth. Admittedly, it is not an unwarranted assumption that Plato has himself no direct personal medical experience. It is also clearly apparent that his medical knowledge has been largely derived not only from contemporary but also from earlier physicians and natural philosophers. His anatomical knowledge, too, is rudimentary and may be safely said to reveal not the slightest hint of systematic dissection. An unfavourable comparison, too, might be drawn between his own failure to undertake detailed empirical research and reproduce the meticulous attention to detail revealed in the case histories presented in the *Epidemics*. Assuredly, the manner in which his pathological and physiological doctrines are expounded in accordance with the general principles of his physics would have earned him severe censure from the author of *De vetere medicina*. Yet his actual procedure is not essentially so very different from that of many of his predecessors who had sought, in similar fashion, to deduce their explanations from their general hypotheses. Both the Hippocratic *Corpus* and the *Anonymus Londinensis* provide abundant evidence of the great variety of medical theories based upon one or more of the four Empedoclean elements or upon one or more of the four primary opposites current in the fifth and fourth centuries. Even Aristotle, it may be noted, who, in sharp contrast to Plato, displays in his biological treatises a keen interest in the multiplicity and variety of empirical phenomena, firmly believes that medicine should derive its first principles from physics.[82] Far from being rudimentary and incoherent, the manner in which Plato combines the medical theories he adopts with his own physical theory is impressive for its systematic and detailed comprehensiveness. In this respect he achieves a far higher degree of comprehensiveness and coherence than any Hippocratic writer one might care to choose for comparison.

Plato, it must be admitted, draws heavily upon 'Sicilian' medicine. But once adopted by him, these doctrines are frequently elaborated and carefully assimilated to accord with his own psychological and teleological beliefs as well as his physical theory. His eclecticism, however, is less wide-ranging than some scholars have imagined. Total departure from this particular body of medical doctrine is comparatively rare and, where it does occur, is almost invariably conditioned by an overriding desire to avoid conflict with other equally firmly held convictions. For example, his decisions to introduce marrow and give it the prime role as the substance of the brain, and to locate the seat of the intellect in the head rather than in the vicinity of the heart, seem to have been conditioned by his theory of the tripartite soul put forward in the *Republic* and his desire to separate the immortal, rational element of the soul from the more basic, appetitive functions of its lowest part, not only physically, but also physiologically. According to Empedoclean belief, the blood not only served as the vehicle of nutrition (as, indeed, it does for Plato), but it also performs important intellectual, psychological and reproductive functions, which Plato wished to associate with the highest element of the soul. Such a duality of function was patently unacceptable to him. Yet, it may be noted, his innovative use of marrow is itself a development fully in accordance with 'Sicilian' principles since the formation of marrow is not essentially different from that of the other tissues.

Plato's critics have failed to recognise the degree of innovation he displays in elaborating the material he takes over. His theory of psychopathology expounded at *Timaeus* 86bff., where he claims that certain psychological disorders are due to physical causes, is remarkable, not only for being fuller and of more detailed application than any previous exposition of this idea, but also for its development upon the basis of his tripartite theory of the soul.[83] His theory that a secondary cause of disease is due to an unnatural reversal of the normal processes of nutrition is most probably an original contribution since there is no clear evidence to suggest that any previous medical writer had put forward such a theory. The detailed application of geometrical atomism to medicine is unique to Plato and its application in physiology and pathology results in several quite original explanations of familiar processes. For example, according to 'Sicilian' medicine digestion is effected by the decomposition (*sēpsis*) of food in the stomach due to the action of the innate heat. Plato's own explanation of this process, while clearly within this tradition, is strongly conditioned by his general physical theory that particles of one element can break up those of another. The tetrahedron, he believes, being the most active and penetrating of the solids, is the principal agent of change. Thus, he holds, in digestion the sharp, highly-mobile pyramids of fire penetrate the food in the belly and cut it up into tiny fragments to form the blood, the vehicle of nutrition.

Although, then, Plato was driven to investigate the physical world primarily for ethical reasons and teleology provides his main motive for studying cosmology and natural science, he nevertheless presents a more detailed and coherent account of natural phenomena than might have been expected from one who regarded the world of becoming as significantly less important than the world of ideas. It is a serious error of judgement, therefore, to dismiss his pathological and physiological theories as rudimentary, incoherent or lacking in originality. Such an assessment, it may be noted, does not appear to have been that of Plato's successors – if we may judge from the *Anonymus Londinensis*, where more attention seems to have been paid to Plato than to any other medical author, not excluding Hippocrates himself.[84]

6

Post-Hippocratic medicine II
Medicine from Lyceum to Museum

Ubi desinit physicus, ibi medicus incipit.
(Prologue, *Dr Faustus* (after Aristotle);1604 recension)[1]

Post [Hippocratem] Diocles Carystius, deinde Praxagoras
. . . artem hanc exercuerunt.
(Celsus, *De medicina*, Proem, 8)

Aristotle was born at Stagira on the north-east coast of Chalcidice
in Thrace. He was thus an Ionian by descent for the peninsula had
been colonised by settlers from Andros and Chalcis. His father
Nicomachus was a member of the guild of the Asclepiadae and
traced his descent from his namesake, the son of Machaon and
grandson of Asclepius. He ultimately became court physician and
friend of Amyntas II, King of Macedon, the grandfather of
Alexander the Great. Aristotle's mother Phaestis was also a
member of an Asclepiad family. If we can trust Galen,[2] the
Asclepiad families trained their sons from childhood in anatomy
as well as in reading and writing. It is possible, therefore, that
Aristotle himself had some such training and it is not unreasonable to assume that it was from his Ionian and Asclepiad
background that he derived his wide-ranging interests in nature
and, especially, in biology. Surprisingly, Aristotle did not join the
hereditary profession of his family, but instead entered the
Academy in his eighteenth year. There is no doubt, however, that
he retained an interest in anatomy and medicine. Diogenes
Laërtius (V, 25) lists two separate works by him on anatomy and
Aristotle himself refers on about twenty occasions to a work
entitled *Anatomai*, 'Dissections', in seven books, which was
apparently an illustrated handbook with a zoological commen-

tary.[3] Diogenes also mentions a treatise on medicine in two books
(V, 25). In addition, it has been claimed that the few lines at the end
of the *Parva naturalia*[4] preserving Aristotle's attitude towards
medicine, which was much discussed in the sixteenth century, are
survivors from a separate, but not extant, treatise of his entitled *De
sanitate et morbo.* (It is conceivable, however, that Aristotle's
comments here may have themselves given rise to the belief in such
a work together with prospective references at *De longitudine et
brevitate vitae* 464b32ff., and *De partibus animalium* 653a8ff.)

Although Aristotle did not choose to follow in his father's
professional footsteps, medicine was manifestly accorded a role
of great importance among the subjects studied within the
Lyceum. The esteem in which it was held by the Peripatetics is
evident in that a history of medicine was compiled by Aristotle's
pupil Meno as a counterpart to the histories of philosophy,
geometry, astronomy and theology written as part of the pro-
gramme for the systematisation of knowledge undertaken by the
Peripatetics.[5] As a result of this activity within the Lyceum,
medicine, like other emergent sciences, became increasingly less
an integral part of philosophy, although philosophical
influences still continued to play a powerful role in its development. It is clearly apparent that Aristotle himself dissected many
animals and he attained a high level of competence as a
comparative anatomist. In general, his knowledge of anatomy is
far superior to that of Plato. His biological and zoological works
reveal a keen interest in empirical phenomena and are impressive
for their close and detailed observations. But if Aristotle's attitude
in this particular respect is vastly different from that of Plato, he
is nevertheless fundamentally in agreement with the latter in his
general attitude towards medicine. Like Plato he is firmly
committed to the belief that the first principles of medicine
should be derived from general philosophical principles. These
principles, it may be noted, are themselves, in Aristotle no less
than Plato, based upon speculative reasoning. This outlook is
clearly apparent in two passages in the *Parva naturalia.* In the
first of these Aristotle remarks:

> It is the function of the natural philosopher also to study
> the first principles of disease and health; for neither health
> nor disease can be properties of things deprived of life.
> Consequently, one might say that most natural philo-

sophers and those physicians who pursue their art more philosophically have this in common: the former end up by studying medicine, whereas the latter begin by basing their medical theories upon the principles of natural science.

(*De sensu* 436a19ff.)[6]

Essentially the same point is made at *De respiratione* 480b24ff. (see Introduction, p. 3).

Like Plato, Aristotle adopted the four element theory. Working initially in the Academy, where the four element theory had previously been accepted as the basis for physical speculation, he most probably adopted it because he saw no cogent reason for a general departure from Plato's teaching. Furthermore, as we have seen, this theory had also firmly established itself in medicine, biology and zoology and all these studies were developing rapidly and systematically upon this basis. A total rejection of this doctrine would have inevitably necessitated their complete revision and severely disrupted their progress. But there is no reason to assume that Aristotle ever contemplated dispensing with this theory.[7]

In agreement with later pre-Socratics and Plato, Aristotle is unwilling to conceive of earth, air, fire and water as irreducible entities – far less as divine beings. For him it was an indisputable fact of experience that these bodies were phenomena involved in genesis and changed into one another.[8] Accepting Plato's strictures in the *Theaetetus* and *Timaeus*, he refers to them as 'the so-called elements' (τὰ καλούμενα στοῖχεια) and criticises Empedocles' concept of them as eternal and unchanging entities on empirical grounds.[9] It might be observed here that he has another good reason for making the simple bodies change into one another. At *De caelo* 305b20ff., in an argument whose target is clearly Empedocles, he maintains that, since the world process is eternal and an infinite body is impossible, the reciprocal generation of the elements is necessary. It is imperative for Aristotle to vindicate the eternity of the world of change in view of his doctrine of natural motion which, unless tempered by this means, would bring about the complete segregation of the simple bodies and a state of complete rest.

Although Aristotle was persuaded to adopt the four element theory, Plato's own particular deduction and construction of the elements clearly did nothing to commend the theory to him. At

De caelo 305b30–307b20 he subjects Plato to a merciless and, at times, unfair attack for his derivation of the elements. Simplicius in his *Commentary*[10] declares that some of these polemics are no better than 'jests'; but others are of a more serious nature and the Neoplatonist Proclus was motivated to write his *Inquiry into Aristotle's Objections against the 'Timaeus'* in refutation of them. It is clear from his criticisms that Aristotle has failed to understand Plato. He is unable to grasp the manner in which Plato has employed mathematical elements, that is, geometrical shapes, as *symbols* to describe physical realities. He misses the essential point of Plato's theory that certain regularities of matter and change can be explained on the basis of geometrical relations existing between the surfaces of bodies that symbolically represent the four elements. At *De caelo* 306a23ff., for instance, he points out that it is impossible for corporeal bodies to be made out of planes, as Plato assumes. According to Aristotle, Plato's cardinal error lies in the introduction of mathematical principles into the realm of physics. At *De generatione et corruptione* 315b30ff., after mentioning the construction of bodies out of planes in the *Timaeus* and adding that he has shown its absurdity elsewhere, he rebukes Plato for his fondness for mathematics, remarking that:

> those who have been more at home in physics are more competent to make hypotheses about the composition of bodies; but those who, by reason of their many discourses, have never made a survey of the real facts, put forward rash speculations on the strength of a slender basis in facts.

Plato, in short, in attempting to explain bodies by surfaces, has sinned against Aristotle's own axiom of scientific explanation which he formulates as follows: 'perceptible things require perceptible principles, eternal things, eternal principles, perishable things, perishable principles and, in general, every subject matter requires principles which are homogeneous with itself.'[11] Whereas an 'eternal' subject like mathematics needs 'eternal' principles, physics, which deals with a perishable and sense-perceived subject matter, requires as its first hypotheses principles of a similar nature. Plato has erred, Aristotle maintains, in seeking to introduce into physics principles which are not germane to this study.

Plato's mathematical derivation of the elements had achieved in a rudimentary form a beginning of mathematical physics. Aristotle, on the other hand, allows no mathematics at all to enter into his theory of the elements and their mutual relations. His desire to separate physics from mathematics in accordance with his methodological axiom has been regarded by historians of science as a retrograde step, since almost two thousand years were to elapse before the close and abiding tie of mathematics and physics paved the way for the development of modern science. Morrow, for example, considers it 'one of the fateful events in the history of Hellenistic Science that Aristotle failed to enter the promising path of physical inquiry explored by Plato in the *Timaeus*'.[12] But Aristotle should not be made to carry the full weight of this responsibility and criticised for having blocked what we, judging from hindsight, might regard as a fruitful development, and for steering Greek science in a more sterile direction. As Solmsen correctly points out:[13]

> it is certainly rash to suppose that, if the Platonic tie between mathematics and physics had not been severed, ancient physics would have developed in a similar direction, arrived at similar discoveries, and by and large entered upon the same triumphant career as the renewal of this tie in the time of Kepler and Galileo opened up for modern science. In any case, the forces that kept ancient science on a different road must have been strong; however powerful the impulse that Aristotle gave to subsequent research, the personal idiosyncrasies of an individual genius can hardly account for the persistent disinclination to use mathematical methods and concepts in the realm of physical or biological inquiry.

Solmsen's argument is given greater weight when we reflect that Aristotle's departmentalisation did not, in any case, sever mathematics from physics once and for all throughout these two millennia. For notwithstanding the dominance of the qualitative theory of matter, the memory of the Platonic concept, which had anticipated in so striking, albeit rudimentary a fashion, the principles which form the basis of theoretical physics in our own day, was not completely expunged by it. On two signal occasions and at times widely removed, this geometrical theory was revived. The first of these revivals occurred at a rather late period of

Neoplatonism and the second some seven centuries later in the twelfth century at Chartres.

Aristotle's own deduction of the elements in the *De generatione et corruptione* is completely in harmony with his methodological tenet. His new concept of matter, devised to meet Eleatic arguments, enables him to remain strictly within the physical realm. In the first book of the *Physics* Aristotle puts forward his general solution to the problem of becoming, which had so vexed his predecessors, and solves the difficulty by maintaining that each separate object in the natural world is a compound, consisting at any given moment of a substratum which is possessed of a certain formal nature: and that, when perceptible things change, change takes place from one contrary to another. This does not entail, as his predecessors had mistakenly thought, that opposite qualities can change into one another (which is a violation of the law of contradiction), but that the substratum which persists throughout the process takes on a new form. Change for Aristotle is from privation to form (e.g. from non-white to white), and substratum, privation and form are his three general principles and presuppositions of genesis.

In the *De generatione et corruptione* Aristotle applies these basic principles of physics to the genesis of the elements. To all appearances he embarks upon his discovery of the elements with a completely open mind with regard both to their number and to their characteristics. What comes to be and passes away, Aristotle agrees, consists of elements. These primary perceptible bodies consist of matter and certain opposites (*De gen. et corr.* 329a25ff.). The elements change into one another, whereas the opposites do not. It must, then, be decided what kinds of opposites compose the body and how many of them there are. (Aristotle proceeds on the assumption that once the relationship between the substrate and the opposites has been determined, it will then be clear what bodies qualify as elements and how many of them there are.) Since he is dealing with perceptible bodies, the opposites must be found among those qualities which make a body perceptible. Each of our senses is associated with its own specific set of qualities. Aristotle, however, declares that only those qualities connected with touch are to be taken into consideration as the principles of perceptible bodies. By this restriction he reduces considerably the number of opposites eligible and rules out such opposites as white and black, sweet and bitter. But even so, a large number is left and he enumerates them as hot and cold, dry and moist, heavy and light, hard and soft, viscous and brittle, rough and smooth, coarse and fine (*De gen. et corr.* 329b18ff.). This number in its turn is further restricted by ruling out immediately heavy and light[14] on the ground that they are neither 'active' nor 'passive', i.e. they have no capacity of acting or of being acted upon. The elements, however, must be reciprocally active and passive, for they mix and change into one another (b24). These latter criteria are fulfilled by the opposites hot, cold, moist and dry. Of these the first pair are active and the second passive. The hot has the capacity to associate things of the same kind, whereas the cold brings together homogeneous and heterogeneous things alike. The moist, being readily adaptable in shape, cannot be confined within limits of its own, while the dry, which is readily determined by its own limits, is not readily adaptable in shape (*De gen. et. corr.* 329b30ff.).

Aristotle now 'discovers' by dint of special pleading that the other pairs of opposites can be traced back to these four basic opposites.[15] These two pairs, we learn, cannot be resolved into one another or reduced to a lesser number. There must necessarily be these four elementary opposites. From them six couples are mathematically possible. But since contraries cannot be paired, it is clear that the actual number of combinations will be four, namely, the hot and the dry; the hot and the moist; the cold and the moist, and the cold and the dry. These four combinations characterise the so-called 'elements': fire is hot and dry, air hot and moist, water cold and moist and earth cold and dry. Each 'element', however, has one predominant quality: of fire it is the hot; of air, the moist; of water, the cold;[16] and of earth, the dry (*De gen. et corr.* 331a3-6). At first sight this seems to be rather a curious decision, since one would naturally be predisposed to expect moisture rather than coldness to be assigned to water. But upon reflection, it can be seen that Aristotle's procedure has been conditioned by his previous correlation of the elements with binary combinations of opposites. If he had characterised water as predominantly moist, as one might have expected, he would then have been left with coldness and dryness to distribute between air and earth, since hotness manifestly characterises the element fire. But air is hot and moist, so neither coldness nor dryness could be its dominant characteristic. Accordingly Aristotle had no alternative but to assign coldness to water.

It would be naïve to believe that Aristotle actually arrived at his doctrine of the four elements by the elaborate process just described. He was clearly not uncommitted when he embarked upon the procedure. He has not arrived by this deductive process at results of which he was previously unaware, but has worked back from conclusion to premiss. (As he does also in similar circumstances in the *De caelo*.) By the time Aristotle came to write the *De generatione et corruptione* the four element theory was already firmly established. His present aim is to establish this system upon a theoretical basis. His procedure is clearly conditioned by certain basic presuppositions. Having established that becoming is a passing from one contrary to another, it became necessary for him to find suitable contraries to inform the substrate and make it change from one 'element' to another. Dealing with perceptible bodies, he had to find these contraries among those opposites that make a body perceptible. Furthermore, only those opposites that are tangible can be taken into consideration. The reasons for this seemingly arbitrary restriction are not immediately apparent and it is noteworthy that, once these four opposites are firmly established as the fundamental attributes of matter, their tangible character becomes decidedly irrelevant. It may, therefore, be suspected - and not without some justification - that Aristotle, far from following the argument where it has led him, was aware of his conclusions beforehand. As Solmsen has pointed out:[17]

> for him tangibility is the conceptual bridge between the 'sense-perceived' elements and the qualities hot and cold, moist and dry. By no other sense function could he find the way to these qualities, and he had reasons - as well as precedents - for considering these closer to the substance of the elements than bright and dark or bitter and sweet.

Aristotle also insists that his elements must be either active or passive and here again his motivation is not apparent until, that is, he turns to discuss the intermutation and mixture of the elements.

Aristotle's correlation of the elements with binary combinations of opposites in this way provides him with a ready explanation of their mutual transformations. The same qualities that constitute the elements account also for their changes. It is a fundamental principle of the *Physics* (see 224a21–226b17) that genesis is from contrary to contrary and the coming-into-being of one contrary involves the destruction of another. Like Plato before him, Aristotle denies that anything can effect any change in or suffer any change from what is identical in character to itself.[18] Four specific combinations of these opposites, then, fashion the substratum into the elements and transformations from one element into another are effected when one of its fundamental qualities is overcome by its contrary or, it may be, when both are so overcome. Transformation takes place most readily between two elements which have one quality in common (331a24ff.), e.g. fire is transformed into air when the dry is overpowered by the moist, and air, in turn, is transformed into water when the hot is overcome by the cold. Water, in its turn, is transformed into earth when the moist is overcome by the dry. To complete the cycle (see 331b2ff.), fire results when the cold of earth becomes hot. It is also possible for two elements taken together to pass into a third. This transformation is effected by each dropping the appropriate quality. For example, fire and water can produce either earth or air, *i.e.* the qualities hot and dry and cold and moist can be recombined either as hot and moist (air) or cold and dry (earth). These transformations can be represented diagrammatically as follows:

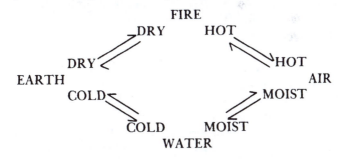

In adopting the four element theory Aristotle is manifestly indebted to earlier Greek physical theory. For his actual correlation of elements with opposites, however, he seems to have been far less indebted to his physicist predecessors than has been been generally assumed, since the role of these four opposites in early Greek physics appears to have been much less influential than has been commonly supposed.[19] Indeed, a close evaluation of our evidence suggests that medicine has exercised here a greater influence than physics. The close affinities between the roles assigned to the opposites in certain of the Hippocratic treatises and Aristotle's own correlation of opposites and elements suggest that one would not be unjustified in finding here further evidence of interaction between medicine and philosophy (see Appendix). It is hard to believe, particularly when Aristotle's own medical background is borne in mind, that the important role played by these four opposites in medicine did not contribute to a very large extent to his decision to give them a role of similar importance in his physics. Thus his keen interest in biology and zoology may well have predetermined, to some considerable extent, his general physical theory. In spite of the dominant position of the elements and the subordination of the role of the opposites within the philosophy of the Academy, in medicine and biology generally the opposites had predominated. Aristotle, then, starting from Plato in physics and from medical theory in biology, doubtless felt it incumbent upon himself to bring the opposites and elements into harmony[20] and developed in the *De generatione et corruptione* his ingenious scheme for the transformation of the elements which, as has been seen, not only brought opposites and elements into harmony, but was also based upon his general theory of genesis and change.

However, when we turn to the biological writings we find, much to our surprise, that Aristotle does not employ this new system for the transformation of the elements but uses instead a correlation of elements and opposites identical to that expounded first by Philistion and subsequently adopted by Diocles. The innate heat of an animal is referred to on occasion as the 'internal fire'.[21] The semen is described as 'wet and waterlike'.[22] In his description of the composition of the tissues, moistness (not coldness!) is associated with water, hardness and dryness with earth.[23] Finally, he considers that the function of the inhaled air is to cool the innate heat.[24] This last theory, in which the function of air is that of a coolant, presents a most striking divergence from the theory of elements expounded in the *De generatione et corruptione*, where air, as we saw, is described as hot and moist. At *De iuventute* 480a28-b6 Aristotle specifically states that air is cold when it enters the body and warm when exhaled only because it has come into contact with the internal heat. It is certain, therefore, that in Aristotle's theory of respiration the essential quality of air is its coldness. Consequently, between Aristotle's biological thought and his physical theory there exists a fundamental discrepancy. The source of this inconsistency can be traced to the pervasive influence of 'Sicilian' medicine and biology. Not even the schematic requirements of his physics are allowed by Aristotle to supersede this fundamental tenet of 'Sicilian' medicine that air is cold.

Although, like Plato, Aristotle firmly believes that the first principles of medicine should be drawn from philosophy, his own outlook is very much more empirical than that of his teacher and in biology generally he displays a far closer attention to the phenomena than is found in Plato. In a famous and oft-quoted passage at *De partibus animalium*, 644b22–645a36, which surely reveals his deep-seated, personal feelings, he presents an impressive vindication of detailed empirical investigation in biology and, at the same time, seeks to allay any initial repugnance caused by its subject matter. He writes:

Of natural substances, some are ungenerated and indestructible throughout eternity, whereas others are subject to generation and destruction. The former [i.e. the heavenly bodies] are precious and divine, but less accessible to knowledge. For the evidence available to the senses by which we might study them and the things we long to know about is very scanty. But concerning perishable things, like plants and animals, we have better means of information because we live amongst them. For, if we are willing to take sufficient trouble, a great deal can be learned concerning each of their kinds. For, even if our comprehension of the heavenly bodies is slight, nevertheless because of the value of that knowledge, it is more pleasing than all our knowledge of the world in which we live; just as a partial glimpse we chance to get of those whom we love is more pleasurable than an accurate view of other things, however many or great they are. On the other hand, our knowledge of the things here on earth has the advantage because it is possible to obtain more and better information about them. Furthermore, because they are nearer to us and more akin to our nature, they make up the balance to some extent as against the study of the things that are divine. Since we have already discussed the things that are divine and set out our

159

opinion concerning them, it remains to speak of animals, without omitting, to the best of our ability, any one of them, treating noble and ignoble alike. For even in those unattractive to the senses, yet to the intellect the craftsmanship of nature provides immense pleasures for those who are able to recognise the causes of things and are naturally philosophically inclined. For, if we take pleasure in studying the likenesses of these things because we are contemplating at the same time the art of the craftsman, for example, the painter or sculptor who made them, it would be strange, absurd even, not to delight more in studying the natural objects themselves, at any rate when we have the ability to discern their causes. Wherefore we ought not to feel a childish disgust at the investigation of the meaner animals. For every realm of nature has something marvellous about it . . . we should approach the investigation of every kind of animal without shame as in all of them there exists something natural and something beautiful. In the works of nature, purpose, not chance is predominant. Purpose, or the end for the sake of which something has been constructed or come to be, has its place among what is beautiful. But if anyone has considered the study of the other animals to be an unworthy pursuit, he ought also to think the same way about himself. For it is not possible to look upon the constituent parts of human beings such as blood, flesh, bones, blood-vessels and the like without considerable disgust. Similarly, in discussing any one of the parts and structures, we must not suppose that the speaker is speaking of the material itself and for its own sake, but for the sake of the whole form. Just as in discussing a house, it is the whole form of the house, not just the bricks and mortar and timber that concerns us. So in natural science, it is the composite thing, the thing as a whole, which primarily concerns us, not the materials, which are never found apart from the thing itself.

Notwithstanding the emphasis here upon careful empirical research it can be clearly seen that Aristotle is committed to the view that biology should be studied in accordance with general philosophical principles; the primary object of inquiry is not the material of any of the parts and structures, but rather their composition and their substance as a whole.

As Lloyd rightly points out,[25] Aristotle's zoological investigations provided him with evidence which appeared to endorse certain aspects of general doctrines which he had himself inherited from Plato. In the first place, his biological researches supplied him with a wealth of data to support the importance they both ascribed to the doctrine of internal finality in nature. This data would have seemed abundantly to confirm that 'in nature purpose is predominant and there is an absence of chance'. Secondly, although Aristotle rejected his teacher's concept of transcendent form, his investigation of individual specimens from the point of view of the species as a whole and his observation of the regularity with which the various natural kinds normally reproduce themselves would have strengthened his belief that forms or species are real and not merely figments of the imagination.

As a result of these careful empirical investigations important advances were made within the Lyceum in both anatomy and physiology. Although there is no evidence of systematic human dissection at this date, Aristotle on several occasions mentions his experiments upon living animals in the course of his physiological investigations.[26] He adopts an analogical procedure and clearly draws inferences regarding the human body from his experience derived from animal anatomy. He observes, for example, in the *Historia animalium* (494b21-4): 'The inner parts [of the body] . . . are unknown, especially those of man; consequently one must refer to the parts of other animals which have a nature similar to that of humans, and examine them.' Like Galen, who was also later constrained to resort largely to animal experiments, Aristotle proceeds by analogy, making inferences regarding the human body from his investigations of animal anatomy. As was seen above, he also made frequent references in his zoological treatises to a book entitled 'Dissections', which was evidently an illustrated work as figures and drawings are expressly mentioned. Since Galen informs us that Diocles of Carystus was, to the best of his knowledge, the first to write a special treatise on anatomy (i.e. animal anatomy) and the latter is said to have made inferences regarding the human womb from his dissections of mules,[27] it is conceivable, given his close connection with the Lyceum (see below), that it was this work to which Aristotle so frequently refers in his own zoological writings. Although Sarton,[28] citing *Hist. an.* 497a32, believes that Aristotle specifically identifies this work as his own, neither here nor elsewhere does the possessive pronoun appear.

Diocles was the most distinguished protagonist of medicine within the Lyceum. Unfortunately only fragments and later testimonies remain of his works,[29] which makes it exceedingly difficult to formulate a comprehensive conception of his medical theories. He was clearly held in the highest regard in the ancient world since Pliny describes him as 'second in time and fame to Hippocrates'[30] and Vindicianus tells us that the Athenians called him 'a younger Hippocrates'.[31] There has been, and continues to be, considerable controversy regarding the date of Diocles' medical activity. It is, however, clear from the surviving fragments that he was greatly influenced by 'Sicilian' medicine. For example, like Philistion, he based his medical theory upon the four element theory of Empedocles and characterised each element with one of the four basic opposites, hot, cold, moist or dry;[32] he believed that respiration took place not only through the nose and the mouth, but also through the pores of the skin and that its purpose was to cool the innate heat;[33] he held that the heart was the seat of the intellect;[34] like Empedocles he believed that digestion was effected by a process akin to putrefaction;[35] and many parallels can be drawn between these two thinkers in their views on embryology[36] and menstruation.[37] In other respects, however, he reveals the influence of Hippocratic medicine.

Because of these 'Sicilian' influences discernible in Diocles' thought, Wellmann, in company with certain other scholars,[38] concluded[39] that Diocles was a contemporary of Philistion and that both were contemporaries of Plato's earlier years, putting them in the first third of the fourth century. This view was widely accepted – apart from one or two dissentients whose opinions were largely disregarded.[40] Even Jaeger initially bowed to the authority of these distinguished predecessors in his early study of the *pneuma* theory within the Lyceum,[41] and accepted that Diocles and Philistion were both sources of Aristotle's physiology. Several decades later, however, upon returning to the study of Diocles, he was persuaded by the coincidences of thought and of language he detected between the fragments of Diocles and Aristotle's own theories and formulations to challenge the accepted view that Diocles and Philistion were contemporaries. Maintaining that Diocles' style was replete with the philosophical terminology of Aristotle, he concluded that the former must have flourished when the Peripatetic school was at its height, i.e. about the end of the fourth century BC.[42] In an article published shortly after the appearance of his book he went even further and maintained that Diocles lived between 340 and 260 BC.[43]

In addition to pointing out close ideological and stylistic resemblances between these two men, Jaeger employs two main chronological arguments to support his thesis that Diocles was a younger contemporary of Aristotle. He maintains that Theophrastus in the fifth chapter of his treatise *De lapidibus* appeals to the authority of Diocles upon a mineralogical question and, in doing so, employs the imperfect tense. Jaeger maintains that this use of the imperfect (ὥσπερ καὶ Διοκλῆς ἔλεγεν, 'as Diocles, too, used to say') seems to indicate that Theophrastus was personally acquainted with Diocles and that the latter was known within Peripatetic circles. He further infers from this use of the imperfect that Diocles was dead at Theophrastus' time of writing. In his subsequent article, however, where he argues for an even later date for Diocles, he changed his mind and suggested instead that the imperfect merely entailed that Diocles was no longer a member of the Peripatetic community of scholars. In the second context,[44] in a discussion regarding the origin of the best vegetables, Athenaeus records that Diocles recommended Antioch as the home of the best cucumbers. Jaeger, reviving an argument first put forward by Rose,[45] thereupon maintained that since Antioch was not founded until 300 BC, Diocles must have written his book in the third, not at the beginning of the fourth century. In this same passage, Diocles is also said to have praised the lettuce of Smyrna and of Galatia. As Galatia was named after the Gauls who invaded Asia Minor in the seventies of the third century BC and settled in that part of the peninsula, Jaeger further maintains that a later date must therefore be assigned to Diocles' death, which he accordingly placed as late as 260 BC.

Jaeger's conclusions have been carefully examined by Edelstein, who accepts his contention that Diocles was a close contemporary of Aristotle and deeply influenced by Aristotelian philosophy, but raises some pertinent objections to Jaeger's later dating of Diocles in his review of the latter's book.[46] Edelstein points out that Pliny in his paraphrase of Theophrastus' *De lapidibus* 5 adds: *quod Diocli cuidam Theophrastus quoque credit.*[47] Since Pliny elsewhere calls Diocles 'second in fame to Hippocrates'[48] his remark that Theophrastus' statement in the present passage refers to a *certain* Diocles entails, therefore, that Pliny, at any rate, did not identify this Diocles with Diocles of Carystus.[49] Edelstein further maintains that it is also unsound to use the reference to Galatia in Athenaeus to support this later date for Diocles. The words καὶ Γαλατία are most probably a later insertion as several scholars had already recognised.[50] Again, as Edelstein points out, in each of the other cases only one place is cited and it is hardly appropriate to mention two places where the best lettuce is grown; furthermore, all the other locations of the origins of the best of the various types of vegetable mentioned are cities not countries.

Edelstein, then, is prepared to accept that Jaeger has established that Diocles was a contemporary of Aristotle and lived until 300 BC,[51] the date of the founding of Antioch, or shortly thereafter (i.e. from *c.* 375–295 BC) – an assessment broadly in accordance with the testimonies of both Galen and Pliny.[52] Jaeger's assumption that Diocles must have been similarly influenced by Aristotle in medicine and zoology as he was in philosophy is also very properly called into question by Edelstein. It does seem prima facie less likely that a medical man who enjoyed the reputation in antiquity of being 'second in fame to Hippocrates' would have been heavily dependent upon Aristotle in this field, too. As was suggested above, his treatise on anatomy, seemingly the first of its kind to be written, may well have been extensively used by Aristotle in his own zoological researches.

If it is correct to accept with Edelstein Jaeger's initial thesis that Diocles was a contemporary of Aristotle, it is not unreasonable to suppose that he would in that case have played an influential role not only in the development of anatomy, but also of physiology within the Lyceum. To be sure, Aristotle's zoological treatises display, by and large, a much more sophisticated level of knowledge than that attained by his predecessors. Aristotle reveals himself as a competent comparative anatomist and has evidently dissected a good many different types of animal. A brief survey of earlier accounts of the heart, to take a convenient example, will serve to illustrate by comparison the great advances made in anatomy in the Lyceum generally.

Although Empedocles had made the 'blood round the heart' the seat of intellectual activity (Frag. 105), he evidently provided no detailed account of the heart itself or of its connection with the vascular system but conceived of the blood as oscillating between the interior and surface of the body through 'tubes of flesh' (Frag. 100). Plato, however, took a major step forward when he explicitly recognised the heart as the focal point of the blood vessels. He ascribed to the heart a new function, too, when he regarded the blood vessels as serving as channels of communication between the brain and heart and thence with every sentient part. In doing so, however, he explicitly acknowledged his ultimate debt in this respect to Empedocles by echoing the latter's own phraseology in the name he gave to these channels (στενωπά, see Empedocles, Frag. 2). At *Timaeus*, 70a–d he describes the heart as the 'knot of the veins and well-spring of the blood':

> The gods stationed the heart, the knot of the veins and well-spring of the blood, which moves vigorously throughout all the limbs, in the guard-room, so that, when passion was roused to boiling-point at a message from reason that some wrong was taking place in the limbs, whether by external action or from desires within, every sentient part should quickly perceive through all the narrow channels [στενωπά] the commands and threats and obediently follow in every way and so allow the noblest part to have command. The palpitation of the heart is caused by the expectation of evil and the excitement of passion. The gods, then, foreseeing that all such passion would come about by means of fire, devised support for the heart in the structure of the lung, making it soft and bloodless, perforated by cavities like a sponge, so that by absorbing breath and drink, and cooling by respiration, it might also provide relief in the heat [of passion]. For this reason they cut air-channels to the lung and set it around the heart as a cushion, so that when passion was at its height, the heart might beat against a yielding body, be cooled down and, being less distressed, might be able to aid the spirited element in the service of reason.

Plato provides here neither a description of the heart's chambers, nor of its functioning. Nor is there any suggestion that the heart is the cause of the movement of the blood. He does, however, recognise some vascular connection between the heart and the lungs, which are given the dual function of keeping the heart from being injured by its violent throbbing when excited and of cooling the innate heat of the heart through respiration. It seems, at first sight, rather strange that respiration should be regarded as only a secondary function of the lungs. But, as Taylor points out,[53] Plato has doubtless been influenced here by the 'Sicilian' belief that respiration also takes place through the pores of the skin (see Chapter 5, p. 108). It is clearly evident that his account of the heart is conditioned more by the constraints of his tripartite psychology than the results of any anatomical investigation. As Solmsen correctly observes,[54] Plato was neither a physician nor a physiologist and when he enters the domain of the physiologist in the *Timaeus* he brings with him firm convictions formed while dealing with altogether different subjects.

While the Hippocratic writings contain several descriptions of the heart, the more sophisticated descriptions are found in treatises which are almost certainly later than Aristotle. The treatise *De nutrimento*, for example, which describes the heart as the centre of the vascular system, differentiates between veins and arteries (Chap. 31) and recognises pulsation as a sign of health or disease (Chap. 48), is rightly regarded by the majority of scholars as a late work probably belonging to the second or even the first century BC.[55] Similarly, the treatise *De corde*, with its impressive descriptions of the auricles, ventricles and valves of the heart is nowadays regarded as Hellenistic in date.[56] The treatise *De carnibus*, however, seems to have been written considerably earlier than these two and the general consensus is that it pre-dates Diocles.[57] It may, therefore, be cited for the purpose of our comparison. Chapter 5 of this treatise contains the following description:

> The heart contains a lot of the glutinous and the cold. Being heated by the hot it became hard, viscous flesh enclosed within a membrane. It was made hollow, but in a different way from the veins. It is situated at the head of the most hollow vein. For there are two hollow veins from the heart. One is called 'artery'; the other one, to which the heart is attached, is called the 'hollow vein'. The heart has the most heat where the hollow vein is situated and it

166

dispenses the *pneuma*. In addition to these two veins there are others ** throughout the body. The most hollow vein, to which the heart is attached, runs through the whole of the belly and the diaphragm and divides towards each of the kidneys. In the loins it branches and shoots up to the other parts and into each leg. But also above the heart in the neck some [vessels] go to the right, some to the left. Then they lead to the head and at the temples each vessel divides. It is possible to enumerate the greatest veins, but, in a word, from the hollow vein and from the artery the other veins branch off throughout the whole body. The most hollow veins are those near the heart and the neck, those in the head and those beneath the heart as far as the hip-joints.

The formation of the parts of the body is described here in terms highly evocative of the accounts of the cosmogonic process put forward by the pre-Socratic philosophers. The heart is recognised as the centre of the vascular system. A distinction is drawn between the two 'hollow' vessels, presumably the vena cava and the aorta. From each of these smaller vessels branch off. The term 'artery' is applied to the aorta, which might suggest that the treatise should be regarded as later than Praxagoras, who is credited with being the first to draw a distinction between veins and arteries (see below). Previously the term 'arteria' seems to have been employed to denote the windpipe or bronchial tubes, not an artery as such.[58] However, in the rest of this passage no clear distinction is drawn between these two different types of vessel: arteries and veins alike – including branches of the 'artery' – are elsewhere all called 'veins'. And although the pulse is recognised (Chap. 6 = VIII.592L.), it is associated with the veins generally. Since, then, with the exception of the aorta (a term not used by our author, but employed by Aristotle (*Hist. an.* 495b8), veins and arteries are not otherwise distinguished, a pre-, not post-Praxagorean date may be assigned to this treatise. (The use of the term 'artery' to denote the aorta, however, is very striking and tempts one to speculate that it might have been this previous application to a vessel newly differentiated from the veins that prompted Praxagoras subsequently to extend its use to refer generally to all other vessels of this type.)

In sharp contrast to the above, Aristotle's description of the heart is much more sophisticated and is manifestly based upon frequent dissection of animals. He expressly refers on one occasion (*Hist. an.* 513a27-30ff.), for example, to the difficulty of distinguishing the chambers of the hearts of very small animals and mentions more than once that he has experimented upon living animals in the course of his physiological investigations.[59] He also prefaces his account of the vascular system (*Hist. an.* 511b13ff.) with a critique of the views of his predecessors and points out that the reason for their mistakes is their failure to base their observations, as he himself does, upon animals which have been first starved and then strangled, thus avoiding the collapse of the most important blood vessels.

The structure of the heart is briefly described by Aristotle at several places in his biological writings.[60] His fullest account is at *Historia animalium*, 496a4ff.:

> The heart has three cavities. It lies above the lung at the point where the windpipe [*arteria*] divides into two. It has a fat, thick membrane where it is attached to the Great Vein and the Aorta. It lies with its apex upon the Aorta. The apex lies towards the chest in all animals which have a chest. In all animals, whether they have a chest or not, the apex of the heart is towards the front. This often escapes notice owing to the change of position of the parts under dissection. The convex end of the heart is above. The apex is largely fleshy and compact in texture and there are sinews[61] in its cavities. In animals - other than man - which have a chest, its position is in the middle of the chest; in man it is more on the left, inclining a little from the division of the breasts towards the left breast in the upper part of the chest. The heart is not large; its shape as a whole is not elongated but somewhat rounded, except that its extremity comes to a point. As has been said, it has three cavities, the largest is that on the right hand side, the smallest that on the left, and the medium sized one is in the middle. All of them, even the two small ones, have a connection leading into the lung. This is clearly visible in respect of one of them. Below, from the point of attachment at the largest cavity there is a connection to the Great Vein.

> Passages also lead into the lung from the heart. They divide, as the windpipe does, and follow closely those from the windpipe throughout the whole of the lung. Those

from the heart are uppermost. There is no common passage, but through their contact they receive the *pneuma* and transmit it to the heart. For one passage leads to the right cavity, and the other to the left.

In the *De partibus animalium* 666b16ff. Aristotle further states that the human heart lies diagonally with its apex inclined to the left, and at *Historia animalium* 513a30ff. he not only informs us that the largest of the cavities, i.e. the right ventricle, is on the right, but also that it is above the rest. It is difficult to see how he could have gained this knowledge without dissection. (The human heart is tilted so that the right ventricle is brought to the front, which is not the case in other animals.) But as there were strong religious taboos against the desecration of the human corpse and even to touch one incurred pollution, it is not surprising that there is no unequivocal evidence of human dissection in ancient Greece before the Alexandrians. Aristotle's knowledge of human internal anatomy is otherwise poor and his anatomical descriptions on several occasions almost certainly entail that they were not based upon an adult human subject. He himself freely admits to an inadequate knowledge of human internal anatomy at *Historia animalium* 494b19ff. and states that he has to refer to the structure of the parts of those animals which resemble man. This difficulty might be resolved, as Ogle suggests,[62] by the assumption that in the present instance Aristotle is basing his knowledge of the human heart upon an aborted human embryo. At *De partibus animalium* 665a30ff. Aristotle explicitly declares that the heart is visible in *aborted* embryos. Although he does not specifically say here that the embryos were human embryos, since it is clear elsewhere that he was able to examine embryos of other animals without awaiting accidental abortion,[63] it seems reasonable to assume that he is speaking in the present context of the human embryo. This assumption, Ogle points out (ibid.) could also explain other errors in Aristotle's account of human anatomy, e.g. his statement that in man there is often, though not invariably, a gall bladder (*De part. an.* 676b30ff.). While its absence is rare in man, the gall bladder is not developed until the liver is already large enough almost to fill the abdomen. His mistaken belief that the human brain is more fluid than that of any other animal (*De gen. an.* 744a27ff.), too, could be explained on this hypothesis, since the brain of an aborted foetus would almost certainly be found in a diffluent condition.

Although Aristotle parts company with Plato and takes what the anatomical investigations of the Alexandrians (see Chapter 7) were subsequently to reveal was a retrograde step in identifying the heart as the seat of the intellect, his recognition of the heart here as the organ from which all the blood vessels arise is of greater precision than Plato's rather vague description of it as the 'knot of the veins'. All vessels (except those of the lung), Aristotle believes, were connected either with the vena cava or with the aorta, which themselves have their origin in the heart. He also seems to have been the first to recognise that the heart consists of more than one chamber, although he makes a celebrated error in maintaining that the hearts of all large animals (including humans) have three chambers.[64] Between the right and left ventricle he inserts a third, medium-sized chamber. Galen, possibly realising that Aristotle's recommended procedure of dissecting after starvation would result in the right auricle and the right ventricle being engorged with blood, while the left side of the heart was virtually empty, believes that Aristotle has mistakenly regarded the right ventricle as consisting of two separate chambers.[65] But since, presumably, it must then be assumed that the lower part of the right ventricle is the largest cavity and the left ventricle is of intermediate size, there is an inconsistency with Aristotle's statement above that the largest cavity is on the right, the smallest on the left, with the middle-sized one between them. (Many other attempts have been made to solve this problem from Vesalius onwards.[66]) While recognising the serious nature of Aristotle's error, Galen seeks to excuse him by pointing out that he was an 'amateur (ἀγύμναστος) in anatomy' and that even 'whole-time professionals' made many mistakes.[67]

It is, unfortunately, impossible to reconstruct Diocles of Carystus' views upon the anatomy of the heart with any high degree of certainty. The evidence we possess is scanty, controversial and has patently been subjected to doxographical distortion. If we accept an emendation of a passage in Theodoret made originally by Diels,[68] who proposed the reading Ἀριστο (τέλης, Διο)κλῆς' to replace the otherwise unknown Ἀριστοκλῆς'[69] and make due allowance for Stoic contamination, then Diocles would appear to have assigned the seat of intellectual activity to the heart 'like Empedocles, Aristotle and the sect of the Stoics'. Diels, in similar manner, emended a second reading in Aëtius,[70] and substituted 'Diocles' for 'Diogenes' in a passage where the subject is said to have located the 'governing principle' (*hēgemonikon*) in the 'arterial, i.e. pneumatic cavity of the heart' (the left ventricle). It has been further maintained by Wellmann[71] that the lengthy fragment incorporated in the Brussels MS of Theodor Priscianus is originally by the hand of Priscianus' master Vindicianus, a contemporary of St Augustine, and that the physician whose doctrines are described here is Diocles. These doctrines are in agreement with those attributed to Diocles in the *Anonymus Parisinus* and Wellmann's standpoint has been generally accepted by scholars. At Chapter 44 of this fragment (p. 234 Wellmann, where a disease accompanied by delirium and described as *phrenetica passio* is held to be caused by a tumour in the heart, which cuts off the blood supply and normal heat, by which the brain provides perception and intelligence), we are told that there are two sides to the brain: the right half providing sensation and the left intelligence. Beneath the brain lies the heart with its two 'ears' or auricles. The heart also has 'bellies' (ventricles), receptacles for the blood and *pneuma* (spiritus) in the separate parts next to the auricles. Although the number of these ventricles is not explicitly stated here, it may be inferred from the context that the author conceives of the heart as comprising two ventricles immediately beneath the two auricles.

This, if our interpretation is correct, is a more sophisticated and accurate view of the heart than the three-chambered model conceived of by Aristotle. But if Diocles had played an influential role in the development of anatomy in the Lyceum, it is curious that Aristotle should not then have himself adopted this more sophisticated conception. If Diocles had identified by animal dissection the two auricles and the two ventricles of the heart, why, then, granted the connection between them, did Aristotle cling so tenaciously to his mistaken belief in a three-chambered heart? It is conceivable, of course, that he may have been influenced here by metaphysical and teleological rather than anatomical considerations and postulated a middle ventricle to serve as the original source of the blood, as Harris has conjectured.[72] Alternatively, it is possible that Diocles is deliberately correcting here Aristotle's mistake concerning the number of the cardiac ventricles.[73] However, before accepting the latter solution it should be noted that elsewhere Aristotle criticises the belief that

171

embryos were nourished in the womb by sucking a bit of flesh (*De gen. an.* 746a19ff.). This criticism, Jaeger has claimed,[74] is specifically directed against Diocles' theory of *kotyledones*, 'breast-like outgrowths . . . made with forethought by nature to give the embryo preliminary exercise in sucking the nipples of the breasts'.[75] Aristotle, for his part, maintains that the dissection of animals disproves this. Although several of the pre-Socratics had subscribed to this belief in intra-uterine breast-like growths,[76] Jaeger's contention that Aristotle's polemic is primarily directed against Diocles should, in our view, be accepted, since it seems unlikely that a man who accepted the validity of making inferences regarding human anatomy from animal dissections (see above, p. 161) would have persisted in holding this strange belief *after* Aristotle had rejected it on these very grounds.

If Jaeger were correct here, we should then have a complete reversal of roles from that suggested by von Staden. Instead of correcting Aristotle on an anatomical point, Diocles is himself corrected by him. However, if it were the case that in anatomy neither man was dependent upon or subordinate to the other and that each, pursuing his inquiries independently over a period of time in the same field of research and within the same milieu, was ready to criticise and correct the other's standpoints with the common aim of furthering anatomical knowledge, then these two apparently conflicting positions could be satisfactorily resolved and our original assessment of Diocles as playing an influential role upon the development of anatomy within the Lyceum could be safely maintained.

The introduction of systematic animal dissection within the Lyceum resulted in a much more accurate knowledge of the internal organs than evidenced previously. In physiology, too, important and influential developments took place. Here, again, it seems a not unreasonable conjecture that Diocles played a leading role. While his own indebtedness to Philistion and the 'Sicilian' medicine is pronounced (see above, p. 162), it is clear that he has developed his physiological theories beyond what he has adopted from Philistion and integrated his 'Sicilian' legacy with Hippocratic elements to form a more comprehensive and better integrated synthesis than that achieved by Aristotle.

Diocles' physiology is based upon the same four opposites that Philistion had previously linked with the four elements.[77] Like Empedocles, he held that the digestive process was a form of corruption (σῆψις) brought about by the action of the innate heat upon the nutriment contained in the stomach. Blood, he believed, was the normal result of this process. However, whenever the heat was excessive, bile was produced; a deficiency of heat, on the other hand, was productive of phlegm.[78] In this manner he brought the four element theory into explicit conformity with the theory of the four humours as it is expounded in the Hippocratic treatise *De natura hominis*. His dietetic prescriptions suggest that, as in this medical work, the prevalence of the individual humours is closely linked with the seasons of the year.[79] Upon the basis of these theories, Diocles put forward a varied account of the causes of disease. Like Philistion[80] and Plato[81] he held that diseases are caused through an imbalance of the elements.[82] He also shared with these two predecessors[83] the belief that diseases occur when the passage of the *pneuma* through the pores in the skin is impeded. Such stoppages, he believed, were due to the influence of the bile and phlegm upon the blood in the veins; whereas the latter cooled the blood abnormally and compacted it, the former, conversely, caused it to boil and curdled it.[84] In either event, the *pneuma* was unable to permeate throughout the body and fever ensued.

The *pneuma* theory, however, not only provided a ready explanation for disease in this way, it also provided a line of escape from a problem which was currently vexing Aristotle and which, as shall be seen, was subsequently to be triumphantly resolved by the Alexandrians upon the basis of their most impressive contribution to medical science, their discovery of the nervous system. This problem, which Aristotle seems to have been the first to formulate in psychophysical terms and for which he sought a solution based upon a single principle of explanation, was to account for the manner in which the soul partakes both in the processes of sense perception and in bodily movement. Being so strongly influenced by 'Sicilian' medical theory, stemming ultimately from Empedocles, who had himself held that the blood around the heart was the organ of thought (Frag. 105), one might have expected Aristotle to have regarded the blood as the intermediary. There is, indeed, some evidence to suggest that he did at one time subscribe to this belief that the blood served as the vehicle of perception.[85] However, after an initial flirtation with this solution, he seems subsequently to have rejected it. He had also adopted from 'Sicilian' medicine the belief that the main function of the blood was to supply the body with nutriment. Thus, for Aristotle the blood was primarily an agent of the nutritive soul. This connection of the blood with nutrition, however, as Solmsen pertinently points out,[86] would not have prevented the latter from conceiving it at the same time as the vehicle of sensation, since he is always keen to find evidence of duality of function in nature.[87] However, what appears to be an explicit reason for quietly rejecting the blood as carrier of the sensations is put forward at *De part. an.* 656b19ff.[88] Here we learn that 'no bloodless part is capable of sensation, nor, indeed, is the blood itself. It is the parts made out of the blood that have this faculty.' Elsewhere in this treatise (650b3ff.) it is explained that the blood is without sensation since it provides nourishment for living beings. As Solmsen says, one might legitimately wonder here whether we have Aristotle's true reason or merely a convenient pretext for the rejection of the blood as the carrier of the sensations in favour of a theory which now seemed to offer greater potentialities.

Although Aristotle stresses that the *pneuma* must have its place in the heart,[89] he does not specify any particular channels through which it might flow to limbs and sense organs and his own application of the *pneuma* doctrine here is somewhat tentative. Later thinkers, however, greatly extended its scope so that ultimately it acquired total control over all the functions Aristotle had initially associated with it. It seems highly likely that Diocles had an important role to play in these developments. At any rate, like Aristotle, he held that the heart was the seat of the intelligence. He, too, located the *pneuma* in the heart – more specifically, it appears, in the left ventricle of the heart[90] – and believed that it issued from thence and spread throughout the body via some of the vessels. It seems likely that he believed that this psychic *pneuma* was given off continuously from the blood under the action of the innate heat and then permeated throughout the entire body.[91] Although Praxagoras is generally credited with the distinction between the arteries and the veins together with the belief that *pneuma* moves through the former and blood through the latter, it should be noted that Galen attributes this distinction both to Praxagoras and to his father Nicarchus.[92] But Diocles, too, seems to have subscribed to these doctrines, since we learn from *Anecdota medica*, 20[93] that both he and Praxagoras regarded the arteries as 'channels through which voluntary motion is imparted to the body' (the *pneuma* is the agent of this motion). The same context ascribes an identical explanation of paralysis to both men, who are said here to have held that it was caused by an accumulation of phlegm in the region of the arteries originating from the heart and the aorta. We learn from this source, too, that Praxagoras and Diocles were also both in agreement upon the causes of epilepsy[94] and apoplexy[95] and attributed each disease to the blocking of the passage of the psychic *pneuma* from the heart through the aorta by an accumulation of phlegm.

Praxagoras held other theories in common with Diocles. Like the latter he held the heart to be the seat of the intelligence. Another 'Sicilian' belief he shared with Diocles is the theory that digestion was effected by the transformation of nourishment into blood by a process of putrefaction brought about by the action of the innate heat. Those scholars who also see here the immediate influence of Diocles are most probably not mistaken. Jaeger, pointing to these affinities, argues that their implication is that 'about twenty years after Aristotle's death the Hippocratic school at Cos was under the dominant influence of the medical department of Aristotle's school.'[96] When one further reflects that of the two great Alexandrians, Herophilus was a pupil of Praxagoras and Erasistratus was manifestly influenced by Peripatetic thought (see Chapter 7), it seems that a persuasive case might, indeed, be made out for the dominance of the Lyceum over the immediately subsequent history of Greek rational medicine. But caution must be enjoined. The causal nexus seems not to have been nearly as strong as Jaeger envisages. Although it may be accepted that Praxagoras reveals in certain respects, like Aristotle and Diocles before him, the continued influence of 'Sicilian' medicine[97] and he, in his turn, undoubtedly influenced Herophilus, it would be quite misguided to regard him merely as a 'Schüler und Nachtreter' of Diocles[98] since elsewhere he reveals a striking independence of thought[99] and, on occasion, stands in marked disagreement with Diocles. Unlike Empedocles, Aristotle and Diocles, for example, he holds that the purpose of respiration is not to cool the innate heat, but rather to provide nourishment for the psychic *pneuma*.[100] Thus he is prepared to depart radically on occasion from 'Sicilian' medicine and, by propounding important and

175

influential theories of his own, forms, as shall be seen in our final chapter, a vital link with the new medicine soon to arise in Alexandria.

7

Early Alexandrian Medical Science

Verique simile est . . . Erasistratum, et quicumque alii non
contenti febres et ulcera agitare, rerum quoque naturam
aliqua parte scrutati sunt, non ideo quidem medicos fuisse,
uerum ideo quoque maiores medicos extitisse.

(Celsus, *De medicina*, Proem, 47)

Ergo necessarium esse incidere corpora mortuorum . . .
longeque optime fecisse Herophilum et Erasistratum, qui
nocentes homines a regibus ex carcere acceptos vivos
inciderint.

(Celsus, *De medicina*, Proem, 23)

In the third century BC Greek rational medicine was transplanted
into Egypt and at Ptolemaic Alexandria it achieved its greatest
success. Expatriate Greek doctors displayed, on the one hand, the
same rational attitudes towards medicine that we have previously
encountered at Cos, Athens and elsewhere in classical Greece; but
being uprooted from their native environments and thus no
longer constrained by traditional customs and attitudes, they also
reflected in their pioneering approach to medicine the new
freedoms they encountered in the new and cosmopolitan city. In
consequence, new levels of sophistication in anatomy and
physiology were attained which were not surpassed until the
Renaissance. In the dedication to his *De humani corporis fabrica*
(Basel, 1543) the great anatomist Vesalius expressed his high
regard for Alexandrian anatomy and his regret at its loss, and
eighteen years later Fallopius echoed this appraisal in his
Observationes anatomicae (Venice, 1561). The outstanding
achievements of the Alexandrians, so highly regarded by these
luminaries of the Renaissance, are well described by a more

recent author as follows:

> In some vital respects the medical achievements of Alexandria, especially in the third century BC, reached a level never achieved before, nor indeed again, until the seventeenth century AD. In medicine, as in mathematics and scholarship, what lies between Ptolemaic Alexandria and the modern world represents a retrogression from the Alexandrian performance.[1]

In spite of its dramatic success it should not be assumed that Alexandrian medicine marks a watershed between the medicine of the classical and Hellenistic eras.[2] Greek rational medicine displays an unbroken line of development after its transference to Alexandria. The ancient sources implicitly recognise this continuity when they include the Alexandrians in their list of the leading exponents of the so-called 'dogmatic school' of medicine,[3] and their assessment is confirmed by Alexandrian adoption of familiar Hippocratic doctrines such as the theory of the four humours[4] and by the manner in which they addressed themselves to particular problems raised previously at Cos or within the Lyceum. It was, significantly, in an area where systematic observation had hitherto been inhibited but could now be pursued without restriction that their most striking discoveries were made.

Alexandria was founded in 331 BC by Alexander the Great. After his death in 323 and the subsequent dissolution of his empire, it became the capital of one of his generals, Ptolemy the son of Lagus, who established the Ptolemaic dynasty there. This first Ptolemy, subsequently named Sōtēr (the Saviour), together with his son Ptolemy Philadelphus (who succeeded him in 285 BC), became immensely enriched by their exploitation of Egypt. The Ptolemies exploited a wide range of commercial monopolies, for example in oil, papyrus and perfume and they imposed high tariffs upon the import of foreign goods. They used this great wealth to raise the city to a position of great power and magnificence. Anxious to enhance both their own reputations and the prestige of their kingdom, they sought to rival the cultural and scientific achievements not only of the other Hellenistic rulers, but even of Athens herself. To further their patronage of the arts and sciences they established the Library and the Museum (an institute for literary studies and scientific research as well as a foundation for the cultivation and worship of the Muses), thereby making the city the centre of Greek culture. Leading philosophers, mathematicians, astronomers, artists, poets and physicians were encouraged to come and work there.

Recently the widespread belief that medical research formed an important part of the activities of the Museum has been called into question.[5] Von Staden, for example, points out that 'there is no evidence that . . . any representative of scientific medicine was associated with the Alexandrian Museum'.[6] In default of clear evidence it is impossible to come to any definite conclusion. Yet one is tempted to speculate that if medical researchers, like their scientific and literary counterparts, were tempted to come to Alexandria because of better research facilities, then it would not be unreasonable to suppose that these facilities were made available for them, too, within the Museum. It would be curious if other leading scholars and scientists pursued their researches there while medical research was uniquely excluded. Again, according to Celsus, criminals were provided for vivisection from the royal gaols.[7] While this information (if true) does not entail that this research was carried out within the Museum, one might nevertheless expect that a practice which contravened so firmly established a taboo among the Greeks would have been more likely to have taken place within a relatively closed intellectual society like the Museum,[8] rather than in a regular *iatreion* in the city, as von Staden suggests.[9] It also seems doubtful that vivisection would do much to enhance in the eyes of his patients a doctor's reputation as a general practitioner. Furthermore the Lyceum, upon which the Museum was closely modelled (see below), itself provided a precedent for anatomical dissection as part of its research activities – of animals, that is, not humans.

At Alexandria rapport was particularly close both with the Lyceum and the medical 'school' at Cos. Although it is recorded[10] that Sōtēr was unsuccessful in his attempts to secure Theophrastus' services, two other Peripatetics, Demetrius of Phaleron and Strato of Lampsacus, undoubtedly spent some time at Alexandria. The former, after his expulsion from Athens, became Sōtēr's legal adviser and seems to have played a major role in setting up the Library,[11] while the latter was employed as the teacher of Ptolemy Philadelphus[12] until his recall to assume the headship of the Lyceum on Theophrastus' death. It seems likely that the Lyceum was influential in the establishment of the Museum as well as the Library, since both of these institutions reflect the traditions of Aristotle's school.[13]

Cos, for its part, was the birthplace of Philadelphus. His mother Berenice had travelled to the island during her pregnancy to avail herself of the best medical care of the day.[14] For some time thereafter the island maintained strong political and cultural ties with Alexandria. It was probably due to Philadelphus' fond affection for his birthplace that the island was favourably assessed for taxation. The scholar-poet Philitas, who was born at Cos, was selected as Philadelphus' first tutor and Philadelphus himself seems to have shared his mother's high regard for Coan medicine, since he chose as his personal physician the Hippocratic doctor Chrysippus the Younger. Coan doctors, it appears, were increasingly drawn to Alexandria to avail themselves of the unprecedented opportunities for research afforded at the Museum. Among these Coan *émigrés* who subsequently achieved distinction at Alexandria was Philinus, a pupil of Herophilus, who settled there in the mid-third century and is credited by Galen with the foundation of the empiricist school of medicine. This Ptolemaic patronage of Coan medicine seems, in fact, to have had an adverse effect upon it since Praxagoras appears to have been the last really important figure to have worked there. After him, Cos ceased to be so important a centre, although the 'school' itself, unlike that at Cnidus, continued during the third and second centuries and even beyond to provide a constant supply of general medical practitioners.

Even before the establishment of the Ptolemaic dynasty, there seems to have been a strong tradition of Coan physicians in service with Macedonian rulers. When Philip II, Alexander's father, suffered severe facial injuries at the siege of Methone in 354 BC, a Coan doctor, Critobulus, achieved great fame for extracting the arrow from his eye and treating the loss of the eyeball without causing facial disfigurement.[15] According to Q. Curtius[16] this same Coan doctor saved Alexander the Great's life when he was critically wounded by an arrow at the siege of the fortress of Multan in 326 BC.[17] Yet another Coan doctor, Hippocrates the son of Dracon, also an Asclepiad, became the personal physician of Alexander's wife, the Sogdian princess Rhoxane and was murdered along with the rest of the royal household in 310 BC by Cassander.[18] The Ptolemies, then, perpetuated a tradition well established among Macedonian ruling circles in employing Coan doctors.

Not all the doctors attracted to Alexandria in the first half of the third century BC by these brighter prospects of research under royal patronage, of course, were Coan. Among them were two men of quite outstanding ability whose work was to lay the foundations for the scientific study of anatomy and physiology, Herophilus of Chalcedon and Erasistratus of Ceos. But although they were not themselves Coans, it may be noted that they each had strong connections with Cos. Herophilus studied there under Praxagoras before moving to Alexandria, while Erasistratus, after a period at Athens studying medicine under Metrodorus, the third husband of Aristotle's daughter Pythias, subsequently went to Cos where he came under the influence of Chrysippus t e Younger, Philadelphus' personal physician. It may have been this personal connection that persuaded him to move to Alexandria.

This widely accepted belief that Erasistratus practised medicine at Alexandria was attacked, however, towards the end of the last century[19] and recently this polemic has been revived by Fraser, who maintains that if it is 'not demonstrably wrong, [it is] at least unjustified by the evidence'.[20] If this contention were correct the implications for the appraisal of Alexandrian medicine would then be considerable. However, Fraser's standpoint has a fundamental weakness in that it fails to give sufficient weight to the evidence of Celsus who informs us in the Proem to his De medicina (Chap. 23) that Herophilus and Erasistratus vivisected criminals received out of prison from the kings.[21] Fraser denies that this evidence entails that both Herophilus and Erasistratus worked at Alexandria about the same time – which would be the natural inference – and maintains that 'Erasistratus, if he, too, was guilty [of human vivisection] may have performed his operations in Antioch – there would be nothing surprising if the Seleucid court emulated the Ptolemaic in this as in other respects.'[22] But as has been rightly pointed out, the balance of probabilities is against this standpoint. There is no evidence at all that human dissection was practised anywhere else in Hellenistic times other than at Alexandria and, in consequence, 'it is far less difficult to believe that Erasistratus, like Herophilus, did his researches there than that there was a second centre [Antioch] where such researches were carried out in the third century'.[23] The claim that Erasistratus worked at Antioch is, in any case, based upon the story that it was he who first diagnosed the illness of Antiochus I as being the result of that young man's passion for his stepmother Stratonice. This tale became one of the most famous love stories of the ancient world. Erasistratus, so most versions of the story relate, finally and after much anxious thought revealed to King Seleucus that his son was in love with his wife. The king, thereupon, out of love for his son, gave him his wife to marry. Wellmann,[24] however, pointed out that the date of this incident, 293 BC, would exclude Erasistratus' participation on grounds of his youth, if the traditional date for his *floruit*[25] is correct. Valerius Maximus (V, 7), whose source was not later than the reign of Augustus, actually offers a choice between Erasistratus and the otherwise unknown mathematician Leptines; while Pliny (*N. H.* VII, 123) credits Erasistratus' father Cleombrotus of Ceos, the palace doctor of Seleucus, with the diagnosis, although elsewhere (XXIX, 5) he attributes it to Erasistratus himself. Followed by Mesk,[26] Wellmann believes that the father's perceptive diagnosis was transferred to his more famous son. Fraser, however, subsequently rejected the traditional date of Erasistratus' *floruit* as given by the chronographers and revived the view that the latter was the doctor in question.[27] But if Erasistratus was the court physician at the time, it is very difficult to understand why his father – let alone the mysterious Leptines – should have been credited with this diagnosis. Thus we may agree with Nutton that the tale is not sufficiently strong 'to contradict the impression given by Celsus and Galen that [Erasistratus'] major work was carried out at Alexandria and certainly does not prove the theory . . . that he worked only under the Seleucids'.[28]

It is exceedingly unfortunate that although each of these medical scientists was the author of several treatises, not a single complete work by either of them has survived.[29] In consequence of this tragic loss we are dependent for our knowledge of this greatly important and fruitful period of medical history, which linked the Hippocratic *Corpus* with the medical works of the Imperial Roman period, upon isolated quotations and reports found in such later medical authors as Rufus of Ephesus[30] and his fellow citizen Soranus,[31] the author of a celebrated work on gynaecology written during the reign of Hadrian or perhaps even a little earlier. Another source, also belonging to the first century AD, is the medical papyrus in the British Museum known as the *Anonymus Londinensis,* which was found to contain material derived ultimately from a history of medicine written by Aristotle's pupil Meno, as his contribution to the systematisation of knowledge being carried out by the Lyceum.[32] The third section of this papyrus (XXI.5-XXIX.32) also contains a general disquisition upon the development of physiology after 300 BC from Herophilus to Alexander Philalethes. A further source of primary importance is the *De medicina* of Cornelius Celsus.[33] This treatise, written most probably during the Principate of Tiberius, is the only surviving part of an encyclopaedic work dealing with agriculture, the military arts, rhetoric, philosophy and law as well as medicine. Here Celsus, apparently with first-hand knowledge, quotes extensively not only from his Roman, but also from his classical Greek and Hellenistic predecessors. But our most important source by far is Galen,[34] who wrote more than four centuries after these two great Alexandrians. Galen was both well acquainted with their works and patently influenced by them, although at times his admiration is replaced by severe attack. Particular hostility is shown towards Erasistratus, who, in Galen's view, had ill-advisedly rejected such traditional Hippocratic beliefs and practices as the theory of the four humours and phlebotomy. A fortunate outcome of Galen's frequent attacks upon Erasistratus, however, is that we have more evidence of his beliefs than we have of those of Herophilus. Although it is stated in the Index of Kühn's edition of Galen that Erasistratus' works had been lost by Galen's own time (vol. XX.228K.) and some scholars have subsequently accepted this viewpoint,[35] it seems more than likely that they were still available to Galen, who quotes a large number of passages from them. The comment made by the latter at *De naturalibus facultatibus,* 1, 7 (II.71K.) also suggests that he was still able to consult them directly. Kühn's indexer has patently misinterpreted a remark made by Galen in *De venae sectione adversus Erasistrateos* 5 (XI.221K.), which actually implies the opposite conclusion.

Notwithstanding the brilliance of the achievements of these two Alexandrians and their paramount importance in the history of medicine, until the last year or so no fully comprehensive editions of their fragments were available to scholars. Previously, the only recourse was to the inadequate German collections by K. F. H. Marx[36] and R. Fuchs[37] of the fragments of Herophilus and Erasistratus respectively. In English our sole resort was to the twin articles by J. F. Dobson in the *Proceedings of the Royal Society of Medicine*,[38] which provided a useful selection of their fragments in translation. Since 1988, however, the modern researcher is at last more fortunately placed with the publication of Garofalo's collection of the fragments of Erasistratus (*Erasistrati Fragmenta*, Pisa, 1988) and now with the appearance of von Staden's splendid *Herophilus: The Art of Medicine in Early Alexandria: Edition, Translation and Essays* (Cambridge, 1989).

The anatomical researches of these two doctors resulted in striking discoveries being made at Alexandria in the third century BC. The immediate cause of this great scientific advance is not hard to discern; for it was at Alexandria that medical researchers first began upon a regular basis to dissect and even vivisect the human body. There is no evidence elsewhere in earlier Greek literature of the systematic dissection of the human corpse. Before the Hellenistic Age it is almost certainly the case that such dissections that were carried out were performed upon animals. Systematic animal dissection seems to have been first introduced within the Lyceum resulting in a much more accurate knowledge of the internal organs than had previously been attained. Knowledge of human internal anatomy, however, had been seriously hampered by superstitious beliefs which still invested the human corpse. Religious scruples, veneration of the dead and dread of the corpse itself had all combined to bring about a deeply entrenched and powerful taboo against human dissection throughout the whole previous history of Greek culture. Although, as has been seen, the influence of Ionian rationalism had played a vital role in challenging superstition and paving the way for the development of rational medicine, it is evident that not all superstitious beliefs were eradicated from the minds of even the most enlightened. Notwithstanding such direct attacks made upon the sanctity of the corpse as Heraclitus' terse declaration that 'corpses are more fit to be cast out than dung'[39] and the later assertion in an unidentified play by Moschion that the laws of burial are simply another product of cultural evolution,[40] traditional attitudes towards the human corpse remained firmly entrenched. Sophocles' tragedy *Antigone* (performed in 441 BC) turns upon the moral issue of whether

Antigone should follow the unwritten laws of the gods and perform a token burial for her brother Polyneices, or yield to the tyrant's edict forbidding burial. Or - to provide a historical rather than a literary illustration - in 406 BC the Athenian generals were impeached and tried *en bloc* for failing to pick up the corpses and survivors after their victory at Arginusae. It is true that Thucydides tells us (II, 52) that during the plague men simply tossed their dead upon another man's funeral pyre and walked away. But this happened at a time when mass disposal of the dead was of paramount importance and the episode is expressly chosen by the historian as a graphic illustration of the breakdown at Athens of normal restraints of religion and piety under the impact of the plague.

At Alexandria, by contrast, there is evidence of a fundamental change in attitude, and dissection of human bodies became a regular feature of anatomical research there. It is recorded that the first Ptolemies even supplied criminals for vivisection from the royal gaols. Doubtless their motivation here as elsewhere was, in part at least, to enhance their regime's prestige by fostering scientific research. The protection and provision of the Ptolemies, however, cannot themselves fully account for these new departures in anatomy since this royal patronage itself presupposes a fundamental change in attitude.

To explain this radically new outlook and account for the well attested practice of human dissection within a Greek city scholars have put forward a variety of suggestions. A philosophical explanation is put forward by Edelstein, who maintains[41] that this change in attitude towards human dissection among learned men and philosophers was due to philosophical teachings which began to take practical effect not long after Aristotle's death; that a change in the philosophy of the fourth century gradually led to a complete transformation of attitudes towards death and the human corpse. Plato, he argues, had taught that the soul was an independent and immortal being which during earthly life carried the body as a mere envelope and instrument to be discarded at death; then Aristotle declared that the soul, though not inseparable and immortal, constituted the purpose and value of the whole organism, implying that after death there was no more than a physical frame without feelings or rights: for Aristotle, therefore, a man's corpse is no longer the man himself.[42] This line of thought, Edelstein maintains, was subsequently adopted by Hellenistic philosophers who relinquished popular ideas about death and popular reverence for and awe of the corpse. From this position, he concludes, it was no large step to the assumption that the dead body could justifiably be used for dissection and anatomical study and maintains that the physicians of Alexandria were the first actually to take this step. However, there is a fundamental flaw in Edelstein's argument in that it cannot explain why it was at Alexandria alone among Greek cities that human anatomy was practised, although there were manifestly other contemporary Greek cities with authoritarian forms of government, equally prestige-conscious, whose intelligentsia were no less *au fait* with current trends in philosophy.

Edelstein's thesis is also rejected by Kudlien,[43] who sees as an important factor in the development of anatomy at Alexandria the influence of a trend towards a stricter concentration upon the exact description of the phenomena manifested in contemporary research. As evidence of this trend, he points not only to the increasing emphasis upon the empirical examination of individual phenomena displayed in the Lyceum after Aristotle,[44] but also to similar manifestations in Pyrrhonian Scepticism which, he believes, had a direct influence upon Herophilus.[45] But it would not be wise to see too much of a sceptic in Herophilus,[46] who not only based his medical theory upon the doctrine of the four humours,[47] but is also described by Ps. Galen as a member of the 'Rational' or 'Dogmatic' school of medicine.[48] Empiricism, however, is hardly a novelty in early Greek medicine and, although it is conceivable that Herophilus could have been influenced by such a 'trend towards greater empiricism', as Kudlien claims, it would be difficult to prove such an influence. In any case, as we shall see, the factors of paramount importance for bringing about these striking developments at Alexandria lie not in any philosophical influence, but elsewhere.

Other scholars have claimed that Egyptian influence[49] was the vital factor and have argued that the Alexandrians derived their knowledge of human anatomy from a study of those abdominal organs that would be available from a mummified corpse,[50] or even from a study of the corpses themselves.[51] The protagonists of these views, however, have overlooked the fact that in Egypt the religious taboos surrounding the dead and the disposal of the body were so strong that it is most unlikely that corpses or even human organs would have been readily available from this source. C. R. S. Harris has similarly suggested that this change in outlook was 'possibly . . . an indirect result of closer acquaintance with the traditional ancient Egyptian practice of embalming and mummification, which entailed the removal of the internal organs from the bodies of the dead and their separate pickling in the so-called Canopic jars'.[52] There is, however, no evidence to suggest that the Greek doctors in Alexandria derived any particular knowledge from Egyptian embalmers, whose own knowledge of anatomy was, in any case, rudimentary. To take a single example: it is difficult to see how the sophisticated Alexandrian description of the anatomy of the brain could in any way have benefited from the experience of the Egyptian mummifier who, as Herodotus informs us,[53] dragged the brain piecemeal with a hook down through the nostrils of the corpse.

Moreover, there existed in early Alexandria wide social barriers between the Greek and native communities and, even had he wished, it would not necessarily have been easy for a Greek doctor to have obtained a 'closer acquaintance' with this Egyptian burial rite.[54] And in any case, human dissection is well attested elsewhere in Alexandria. Although there seems to be a strong likelihood that the Egyptian practice of embalming was influential in the development of this new outlook at Alexandria, this influence was, in all probability, much more indirect than even Harris envisages. The transplantation of Greek medicine, fostered by the stimulus of the excellent facilities for advanced research afforded by the Ptolemies, into a different cultural environment, where the opening up of the human body was not invested with the inhibitions in vogue in mainland Greece[55] but, on the contrary, was regarded as the best and most perfect way to perform an ancient burial rite,[56] resulted in a situation highly beneficial to the development of anatomical research. As von Staden usefully reminds us,[57] there is other evidence that 'inveterate Greek taboos' were violated in the 'frontier' environment of the newly established city. Philadelphus himself disregarded another deep-seated Greek taboo and followed Egyptian precedent when he incestuously married his older sister Arsinoe II in c. 276 BC.[58]

Celsus, however, speaks not only of human dissection at Alexandria but also specifically records that Herophilus and

Erasistratus actually vivisected criminals supplied from the royal prisons:

> Moreover, since pains and various kinds of diseases arise in the interior parts, the Dogmatists think that no one can apply remedies for them who is ignorant of the parts themselves. Therefore it is necessary to cut into the bodies of the dead and examine their viscera and intestines. They hold that Herophilus and Erasistratus did this in by far the best way when they cut open live criminals they received out of prison from the kings and, while breath still remained in these bodies, they inspected those parts which nature had previously kept enclosed.
>
> (*De medicina*, Proem, 23ff.)

Celsus further tells us that the Dogmatists defended this viewpoint against the charge of inhumanity by claiming that the good outweighed the evil: 'nor is it cruel, as most people state, that remedies should be sought for innocent people of all future ages in the execution of criminals, and only a few of them.'[59]

Furthermore, the Christian writer Tertullian, writing over a century later, preserves some additional evidence upon this matter when he describes Herophilus as 'that doctor, or rather, butcher, who cut up innumerable human beings so that he could investigate nature and who hated mankind for the sake of knowledge,' and adds, 'I do not know whether he investigated clearly all the interior parts of the body, since what was formerly alive is altered by death, not a natural death, but one which itself changes during the performance of dissection.'[60] It is evident from Tertullian's additional comment here that he is referring to vivisection.[61]

This charge of vivisection levelled against the two great Alexandrian anatomists has aroused vigorous controversy and scholars of an earlier generation, especially, have sought to discredit the evidence on which it is based.[62] (Most recent writers, however, have been prepared to accept the charge as accurate.[63]) Crawfurd, for example, maintains[64] that if human dissection had been practised, the mistaken belief that the arteries contained only air would have ceased to be held. But this argument had already been refuted by the Victorian scholar Finlayson,[65] who had pointed out that vivisection of animals was regularly practised before the time of Galen and yet this belief undeniably survived until the second century AD, when Galen himself showed by careful experiments in animal vivisection that the arteries of living creatures carry blood continuously. Dobson produces a different argument and contends that Erasistratus is cleared of the charge of vivisection by Galen himself.[66] The latter criticises his Hellenistic predecessor at *De placitis* 7, 3 (V.604K.) on the grounds that, if he had experimented frequently, as he himself had done, also upon living creatures, he would have been in no doubt that the function of the 'thick membrane' (the *dura mater*) was protective. But this criticism does not entail that Erasistratus had never dissected living animals and, a fortiori, that 'it is inconceivable that he should have dissected living men,' as Dobson concludes, but only that Galen thought that he had failed to carry out the appropriate animal vivisections, which would have shown that the function of the *dura mater* is not to serve as the source of the nerves, but rather to provide protection for the *cerebrum*.[67] Other equally persistent arguments have been employed to rebut this charge of vivisection. It is pointed out, for example, that prejudice against human dissection excites rumours and calumnies[68] and the charge of human vivisection has been made in more recent times, e.g. against Vesalius and Fallopius. This same charge is also brought against Archigenes and even Galen himself, of whom it is certainly not true.[69] But the strongest argument of all is the appeal to Galen's apparent silence on this matter.[70] It is argued that the latter, who refers on several occasions to his predecessors' good fortune in being able to practise anatomy upon human bodies, would hardly have failed to mention, either in envy or by way of disapproval, this additional feature of human vivisection. If the Alexandrians had actually vivisected human beings, it is contended, then it is most unlikely that this gruesome innovation would not have been known to Galen and left unrecorded by him.

This controversial matter is most difficult to resolve. Whereas the repetition of charges of vivisection at a later date does not entail that the original charge was not justly made, it must be conceded that the last argument is not without some weight. However, Galen himself at *De ordine librorum suorum* 2 mentions that he dealt with the question of vivisection in a treatise that is no longer extant. While this treatise may, as some have argued, have confined itself solely to animal vivisection, here would surely have been the logical place for him to have mentioned human vivisection, too, had it occurred.[71] In the final analysis, then, it would perhaps be unwise to put too much weight upon an argument from silence and the positive statements of Celsus and Tertullian cannot easily be set aside. Celsus, we may note, disagrees with the Dogmatists and gives his own views later in the Proem (74-5):

> But to cut open the bodies of the dead is necessary for medical students. For they ought to know the position and arrangement of its parts - which the dead body exhibits better than a wounded living subject. As for the rest, experience will demonstrate it rather more slowly, but much more mildly, in the actual treatment of the wounded.

Celsus' own position, then, is an intermediate one: like the Dogmatists he approves of dissection and like the Empiricists he is hostile to vivisection.[72] But notwithstanding his antipathy towards vivisection, his account is otherwise restrained and he evidently does not doubt the tradition. Tertullian's evidence is, by contrast, less restrained and some scholars have contended that his *odium theologicum*, his total opposition to the scientific investigations of pagan researchers, inevitably diminishes the value of his evidence.[73] But these scholars have overlooked the fact that Christian polemic here is patently based upon Methodist doctrine, which in this respect, like that of the Empiricists, was opposed to anatomical dissection. Tertullian is here undoubtedly reproducing the views of Soranus, on whose work the *De anima* is largely based.[74] Since both Celsus and Soranus, then, evidently believe in the tradition of human vivisection at Alexandria, this positive evidence should be accepted in preference to the negative evidence of Galen's apparent silence. In the last resort, Galen may, conceivably, have chosen not to publicise a practice which was so likely to arouse widespread repugnance against medicine.

At Alexandria, then, for the first time, the irrational taboos which had inhibited investigation of the human corpse were, at least for a brief period and for whatever reason, overcome. The practice of systematic dissection of humans became established there and provided a powerful impetus to the development of scientific medicine. Although Herophilus was the author of at least eleven treatises covering a wide range of medical experience

– all of them unfortunately lost – it was in anatomy, to which he devoted three treatises, that he made his greatest contribution to medical science. He conducted important investigations of the brain, eye, nervous and vascular systems, the liver, and the sexual organs. Galen tells us unequivocally that he practised human dissection. In his treatise *De uteri dissectione* 5 (II.895K.), for example, he informs us that Herophilus' knowledge acquired through anatomical investigation was exceedingly precise, and adds that he had derived most of this knowledge not, as was generally the case, from brute beasts, but actually from human beings.

In the course of his anatomical researches into the brain Herophilus not only distinguished the *cerebrum* (*enkephalos*) from the *cerebellum* (*parenkephalis*),[75] as Aristotle had done previously,[76] but also demonstrated the origin and course of the nerves from the brain and spinal cord. He specified the 'fourth ventricle' or the 'cavity' of the *cerebellum* as the seat of the intellect.[77] This cavity in the rear portion of the floor of the fourth ventricle he aptly compared to the cavity in the pens in use at that time in Alexandria (the *anaglyphē kalamou*),[78] and the Latin translation of this term, *calamus scriptorius* or *calamus Herophili*, remains in current medical use. The three membranes of the brain were also recognised by Herophilus and designated as 'chorioid' (*chorioeidē*) because he imagined them to resemble the chorionic envelope surrounding the foetus.[79] He observed, too, the depression in the occipital bone where the sinuses of the *dura mater* meet and likened it to the trough or reservoir (*lēnos*) of a wine-press.[80] (The Latin translation, *torcular Herophili*, is also still in use.[81]) His description of the plexus of the arteries at the base of the brain (the *rete mirabile*) as the 'retiform plexus' (*diktyoeides plegma*)[82] affords evidence of his dissection of animals since it is found only in certain ungulates and does not exist in human beings. From this description it has been inferred that Herophilus had never actually dissected a human brain.[83] But Galen, who is our source for this information, is himself speaking of animals, and the same may have been true of Herophilus. There is no reason to suppose that he believed it to exist in humans also.[84]

Herophilus' most impressive contribution to anatomy, however, is to be found in his investigation of the nervous system. As was seen above,[85] his teacher Praxagoras had previously addressed himself to the question of how voluntary movement was transmitted from the seat of the intelligence to the bodily extremities. He had answered this question by conjecturing that some of the arteries, which he believed served as vessels for carrying the psychic *pneuma*, became progressively thinner until their walls ultimately fell together and their *lumen* disappeared. To describe this final, attenuated part of the artery through which he believed the vital motions were transmitted,[86] he employed the term *neuron* – implying, presumably, that it resembled a sinew. Galen tells us[87] that it was by the operation of these *neura* that Praxagoras accounted for the movements of the fingers and other parts of the body. Thus, as Solmsen perceptively points out,[88] Praxagoras became the discoverer of the nerves 'in a rather Pickwickian sense', i.e. while

> he did not in actual fact find or identify a nerve . . . he evidently wondered to what kind of organ the extremities of the body owe their movement, identified this organ to his satisfaction, described it, and discussed its connection with the center of vitality and energy.

Although, then, Praxagoras did not himself actually isolate and identify the nerves as such, he nevertheless played an important role in their discovery a generation later by Herophilus.

It was Herophilus who transferred to the nerves the function that Praxagoras had attributed to the arteries and thereby, after many ingenious theories and speculations on the part of his predecessors, finally and triumphantly identified the means through which the soul participates in the processes of sense perception and bodily movement. It was, he discovered, essentially one and the same organ which provided the answer to both questions. Reviewing the history of this problem, Solmsen points out[89] that Aristotle may be singled out as the first thinker to formulate both questions in psychophysical terms and to resort to the same principle of explanation for both of them. In the period between him and Herophilus the *pneuma* doctrine had come to exercise a dominant role in physiology and had become the instrument of soul. Herophilus' discovery of the nervous system proved that those who had looked for an identical answer to both problems were correct. Having discovered the nerves and demonstrated that they originated from the brain, the Alexandrian then proceeded to draw a distinction between the

sensory and the motor nerves[90] and succeeded in tracing the optic
nerves from brain to eye.[91] These latter nerves, Galen tells us, he
called *poroi* ('paths') because in them alone is the passage visible
through which the *aisthētikon pneuma* passes.[92]

His careful anatomical researches also enabled Herophilus to
make some striking advances in the knowledge of the anatomy of
the eye.[93] Aëtius of Amida, a medical writer of the sixth century
AD, whose own writings on the eye are of high quality, tells us
that Herophilus devoted a treatise specifically to this topic.[94] The
Alexandrian's main contribution seems to have been to establish
that the eye had four tunics rather than the three previously
recognised[95] and to have devised a technical nomenclature for the
different parts of the eye, which he based upon graphic similes
drawn from everyday experience. For example, he described the
posterior surface of the iris as 'like the skin of a grape';[96] the third
tunic of the eye, enclosing the vitreous humour, which had
previously been called 'arachnoid' (i.e. like a spider's web), he
likened to a 'drawn-up casting-net' (*amphiblēstros anaspōme-
nos*)[97] and the Latin translation of this description of it as 'net-
like' (*amphiblēstroeidēs*), i.e. 'retiform' – hence the retina,
remains in current medical use.

Descriptions of the four tunics of the eye (the fourth being the
lens capsule) are preserved in Rufus and in Anonymus Pseudo
Rufus. The former account is frequently cited in histories of
science and histories of ophthalmology, where it is commonly
believed that the description stems primarily from Rufus himself,
and thus affords evidence of the sophisticated level of knowledge
of the anatomy of the eye attained in the first century AD. Rufus
tells us:

> Of the tunics of the eye, the first which is visible has been
> named the 'horn-like' [i.e. the cornea]; of the others, the
> second is called the 'grape-like' and 'chorioid'; the part
> lying beneath the 'horn-like' is called the 'grape-like'
> because it resembles a grape in its external smoothness and
> internal roughness; the part beneath the white is called
> 'chorioid' because, being full of veins, it resembles the
> chorioid [membrane] that encloses the foetus. The third
> tunic surrounds the 'glass-like' humor [i.e. the vitreous
> humor]: on account of its fineness its ancient name is
> 'arachnoid' [i.e. like a spider's web]. But, since Herophilus

likens it to a drawn-up casting-net, some also call it 'net-like' [i.e. retiform, hence retina]. Others also call it 'glass-like' from its humor. The fourth tunic encloses the crystal-line humor; originally it was without a name, but later it was called 'lentiform' (like a lentil, hence lens) on account of its shape and 'crystalline' because of the humor it contains.

(De corporis humani partium appellationibus 153 (p. 154, 1 Daremberg-Ruelle)

The second and longer account is preserved in the treatise *De anatomia hominis partium*, which was originally believed to have been written by Rufus but subsequently found not to be a genuine work. Here we learn:

There the web of the tunics which compose the eye is as follows: the one positioned in front of all the others is called 'first' by virtue of its position and 'white' because of its colour. The first tunic is called the 'white'. This same tunic is called the 'horn-like' [cornea], whether because of its elasticity or because the adjacent humor within shines through it as though through horn or because, like horn, it is divided into individual layers. The second tunic closely adheres to the first as far as the so-called corona [i.e. the rim of the cornea where it joins the sclerotic]. It preserves its distance relative to its own middle and has a circular perforation. The perforated body is smooth externally where it joins the cornea, but is rough by reason of the parts on the interior surface, being formed of a tissue of vessels, 'like the skin of a grape', as Herophilus says. It is called the 'second' tunic because of its position, 'perforated' by reason of its constitution, 'grape-like' from its resemblance and 'chorioid' because it is furnished with blood vessels like the chorion. The third coat arising from the same passage [i.e. the optic nerve] encloses a humor similar to the white of an egg, the so-called 'glass-like' humor [i.e. the vitreous humor]. This tunic is exceedingly fine. It is called 'glass-like' from the coagulation of the humor, 'web-like' from its fineness and 'net-like' [retiform] on account of the interweaving of the vessels and its shape. For from a narrow beginning it widens and becomes hollow towards the point where it receives the fourth tunic, which surrounds the

humor resembling crystal [i.e. the aqueous humor]. One half of this tunic peeps out unbroken at the aperture of the second; the other half is joined to the arachnoid. This tunic, then, is called 'disk-like' and 'lentiform' from its shape, but 'crystalline' from the congelation of the humor. Some anatomists do not think it right to call this a tunic, but say that it is a kind of integument-like coagulation.
(Anonymus Pseudo Rufus, *De anatomia hominis partium*,
9 (p. 170 Daremberg-Ruelle)

As can be plainly seen these two accounts are essentially in harmony. The second, however, is the fuller and more accurate and patently does not stem from the first. The two accounts are clearly independent of each other and share a common source. It is noteworthy that each of them refers to Herophilus specifically by name; but in two entirely different contexts. In Rufus' account, the simile drawn between the third tunic of the eye and the casting-net is specifically attributed to Herophilus, whereas in the second account, it is the analogy between the posterior part of the iris and the skin of a grape that is directly attributed to him. As was seen above,[98] Herophilus described the three membranes of the brain as 'chorioid' because he thought they resembled the chorionic envelope surrounding the foetus. In both descriptions of the tunics of the eye the same analogy is employed, this time applied to the second tunic. In consequence, it is difficult to believe that Herophilus is not here the source of the simile. Furthermore, Pseudo Rufus tells us that not all anatomists were prepared to regard the lens capsule as a tunic. But as we have already seen, Herophilus' specific innovation was to identify the capsule as the fourth,[99] and therefore the description of this tunic would also seem to stem ultimately from him. Considered in isolation, these passages in Rufus and Pseudo Rufus might seem to provide merely a couple of pieces of isolated information as to Herophilus' views upon the anatomy of the eye.[100] Closer analysis and careful comparison, however, reveal that in fact, they preserve a detailed account of Herophilean ophthalmology, going back ultimately to his treatise 'On the eyes', which must have exercised a considerable influence upon later ophthalmology in general and upon Rufus in particular, who, quite undeservedly, has been given the credit for much of Herophilus' pioneering investigations. The same careful approach is revealed by Herophilus' work on the liver. His description of this organ, which appeared in the second book of his work *De dissectione*, provides further evidence both for his dissections of humans and for his interest in comparative anatomy. Galen has preserved in his treatise *De anatomicis administrationibus* 6, 8 (II.570K.) a lengthy fragment from Herophilus' account:

> The liver is not the same in all men both with respect to its size and the number of its lobes. At any rate, Herophilus, writing about it most accurately, reports as follows in these very terms: 'The human liver is of good size and larger than that in certain other creatures comparable in size to man. At the point at which it touches the diaphragm, it is convex and smooth. But, where it touches the stomach and the convexity of the stomach, it is concave and irregular. It resembles here a kind of fissure [i.e. the portal fissure], at which point, even in embryos, the vessel from the navel is rooted in it. The liver is not alike in all creatures, but differs in different animals both in breadth, length, thickness, height, number of lobes and in the irregularity of the frontal part, where it is thickest, and in the relative thinness at the surfaces that encircle it. In some creatures the liver has no lobes at all, but is entirely round and not differentiated. But in some it has two lobes, in others more, and in many even as many as four.' Herophilus, therefore, was right in his account and, besides, he wrote truly in this same second book of his work, *De dissectione*, that in the case of a few men and not a few other creatures the liver occupies a part of the left side. He himself mentioned only the hare, leaving it to us to investigate the other animals also.[101]

It may be inferred from the above account that Herophilus is primarily interested in the human liver; otherwise, as Fraser suggests,[102] he would himself have investigated the number of animals in which the liver was known to occur on the left hand side. Fraser is correct here[103] to accuse the German scholar M. Simon of giving a false emphasis when he declares that Herophilus has drawn the majority of his inferences from observation of animal livers.[104] It is apparent from this fragment that Herophilus had dissected a good many livers, both human and animal.

Although it was the traditional view that the liver was the starting point of the veins,[105] and even Galen himself subscribed to this mistaken belief, Herophilus cautiously confessed his uncertainty upon this matter.[106] He also described the 'great vein' (i.e. the portal vein) which grows from the portal fissure and extends obliquely downwards near the middle of the *dōdeka-daktylos ekphysis* (the 'growth of twelve fingers' breadth', i.e. the duodenal process – the name he gave to 'the beginning of the intestine before it becomes twisted').[107] Nothing else has survived of his views on the hepatic vascular system. It is unfortunate that we have no evidence of any view held by Herophilus on the relation of the liver to digestion or *haematopoiesis*, the formation of blood. He did, however, isolate certain 'veins' ending in glandular bodies which serve to nourish the intestines themselves, but do not pass to the liver.[108] These 'veins' seem to have been the lacteals or chyle vessels, and in isolating them Herophilus to some extent anticipated the work of the Italian anatomist Gasparo Aselli, who explained their function in the seventeenth century.[109]

Some evidence of Herophilus' investigations of the reproductive organs has survived which reveals that here, too, his dissections included human subjects, both male and female. His discoveries mark a considerable advance upon the rather primitive beliefs previously held. Aristotle, for example, believed that the production of the seed was completed in the blood vessels and assigned no role in this function to the testicles, which he compared to the stone weights women hung on their looms when weaving.[110] Herophilus, however, believed that both the testes (which he termed *didymoi* or 'twins') and the spermatic vessels were primarily responsible for the formation of semen.[111] (Galen, it may be noted, is critical of Herophilus for attributing a greater role to the spermatic vessels than to the testes, but he does make the point that he was not as mistaken as Aristotle in this matter.) Although Herophilus' anatomical knowledge of the male reproductive organs is patently an advance upon that of Aristotle he still agrees with the latter in adopting the haematogenous theory of the seed, the belief that the human semen is a product of the blood, a form of surplus nutriment – a theory which I sought to show earlier can be traced back to Empedocles as its first proponent.[112] It seems possible that Herophilus believed that his dissections enabled him to confirm this theory. According to the

197

treatise *De semine*, which is widely considered to be the work of Vindicianus in the fourth century and which survives only as a fragment in a Latin MS at Brussels, Herophilus declared that:

> dissection supports this theory. For, whereas the interior parts of the seminal vessels remote from the genitals are seen to be blood-red . . . those lower down have the colour of semen. This proves that the blood enters into the seminal ducts and then, through the power of these ducts, becomes white and . . . is transformed into the quality of semen.[113]

Herophilus not only recognised that the testes performed an important function in the generation of semen, he also distinguished between the various parts of the spermatic duct system. It seems likely that it was he who identified and named the epididymis, the narrow, convoluted structure which lies on the outer surface of the testis (hence its name), created by the union of the seminiferous tubules and forming the commencement of the seminal duct or *vas deferens*. The dilations (*ampullae*) of these two *vasa deferentia* were also identified by him and called 'varicose or varix-like assistants' (*parastatai kirsoeideis*); 'varix-like' because their dilations resembled those of varicose veins and 'assistants' because they assist both in the transportation and the production of semen.[114] He also identified the two seminal vesicles (*vesiculae seminales*) which serve as reservoirs on each side of the male reproductive tract for the external secretion of the testes conveyed by the *vas deferens*. To these vessels he gave the name 'glandular assistants' (*parastatai adenoeideis*).[115]

In similar fashion Herophilus investigated the female reproductive organs. He described accurately the uterus, the ovaries and the Fallopian tubes. He rejected the traditional belief in a two-chambered uterus, but in the case of the latter organs followed common precedent more closely in seeking to elucidate their structure and function by analogy with the male organs. The ovaries, which he also calls *didymoi*, are said to 'differ only slightly from the testicles of the male', while the 'seminal ducts' (i.e. the Fallopian tubes) are likened to the seminal vessels of the male in that their first part is twisted and practically all the rest towards the end is 'curled' (*kirsoeideis*), i.e. varicose.[116] Elsewhere, we learn that he described the Fallopian tubes as *apophyseis mastoeideis*, i.e. 'mastoid' or 'breast-like' growths, and compared their shape to the curve of a semicircle.[117] Simon, in accordance with his general thesis that Herophilus did not systematically dissect humans,[118] has argued that this account of the Fallopian tubes can only have been derived from animal dissection, and claims that Herophilus is recorded as having specifically said so himself elsewhere (i.e. at Galen, *De semine* 2, 1 IV.596K.). But in this passage, which is derived from the third book of his work *De dissectione*, Herophilus simply declares that the ovaries are of great size in the case of mares. The natural inference from this observation is that mares represent an exception in the relative size of their ovaries.[119] And in any case, as has already been seen, Galen explicitly tells us elsewhere that Herophilus practised human dissection and records in his own treatise *De uteri dissectione* 5 (II.894-5K.) the latter's erroneous belief that the ovarian arteries and veins are not present in all women,[120] which certainly seems to entail that Herophilus had dissected human females. Although Herophilus failed to recognise the true function of the Fallopian tubes and, misled by his use of the analogy of the male model, believed that they 'grew into the fleshy part of the neck of the bladder, just like the seminal vessels of the male',[121] his careful dissections of the human female enabled him to make conspicuous advances upon the attainments of his predecessors.

Sadly, no description by Herophilus of the structure of the heart has survived. The scattered references in secondary sources are insufficient to enable us to piece together a composite picture. He had evidently dissected the heart and seems to have had some knowledge of its valves since Galen judges his description of them to be inadequate compared with the accuracy attained by Erasistratus.[122] In the same passage Galen attributes to him the term 'nerve-like processes' which he apparently applied to the 'rims' or 'edges' (*perata*) of the membranes of the 'mouths' of the heart. Elsewhere,[123] we learn that in contrast to Erasistratus and Galen himself, he considered the auricles to be part of the heart, not merely the terminal processes of the vena cava and the pulmonary vein.

His interests in the anatomy of the vascular system, however, were clearly not confined to the heart. He also described the subclavian vein and the carotid arteries as well as other vessels of the head, abdominal cavity, and reproductive organs. Praxagoras had previously distinguished between veins and arteries, maintaining that arteries contained not blood, but *pneuma*,[124] and emerged from the left ventricle of the heart, whereas veins emerged from the right. Herophilus, however, taking up this interest of his master, drew more precise anatomical distinctions between these vessels and was the first to point out that the coats of the arteries were six times thicker than those of the veins.[125] He also noted that in dead bodies veins, when emptied of blood, collapse, whereas arteries do not.[126]

According to Rufus,[127] it was Herophilus who gave the name 'artery-like vein' (*phleps artēriōdēs*) to our pulmonary artery:

> Herophilus calls the thickest and largest vessel that proceeds from heart to lung 'artery-like';[128] for in the lungs the situation is the opposite of the other parts. On the one hand, the veins are strong and very close in nature to the arteries, whereas the arteries are weak and very close in nature to veins.

This distinction, whereby the pulmonary artery was called the *phleps artēriōdēs* and the pulmonary vein the *artēria phlebōdēs*, was held by Erasistratus and subsequently adopted by Galen. In its more familiar Latin form (*vena arterialis* and *arteria venalis*) it was dominant in anatomy until the Renaissance.

Having drawn these careful distinctions between veins and arteries, Herophilus must, one would suppose, have had a very strong motive indeed for calling the pulmonary artery a vein – albeit a vein which resembled an artery. This motivation might be found in the assumption of some scholars who believe that it is 'unlikely that Herophilus would have held views radically different from those of his own teacher'.[129] Thus, having adopted Praxagoras' theory that the arteries contain *pneuma* and the veins blood, but having also differentiated between these two types of vessel, he would then have been constrained to introduce the saving clause that in the lungs the situation was reversed. Scholarly opinion, however, is deeply divided on the matter of the content of Herophilus' arteries and standpoints have been adopted with a confidence which cannot be sustained by the nature of the evidence. In contrast to the above view, it has been equally positively stated that Herophilus 'definitely repudiated the conception of his master, Praxagoras, and his younger contemporary, Erasistratus, that the arteries contained only *pneuma*'.[130]

The key text on this issue occurs in the treatise *An sanguis in arteriis natura contineatur* 8 (IV.731K.), where Galen, arguing against Erasistratus that *pneuma* can be present in the body without necessarily being distributed from the heart through the arteries, cites predecessors, including Herophilus, who had thought that *pneuma* could enter the body everywhere through the skin:

> So that, whenever they are at a loss how the *pneuma* is to be carried from the heart to the whole body *if the arteries are filled with blood,* it is not difficult to resolve their perplexity by asserting that it is not forced, as they say, but is drawn and not only from the heart but from everywhere, as was the opinion of Herophilus.
>
> (my italics)

It has been held that this passage immediately and conclusively establishes that Herophilus held that the arteries contain blood.[131] But among the other names cited here by Galen is that of Praxagoras himself, who certainly did not subscribe to the belief that the arteries are filled with blood.[132]

It transpires, then, that Galen's testimony here does not allow us to establish beyond any doubt the matter of the content of Herophilus' arteries. Circumstantial evidence, however, does seem to suggest that he did, in fact, part company with his master in this respect. In the first place, it should be noted that if Herophilus agreed with Praxagoras and Erasistratus that the arteries contained (only) air, then it is strange that he should not have been attacked anywhere by Galen for holding this belief. Galen's prime target here is always Erasistratus with Praxagoras serving in a subsidiary role. This is an argument from silence of course; but none the less a strong one. In the last chapter of *De dignoscendis pulsibus* 3 (VIII.947K.) Erasistratus and Praxagoras are both clearly identified as subscribing to the view that the arteries contain air. Although Herophilus is cited frequently by Galen in this chapter, nowhere is there any suggestion that he shared their views on the content of the arteries. Secondly, we learn from *Anonymus Londinensis* XXVIII, 47ff. (p. 110J.), where the papyrus is in fairly good condition, that Herophilus held that more absorption (*anadosis*) takes place in the arteries than in the veins: what is absorbed is *trophē* and it is clear that by *trophē* the author here means nutriment, not in its raw, unconcocted form, but in the form of blood. It is salutary to compare this passage where it is stated that: 'Herophilus . . . has taken the opposite view [i.e. from the author]. For he thinks that more absorption takes place in the arteries and less in the veins' with an earlier passage in the papyrus (XXVI, 31ff.), where we learn that Erasistratus denied that there is absorption from the arteries because there is naturally no blood in them but only air: 'Erasistratus, however, does not think that absorption takes place from the arteries. For he says that they do not naturally contain blood – that is nutrient – but breath.' Herophilus held the former view, we are further informed, because, although an equal absorption takes place into each type of vessel, the pressure which produces the pulsation in the arteries also brings about a greater degree of absorption within them. This testimony is all the more trustworthy since at this point in the *Anonymus Londinensis* Herophilus is being criticised. (The author's own view is that there is more *anadosis* from the veins than from the arteries because veins, having one covering only, are of a wider capacity than the arteries and thus allow a greater absorption to take place into them (see XXVIII, 28ff.) and also, since the veins contain more blood than air, it is likely that more absorption occurs in a vein than in an artery.) If, then, Herophilus did actually believe that the arteries contained blood,[133] there would seem to be no apparent reason for him to deny arterial status to the pulmonary artery which would fulfil all of his criteria for an artery. In that case, one might legitimately wonder whether Rufus might not be in error here and whether an alternative scenario might not offer better historical sense, that is, having drawn clear anatomical distinctions between veins and arteries, Herophilus applied this distinction consistently throughout (even within the lungs). Later, however, when Praxagoras' concept of *pneuma*-filled arteries, together with his belief that vessels originating in the left heart were arteries and those from the right veins, was revived by Erasistratus, the Herophilean distinction between veins and arteries strictly upon anatomical grounds proved a serious stumbling-block so far as the lungs were concerned and led to this influential saving device (introduced by Erasistratus (?) or by the Erasistrateans (?)) whereby the (modern) pulmonary artery is held to be a vein which happens to resemble an artery and the pulmonary vein an artery which resembles a vein.[134]

Herophilus' careful dissections provided him with a much more accurate knowledge of the internal organs of the human body than that of his predecessors and he applied this knowledge in his explanations of physiological functions. Although in some respects he surpassed the achievements of his predecessors, he was more traditional and less innovative in this field than in anatomy and seems, for example, to have continued to accept the firmly established - and philosophically influenced - humoral theory as the basis of his theory of health and illness.

Having drawn a clear distinction between veins and arteries, Praxagoras had restricted pulsation to the arteries alone and had given to the pulse an important role in diagnosis and therapy. His pioneering investigations were subsequently developed by Herophilus. Galen, who is our main source of information here, clearly regards Herophilus' work as inaugurating a new era.[135] Although indebted to Praxagoras, Herophilus in several important respects departs markedly from his master's standpoint. For example, Praxagoras believed that the arteries possessed the power to pulsate independently of the heart.[136] Herophilus, however, rejected this view and maintained that the arteries' power of pulsation was derived from the heart[137] - although he failed to recognise that it was caused by the pumping action of the heart. (For recognition of this we have to wait until Erasistratus took up the inquiry later.) Although Praxagoras' discovery that only arteries pulsate was an important innovation, pulsation in his view was still not differentiated from other cardiac and arterial movements, muscular in origin, which differed only quantitatively from the pulse and from one another.[138] Herophilus, however, distinguished the pulse from these and other phenomena, and having isolated it as a specific physiological reaction, thereby became the first to recognise its full importance as a clinical sign in diagnosis and prognosis. He also developed a systematic (but largely fanciful) classification of different types of pulse employing the four main indications of size, strength, rate and rhythm.[139] To differentiate the numerous subdivisions of the latter, he employed a musical terminology apparently derived from his contemporary, the Peripatetic philosopher and musicologist Aristoxenus of Tarentum.[140] He produced an elaborate theory of a tetrapartite development of human pulse rhythms, distinguishing certain cardiac rhythms as characteristic of different periods of life, namely childhood, adolescence, maturity and approaching senescence. He was also keenly interested in deviations from these normal rhythms. He identified three main types of abnormal pulse – the 'pararhythmic', the 'heterorhythmic' and the 'ekrhythmic'. Of these the first indicates merely a slight divergence from normality, the second a greater and the third the greatest.[141] Some further light is thrown upon these terms by the pseudo-Galenic treatise *Definitiones medicae* 220.[142] Its author, citing Bacchius and Zeno, two disciples of Herophilus, here distinguishes the 'pararhythmic' pulse as one which does not possess the rhythm characteristic of the age of the patient, the 'heterorhythmic' as possessing the rhythm of another age and the 'ekrhythmic' as possessing a rhythm which does not correspond to any age. For other types of abnormal pulse Herophilus devised metaphorical terms derived from their supposed resemblance to the gait of certain animals such as 'capering' (*dorkadizōn*, i.e. like a gazelle),[143] 'crawling' (*myrmēkizōn*, i.e. like an ant)[144] and others, which remained in use for centuries afterwards.

Herophilus is also credited by Marcellinus, a physician of the first century AD, with the first known attempt to measure the frequency of the pulse by means of a portable water-clock or clepsydra. His account gives us some idea of the manner in which his theory of the four stages of human life was given clinical application:

> Herophilus demonstrated that a man has a fever when his pulse becomes more frequent, larger and more forceful, accompanied by great internal heat. If the pulse loses its forcefulness and magnitude, an alleviation of the fever ensues. He says that the increased frequency of the pulse is the first symptom of the beginning of a fever and was so confident in the frequency of the pulse that, using it as a reliable symptom, he prepared a clepsydra with the natural pulses of each age. He then went to the patient's bedside, set up the clepsydra, and took hold of the fevered pulse. And in so far as a greater number of pulse-beats occurred than was natural, relative to the time required to fill the clepsydra, to this degree was the greater frequency of the pulse revealed – that is to say, the patient had more or less fever.[145]

Although it is hard to envisage how the apparatus could have been calibrated with the requisite degree of sophistication to cater accurately for the various age groups, it is difficult to believe that this story is a complete fabrication. The absence of any record of the subsequent use of this device would seem to suggest that the innovation was hardly a spectacular success.

Finally, another field in which Herophilus was innovative is that of medical terminology. Before the Hellenistic period there is little evidence of a developed use of technical terminology in Greek medicine. The usual Greek practice was to adapt existing words of common speech rather than invent new terms. Herophilus, however, as has already been seen above, became something of a pioneer in this field in the sense that he introduced into medicine as new technical terms several expressions, largely metaphorical in character and drawn mainly from everyday life, in order to describe internal parts of the human body newly discovered in the course of his anatomical investigations. Several of these terms have survived and some of them remain in current medical use. For example, he called the slender, pointed process from the lower side of the temporal bone at the base of the skull the 'styloid' process because of its resemblance to the pens (*styloi*) used in Alexandria at that time to write on wax tablets. He also called this process 'pharoid' ('lighthouse-like') because of its resemblance to the shape of the famous lighthouse in the Bay of Alexandria.[146] We have already encountered the terms *calamus scriptorius*, *torcular Herophili* and the *chorioid plexus*, all of which stem from his account of the anatomy of the brain. His graphic account of the tunics of the eye and his newly coined terminology to describe the different types of pulse and the male and female reproductive organs have all been discussed above.[147]

The second of the two great Alexandrians, Erasistratus, shares the anatomical and physiological preoccupations of Herophilus. He, too, reveals a keen interest in the structure and functions of the brain, heart and eyes, and in the vascular, nervous, respiratory and reproductive systems. In several respects his work displays marked advances upon that of his predecessor. This is especially apparent in his description of the nervous and vascular systems and in his views upon the significance and structure of the heart. Even Galen remarks that Erasistratus' accurate account of the valves of the heart made it superfluous for him to describe them himself.[148] We are greatly indebted to Galen for providing in the *De placitis* 6, 6 (V.548-50K.) the following verbatim account derived from Erasistratus' treatise *De febribus*:

The phenomenon how membranes adhere to the mouths of vessels which the heart employs in the service of introducing and expelling its material is examined by Erasistratus in his work *De febribus*. Some have had the effrontery to deny the existence of these membranes and claim that they were invented by a follower of Erasistratus to establish his doctrine. But knowledge of them is so widespread amongst doctors that anyone who was not aware of them would seem to be utterly out of date. There are at the mouths of the vena cava three membranes which in their arrangement are very like the barbs of arrows – whence, I imagine, some of the Erasistrateans call them 'tricuspid'. At the mouth of the 'vein-like artery' (which is what I call the divided vessel leading from the left ventricle of the heart into the lungs) the membranes, though very similar in shape, are unequal in number. For to this mouth alone, only two membranes adhere. Each of the other two mouths has three membranes, all of them sigmoid. As Erasistratus says in his explanation of the phenomenon, each of the two mouths evacuates material, the one evacuates blood to the lung, and the other *pneuma* into the whole living creature. These membranes, in his opinion, perform a reciprocal service for the heart, by alternating at the appropriate times – those which adhere to the vessels which lead matter into the heart from the outside, are tripped by the entrance of the material and, falling back into the cavities of the heart, by opening their mouths, give an unimpeded passage to what is being drawn into their cavity. For, he says, material does not rush in spontaneously, as into some inanimate vessel; but the heart itself, dilating like a coppersmith's bellows, draws the material in, filling itself in diastole. Membranes, which, he said, lie on the vessels that lead material out of the heart, are considered by Erasistratus to behave in the opposite way. For they incline outwards from within and, being tripped by the material passing out, open their mouths in proportion[149] to the amount of the material furnished by the heart. But for all the rest of the time they firmly close their mouths and do not allow any of the material which has been emitted to return. So, too, the membranes upon the vessels which lead material into the heart close their mouths whenever the heart contracts and do not permit any of the material drawn in by it to flow back again to the outside.

Erasistratus was probably the first person to discover the co-ordinated function of all four main valves of the heart.[150] It has been suggested that it was he who actually discovered and named the tricuspid and bicuspid valves.[151] But while he may have indeed discovered them, it should be noted that Galen here specifically attributes the introduction of the former term to 'some of the Erasistrateans'.[152] It is evident from the above account that the Alexandrian had a clear knowledge both of their form and function and regarded them correctly as mechanisms for maintaining the flow in one direction. The tricuspid valve at the entrance to the right ventricle allows the blood to enter it, but not to relapse into the right auricle and vena cava, while a second semi-lunar valve (the pulmonary valve) at the base of the 'artery-like vein' (i.e. the pulmonary artery) allows blood to flow out towards the lungs, but not back into the heart. Similarly, two valves, the bicuspid (i.e. mitral) and the semi-lunar (aortic), control the flow into and out of the left side of the heart, though in this case, according to Erasistratus, it is *pneuma* that enters and leaves.

Consequent upon his discovery of the tricuspid and bicuspid valves, Erasistratus was led to consider the heart as a kind of double pump, 'a two-stroke (i.e. combined suction and force) pump with double action (since it is designed to move two different fluids, blood and *pneuma*, simultaneously)'.[153] It has been maintained that

> if ever a discovery came too early, it was this one of the heart as a pump. Veins and arteries were seen as sets of independent, dead-end canals; blood and air were supposed to slowly seep (sic) towards the periphery, where they were used up. So there was no need for a busy, powerful, one-way pump, in fact it was an embarrassment. . . . The heart as a pump made no sense really, until Harvey.[154]

But this is, surely, too extreme a standpoint. Admittedly Erasistratus has sadly underestimated the heart's vital capacity, but his conception of it as a pump was in no way an embarrassment to him – quite the reverse, in fact, since blood and *pneuma* had to be

207

pumped through increasingly fine capillaries to the furthest parts of the body.

Lonie makes the interesting suggestion[155] that Erasistratus might well have actually seen in operation the pump with two alternating sets of valves invented by his Alexandrian contemporary Ctesibius, which is described in the *Pneumatica* of Hero of Alexandria (see Figure 7a and b).[156] This suggestion has been taken up by Majno, who asserts[157] that Erasistratus' realisation that the heart is a pump 'may have been helped by . . . discussion with a colleague . . . who had just invented the flap-valve and the force-pump'. If Erasistratus had been influenced in his conception of the functioning of the heart as a result of his observation of the operation of this pump, we could then point to a rare instance of the fructification of Greek science by contemporary technology. But as Lonie himself has to acknowledge, the differences between heart and pump are considerable and it is noteworthy that the comparison the Alexandrian actually employs is that of a smith's bellows,[158] which is in fact a better analogy. Unlike the bellows, however, the heart has the capacity to dilate and contract by its own innate force. The arteries, on the other hand, were likened by Erasistratus to a skin bag[159] and held to be passively and directly dilated by the heart's contraction. Thus, he correctly believed that whereas the heart fills because it is dilated, the arteries are dilated because they are filled.

So impressed have been some scholars at Erasistratus' description of the blood vessels and his account of the structure and operation of the heart that they have claimed that the Alexandrian came near to or even actually anticipated Harvey's discovery of the circulation of the blood.[160] But such claims are quite unwarranted. Like Praxagoras before him, Erasistratus believed that the arteries contained not blood, but *pneuma*. Furthermore, like other ancient physiologists – not excluding Galen himself – Erasistratus believed that the blood was entirely consumed in the replacement of wasted tissue. The supply of blood was conceived as analogous to that of an irrigation system[161] and in an irrigation system the dry earth consumes the water in its runnels. Blood as pure nutriment is similarly consumed by the tissues and organs. It was this widespread and deep-seated belief, then, in the total consumption of the blood which precluded any suggestion of its being recycled.

Erasistratus was acquainted with the pulmonary artery and

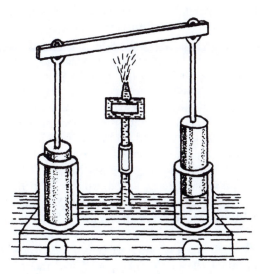

Figure 7a Ctesibius' double force-pump (known as the 'fire engine' because Hero refers to it as 'the siphon used in conflagrations'). This frequently used illustration (re-drawn with slight modification by Elizabeth Lazenby) is taken from G. B. Aleotti d'Argenta, *Gli Artifitiosi et Curiosi Moti Spiritali di Herrone*, 1589, Ferrara, Baldini, no. 27.

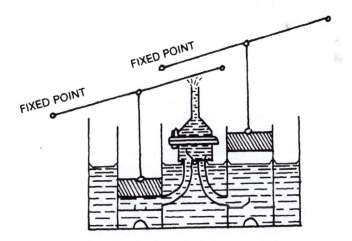

Figure 7b Scheme of the pump as described by Vitruvius. Re-drawn with slight modification by Elizabeth Lazenby after A. G. Drachmann, *Grosse Griechische Erfinder*, 1967, Zurich, Artemis Verlag, Fig. 8.

recognised its function of conveying blood from the right ventricle to the lung. Each contraction of the heart pumped blood through this 'vein resembling an artery' into the lungs. No evidence has survived to reveal what he thought happened to this blood. Possibly he may have believed, as did Galen after him, that it was totally consumed by these organs. Some scholars, however, have suggested that Erasistratus might have anticipated both the thirteenth-century Persian commentator on Avicenna, Ibn al-Nafis,[162] and the sixteenth-century Catalan scholar Michael Servetus, and discovered the lesser or pulmonary circulation. They rest their case upon a somewhat obscure passage in Galen's treatise *De locis affectis* 5, 3 (VIII.311K.). But the reference here is patently to a morbid condition resulting in the spitting of blood and not to any natural process of circulation of the blood. There can be no question here of a pulmonary circulation.

Although in the course of his investigations into the structure and operation of the heart Erasistratus had made striking discoveries consistent with the later discovery of the circulation of the blood, it would be quite misguided to claim that he in any way anticipated this discovery. A fundamental difference, of course, between Erasistratus and Harvey was that the former believed that, while the veins contained blood, the arteries were normally filled with *pneuma*. The phenomenon of arteries of dead animals empty or almost empty of blood had been noted earlier in the history of Greek medicine and his own dissections of corpses would have seemingly confirmed this belief.[163] Erasistratus, however, had not failed to observe that the arteries of living creatures spurt blood when cut and to account for this phenomenon he invoked the principle of *horror vacui* (see pp. 214ff.), maintaining that when an artery was severed, the *pneuma* it contained escaped unperceived and created a vacuum whose pull drew blood from the veins through certain fine capillaries (the *sunanastomōses*) which were normally closed. This blood then spurted out of the artery after the escaping *pneuma*.[164] It is widely believed that this ingenious hypothesis was not disproved until some four and a half centuries later, when Galen showed by careful experiments in animal vivisection that the arteries of living creatures carry blood continuously and that this is their normal condition and not the result of disease or damage. (Galen's procedure was to isolate and tie off with ligatures a portion of an artery of a living animal so that no blood could flow into or out of it and then open it to demonstrate that it was always found to be full of blood.) However, as Galen's account reveals,[165] Erasistratus himself had already been faced with this rather obvious objection to his theory (levelled perhaps by the Herophileans?) and had argued that the very act of cutting was enough to cause the evacuation of the *pneuma* and the flooding of the artery with blood.

Although Herophilus was the actual discoverer of both sensory and motor nerves, since Erasistratus carried the inquiry into the brain and nervous system considerably further than he had done, the latter's subsequent achievements have put the work of his predecessor in the shade. His description of the structure of the brain reveals a greater accuracy than that attained by Herophilus, as can be seen from Galen's verbatim account in the *De placitis Hippocratis et Platonis* 7, 3 (V.602K.):

> [Erasistratus'] account is as follows: 'I examined also the nature of the brain. It is divided into two parts, like that of other animals, and has a ventricle situated longitudinally along each side. These two ventricles are connected by a passage and come together where the two parts of the brain are joined. From here they lead into the so-called *epencranis* [i.e. the *cerebellum*] and there is another small ventricle. Each of the two parts of the brain is divided off by the membranes, for the *epencranis* has many more still and is furnished with many intricate convolutions. In consequence, the observer learns that just as the deer, the hare, or any other animal that excels others in running is well provided with muscles and sinews useful for this function, so man, too, since he is far superior to other animals in intellect, has a very convoluted brain. All the nerves grow out of the brain, and, speaking generally, the brain seems to be the source of bodily activity. For the sensory channel from the nostrils opens onto it as do those from the ears. The channels which lead to the tongue and the eyes also grow out of the brain.'

From this description, which seems to have been based upon dissections performed upon human, as well as upon animal, brains, it can be seen that Erasistratus, like Herophilus, distinguished the *cerebrum* (*enkephalos*) from the *cerebellum* (which he called *epenkranis* not *parenkephalis*, as the latter had done). He also described in some detail the cerebral ventricles or cavities within the brain. Herophilus, having shown clearly by dissection that the nerves originate in the brain, had specified the fourth ventricle of the *cerebellum* as the central organ of intellectual activity. It seems likely that Erasistratus was in agreement with this viewpoint for, as has just been seen, his observations that the *cerebellum* of the human brain has more convolutions than that of other animals had led him to the conclusion that the number of convolutions varied according to the degree of intellectual development.

Erasistratus was also in agreement with Herophilus that the brain was the starting point of all the nerves[166] and, like his fellow Alexandrian, he differentiated between the sensory and motor nerves. Initially, at any rate, he seems to have regarded them as hollow vessels serving as channels for the psychic *pneuma*.[167] Galen informs us that until late in life Erasistratus believed that all the nerves sprang from the *dura mater* itself, since he had seen only those parts of the nerve which issue from it and had discovered in the course of his vivisections that incisions into this membrane adversely affected the motor ability of living creatures; but greater leisure for research in old age enabled him to perform more accurate dissections and he succeeded in tracing the nerves into the interior of the brain itself, concluding that the core of the nerves sprang from the *cerebrum*.[168]

Before beginning his citation of Erasistratus' views on the brain, Galen explains that each nerve has an inner part as well as two envelopes and compares this inner part to the 'pith' or 'heartwood' of a tree: *to meson . . . analogon tē tōn dendrōn enteriōnē*.[169] Taking up this analogy a few sentences later, he further informs us that 'the pith, as it were (*tēn hoion enteriōnēn*), sprang from the brain.' Upon the basis of this report it has been widely believed that Erasistratus in his old age renounced his theory that the nerves were filled with psychic *pneuma* and replaced it with the belief that they contained marrow or brain substance.[170] This view that Erasistratus fundamentally changed his mind about the nerves with such radical implications for his whole pneumatology and a good deal of his physiology has been aptly described by Solmsen as 'on the point of becoming the vulgate' and is rightly attacked by him.[171] Solmsen contends that this belief rests upon a patent misunderstanding of Galen's text.

He argues that the latter's use of the word *enteriōnē* has totally misled those scholars who see so fundamental a change in Erasistratus' outlook and points out that the usual Greek word for marrow is *myelos*. (He might have strengthened his case by adding that their error has doubtless been fostered by the Latin translation in Kühn of *enteriōnē* as 'medulla', which has 'marrow' as one of its meanings.) Solmsen further maintains that the use of this term carries no implication whatsoever for the *substance* of the nerves, that it is introduced here by Galen himself, and unequivocally designated by him as a comparison or analogy. He contends that Erasistratus' new discoveries relate not to the content, but to the starting point of the nerves, and cogently observes that, if the Alexandrian had changed or renounced his theory regarding the psychic *pneuma*, it would then be difficult to explain the prevalence of this doctrine throughout many later centuries. Thus we may with reasonable confidence dismiss the belief that Erasistratus in his old age made a discovery which totally subverted his pneumatology and endorse Solmsen's standpoint that, in the light of all we know, Erasistratus remained to the end of his life unshaken in his belief that the psychic *pneuma* continued to be passed out from the brain – indeed, now from the inner part of the brain, which is a much more satisfactory idea.

However, although it may be agreed that this theory of marrow-filled nerves rests upon no more firm a foundation than a simple misinterpretation of Galen's text, two of Solmsen's arguments arouse misgivings. In the first place, is one entitled to assume so confidently that Erasistratus' new discoveries relate not to the content, but exclusively to the starting point of the nerves? It is difficult to believe that when Erasistratus, as a result of his more accurate dissections, had to his own satisfaction traced the core of the nerves to the interior of the brain, he did not also, in the course of these dissections, make a cross-section of a nerve, which would have enabled him to correct his prior assumption that the nerves were hollow. Again, Solmsen's contention that the word *enteriōnē* carries no implication at all for the substance of the nerves seems over-confident. Admittedly the analogy is Galen's, and there is no evidence to suggest that Erasistratus himself used this precise term. But if Erasistratus had actually made such a cross-section, then Galen's *enteriōnē* would describe very adequately indeed what he must then have found.

Whereas the concept of marrow-filled nerves seems quite incompatible with Erasistratus' pneumatology, there does not seem to be any reason why this newly discovered pithy core of the nerves should not have been regarded as permeated with passages so as to enable that lightest of substances, the psychic *pneuma*, to pass freely down them.[172] In this connection, it should not be overlooked that Galen himself has no difficulty in reconciling the physiology of the nerves described here (*enteriōnē* and all) with the belief in *pneuma* flowing through them.

Erasistratus seems not only to have displayed a greater interest in physiology than his fellow Alexandrian did, but also to have been more innovative. (Galen's disapproval and frequent criticisms of Erasistratus for his radical departures from traditional Hippocratic concepts has resulted in more information being preserved.) Once again the influence of philosophy may be detected. Erasistratus seems to have based his physiology directly upon a corpuscular theory derived from the Peripatetic philosopher Strato of Lampsacus,[173] who had worked in Alexandria until his recall to Athens. As Diels pointed out in an important essay,[174] in the Preface to the *Pneumatica* of Hero of Alexandria a theory of suction is described which is identical to that employed by Erasistratus. Both engineer and doctor hold that matter consists of tiny particles interspersed with void, that virtually all bodies contain minute void interstices (but no 'large void' exists naturally), and that, should such a large void occur anywhere in the world, then the surrounding matter, unless prevented in some way, would immediately rush in to fill it. This theory seems unlikely to have been invented by doctor or engineer. Indeed, Hero himself ascribes it to 'those who have studied natural philosophy'. Diels, therefore, pointing to the tradition linking Erasistratus with the Lyceum and the agreement between a passage in Hero's Preface and a fragment which Simplicius attributes to Strato,[175] persuasively concludes that the theory in question is derived from the latter.[176]

Like Strato,[177] then, Erasistratus conceived of his particles as very small, imperceptible, corporeal entities partially surrounded by a vacuum in a finely divided or discontinuous condition. He combines this corpuscular theory with the doctrine of the *pneuma*. An important factor in persuading him to adopt this latter concept must have been the influence, not only of Aristotle, but also of such doctors as Diocles, Praxagoras and Herophilus in whose medical theories the *pneuma* plays so fundamental a role. It is worth recalling, too, that Strato also seems to have adopted this theory.[178] Upon the basis of these two theories, Erasistratus sought to assign natural causes to all phenomena and rejected the widely prevalent idea that there were certain hidden, unexplained forces, such as the power of attraction of certain organs, postulated by many medical theorists in order to account for such physiological processes as the assimilation of food and the secretion of humours. For this belief Erasistratus substituted the theory of *pros to kenoumenon akolouthia* – the *horror vacui* derived from Strato,[179] whereby those empty spaces which suddenly form in a living body are continually filled.

As several scholars have persuasively argued, Erasistratus may also have derived his experimental method from Strato. The *Anonymus Londinensis* preserves some evidence of his methodology and describes an experiment carried out by him (col. XXXIII),[180] which anticipates that performed in the seventeenth century by the Paduan professor Santorio of Capo d'Istria, which is generally considered to mark the beginning of the modern study of metabolism. In order to prove that living creatures give off certain invisible emanations, Erasistratus recommended that a bird or similar creature should be weighed and then kept in a vessel for some time without food. It should then be weighed again together with all the excrement that had been passed. A great loss of weight would then be discovered 'proving' that the creature had given off matter invisibly.

Sufficient evidence has survived to enable us to see how Erasistratus employed these mechanical ideas to explain organic processes. For example, in the case of digestion, he rejected the Hippocratic and Peripatetic belief that food underwent a qualitative change ('concoction') in the stomach under the action of the 'innate heat'.[181] Instead, he sought to explain the digestive processes as far as possible in mechanical terms, and held that food, once in the stomach, was subjected to mechanical action and torn to pulp by the peristaltic action of the gastric muscles.[182] (His accurate description of the structure and function of these muscles has survived.) This nutrient, he maintained, was then squeezed out in the form of chyle through the walls of the stomach and intestines into the blood vessels communicating with the liver, where it was transformed into blood.[183] During this process the biliary contents were separated off[184] and passed

215

to the gall bladder, while the pure blood from the liver was conveyed via the vena cava to the right ventricle of the heart. From there it was pumped into the lungs through the so-called *phleps arteriōdēs*, the 'vein resembling an artery', i.e. our pulmonary artery, and distributed generally throughout the venous system as nourishment to repair the bodily wastage which, as he had so vividly demonstrated, took place not only visibly but to some extent invisibly.

The supply of nutriment to each particular bodily part, Erasistratus held, was effected by a process of absorption (*diadosis*) through extremely fine pores (*kenōmata*) in the walls of the capillary veins contained within it. The particles of nourishment were able to pass through these very fine and ultimate branches of the venous system to fill, in accordance with the principle of *horror vacui*, those spaces left empty by the evacuations and emanations. The Alexandrian had made the striking discovery that all organic parts of a living creature were a tissue composed of a 'triple weaving' of vessels, of vein, artery and nerve (the *triplokia ton angeiōn*), vessels so fine that they could only be apprehended by reason.[185] Some tissues, however, like the brain, fat, liver, lung and spleen, Erasistratus held, were different in that they had a deposit of nutriment 'poured-in-beside' these vessels.[186] This deposit of nutriment he called the *parenchyma* – a term which is still used in modern physiology to denote the cells that fill the spaces between the vessels and fibres of connective tissues. This attempt by Erasistratus to account for nutrition and growth in purely mechanical terms was not to the liking of Galen, who accuses him of conceiving the growth of living creatures to be akin to that of a sieve, rope, bag or basket, each of which has woven on to its margins additional material similar to that of which it is composed.[187]

Disease was explained by Erasistratus upon the basis of this theory of nutrition. Its main cause was held to be *plethōra*, i.e. the flooding of the veins with a superfluity of blood engendered by an excessive intake of nourishment.[188] As *plethōra* increased, the limbs began to swell, then became sore, more sluggish and harder to move. Should *plethōra* increase still more, the superfluous blood was then discharged through the *sunanastomōses*, the fine capillaries, which were closed under normal conditions, into the arteries, where it was compressed by the *pneuma* being constantly pumped from the left ventricle of the heart. This compressed blood collected in the extremities of the arteries and caused there local inflammation accompanied by fever. Moreover, since the flow of the *pneuma* was impeded by the presence of this blood in the arteries, it could not perform its natural functions. As examples of diseases brought about in this way by *plethōra*, he mentions ailments of the liver, spleen and stomach, coughing of blood, phrenitis, pleuritis and peripneumonia.

As treatment for *plethōra*, Erasistratus recommended primarily starvation on the grounds that the veins, when emptied, would more easily receive back the blood which had been discharged into the arteries. Unlike many of his contemporaries, he did not resort freely to phlebotomy,[189] but employed it only upon rare occasions. In general, he preferred prevention to therapy and in a separate treatise stressed the importance of hygiene. He was opposed to violent remedies, especially purgatives, preferring in their stead carefully regulated exercise and diet.[190]

Impressive results, as has been seen, were achieved by these two Alexandrians, who had the imagination to realise the need to dissect and even vivisect humans as well as animals. Working fully within the tradition of Greek rational medicine,[191] yet at the same time within a new and stimulating environment, they were fortunate in having the protection and patronage of the Ptolemies which enabled them to overcome the deeply entrenched and irrational taboo which had inhibited the investigation of the human corpse in Greece proper. As a result of their radical innovation of systematic human anatomy, striking advances were made in the knowledge of the human heart, brain, eye, liver, vascular, nervous, and reproductive systems. In physiology, however, as might be expected, they were less successful although this study clearly benefited from now being firmly based upon a more accurate knowledge of the structure and location of the internal parts of the human body. In consequence, some - but by no means all - traditional theories were renounced, some misconceptions corrected, and some new and potentially fruitful areas opened up for further investigation. On the debit side, however, certain of their new physiological theories, although more accurately based anatomically, were, in the final analysis, hardly less speculative than those that they replaced and were invested with a spurious authority by the impressive anatomy upon which they were founded.

It was in anatomical research, then, that they achieved their greatest success. Their careful dissections not only provided the basis and stimulus for investigations undertaken by Galen some four centuries later, but also led to a plethora of discoveries of a range and sophistication unparalleled until the seventeenth century. Their activities, however, were not confined solely to anatomical and physiological research. It should not be overlooked that they were both practising physicians, too. Reference has already been made to Herophilus' use of a portable clepsydra at the patient's bedside[192] and to his use of an embryotome to cut the foetus to pieces within the womb.[193] He evidently placed a heavy reliance upon drugs, which, Galen tells us,[194] he described metaphorically as 'the hands of the gods'. He also resorted frequently to phlebotomy and stressed the importance of diet and exercise for the maintenance of health. Erasistratus similarly emphasised the importance of these two factors for good health but, in contrast to Herophilus, only rarely had recourse to phlebotomy – doubtless as a result of his decision largely to disregard the influential theory of the four humours.[195] In surgery, however, he appears to have been less restrained. We are told, for example, that he even opened the abdomen in a case of dropsy in order to apply remedies directly to the liver.[196] Like Herophilus, he was evidently interested in the development of technical aids and is credited with the invention and introduction into surgery of a catheter for draining the bladder. This catheter, which was named after him, was shaped like the Roman letter S.[197]

Herophilus and Erasistratus themselves represent the culmination of Alexandrian medical science. They were followed by an almost immediate decline. They each founded medical schools and the names of some of their followers have survived.[198] None of these, however, was able to equal the pre-eminence of his master. The two rival schools seem to have largely dissipated their energies in sophistry and unrewarding sectarian strife. The practice of human anatomy, too, did not continue as a permanent legacy of Alexandrian medical science. Our evidence again is scanty, but it is clear from a remark made by Rufus, who himself considered human dissection to be the ideal, that by the first century AD this practice was already a thing of the past: 'We shall try to teach you,' says Rufus, 'how to name the internal parts by dissecting an animal that closely resembles man. . . . In the past they used to teach this, more correctly, upon man.'[199] It has been maintained, however, that in Galen's own day (second century AD) human dissection continued to be practised at Alexandria.[200] But the evidence upon which this assessment is based is drawn from Galen's *De anatomicis administrationibus*, where the latter is discussing osteology:

> Let it be your serious concern not only to learn accurately from books the shape of each bone, but also to carry out a keen visual examination of the human bones. This is very easy at Alexandria inasmuch as the physicians there employ visual demonstration in teaching osteology to their pupils. For this reason – even if for no other – try to visit Alexandria.[201]

This evidence, however, seems to suggest the opposite conclusion in that the importance of the study of the human skeleton is stressed precisely because knowledge of human anatomy was no longer based upon the dissection of the human corpse, but upon other creatures, like the barbary ape, which resembled the human animal. Thus it was only through an accurate knowledge of the human skeleton that the proper morphological analogies could be drawn.[202]

It is difficult to account for the puzzling abandonment of a practice whose introduction had resulted in such striking successes. In default of firm evidence one can only conjecture. As has been seen, human dissection had never been generally accepted as an essential part of medical practice in Greece and there existed deeply entrenched and abiding irrational prejudices against it. At Alexandria, however, these prejudices were temporarily overcome thanks partly to the protection and provision of the first Ptolemies, who were keen to foster the prestige of their regime by encouraging medicine as well as the other arts and sciences. But had human vivisection and dissection aroused at an earlier date the sort of odium which is in evidence later, then it could well have been the case that subsequent Ptolemies, with Macedonian sensitivity to any charge of barbarism, withdrew their patronage from an activity which, instead of winning renown, was now bringing their regime into disrepute.[203]

Appendix

The role of the opposites in pre-Aristotelian physics

An appraisal of the role of the four opposites, hot, cold, moist and dry in Milesian physics is difficult since direct evidence of Milesian thought is extremely meagre and we are almost exclusively dependent upon secondary sources. While it is true that these sources do ascribe to these four opposites an important role in Anaximander's cosmology[1] and this evidence has been widely accepted at face value,[2] the accuracy of the evidence of Aristotle and Theophrastus and the doxographical sources dependent upon them has been challenged.[3] Whether or not one is prepared to accept this challenge in its entirety,[4] the claim that Aristotle's attempt to show that his predecessors held these opposites to be principles was motivated by his desire to find in pre-Socratic thought presentiments of his own theory of Form and Privation[5] is most persuasive.[6]

Notwithstanding these misgivings, some scholars are still prepared to accept as reliable Peripatetic evidence concerning the role of these opposites in Milesian cosmology.[7] Others, however, firmly reject this evidence.[8] There is, then, a fundamental dichotomy in scholarly opinion as to whether the hot, the cold, the moist and the dry were themselves used in cosmological theory as early as Anaximander. The view that the entities which separate off from Anaximander's first principle, the *Apeiron*, are the hot and the cold, the dry and the moist, rests upon a single testimony of Simplicius (*In phys.* 150. 24 *D.K.*12A9). Elsewhere (*In phys.* 24. 13ff.) Simplicius, like Aristotle, leaves undetermined the precise nature of these entities. In this one passage, however, they are specified as the opposites, 'the hot, the cold, the dry and the moist and the rest'. But, as even Kahn has to acknowledge,[9] Simplicius is here clearly 'more concerned to explain Aristotle's

220

APPENDIX

text than to describe Anaximander's doctrine in detail'. Kahn argues, however, that although it is possible that Simplicius himself has supplied the second pair, the first pair was certainly given by Theophrastus and he supports his standpoint by citing two doxographical passages, namely Aëtius, II 11, 5 (*D.K.* 12A17a) and the pseudo-Plutarchean *Stromateis* 2 (*D.K.*12A10), which certainly seem to suggest that the hot and the cold were mentioned by Theophrastus in his account of Anaximander. But even if it is accepted that Theophrastus did speak of this pair of opposites in describing Anaximander's cosmology, we are still left with the extremely difficult question whether this mention of the hot and the cold represents a direct report of Anaximander or a reformulation of his thought in terms of the opposites.

This problem has been examined by Lloyd,[10] who believes that some light might be shed by examining the context of these two doxographical sources. Aëtius tells us here that 'Anaximander said that the heavens are formed from a mixture of the hot and cold.' But as Lloyd points out, all other reports of Anaximander's views of the nature of the heavenly bodies are basically agreed that they are rings of fire enclosed in tubes of *aēr*, which have openings at certain points through which the fire shines. Given this set of reports that Anaximander held that the heavens contain a series of rings composed of fire and opaque mist, and granted that Aristotle and the doxographers sometimes reformulated pre-Socratic theories in terms of the neater opposition of the hot and the cold, there is, then, as Lloyd maintains, a distinct possibility that Aëtius' report is just such a reformulation. Similarly, it is possible that the reference to the hot and the cold in the pseudo-Plutarch passage represents a comment upon Anaximander's theory rather than a verbally accurate report. In this passage of the *Stromateis*, which is our only surviving evidence of Theophrastus' account of Anaximander's cosmogonical process, it is stated that there separates off from the *Apeiron* 'that which is capable of generating the hot and the cold' (τὸ . . . γόνιμον θερμοῦ τε καὶ ψυχροῦ). As Kirk points out,[11] 'the nature of the hot (substance) and cold (substance) thus cryptically produced appears from what follows: they are flame and air-mist (the inner part of which is assumed to have condensed into earth).' Thus, as Lloyd says, Holscher's view that what was produced from the *Apeiron* was not 'the hot' and 'the cold' as

221

such, but rather such opposed substances as flame and mist, seems to have the balance of probability in its favour.

The first extant philosophical text in which these four opposites are explicitly mentioned is a fragment of Heraclitus preserved in a scholion of Tzetzes: 'Cold things heat themselves, the hot cools, the moist dries, the parched is made wet' (Scholia ad Exeg. in Iliadem p. 126 Hermann D.K. 22B126). It is uncertain whether this fragment has any specific cosmological import.[12] After a careful analysis, Kirk has suggested that the mention of the opposite things is (merely) intended to demonstrate that, in spite of their apparent differentiation, they form an essential unity.[13] A wider view than Kirk's is taken by Kahn, who does find the fragment of cosmological significance.[14] But there is no suggestion in the remaining fragments that the opposites play any special role in Heraclitus' physics and Fragments 31 and 36 suggest that physical change was conceived broadly in terms of the intermutation of the cosmic masses, fire, earth and water. Nor is there any hint that Heraclitus employed a special mechanism of change based strictly upon the opposites themselves. As Kirk further points out, 'one of the strangest features of his system is the lack of explicit interrelation between his special analysis of cosmological change . . . and his general analysis of change as between opposites.'[15]

It is not, in fact, until the fifth century that these opposites are encountered unequivocally playing important cosmological roles. The fragments of Anaxagoras of Clazomenae reveal that they were employed in the composition of both elements and tissues.[16] However, it is apparent that these four opposites play here neither exclusive nor primary roles, but take their place in a wider inventory of opposites, which includes the rare and the dense and the bright and the dark. In Empedocles' thought, too, as has been seen (Chapter 3), certain opposites, including the hot and the cold, are connected with the four elements and others are, apparently, allowed independent activity to effect processes like nutrition. Kahn has argued[17] that 'if the complete poem of Empedocles had survived we might see that his theory was as fully articulated as that of Aristotle' and adds that other fragments permit us to catch a glimpse of the causal roles ascribed to the hot and cold, the dense and rare, and to the qualities of taste – bitter, sweet and others (citing Fragments 65, 67, 75, 90 and 104). But the fact remains that Fragment 21, where fire (more precisely, the sun) is described as white and hot, water (rain) as dark and cold, while earth is associated with solid things,[18] is the only surviving fragmentary evidence for the association of opposites and elements. Kahn's thesis, therefore, does not rest upon very substantial foundations.

Nor is there any evidence in the *Peri Physeōs* to suggest, as some scholars have claimed, that Empedocles' procedure was to take over these four opposites and attach them to the appropriate specific cosmic mass.[19] But as was seen above, Philistion, who is manifestly deeply influenced by Empedocles, does explicitly make this identification of opposites with elements and some fifth-century philosophical theory evidently *did* assign a definite and primary role in physics to these four opposites. For the author of *De vetere medicina*, who is much concerned to counter the intrusion of 'newfangled' philosophical hypotheses into medicine, specifically cites, as an example of such a postulate, the belief that there are four 'powers' active in the human body, the hot, the cold, the moist, and the dry.[20] He also explicitly names Empedocles as a representative of this objectionable influence of the philosophical approach to medicine. This evidence is difficult to reconcile. It could, conceivably, be the case that Philistion did not himself originate the identification of these opposites with the elements and here, as elsewhere, was influenced by Empedocles, who might himself have arrived at this neater correlation of opposites with elements subsequent to writing his physical poem.

In this connection it should not be overlooked that Empedocles' younger contemporary Diogenes of Apollonia,[21] in seeking to accommodate the four element theory to his own monistic hypothesis, maintains that earth, air, fire and water are merely temporary modifications of his one everlasting *archē*.[22] Diogenes attacks Empedocles' conception of different immutable elements and maintains that interaction of any kind between absolutely and essentially distinct substances is impossible. Without an underlying unity to allow for mutual transformation, the kind of interaction necessary to produce organisms like plants and animals would be impossible. Biological change such as that envisaged by Empedocles whereby bone and flesh arose from the juxtaposition of totally different substances[23] simply could not occur. Since earth, air, fire and water are expressly itemised in this fragment as being among the 'things existing in this world now' and the hot, cold, moist and dry appear among the modifications of his first principle, aēr, described in Fragment 5, it seems likely that Diogenes correlated these four opposites with the four 'elements'. Anaximenes, whose monistic hypothesis had been revived by Diogenes, appears to have accounted for different degrees of heat and cold upon the basis of differences in the density of his archē,[24] and it is conceivable that Diogenes adopted a similar explanation.

After Diogenes, however, the role of these four opposites becomes even less important in physics. The Atomists regarded them merely as temporary sensations experienced by the percipient subject. In a well known fragment Democritus declares that hot and cold and bitter and sweet have their names by convention.[25] They have no physical reality per se, but are correlated with specific atomic shapes. The atoms which produce these sensations within us by means of their shape are themselves devoid of these qualities. Plato is essentially in agreement with the Atomists. Although, as was suggested in the previous chapter, 'Sicilian' medicine may have been introduced into the Academy by Philistion, Plato's debt to him seems to lie strictly in medical matters, in physiology, and the aetiology of disease, rather than in physics. Plato does not follow Philistion in endowing the elements each with one of these four opposites. For him, like the Atomists, the hot, the cold, the moist and the dry have no independent existence among physical things; they are reduced to the status of transitory sensations, which arise between the objects perceived and the percipient. Sensible qualities for Plato, as well as Democritus, are 'affections of the sensitive part undergoing alteration, from which comes the perception; not even cold and heat have an objective character, but the atom as it moves brings about an alteration in us also'.[26] In answer to the question in what sense is fire called hot, Plato declares:

We are all aware that the sensation is a piercing one. The fineness of its edges, the sharpness of its angles, the smallness of its particles, and the speed of its movement – all of which give it the force and penetration to cut into anything it encounters – can be explained when we remember the formation of its figure; and we may conclude that its special ability to penetrate and disintegrate our bodies gives what we call 'heat' its quality and name.

(*Timaeus* 61d5ff.)

The sensation of cold is explained upon similar lines - except that it is not linked so precisely with one particular 'element' and its shape. Basically, the same principle of explanation is put forward for the other opposites which are depicted as effects produced by the geometrical shape of the 'elements' upon the relevant sense organs.

Aristotle's own approach displays a much greater similarity to that of Philistion than to that of Plato. Unlike the former, however, Aristotle connects each of the elements with two of the opposites. So, notwithstanding his demonstrable debts to 'Sicilian' medicine, the influence of Philistion upon him in this respect should not be overstressed. Philistion's specific association of fire with the hot, air with the cold, earth with the dry, and water with the moist seems to have had a greater influence upon Stoic[27] than upon Peripatetic philosophy. Furthermore, it should not be overlooked that in Aristotelian physics air is hot and not cold, as Philistion maintained. Aristotle's procedure in associating binary combinations of opposites with each element has far closer parallels in the Hippocratic *Corpus* than it has with Philistion. In the treatise *De carnibus*, for example, the qualities cold and dry are associated with earth, warm and moist with air, while the 'moistest and the thickest' are correlated with water. Almost every Hippocratic work poses difficult questions over dating and the *De carnibus* is no exception. Although several scholars follow Littré in holding that this work was written after Aristotle,[28] the correlation of elements and opposites found here looks much more primitive and less comprehensive than the relatively sophisticated schema put forward by Aristotle. Furthermore, Littré's dating is based upon his general theory that all Hippocratic treatises which find the origin of the blood vessels in the heart must be later than Aristotle.[29] But unfortunately, Littré overlooked *Timaeus* 70b, where the heart is described by Plato as the 'tie of the blood-vessels and the fountain-spring of the blood which runs through all the limbs'. Thus there is no major obstacle to holding the work as earlier than Aristotle.[30]

At *De victu* I, 4 fire is defined as hot and dry, and water as cold and wet - but at least one scholar has claimed that this treatise has undergone Peripatetic influence.[31] Even closer parallels with Aristotle's ascription of opposites to elements in the *De generatione et corruptione* are found in *De natura hominis*, Chapters 1-6. Here are employed precisely the same binary combinations of opposites. They are correlated, however, not with the elements, but with the four humours, blood being considered as warm and moist; phlegm, cold and moist; black bile, cold and dry;, and yellow bile, warm and dry. (These humours, however, have the elements air, water, earth and fire as their respective counterparts.) The reference to Melissus in the first chapter of this treatise provides a *terminus post quem* for the theories expounded in these opening chapters and in the *Anonymus Londinensis* XIX, 9 the same doctrine of the humours is ascribed to Polybus, the pupil and son-in-law of Hippocrates. (And Aristotle himself attributes to Polybus the vascular system described in Chapter 11 (VI, 58-60L.) of the treatise).[32] Although there are some divergences in detail, the general consensus among scholars is that this work, too, was written prior to Aristotle.[33]

Thus Hippocratic medicine, it would appear, provides much closer approximations to Aristotle's use of binary combinations of these four opposites than can be found in the physics of his predecessors. Given, then, Aristotle's own medical background and his deep interest in biology, it seems that we may therefore be not unjustified in seeing here a further important influence of medicine upon philosophy.

Notes

Introduction

1 See Chapter 2, p. 32.
2. Hett's translation (Loeb edn, 1957 with slight modification. The same observation is made by Aristotle at *De sensu* 436a18ff. Even if Aristotle is referring to the contemporary state of affairs and is not expressly referring to the earlier period, his remarks would apply a fortiori to that earlier period.
3 Burnet, 1930, p. 201 n. 4. See Chapter 2, p. 46.
4 'A studio sapientiae disciplinam hanc separavit' (*De medicina*, Proem, 8). It seems doubtful whether we shall ever know for certain what prompted Celsus to make this curious assessment. Philosophical speculation is prominent in many of the treatises of the Hippocratic *Corpus*. Some scholars believe that Celsus had in mind here the treatise *De vetere medicina*. Mudry, 1982, p. 64 makes the interesting suggestion that Celsus' comment here has a purely literary connotation and that he is claiming that Hippocrates was responsible for the advent of a specific medical literature separate from the writings of the philosophers.
5 op. cit., 13.
6 For Celsus' account of the dogmatic sect see *De medicina*, Proem, 13-26.
7 Parker, 1983, p. 238.

1 Pre-rational and irrational medicine in Greece and neighbouring cultures

1 See Wilson and Reynolds, 1990, pp. 185-98.
2 Egyptian medicine enjoyed an almost legendary reputation from earliest antiquity. According to Herodotus (II, 84) each physician specialised in a single disease and no more. Egyptian doctors were employed as court physicians by the Persian kings (Xenophon, *Cyropaedia, passim*; Herodotus, III, 1 and 129. See too the report inscribed upon the statue of the Egyptian priest/physician Uzahorresenet (trans. by J. H. Breasted, 1930, vol. I, pp. 17ff.), who had

been sent by Darius I to Saïs to restore the House of Life, a school for the training of physicians. Egyptian medicine is described at *Odyssey* IV. 220-32 as the most skilful in the world. The high esteem, generally, in which Egyptian medicine was held among the Greeks has given rise to the claim by modern scholars that Greek medicine was considerably influenced by the Egyptians, e.g. Steuer and Saunders, 1959; Saunders, 1963; Lefebvre, 1956, p. 2; Breasted, 1930, vol. I, pp. 16-17; Ghalioungui, 1973; and Iverson, 1953. But see, for example, Allbutt, 1921, p. 133; Sigerist, 1951, vol. I, pp. 356-8; Fraser, 1972, vol. I, pp. 344ff.; and Thivel, 1981, p. 320, who are more sceptical about Greek medical debts to Egypt. See p. 10 below.

3 These comprise the *Ebers Papyrus*, the *Edwin Smith Surgical Papyrus*, the *Hearst Papyrus*, Berlin Papyrus 3038, the *London Papyrus*, *Carlsberg Papyrus* VIII, and *Chester Beatty* VI. For the Egyptian medical papyri generally see Grapow *et al.*, 1954-62.

4 Breasted, 1930, vol. I, p. 14.

5 See Dawson, 1953, vol. I, p. 58.

6 Sigerist, 1951, vol. I, p. 355.

7 See the references cited in n. 2 above.

8 Diodorus Siculus (I, 25) attributes this cult practice of healing by dreams to Isis.

9 For example, Egyptian *natron* (a sodium carbonate used by the Egyptians mostly for embalming and known to the Greeks as *nitron* or *litron*) occurs in several drug prescriptions recommended in *Epidemiarum Liber* II (II.6, 9, 29; V.134, 138L.), and in *De internis affectionibus* 26, 31, 51 (VII.236, 248, 294L.). Egyptium alum (στυπτηρίη) is recommended in several Hippocratic treatises (*Epidemiarum Liber* V, 69 (V.244L.); VII, 66 (V.430L.); *De ulceribus* 14, 17-18 (VI.416, 422L.); *De haemorrhoidibus* 7 (VI.442L.); *De fistulis* 7 (VI.454L.); *De natura muliebri* 97 (VII.414L.); *De morbis mulierum* I, 23, 63, 75, 78 (VIII.62, 130, 166, 178L.), and *De superfetatione* 33, 35 (VIII.504, 506L.). Egyptian beans are also recommended for dietary purposes (*De victu acutorum* 21 (II.502L.)). For further references see Kühn and Fleischer, 1986-9, *s.v.* Αἰγύπτιος, Thivel, 1981, p. 320, and the excellent account of Alexandrian and Greek medicine in von Staden, 1989, Chap. 1, pp. 16ff.

10 The Egyptian thistle, white Egyptian oil, Egyptian salt, Egyptian saffron, Egyptian unguent, Egyptian acorn (βάλανος) and the 'purse tassels' from Egyptian cornfields are recommended for use in douches, uterine purges and in pessaries to bring on menstruation or induce childbirth. See especially *De morbis mulierum* I, 37, 74, 75; II, 126, 181, 203 (VIII.90, 160, 166-8, 176, 186-8, 270, 364, 390L.) and *De natura muliebri* 7, 32-4, 109 (VII.322, 360, 366, 372, 431L.). See further Kühn and Fleischer, 1986-9; Thivel, 1981, p. 320; and von Staden, 1989, Chapter 1, pp. 16ff.

11 See Le Page Renouf, 1873, pp. 123-5, and Iverson, 1939, pp. 1-31. The parallels here seem particularly close. For example, the

Carlsberg Papyrus VIII.4 (Iverson, 1939, pp. 21-2) contains the following prognosis:

Another, to distinguish a woman who will give birth from one who will not give birth: you shall let an onion bulb . . . remain the whole night [on her vulva?] until dawn. If the smell passes through her mouth, she will give birth; if . . . [lacuna], she will not give birth.

A similar test to determine whether a woman will conceive is described in the Hippocratic treatise *De sterilibus* (= *De morbis mulierum* III, 214 (VIII.416L.):

Another: clean off a clove of garlic all around, snip off its head, and insert it into the womb; and on the following day see whether she smells of garlic through her mouth; if she smells, she will conceive; if not, she won't.

For other Egyptian birth prognoses see Grapow *et al.*, 1954-62, IV.1, pp. 272-6.

12 See Lefebvre, 1956, p. 90.
13 By Iverson, 1953, pp. 163-71, who compares wounds in the head described in the *Edwin Smith Papyrus* and in the Hippocratic treatise *De vulneribus in capite*. See, however, Majno, 1975, p. 499, n. 283.
14 For other (dubious) parallels drawn between Egyptian and Greek medicine see Ebbell, 1937, p. 129; Steuer, 1948; Steuer and Saunders, 1959. See also Saunders, 1963, pp. 20-3 and J. R. Harris, 1971, Chap. 5.
15 With Thivel, 1981, p. 320.
16 See, for example, *De vetere medicina*, Chapter 3, and Plato, *Republic* 405aff.
17 Pliny the Elder, however, considers the possibility that the art of medicine was invented by the Egyptians (*N.H.* VII, 56, 196; but see XXIX, 1ff.).
18 See von Staden, 1989, p. 4, who cites here Diodorus Siculus I, 182.
19 See Fränkel, 1960, pp. 331ff. and Frazer, 1972, pp. 235-8.
20 Fränkel, 1975, p. 118.
21 Lloyd, 1987, p. 17 n. 52.
22 Elsewhere in Homer wounds are treated without recourse to chants and charms. But here too, we may note, the healers are frequently of semi-divine status like Podalirius and Machaeon, the sons of Asclepius, and Achilles, who learned medicine from the Centaur Chiron. When Patroclus treats the wound of Eurypylus (*Il.* XI. 829ff.) he apparently does so upon the basis of knowledge learned from Achilles.
23 *History of the Peloponnesian War* II. 47.
24 Pliny, *N.H.* XXV, 23, 58.
25 There is a famous etching of the island of San Bartolemmeo by Piranesi.

26 I.G.II²4960a.
27 See Semeria, 1986, pp. 931-58.
28 The burning of the temple is not explicitly attributed by Pliny to Hippocrates. Strabo (*Geographia* XIV, 2, 19) is aware of the tradition of Hippocrates' use of the Coan *iamata*, but makes no reference to the burning of the temple. In a similar tale told some three centuries earlier by the physician Andreas, Hippocrates is represented as having burned not the temple at Cos, but the library at Cnidus. See [Soranus] *Vita Hippocratis* 4 (Ilberg, 1927, p. 175).
29 Littré, 1839-61, vol. I, p. 9.
30 Andreas' substitution of the destruction of a library for that of a temple may well indicate his own dissatisfaction with the story.
31 Herzog, 1899, pp. 204ff. See too Herzog, 1931, pp. 148ff.
32 Herzog, 1931, p. 148. (*Arch. Anz.* (1903) pp. 198-9.)
33 For a clear statement of this view see, for example, Tuke, 1910-11, pp. 517-19 - cited by Withington, 1921, p. 192.
34 For a recent statement of this view see Sherwin-White, 1978, p. 261.
35 W. D. Smith, 1990, p. 9.
36 Sherwin-White, 1978, p. 261.
37 W. D. Smith, 1990, p. 11.
38 XLVIII, 17. See Lloyd, 1979, p. 45 n. 193.
39 Edelstein and Edelstein, 1945, vol. II, p. 112 n. 4; Lloyd, 1979, p. 41.
40 Parker, 1983, p. 249.
41 See *De morbo sacro*, Chapter 4, where it is implied that there is no incompatibility between what the author regards as true religious belief and rational medicine. Lloyd, however (1979, p. 46 n. 197), points to one case (Case 48, Herzog, 1931, p. 28) where the god forbids a patient to follow a treatment recommended by a doctor; but as the prescribed treatment involved cautery this interdiction may have been due to the drastic nature of that treatment. Yet, at a later date, Aelius Aristides provides several instances where the diagnoses and therapies of ordinary physicians are overruled by the god.
42 Edelstein and Edelstein, 1945, vol. II, p. 139.
43 See too Diodorus, Frag. XXX.43 (Dindorf), where it is observed that 'when the doctors' therapy fails, their patients resort to incantations and prayers' and Pliny, *N.H.* XXX, 98.

2 Ionian natural philosophy and the origins of rational medicine

1 At *De decenti habitu*, Chapter 6, however (IX.235L. - where the text is corrupt), it seems to be suggested that, though physicians are the agents, the gods are the real cause of cures in medicine and in surgery. The author of *De victu* IV, Chapters 89 (VI.652L.) and 90 (VI.656L.) prescribes prayers as a third remedy after exercise and diet. Mansfeld, 1980, p. 378, believes that the resort to prayer in these passages represents only an apparent exception to the normal

NOTES

Hippocratic outlook and that the attitude of our author towards
such matters is (otherwise) 'an enlightened and critical one'. He
cites Chapters 87 (VI.642L.) in support of his contention, but the
attitude revealed here does not seem to be in any way inconsistent
with that displayed in Chapters 89 and 90. Joly, it may be noted, is
equally unpersuasive in suggesting that the author has transferred
these prayers (complaisamment) from his source (1967, ad loc. and
1960, p. 171).

2 Euripides, it may be noted, in a famous fragment (Frag. 910 Nauck =
   D.K.59A30) speaks of the happiness of the man who devotes his life
   to the study of 'the ageless order of the undying nature, whence it
   was composed and in what way'.
3 Aëtius records that Pythagoras himself was the first to use this term
   (I 3, 8 D.K.58B15).
4 Excepting, of course, the creation myth in the Timaeus. See Chapter
   5.
5 There is a good discussion of this background in Lloyd, 1979,
   pp. 264-7.
6 Theaetetus 155d.
7 Metaphysics 982b12ff.
8 Aristophanes, Pax 376.
9 Iliad XIII. 43.
10 Iliad I. 46-53. See above, Chapter 1, p. 11.
11 Metaphysics 983b17ff. (D.K11A12).
12 See Aristotle, De caelo 294a28ff. (D.K.11A14); Metaphysics 983b17ff.
   (D.K.11A12).
13 See Aëtius, II 20, 1; II 24, 2; II 25, 1 and II 29, 1 (D.K.12A21, 22).
14 See Hippolytus, Ref. I, 7, 4 (D.K.13A7); Aëtius II 14, 3-4
   (D.K.13A14) and II 22, 1 (D.K.13A15).
15 Aëtius II 13, 10 (D.K.13A14).
16 Physics, 203b13ff. (D.K.12B3, and 12A15).
17 Ref. I, 6, 1 (D.K.12B2, and A11).
18 Aëtius, I 7, 13 and Cicero, De natura deorum, I, 10, 26 (D.K.13A10).
   The dictum 'all things are full of gods', cautiously attributed to
   Thales by Aristotle (De anima 411a7ff. D.K.11A22), should also be
   considered within this context. The interpretation of this assertion
   is highly controversial, but it could very well entail both that
   Thales, like his Milesian successors, considered his own first
   principle, water, to be divine and that he regarded all natural
   phenomena also as divine. Aristotle, it should be noted, connects
   this dictum with the belief of other thinkers that 'soul is mingled in
   the whole' and, earlier in the De anima (405a19ff. D.K.11A22), he
   tells us that Thales seems to have identified soul and life with the
   cause of motion if he said that the Magnesian stone possesses soul
   because it makes iron move.
19 Hippolytus, Ref. I, 7, 1 (D.K.13A7) and Augustine, De civitate dei,
   VIII, 2 (D.K.13A10).
20 Aëtius, I 3, 20 (D.K.31B6).
21 Fragment 21.12.

22 Fragments 21.12, 23.8.
23 In Fragment B6 the four elements are actually named as Zeus, Hera, Aidoneus and Nestis. See Arist. *De gen. et corr.* 331621 (*D. K.* 31A40).
24 See Fragment 8 (*D.K.*64B8).
25 Vlastos, 1952, pp. 116, 117 (reprinted in Allen and Furley, 1970, p. 119).
26 Jaeger, 1939-45, vol. III (4), p. 4.
27 Herodotus mentions at Histories VII, 99 the tradition of emigration from Dorian Epidaurus to Cos, and Cnidus itself claimed descent from Sparta.
28 It should not be overlooked that Halicarnassus, Herodotus' birthplace, was also a Dorian foundation, settled originally by Dorian colonists from Troezen (VII, 99). Thus the development of Greek historiography affords a striking parallel to that of rational medicine in Greece in that both fields of inquiry originated in Dorian settlements, both are expounded in Ionic and both owe their impetus to Ionian natural philosophy.
29 That is, in the modern sense of the word: in the Hippocratic *Corpus* the term 'epidemic' denotes a disease that visits a region from time to time, a disease observable in a given place during a given time.
30 See *De natura hominis* 9, 44ff. and *De flatibus* 6, 19. The outbreak of winter coughing at Perinthus, described in clinical detail in *Epidemiarum Liber* VI, 7 is similarly linked with atmospheric changes. See also Galen's comments (Wenkebach and Pfaff, 1956, p. 386, *Corpus Medicorum Graecorum* V, 10, 2, 2). This outbreak has been widely regarded since Littré (1839-61, vol. V, pp. 330-6) as a specific epidemic (in the modern sense) of a single disease. Grmek, however (1989, p. 320), has persuasively argued that the description here embraces not one, but several diseases, and that the Hippocratic writer is offering in reality 'an overview of the climatic conditions and seasonal endemic and epidemic diseases that prevailed in Perinthus over a specific winter and spring'.
31 For the relationship between Thucydides and contemporary medicine see, in particular, Longrigg, 1992a, pp. 30ff., and, generally, Rechenauer, 1991, *passim.*
32 See Diodorus Siculus (XII, 58, 6) and Longrigg, 1992a, p. 43 n. 32.
33 For references see Longrigg, 1992a, p. 42.
34 XII, 45, 2.
35 Diodorus Siculus, XII, 58.
36 XIV, 70, 4.
37 For Herodotus' attitude in this respect see especially Lloyd, 1979, pp. 30ff.
38 All three of the above examples are discussed by Lloyd, 1979, pp. 30ff.
39 *De morbo sacro*, Chapter 1. See especially van der Eijk, 1990, p. 113.

40 As Green appositely remarks (1990, p. 489) 'there could be no better simultaneous demonstration of the glories and shortcomings of Greek medicine.'

41 Jaeger, 1947, p. 31 n. 44.

42 See van der Eijk, 1990, p. 117.

43 See, for example, von Wilamowitz-Moellendorff, 1901, pp. 16ff.; Diller, 1934, pp. 94ff.; Grensemann, 1968b, pp. 7-18.

44 See Halliday, 1910-11, pp. 95-102, who points out that this is unlikely to have been a true Scythian belief.

45 Lloyd, 1979, p. 25.

46 This mode of argument is nowadays more usually called the 'denial of the consequent', i.e. if A, then B; but not-B, therefore not-A.

47 See, generally, Lonie, 1981, pp. 110ff.

48 Clarke, 1963a, p. 303.

49 There is a discussion and partial translation of this text by King 1983, pp. 109-41.

50 See, generally, Simon, 1978.

51 See especially the discussions in Simon, 1978, Chapter 11 and Lloyd, 1979, Chapter 1.

52 Lloyd, 1987, p. 28.

53 See Aëtius, I 3, 4 (D.K.13B2) and Longrigg, 1964, pp. 1-4.

54 See, for example, Clement, *Stromateis* VI, 16 (D.K.22B36); Stobaeus, *Florilegium* III 5, 7 (D.K.22B117), and ibid., III, 5, 8 (D.K.22B118).

55 Burnet, 1930, p. 201 n. 4, cited in Introduction, p. 3.

3 Philosophy and medicine in the fifth century I

1 Some scholars translate φῦμα as 'tumour' and believe that Atossa was suffering from breast cancer, e.g. Kôrbler, 1973, pp. 8-10 but it seems more likely that her affliction was an inflammatory mastitis. See Sandison, 1959, pp. 317-22 and Grmek, 1989, pp. 350ff.

2 A sceptical attitude towards the circumstantial details of Herodotus' account is taken by Griffiths, 1987, pp. 37-51.

3 Heidel, 1941, p. 42.

4 For these descriptions see C. R. S. Harris, 1973, p. 5 n. 2.

5 Harris himself more persuasively describes him as 'one of the great pioneers of rational . . . medicine' (1973, p. 9).

6 Iamblichus, *V.P.* 104 (D.K.67A5) and Philoponus, *In de anima* 405a 29, p. 88 (Hayduck).

7 Diogenes Laërtius, VIII, 83 (D.K.24A1).

8 Wachtler, however (1896, p. 104), stoutly denied this.

9 Brotinus is variously described as the father-in-law of Pythagoras or as married to a female pupil of Pythagoras (D.K.17.1). See n.19 below. The two others named here are listed as Pythagoreans by Iamblichus, *V.P.* 267 (D.K.58A1).

10 See Zafiropulo, 1953, p. 60; Sambursky, 1956, p. 53. According to Burnet (1930, p. 193) 'he was intimately connected with the society.'

11 See, for example, Heidel, 1941, p. 45; Vlastos, 1953, p. 344 and Guthrie, 1962, p. 341.
12 Burnet, 1930, pp. 194ff.
13 Ross, 1924, Note on *Metaphysics* 986a27ff.; Heidel, 1940, p. 4.
14 See Vlastos, 1953, p. 344 n. 25.
15 Vlastos, 1953, p. 345.
16 Lloyd's dating of Alcmaeon 'about the middle or end of the fifth century' (reported by Guthrie, 1962, p. 342 n. 1) is in my opinion a little too late.
17 *De elem. sec. Hipp.* I, 9 (I.487K., 54,18 Helmr. *D.K.*24A2).
18 Diogenes Laërtius, V, 25.
19 Some MSS record his name as Brontinus.
20 Diogenes Laërtius, VIII, 83 (*D.K.*24B1). The text of this fragment is highly controversial and almost certainly corrupt. I follow here Wachtler's suggestion (1896, pp. 34-8). See app. crit. in Diels and Kranz, 1956 for other suggestions. The contrast, however, between divine and human knowledge is not affected.
21 It may be noted that, unlike the Pythagorean opposites, which were predominantly a set of semi-abstractions, Alcmaeon's own list comprises an indefinite number of physical qualities drawn from the world of experience.
22 Simplicius, *In physica* 24. 13 (*D.K.*12B1).
23 See Simplicius, *In physica* 32. 3 (*D.K.*31B98); Aëtius, V 22, 1 (*D.K.*31A78) and Theophrastus, *De sensibus* 10-11 (*D.K.*31A86).
24 *Anonymus Londinensis* XX, 25.
25 Its attraction for the latter was particularly strong, for his ethical theory of pleasure and pain, most fully expounded in *Republic* IX and in the *Philebus*, but equally implied in the *Protagoras*, *Gorgias* and *Timaeus*, represents an attempt to apply this medical theory in psychology.
26 Lloyd, 1975b, pp. 116ff.
27 As C. R. S. Harris has suggested, 1973, p. 6.
28 Lloyd, 1975b, p. 118 n. 22.
29 Lloyd, 1975b, p. 125.
30 In Empedocles' case the seat of the intellect is the blood round the heart (*D.K.*31B105).
31 *S.V.F* II.897. See Solmsen, 1961, p. 195.
32 Stella, 1939, p. 271.
33 *Apud* Oribasium III, 156 *C.M.G.* VI, 2, 2 (*D.K.*24A17).
34 Olivieri, 1919, p. 34.
35 Adopting here Reiske's emendation for the MSS ὁμόρους.
36 See Fredrich, 1899, p. 67.
37 C. R. S. Harris, 1973, p. 8.
38 See Tannery, 1887, p. 223; C. R. S. Harris, 1973, p. 8; and Lloyd, 1975b, p. 126.
39 *D.K.*28B1, 30.
40 *D.K.*28B8, 53ff.
41 See Table 1.
42 Simplicius, *In phys.* 152. 18 (*D.K.*64B6).

NOTES

43 ibid., 153. 12.
44 Alexander in his commentary on *Metaphysics* 984a3ff. (26. 21,
   *D.K.*38A6) tells us that Hippon used τὸ ὑγρὸν as a general term
   without specifying whether he meant water like Thales or air like
   Anaximenes and Diogenes. Simplicius (*In phys.* 23. 22 *D.K.*38A6),
   however, does not hesitate to link him with Thales in declaring
   water to be the 'αρχή.
45 This association of the living with wetness and the dead with
   dryness is, of course, an archaic one: see, for example, Homer,
   Odyssey VI. 201; *Iliad* IV. 487 and, generally, Onians, 1951,
   pp. 254ff. and Lloyd, 1966, pp. 45ff.
46 See Menon, *Anonymus Londinesis* XI, 22 (*D.K.*38A11), where these
   arguments are too specific simply to be the result of Peripatetic
   conjecture.
47 See Aristotle, *De anima* 405b2ff. (*D.K.*31A4) and also Hippolytus,
   Ref. I, 16 (*D.K.*38A3). It is possible, however, that this particular
   physiological argument, too, was used in the sixth century. Aristotle's own knowledge of Thales' views is indirect and, although they
   reached him in an abbreviated form, they nevertheless appeared to
   fit his own idea of a material cause. At *Metaphysics* 983b17ff.
   (*D.K.*11A12) he includes this argument from the nature of the seed
   amongst his explicit physiological conjectures as to why Thales
   may have been led to put forward water as his αρχή. Burnet (1930,
   p. 48) objected to these conjectures on the ground that at the time of
   Thales the prevailing interests were not physiological but meteorological. But it is much too exaggerated a generalisation to maintain
   that the sixth-century thinkers were exclusively interested in
   meteorological phenomena. Much of the pre-philosophical
   speculation in Greece has a strong genealogical colouring and the
   analogy of physiological reproduction is in evidence (see Onians,
   1951, pp. 247ff.). Moreover, as Baldry has pointed out (1932, p. 28),
   'an interest in birth and other phenomena connected with sex is a
   regular feature of primitive societies long before other aspects of
   biology are even thought of.'
48 *De generatione et corruptione* 324b26 (*D.K.*31A86). See further
   Longrigg 1963, Appendix B.
49 Fragment 17, 22ff.
50 S. in Gregor. Naz. XXXVI 911 Migne (*D.K.*59B10).
51 *In phys.* 460. 4ff. (*D.K.*59A45).
52 See, for example, Jaeger, 1947, p. 156; Vlastos, 1950, pp. 31–57;
   Longrigg, 1963, p. 158 and Kucharski, 1964, p. 153.
53 See Vlastos, 1950, p. 32.
54 *In phys.* 460.28.
55 On this point see Jaeger, 1947, p. 157; Longrigg, 1963, p. 159 and
   Kucharski, 1964, p. 138.
56 For Aristotle's assessment of Hippon see *Metaphysics* 984a3ff.
   (*D.K.*38A7) and *De anima* 405b1ff (*D.K.*31A4).
57 For his role, however, in the development of the semen theory

GREEK RATIONAL MEDICINE

which was dominant in antiquity to Galen and beyond see Longrigg 1985a, pp. 277ff.

58 According to Diogenes Laërtius (X, 13 *D.K.*67A2), Epicurus declared that there never was such a philosopher as Leucippus and this statement has, surprisingly, been accepted by some scholars and a considerable controversy has arisen (for details see *D.K.* vol. II, notes to pp. 71-2). It seems more likely that Leucippus was overshadowed by Democritus and Diogenes' remark stems from a disparaging remark by Epicurus (see Burnet, 1930, p. 330 n. 2).

59 Celsus also says that, according to some, Hippocrates was a student of Democritus (*De medicina*, Proem, 8). The Suda elsewhere, however, states that Hippocrates was a pupil of Democritus' pupil Metrodorus of Chios.

60 See Diogenes Laërtius IX, 42 (*D.K.*68A1) and Hippocrates, IX.350L.

61 Letters of Hippocrates, IX. 320L. and W. D. Smith, 1990. See, generally, Pohlenz, 1917, pp. 348-53; Temkin, 1985, pp. 455-64; and Pinault, 1983 and 1992.

62 Aristotle, *De respiratione* 471b30ff. (*D.K.*68A106). See too *De anima* 404a9ff., where Aristotle mentions both Leucippus and Democritus as holding this belief.

63 Aëtius, V 25, 3 (*D.K.*67A34).

64 For Empedocles' theory of sex differentiation see Longrigg, 1964b, pp. 297-300.

65 It has been maintained that Anaxagoras and not Democritus was the true originator of the pangenesis theory. See, for example, Pohlenz, 1953, p. 437. (Lesky, 1951, p. 1276 also admits that Anaxagoras must have held this theory, but she does not elaborate the point and elsewhere regards Democritus as the real originator of the theory (pp. 1294-7).) However, as Lonie points out (1981, p. 66 n. 84), if Anaxagoras did hold this theory, he did not make it explicit or, apparently, provide supporting arguments.

66 See *De genitura*, Chapters 3 and 8-11; *De aere aquis locis* 14.5 = II,66.1L. and *De morbo sacro* 2 = VI,364.19L.

67 Diogenes Laërtius, VIII, 59 (*D.K.*31B111).

68 See Longrigg, 1993, pp. 37ff.

69 See Karsten, 1838, p. 148 and Mullach, 1881, vol. III, p. 14.

70 By Karsten, 1838, p. 71.

71 See Simplicius, *In phys.* 32. 3 (*D.K.*31B98); Aëtius, V 22, 1 (*D.K.*31A78) and Theophrastus, *De sensibus* 10-11 (*D.K.*31A86). According to a later source (Caelius Aurelianus, *Morb. chron.* I, 5 *D.K.*31A98) he held that pathological madness had a natural, somatic origin and was caused by an 'unbalanced nature', i.e. of the elements in the blood.

72 For whiteness associated with this element see Frag. 21.3; Theophrastus, *De sensibus* 7 (*D.K.*31A86), and 59 (*D.K.*31A69a).

73 For the hardening role of fire see Aëtius, III 16, 3 (*D.K.*31A66); [Aristotle] *Problems* 24. 11 937a11, and Plutarch, *De primo frigido* 19, 4 p. 953e (*D.K.*31A69).

74 *In de anima* 68. 5 Hayduck (*D.K.*31B96).

75 *In de anima* 178. 6 Hayduck.

76 *De sensibus* 23 (*D.K.*31A86).

77 *In de anima* 68. 5, 178. 6.

78 Aëtius V 22, 1 (*D.K.*31A78), V 26, 4 (*D.K.*31A70).

79 Theophrastus, *De sensibus* 7 (*D.K.*31A86) and Frags 84, 85 and 109.

80 Or 'round-eyed baby girl'.

81 Or 'fine linen (swaddling clothes)'.

82 I discuss this matter in my Oxford research thesis 'The Sun and the Planets' (1960) Appendix D, pp. 203–6. See too the discussion in O'Brien (1970, pp. 140ff.), who provides (p. 157 n. 3) a bibliography of earlier interpretations of Empedocles' theory of vision.

83 Simplicius describes the process in Peripatetic terminology (*In phys.* 371. -33.*D.K.*31B61). For the concept of σῆψις in Empedocles see Aristotle, *De gen. an.* 777a7 (*D.K.*31A68); Plutarch, *Quaest. nat.* 2, 912C (*D.K.*31B81) and [Galen] *Definitiones medicae* 99 (XIX.372K. and *D.K.*31A77).

84 For evidence that Empedocles subscribed to this concept see Aëtius IV 22, 1 (*D.K.*31A74); V 27, 1 (*D.K.*31A77); V 24, 2 and V 25, 4 (*D.K,*31A85). See too Longrigg, 1965, pp. 314–15; O'Brien, 1970, p. 167 n. 131; and Longrigg, 1974, p. 173.

85 Simplicius, *In phys.* 371. 33. See p. 215n. 183.

86 With Guthrie, 1965, p. 213 n. 2.

87 See Theophrastus, *De sensibus* 3 (*D.K.*28A46).

88 See, for example, Philolaus (*Anon. Lond.* XVIII, 8 *D.K.*44A27); Hippon (Aristotle, *De anima* 405b24ff. and Philoponus, *De anima* 92, 2 *D.K.*38A10) and Diogenes (Aëtius, V 15, 4 *D.K.*64A28).

89 See, for example, *De natura hominis* 12; *De victu* 2, 60–2; *De carnibus* 2ff., 6 and *De corde* 6; and, for Philistion: Galen, *De usu respirationis* 1, 1 (IV.471K.); for Plato: *Timaeus* 79b–79c; for Aristotle, *De partibus animalium* 650a3ff., *De anima* 416b28ff., *De iuventute* 470a19ff. and *De generatione animalium* 732b31ff., 733b1ff. See, generally, Solmsen, 1957, pp. 119–23.

90 See Longrigg, 1965, pp. 314–15.

91 See *Timaeus* 70d, 78e and 79e.

92 Galen, *De usu respirationis* 1, 1 (IV.471K.).

93 See *De partibus animalium* 668b34ff. and *De respiratione* 475b17ff.

94 Namely, Philolaus, Hippon and Diogenes. (For references see n. 88 above.)

95 Solmsen, 1950, p. 454.

96 Solmsen, 1965, p. 137 n. 78 (but see Longrigg, 1985a, p. 285 n. 21).

97 Another instance of Empedocles' exploitation of word play in a biological context may be seen in his use of the word *amnion* 'sheepskin' to describe the fine inner membrane surrounding the foetus (Rufus, *De corp. hum. part. app.* 229 p. 166 Daremberg *D.K.*31B70 and Pollux, *Onomasticon* ii 2225, i 155.8 Bethe - not cited in *D.K.*). In Homer, however, this word is used of the bowl in which the blood of the sacrificial victims is collected (see *Od.* III. 444 and *schol. in loc.*). The Hippocratic treatise *De natura pueri* 14ff.

describes how the mother's blood is drawn into the foetal membrane where it coagulates to form the flesh of the growing embryo.

98 See Diels and Kranz, 1956, vol. I, p. 283 note *ad loc.: sicher Empedokles gemeint.*

99 Guthrie, 1969, p. 303.

100 See, for example, Macrobius, *In Somnium Scipionis* I 14, 19 (Diels, 1879, p. 213); Tertullian, *De anima* 5 (Diels, 1879, p. 212), and Galen, *De placitis Hippocratis et Platonis* 2, 8 (V.283K.).

101 While the evidence is not conclusive that Diogenes was actually a doctor, we seem to have some indications of his medical interests. We learn from Theophrastus (*De sensibus* 43 *D.K.*64A19) and from the anonymous author of a medical treatise ([Galen] *De humoribus* XIX.495K. *D.K.*64A29a) that Diogenes believed in the possibility of diagnosis by the tongue and the patient's colour. It is possible that the Diogenes cited by Galen as the author of a medical treatise on diseases, their causes and remedies, may have been the Apolloniate (*On Medical Experience* 22, 3, translated from the Arabic by R.Walzer). In his commentary upon the *Epidemics* (*In Hippocratis Epidemiarum Libros VI, Commentarius* 2 (XVII.1006K. = *D.K.*64B9)) Galen further informs us that while almost all the doctors are agreed that the male was not only formed before the female but was also the first to move, Rufus said that Diogenes alone disagreed with this. (Rufus' assertion, incidentally, is inconsistent with that of Censorinus at *De die natali* 9, 2 *D.K.*64A26.) This passage is by no means conclusive in itself that Diogenes was a doctor but it seems to suggest that Galen regarded him as such.

102 This idea Diogenes may have derived from Heraclitus, see Stob. *Flor.* III 5, 7 (*D.K.*22B117) and ibid. III 5, 8 (*D.K.*22B118).

103 But see, however, Aëtius, IV 5, 7 (*D.K.*64A20), where he is said to have situated the seat of the intellect in the heart. Some scholars, however, have found this testimony unacceptable and have suggested that 'Diocles' should be substituted in place of the MSS 'Diogenes' (see Chapter 6, p. 171 and n. 70).

104 See Longrigg, 1985a, p. 279.

105 See *De generatione animalium* 726b1-11, and 735b32ff.

106 See ibid., 736a14ff. and Galen, *De semine* 1, 5 (IV.531K.).

107 See, for example, Vindicianus, *Fragmentum*, para. 1 (Wellmann, 1901, p. 208).

108 For the influence of this conception of the semen via Aristotle upon the Stoics, see Lesky, 1951, pp. 1388ff. and Hahm, 1977, p. 70.

109 See *De semine* 1 & 2 *passim* (IV.512-651K.).

110 See, for example, Pohlenz, 1938, pp. 39ff. and Lesky, 1951, pp. 1345ff.

111 Jaeger, 1913, pp. 29-74, esp. 51-7.

112 Solmsen, 1957, p. 120.

113 For the development of the doctrine of the *pneuma* generally see especially Verbeke, 1945.

4 Philosophy and medicine in the fifth century II

1 The actual mention of Empedocles here in Chapter 20 was not in fact realised until Littré discovered this citation in MS A. This restoration provides an important indication of the date of *V. M.* See the discussions in Longrigg, 1989, p. 15 n. 55 and Jouanna, 1990, p. 84.

2 In assigning a restricted sense to 'nature' here I am in agreement with Jouanna, 1990, p. 146 n. 5.

3 Plutarch, *Pericles* 26ff. (*D.K.*30A3).

4 Diogenes Laërtius, IX, 24 (*D.K.*30A1).

5 See Chapter 3, p. 64.

6 See Chapter 3, p. 64.

7 See Chapter 3, p. 77.

8 See Jouanna's perceptive remarks (1965, pp. 306-23).

9 Jouanna, 1965, p. 309.

10 For further similarities see Jouanna, 1965, p. 310.

11 Aëtius, IV 9, 15 and V 28 (*D.K.*31A95). See too Theophrastus, *De sens.* 9, 10, 16 (*D.K.*31A86). Burnet, however, believes (1930, p. 326) that Melissus' reference here is to Anaxagoras' theory that perception always involves pain (see Theophrastus, *De sens.* 29 (*D.K.*59A92) and Aristotle, *E.N.* 1154b7).

12 Diller, 1941, p. 366.

13 Jouanna, 1965, pp. 321ff.

14 With Jouanna, 1965, p. 322.

15 For the influence of Empedocles upon *De natura hominis* see Fredrich, 1899, pp. 28-32; Diepgen, 1949, pp. 81ff.; and the editions of Villaret, 1911, pp. 65ff. and Jouanna, 1975, pp. 43ff.

16 See Chapter 3, p. 53.

17 Chapters 7ff.

18 See Schöner, 1964, p. 100.

19 Lonie, 1981, p. 60. See too Grmek (1989, p. 1) who describes the theory of the humours as 'at once the logical consequence of Ionian philosophy and a . . . reflection of the pathological and clinical features of the ills actually suffered by Mediterranean populations'.

20 Langholf (1986, pp. 3-30), however, argues that the *De flatibus* was known to Callimachus, that it is this work that is referred to at *Anonymus Londinesis* V, 35-VII, 40, and that consequently it may be identified as a genuine work of Hippocrates.

21 The influence of Diogenes may also be detected in the account of the venous system outlined in *De morbo sacro*, Chapter 3. Aristotle preserves Diogenes' own account at *Historia animalium* 511b30ff. (*D.K.*64B6). The similarities between the two accounts are clearly apparent.

22 Lonie, 1981, p. 63. See too Heidel, 1941, p. 18 who makes the same observation.

23 Wellmann, 1929a, pp. 297-330.

24 Fredrich, however (1899, p. 48 n. 1), is of the opinion that *De morbis* IV was earlier, though by the same author, while Joly (1970, p. 12) now believes that the two works were originally separate, but

later combined and issued as a single work. Kahlenberg (1955,
pp. 252-6) seems to be alone in attacking the belief in a single
authorship.
25 *Nat. an.* XII. 18-20 (*D.K*.68A153-5).
26 Aëtius, V 22, 1 (*D.K*.31A78).
27 Wellmann, 1929a, pp. 306-9.
28 Aëtius, V 3, 6 (*D.K*.68A141).
29 Lesky, 1951, pp. 1294-7.
30 Wellmann, 1929a, p. 304.
31 Lonie, 1981, p. 253.
32 *Nat. an.* XII. 16 (*D.K*.68A151).
33 Aristotle, *De generatione animalium* 764a6ff. (*D.K*.68A143).
34 For the eclectic nature of his borrowings from earlier pre-Socratic
philosophers see especially Lonie, 1981, pp. 126ff.
35 For these philosophical influences see especially Joly, 1960,
pp. 23ff., 89, 205; Kucharski, 1964, pp. 153-61; and Peck, 1926,
p. 69.
36 *De medicina*, III 4, 15.
37 On the relationship between Empedocles and Diogenes see Chapter
3, p. 79.
38 Heidel, 1941, p. 18.
39 Lonie, 1981, p. 61.
40 For a similar case with a happier outcome see *Epidemiarum Liber*
III, Case 10 (III.130L.).
41 With Mansfeld, 1980, p. 381, who observes, 'it is the enlightened
theoretical attitude which makes the enlightened empirical attitude
possible.'
42 See, for example, Plato, *Apology* 18bff. and Aristophanes, *Nubes*
187ff.
43 Festugière, 1948, p. 43.
44 Considerable controversy has arisen over the import of this phrase:
whether the sensation here referred to is that of the doctor tending
the patient or, conversely, that of the patient's body itself. For a
recent discussion see Jouanna, 1990, p. 174.
45 See Guthrie (1962, p. 344), who is here paraphrasing Cornford.
46 Sextus is only one of several authors to preserve this fragment. He
quotes these lines in whole or part no less than four times (*Adversus
mathematicos* VII, 49 and 110; VIII, 326; *Pyrrhoniae hypotyposes* II,
18). They are also quoted by Plutarch, Galen, Proclus, Diogenes
Laërtius, Epiphanius and Origen. For full references see Karsten,
1830, p. 51. Fränkel analyses these sources (1925, pp. 174-92).
47 See Sextus, *Adversus mathematicos* VII, 49.
48 ibid., p. 110.
49 See Reinhardt, 1916, p. 118 and Fränkel, 1925, p. 190.
50 As Barnes has persuasively suggested (1982, p. 138).
51 ibid., p. 139. These affinities between Xenophanes, Alcmaeon, and
De vetere medicina were pointed out earlier by Fränkel, 1925,
pp. 190-2 and 1974, pp. 118-31.
52 *Prometheus Vinctus* 442-68, 478-506.

53 *Antigone* 332-71.

54 *Supplices* 201-13.

55 Sextus, *Adversus mathematicos* IX, 54 (*D.K.*88B25).

56 Guthrie, 1969, p. 62.

57 Cornford, 1952, p. 42.

5 Post-Hippocratic medicine I

1 Wellmann, 1901, p. 68.

2 Burnet, 1930, pp. 200ff.

3 The Suda *s.v.* Acron.

4 Wellmann, 1901, p. 70.

5 See the Ps. Galenic treatise *Introductio seu medicus* 4 (XIV.683K. = Wellmann, 1901, p. 108).

6 See Diogenes Laërtius, VIII, 8, 86.

7 See, for example, Burnet, 1930, p. 228; Kirk, 1954, p. 154 and Raven in Kirk and Raven, 1957, p. 329.

8 See Chapters 1 and 20.

9 The qualities of earth are given as 'heavy and hard' by Aristotle at *De generatione et corruptione* 315a11ff.

10 See Fragments 65, 67, 75, 90 and 104.

11 See *Anonymus Londinensis* XX, 25 (Wellmann, 1901, p. 110) and Galen, *De usu respirationis* 1, 1 (IV.471K. = Wellmann, 1901, p. 112).

12 Wellmann, for example, remarks 'seine Atmungstheorie ist empedokleisch' (1901, p. 111). See too Burnet, 1930, p. 245.

13 On this fragment see especially Last, 1924, pp. 169-73; Furley, 1957, pp. 31-4; Booth, 1960, pp. 10-15 and, most persuasive in my view, O'Brien, 1970, pp. 140-79.

14 VIII, 8, 86 Frag. 2 Wellmann, 1901, p. 110.

15 See Athenaeus, II, 59ff.

16 Although the authenticity of the Seventh Letter is much disputed, the information it provides may nevertheless be accurate. For discussions of this controversy see Edelstein, 1966 and, more recently, Brisson, 1987.

17 For Plato's description of the varieties of the primary bodies see *Tim.* 57c6-d7, 58c5.

18 For Empedocles' amalgamation of these theories see Chapter 3, p. 53.

19 For Philistion's influence upon Plato see Fredrich, 1899, pp. 46-8; Wellmann, 1901, pp. 81-5, and Jaeger, 1938a, pp. 8-11, 211-13. Another instance of the direct influence of Philistion upon Plato may be seen at *Timaeus* 70c (see too 91a), where Plato puts forward the mistaken belief that some part of what is drunk passes down the windpipe and enters the lungs. Philistion is cited as an advocate of this theory by Plutarch (*Quaestiones conviviales* VII, 1, 699bff. (Wellmann, 1901, p. 112)). This misconception was widely held in antiquity; but in view of Plato's declared belief that the function of this liquid is to cool the heart, it seems likely that he is directly

dependent upon Philistion here. See Lonie's comprehensive discussion of this matter (1981, pp. 361ff).

20 Cornford, 1937, p. 336.

21 Solmsen, 1950, p. 457 n. 89.

22 ibid., p. 454.

23 At *Anon. Lond.* XI, 14, however, it is recorded that Thrasymachus of Sardis held that blood was the cause of disease when it was changed, due to fluctuations of temperature, into phlegm, bile or pus. This theory has certain affinities with the Platonic doctrine. Unfortunately, since no other information regarding Thrasymachus has survived, it is impossible to say whether he influenced Plato or was himself influenced by him.

24 During and Owen, 1960, p. 219.

25 See Longrigg, 1985c, pp. 109ff.

26 Taylor, 1928, p. 11.

27 Diogenes Laërtius, VIII, 79 *D.K.*47A1.

28 See the construction and its proof given in full by Eutocius of Ascalon in Archimedes, *Sphaer. et Cyl.* II (iii, 84 Heib. *D.K.*47A14).

29 *In Ptol. harm.* p. 56 Düring. *D.K.*47B1.

30 IV 1, 139. See Iambl., *D. comm. math. sc.* 11, p. 44. 10 Fest. *D.K.*47B3.

31 See, for example, *De fin.* V, 87; *Tusc. disp.* I, 39 and *De republica* I, 10.

32 See Aristotle, *Metaphysics* 986a2ff.

33 This belief is clearly apparent at *Republic* 500c9 and *Timaeus* 47b-c, 90c-d. It also appears in the *Gorgias* 507e6, where Socrates does not claim the idea as his own, but appeals to the authority of 'the wise', whose identification with the Pythagoreans has been widely and correctly recognised. See, for example, Delatte, 1922, p. 100.

34 See Longrigg, 1985c, pp. 102ff.

35 Cicero, *De oratore* III, 34, 139 *D.K.*44A3.

36 By Cornford, 1937, p. 167.

37 *Phaedo* 97bff. See too Aristotle, *Metaphysics* 985a18 *D.K.*59A47, where this criticism is repeated.

38 See Taylor, 1928, p. 353.

39 *Physics* 198b17ff.

40 See Porphyry, *In Ptol. harm.* p. 92 (*D.K.*47B2), who preserves here a fragment of the latter's work *On music.*

41 See Aristotle, *De generatione animalium* 736b30ff. *D.K.*59A107.

42 Crombie aptly describes it (1963, vol. 2, p. 224) as 'the ghost of the Pythagorean "unlimited", the germ of Aristotle's "matter" and of Locke's "something, I know not what" '.

43 Solmsen, 1960, p. 49.

44 Cornford, 1937, p. 210.

45 It is noteworthy, however, as Sambursky points out (1962, p. 30) that he upholds one of the Atomists' principles when he maintains that shape is the determining factor for the physical behaviour of the elements.

46 8, 25 *D.K.*58B1A.

NOTES

47 For a survey of these conflicting views see Guthrie 1962, p. 201 n. 3, who is himself prepared to accept that this account contains some genuinely early Pythagorean elements.

48 Popper 1952, pp. 150ff. and 1966, vol. I, pp. 248-53.

49 Of the fifth regular solid, the dodecahedron, Plato merely says (55c) that 'the god used it for the whole, making a pattern of animal figures upon it.' (The reference here is most probably to the twelve signs of the zodiac and the other constellations.) The dodecahedron is not constructed like the other regular solids. Its pentagonal faces, in any case, cannot be formed out of either of the two elementary triangles. It is used by Plato to denote the spherical heavens. It seems that he has in mind here a flexible dodecahedron capable of expansion into a spherical shape. There is a similar idea in the *Phaedo* 110b5, where Socrates points out that if the earth were seen from above, it would resemble 'those balls made out of twelve [pentagonal-shaped] pieces of leather'.

50 Plato thus weaves together the four element theory of Empedocles, Pythagorean mathematics and Democritean atomism. It is noteworthy that more than two thousand years before Dalton, each element is given a corpuscular structure of its own. It is also of interest to observe that whereas in the *Timaeus* the tetrahedron is the corpuscle of fire, the French mathematician and philosopher Gassendi made it the corpuscle of frost. Both he and Plato rather naïvely account for the sensation of prickling by the sharpness of the angles of this figure.

51 See Longrigg, 1985c, pp. 109ff.

52 *Timaeus* 57a.

53 See Longrigg, 1985c, pp. 101ff.

54 *Timaeus* 73a3-8. One is reminded here of Diogenes' association of lower intelligence, in the case of birds, with rapid digestion (Theophrastus, *De sensibus* 44 D.K. 64A19).

55 In Fragment 34 Empedocles also uses the illustration of the baker in an unspecified context. It is possible that these words are also derived from an account of bone and that Plato has followed Empedocles in using this simile here too.

56 For the hardening role of fire in Empedoclean physics see Aëtius, III 16, 3 (*D.K.*31A66), [Aristotle] *Problems* 24, 11, 937a11 and Plutarch, *De primo frigido* 19, 4, 953e (*D.K.*31A69).

57 Taylor, 1928, p. 528.

58 See Aristotle, *De partibus animalium* 640a18ff. (*D.K.*31B97). On the implications of this text see Longrigg, 1973, p. 315.

59 All liquids contain an admixture of fire, see 59c.

60 Taylor, however (1928, p. 531), disagrees.

61 See *De locis in homine* 4 and Solmsen, 1950, p. 447.

62 Censorinus, *De die natali* 5, 2 (*D.K.*38A12).

63 Theophrastus, *De sensibus* 11 (*D.K.*31A86).

64 Aëtius, V 3, 3 (*D.K.*24A13).

65 Aristotle, it may be noted, who is always happy to find a duality of function, has no such reservations.

66 See Cornford, 1937, pp. 308ff., 311.
67 Galen, *De placitis Hippocratis et Platonis* 8, 8 (V.711K.). See too Aristotle, *De respiratione* 472b12ff.
68 At 68b red is described as the colour of fire gleaming through moisture.
69 Plato may have derived this idea from the Atomists, but it is already implicit in Empedocles.
70 Strictly speaking, it is implied elsewhere (78eff.) that the fire particles alone possess this function of cutting up the food. Here, however (81b-d), this capacity seems to be extended more widely.
71 This theory, too, seems to have been derived from Empedocles. See Aristotle, *De generatione et corruptione* 333a35 (*D.K.*31B37) and Aëtius, V 27, 1 (*D.K.*31A77).
72 Here Empedocles' original biological metaphor is adopted but reapplied to the components of the 'elements' rather than to the elements themselves.
73 Blood is formed by the action of the innate heat upon food and drink in the stomach and contains particles suitable for the nourishment of all the other tissues (*Tim.* 80dff.).
74 At 74c5-d2 flesh is described as a composition of water, fire and earth along with a ferment of acid and saline.
75 Taylor, 1928, pp. 11, 592, 599.
76 See *Anon. Lond.* XVIII, 41ff. (*D.K.*44A27), where Philolaus is said to have appealed to etymological support for his view.
77 See *Timaeus* 85b, where inflammations are held to be caused by bile, not phlegm.
78 See Wellmann, 1901, pp. 9ff.
79 See, for example, Heraclitus (Stob. *Flor.* III 5, 7 *D.K.*22B117 and ibid. III 5, 8 *D.K.*22B118); Empedocles (Caelius Aurelianus, *De morbis chronicis* 1 *D.K.*31A98); Democritus (Stob. *Flor.* III 1, 210 *D.K.*68B191); *De morbo sacro* 1; *De flatibus* 14; *De virginum morbis*.
80 For a valuable corrective to their attitude, however, see Miller, 1962, pp. 175-87 and Lloyd, 1968b, pp. 78-92.
81 Rivaud, 1925, pp. 114-15.
82 See *De sensu* 436a19ff. and *De respiratione* 480b24ff. (See also Introduction, p. 3 and Chapter 6, p. 150.)
83 With Lloyd, 1968b, p. 87.
84 Pointed out by Lloyd, 1979, p. 97 n. 203.

6 Post-Hippocratic medicine II

1 See Schmitt, 1985, p. 15.
2 Galen, *De anatomicis administrationibus* 2, 1 (II.280K.).
3 See, for example, *Hist. an.* 497a32; 509b23; 510a30; 511a13; 525a8; 565a13; 566a15 and *De gen. an.* 746a15.
4 *De respiratione* 480b22-30.
5 See Jones, 1947.
6 Hett's translation (Loeb edn, 1957) with slight modifications.

7 As Solmsen remarks (1960, p. 285), 'it is a measure of the hold which the doctrine had gained over his thought that not even the discrepancy between the number of the elements and that of natural movements (see *De caelo*, 302b5ff.) weakened his confidence.'
8 See Longrigg, 1985c, pp. 109ff.
9 *Metaph.* 989a19ff.
10 Simplicius, *In de caelo* 665.25 (Heiberg, 1894).
11 See *De caelo* 299a2ff.; 306a10ff.; *Metaph.* 1000a5-9; 1000b20-1001a34; 1060a27-36; 1075b13-14; *Anal. Prior.* 46a17ff and *Anal. Post.* 71b19-25.
12 Morrow, 1969, p. 154.
13 Solmsen, 1960, p. 261.
14 These two qualities, we may note, play a vital role in the deduction of the elements at *De caelo* 311a15ff.
15 *De generatione et corruptione* 329b32-330a26.
16 Aristotle is frequently inconsistent in this matter. At *Meteorol.* 382a3ff. water's dominant quality is said to be the moist and this is the view adopted throughout the whole of the *Meteorologica. De generatione et corruptione* 334b34ff. itself implies that water is predominantly moist.
17 Solmsen, 1960, p. 351.
18 *Timaeus* 57a3ff. and *De gen. et corr.* 323b18ff.; 323b29ff.; 324a5ff.
19 *Pace* Solmsen, 1960, p. 342, who declares that 'hot and cold, moist and dry are very familiar characters to students of ancient philosophy. . . . From the beginning of physical speculation . . . they have . . . persistently played important roles.'
20 For Diocles' subsequent correlation of the humoral theory with the element theory see below, n. 78.
21 *De resp.* 473a4; 474b12; 478a16-17 and *De anima*, 416a9-10.
22 *De generatione animalium* 737a11-12; 747a18.
23 See esp. *De part. an.* 651a33; 653a22-4 and *De resp.* 477b24.
24 *De resp.* 475b15ff.; 478a28ff.; *De part. an.* 642a31ff.; 668b33ff.
25 Lloyd, 1968a, p. 91.
26 See *De resp.* 471b20ff.; *De progressu animalium* 708b4ff. and *Historia animalium* 519a25ff.
27 *De anatomicis administrationibus* 2, 1 (II.282K.) and Aëtius, *Plac.* V 14, 2ff. (Diels, 1879, p. 425, 3) and Diokles, Frag. 29 (Wellmann, 1901).
28 Sarton, 1952, vol. I, p. 538.
29 Collected by Wellmann, 1901, pp. 117-207.
30 *N. H.* XXVI, 10: 'secundus aetate famaque extitit' = Diokles, Frag. 5 (Wellmann, 1901).
31 'Iuniorem Hippocratem' Chap.2 = Diokles, Frag. 2 (Wellmann, 1901).
32 Galen, *De methodo medendi* 7, 3 (X.462K.) = Diokles, Frag. 7 (Wellmann, 1901).
33 Galen, *De usu respirationis* 1 (IV.471K.) = Diokles, Frag. 15 (Wellmann, 1901).
34 Diokles, Frag. 14 (Wellmann, 1901).

35 See Aristotle, *De gen. an.* 777a7ff. (*D.K.*31B68) and Plutarch, *Quaest. nat.* 27 912c (*D.K.* 31B81) and Ps. Soranus, *Quaest. med.* 61 (= Diokles Frag. 22 Wellmann, 1901, p. 125.

36 See Oribasius III, 78 (*D.K.*31A83 and Diokles Frag. 175 Wellmann, 1901, p. 199).

37 See Soranus, *Gyn.* I, 21 p. 14, 9 (*D.K.*31A80 and Diokles Frag. 171 Wellmann, 1901, p. 196).

38 See Fredrich, 1899, pp. 171, 196 and Wilamowitz-Moellendorff, 1902, vol. II, p. 277.

39 Wellmann, 1901, pp. 66ff.

40 Rose, 1863, pp. 379-89 and Ideler, 1834, vol. I, p. 157.

41 Jaeger, 1913, pp. 29-74.

42 Jaeger, 1938a.

43 Jaeger, 1938b, pp. 1-46. The views expressed in both the book and in this paper are summarised by Jaeger in an article published two years later, 'Diocles of Carystus: a new pupil of Aristotle', 1940, pp. 393-414.

44 Athenaeus, II, 59a = Diokles, Frag. 125 (Wellmann, 1901).

45 Rose, 1863, pp. 379-80.

46 Edelstein, 1940, pp. 483-9.

47 *N. H.* XXXVI, 53.

48 *N. H.* XXVI, 10 = Diokles Frag. 5 (Wellmann, 1901).

49 So too Kudlien (1963, pp. 456-64), who argues, however, for a much earlier date, placing Diocles' *floruit c.* 360 BC. But he has not refuted all of Jaeger's arguments pointing to Aristotle's influence upon Diocles.

50 See Kaibel's edition of Athenaeus, app. crit. *s.v.* Γαλατεία; Jacoby, too, regards these words as an obvious interpolation (*apud* Jaeger, 1938b, p. 203 n. 2).

51 In consequence Edelstein rejects on chronological grounds (1940, p. 486 n. 4) Jaeger's identification (1938b, pp. 13ff.) of Diocles of Carystus with the Diocles mentioned in the will of Strato. He also points out that if Jaeger's later position were adopted then further doubt would be cast upon the authenticity of the so-called 'Letter of Diocles to Antigonus' since Diocles could hardly have written to the king around 305/4 (1938a p. 79) if he was at that time only 35 years old and at the beginning of his career. Since Edelstein wrote, Heinimann has published an article attacking the authenticity of this letter (1955, pp. 158-72).

52 Galen, *De uteri dissectione* 10 (II.905K.) = Diokles, Frag. 26 (Wellmann, 1901): μικρὸν ὕστερον Ἱπποκράτους and Pliny, *N. H.* XXVI, 10 = Diokles, Frag. 5 (Wellmann, 1901): *secundus aetate famaque sc. Hippocratis.*

53 Taylor, 1928, p. 503.

54 Solmsen, 1961, p. 159.

55 See, for example, Diller, 1936, pp. 178-95; Kudlien, 1962, pp. 419-29 and 1968a, col. 1101; Joly, 1972, pp. 132ff. Deichgräber, 1973, p. 12. Duminil (1983, p. 54) believes that the treatise was not prior to Nicarchus, the father of Praxagoras.

56 See Lonie, 1973, *passim*.
57 See Appendix, n. 30.
58 See, for example, Sophocles, *Trachiniae* 1054; [Hippocrates] *Epidemiarum Liber* VII,12, 25 (V.388, 394L.); Plato, *Timaeus* 70d2, 78c4-5 and Aristotle, *Hist. an.* 493a8ff.
59 *De resp.* 471b20ff.; *De progressu animalium* 708b4ff. and *Hist. an.* 519a25ff.
60 *Hist. an.* 496a4ff.; 513a30ff. and *De partibus animalium* 666a6ff.
61 C. R. S. Harris suggests (1973, p. 161) that in his dissections of larger animals Aristotle 'may have been struck by the sinew-like attachments of the valves, the musculi papillares and the chordae tendinae'.
62 Ogle, 1882, pp. 149, 195.
63 See *De gen. an.* 764a34ff.; 779a8ff. and *De part. an.* 666a19ff.
64 See too *De part. an.* 666b22-3 and *Hist. an.* 513a27-30.
65 Galen, *De venarum arteriarumque dissectione* 9 (II.817K.).
66 See the discussion in C. R. S. Harris, 1973, pp. 126ff.
67 Galen, *De anatomis administrationibus* 7, 10 (II.621K.).
68 Aëtius IV 5, 6-8, Diels, 1879, p. 204 n. 1.
69 See too Vindicianus, *De semine* 41 (Wellmann, 1901, p. 233). Wellmann himself adopts Diels' suggestion (p. 14).
70 IV 5, 7 *apud* Plut., *Epit.* IV, 5 (Diels, 1879, p. 391). See Chapter 3 n. 103.
71 Wellmann, 1901, pp. 3-14. Cf. too Rüsche, 1930, p. 143 n. 3 and Jaeger, 1938a, pp. 187-211.
72 C. R. S. Harris (1973, p. 133), where he cites *De part. an.* 666b23-33.
73 See von Staden, 1989, p. 172.
74 Jaeger, 1938a, pp. 165ff.
75 Soranus, *Gynaecia* I 14, 2 (*C.M.G.* IV, p. 10 Ilberg) = Diokles, Frag. 27 (Wellmann, 1901).
76 See, for example, Aristophanes, *Epit. hist. anim.* I, 78 (*D.K.*64A25) and Aristotle, *De gen. an.* 740a33ff., and 746a19ff. (*D.K.*68A144).
77 Galen, *De methodo medendi* 7, 3 (X.462K.) = Diokles Frag. 7 (Wellmann, 1901).
78 Galen, *De naturalibus facultatibus* 2, 8 (181 Helmreich = II.110K.) = Diokles, Frag. 8 (Wellmann, 1901). See too Vindicianus, *De semine* 2 = Diokles, Frag. 9 (Wellmann, 1901).
79 Oribasius, III, 168ff ≡ Diokles, Frag. 141 (Wellmann, 1901).
80 *Anon. Lond.* XX, 25.
81 *Timaeus* 81e.
82 Aëtius, V 30, 2 = Diokles, Frag. 30 (Wellmann, 1901) = Diels, 1879, p. 443.
83 *Anon. Lond.* XX, 47 and *Timaeus* 84d.
84 Frags 40, 43, 51, 59 and 63 (Wellmann, 1901).
85 See *De somn.* 461b11, b17; *De part. an.* 656b3ff. and Solmsen's discussion of these passages (1961, pp. 171ff.).
86 Solmsen, 1961, p. 172.
87 See *De part. an.* 688a22-25, where nature is said frequently to fulfil a dual role.

88 See Solmsen, 1961, p. 172.
89 *De an. mot.* 703a13ff.
90 Diokles, Frag. 57 (Wellmann, 1901) and n. 70 above.
91 See Longrigg, 1975c, p. 228 n. 62.
92 Galen, *De plenitudine* 11 (VII.573K.).
93 *Anecdota medica* 20 (p. 550 Fuchs) = Diokles, Frag. 57 (Wellmann, 1901) = Praxagoras, Frag. 75 (Steckerl, 1958).
94 ibid. 3 (p. 541 Fuchs) = Diokles, Frag. 51 (Wellmann, 1901) = Praxagoras, Frag. 70 (Steckerl, 1958).
95 ibid. 4 (p. 542 Fuchs) = Diokles, Frag. 55 (Wellmann, 1901) = Praxagoras, Frag. 74 (Steckerl, 1958).
96 Jaeger, 1938a, p. 225 and 1940, p. 406.
97 See Wellmann, 1901, p. 11 and Jaeger, 1938a, pp. 225, 233.
98 See Wellmann, 1901, p. 11 (endorsed by Jaeger, 1938a, p. 225 but attacked by Steckerl, 1958, p. 34).
99 See, for example, Galen, *De naturalibus facultatibus* 2, 9 = II.141K. = Praxagoras, Frag. 21 (Steckerl, 1958), where he is said to have subscribed to ten humours (excluding the blood). Galen adds here, however, that Praxagoras does not entirely depart from the teaching of Hippocrates, since he divides up into species and varieties the humours he considers to have been first mentioned by Hippocrates.
100 Galen, *De usu respirationis* 1 (IV.471K.) = Diokles, Frag. 15 = Praxagoras, Frag. 32 (Steckerl, 1958).

7 Early Alexandrian medical science

1 Fraser, 1972, vol. I, p. 341.
2 See Green, 1990, p. 480, who draws a useful parallel with the development of astronomy. Mathematics affords an equally valid parallel.
3 See, for example, Celsus, *De medicina*, Proem, 13ff. and Ps. Galen, *Introductio seu medicus* 4 (XIV.683K.). On the 'Dogmatic school' see Introduction, p. 4.
4 For Herophilus' adoption of this theory see p. 186; (for Erasistratus' rejection of it, however, see p. 183).
5 See Fraser, 1972, vol. I, pp. 317, 357.
6 Von Staden, 1989, p. 458.
7 See p. 188.
8 With French (1978, p. 153), who points out that the existence of the medical school would itself have provided 'mutual support within a group to preserve an unpleasant practice'.
9 Von Staden, 1989, p. 27.
10 Diogenes Laërtius, V, 37.
11 Green, 1990, p. 86ff.
12 According to Diogenes Laërtius, V, 88 Strato was paid 80 talents to tutor the young prince.
13 Fraser, 1972, vol. I, p. 320.
14 *Marm. Par.* (*F. Gr. Hist.* II B239) B19 (309/8).

15 Pliny, *N. H.* VII, 37, 124: 'magna et Critoboulo fama est, extracta Philippi regis oculo sagitta, et citra deformitatem oris curata orbitate luminis.' See Prag *et al.*, 1984, pp. 60-78 and Prag, 1990, pp. 237-47.

16 *History of Alexander* 9. 5. 22-9. 6.

17 According to Arrian, however (*Anab.* 6. 11. 1), this operation was performed by another Coan doctor, Critodemus, an Asclepiad and a member of the Hippocratic school. See too Curtius Rufus 9, 5, 25.

18 Suda *s.v.* Ἱπποκράτης τέταρτον.

19 See Susemihl, 1891, vol. 1, p. 800 n. 129 and Beloch, 1904, vol. 3, 2, pp. 473ff. and 1927, vol. 4, 2, pp. 564-5.

20 Fraser, 1969, p. 518.

21 'Nocentes homines a regibus ex carcere uiuos inciderint.'

22 Fraser, 1972, vol. I, p. 349. See also Fraser, 1969, p. 531.

23 Lloyd, 1975a, p. 175.

24 Wellmann, 1900, pp. 380ff. and 1907, col. 333f.

25 Given by Eusebius (*Chron.* p. 200 Karst.) and St Jerome (p. 131 Helm.).

26 Mesk, 1913, pp. 366-94.

27 Fraser, 1969, pp. 534ff.

28 Nutton, 1979, pp. 195-6.

29 The only surviving example of an Alexandrian medical work is the commentary upon the Hippocratic treatise *De articulis* (*Peri arthrōn*) dating from the last generation of Ptolemaic Alexandria.

30 See Daremberg and Ruelle, 1879.

31 See Ilberg, 1927 and Temkin, 1956a.

32 See Diels, 1893a and Jones, 1947.

33 See F. Marx, 1915 and Spencer, 1935-8.

34 For convenience and brevity references to Galen will be cited according to the comprehensive edition of Kühn, *Claudii Galeni Opera Omnia*, 20 vols in 22, Leipzig, 1821-33. This edition is gradually being superseded by the *Corpus Medicorum Graecorum* edition (various editors, Leipzig and Berlin, in progress since 1914). References to these more modern editions will be made where relevant.

35 See Allbutt, 1921, p. 156 and Dobson, 1926-7, p. 825 (21).

36 See K. F. H. Marx, 1838 and 1840.

37 Fuchs, 1892.

38 Dobson, 1925 and 1926-7.

39 Plutarch, *Quaestiones conviviales* IV, 4, 3, 669a (*D.K.*22B96).

40 See Frag. 6.30-3 Nauck. The date of this play is uncertain. It is now thought to belong to the third century. But this passage certainly reflects attitudes propounded in intellectual circles during the fifth-century Enlightenment.

41 Edelstein, 1967, p. 275ff. Edelstein's thesis has been accepted by Phillips, 1973, p. 140 and French, 1978, p. 153.

42 Edelstein cites here (1967, p. 278) *De partibus animalium* 640b36ff.

43 See Kudlien, 1969, p. 87 and 1968b, p. 42.

44 Von Staden similarly suggests (1989, p. 124) that Aristotle's method

of biological research may have served here as the model for Herophilus and provided him with 'useful ways of reconciling observational activity with the construction of anatomical theory'.

45 See Kudlien, 1964, pp. 1–13. Kudlien's standpoint has subsequently been adopted by Potter, 1976, p. 59.
46 With von Staden, 1975, p. 197 n. 57.
47 See Galen, *De placitis Hippocratis et Platonis* 8, 5 (V.685K.) and Celsus, *De medicina*, Proem., Chapter 15.
48 Ps. Galen, *Introductio seu medicus* 4 (XIV.683K.).
49 See, generally, von Staden, 1989, Chapter I 'Alexandrian and Egyptian medicine'.
50 See, for example, M. Simon, 1906, vol. II. pp. xxxixff. It is worth observing here that according to Herodotus (*Histories* II, 86ff.) in all but the most expensive types of embalming the intestines are not removed from the body but are dissolved within it.
51 See G. Elliott Smith, 1914, p. 190.
52 C. R. S. Harris, 1973, p. 177.
53 Herodotus, *Histories* II, 86ff.
54 See Fraser, 1972, vol. I, p. 351.
55 Kudlien also points to the absence of these 'traditionelle Hemmungen' (1969, p. 87). He should, however, have stressed not only the absence of these inhibitions at Alexandria, but also the actual treatment of the corpses there. Vivian Nutton has suggested to me privately that the Greeks, who regarded mummification as a desecration of the corpse, might well have come round to the view that if the Egyptians could treat their own dead in this manner, then they themselves could do the same (see now Nutton, 1992, p. 30 n. 65). It is possible that they were influenced in this way and there is evidence to suggest that the Alexandrian Greeks regarded themselves as superior to the native inhabitants. Unfortunately, we are unable to determine the nationality of the corpses dissected by the Alexandrians. I also wonder whether the Greeks are likely to have been so selective in their general attitudes towards the human corpse.
56 Herodotus, *Histories* II, 86ff.
57 Von Staden, 1989, p. 29.
58 For a contemporary and very forthright Greek reaction to this marriage see Sotades, Fragment 1. For conventional Greek attitudes towards incest generally see Aeschylus, *Suppliant Women, passim*; *Prometheus Vinctus* 853ff.; Sophocles, *Oedipus Rex* 1182, 1248, 1357ff., 1403ff., 1496ff.
59 Celsus, *De medicina*, Chap. 26.
60 *De anima* 10.
61 In a later passage (25) Tertullian condemns the use of the *embryosphaktēs* (*vel sim.*) – a bronze spike for killing the embryo within the womb – and tells us that among those doctors who used this device was Herophilus 'the dissector of adults, too' – *et maiorum quoque prosector* – which in its context seems also to suggest vivisection.

Diels, it may be noted, actually proposes the emendation *vivorum* (1879, p. 206 n. 2).

62 See, for example, Allbutt, 1921, p. 147 n. 3; Dobson, 1925, pp. 25ff., and Singer, 1925, pp. 34ff. Greenhill (1843, p. 109), however, took a sturdily independent line.

63 A recent exception, however, is Scarborough, 1976, pp. 25-38.

64 Crawfurd, 1919, p. 554 rt col. See too Allbutt, 1921, p. 147 n. 3.

65 Finlayson, 1893, p. 326.

66 Dobson, 1925, p. 26.

67 The same misinterpretation of this passage is repeated by Fraser, 1969, p. 532 n. 37 and 1972, vol. II, p. 507 n. 76 and, most recently, by Scarborough, 1976, p. 31.

68 See, for example, Dobson, 1925, pp. 25ff. and Singer, 1925, pp. 34ff.

69 See Johannes Alexandrinus' (seventh century AD) commentary on [Hippocrates] *De natura pueri* in Dietz, 1834, p. 216 (cited by Greenhill, 1843, p. 109).

70 For this argument see especially Singer, 1925, p. 34 and, most recently, Scarborough, 1976, pp. 26ff.

71 See von Staden, 1989, p. 151. Nutton has pointed out to me that an unedited Arabic translation of a Galenic text entitled 'On Vivisection' has survived. It will be interesting to see whether it throws any further light upon this issue.

72 In *De medicina*, Proem, 40-2, Celsus records the strong condemnation of vivisectionists by the Empiricists, who revile them as 'pirates' and 'cut-throats'.

73 See, for example, Singer, 1925, p. 34 and Lloyd, 1973, p. 76.

74 See Diels, 1879, p. 207 and Waszink, 1947, pp. 25ff.

75 Galen, *De usu partium corporis humani* 8, 11 (III.665K.).

76 Both terms are employed by Aristotle in *Historia animalium* 495a10ff. For Aristotle's view of the brain see Clarke, 1963b, pp. 1-14 and Clarke and Stannard, 1963, pp. 130-48.

77 Ps. Rufus, *De anatomia hominis partium* 74 (p. 185 Daremberg-Ruelle); Aëtius, IV 5, 4; Galen, *De usu partium* 8, 11 (III.667K.). For reactions to this 'epochmaking discovery' within the Lyceum and Stoa, where the seat of the *hegemonikon* was held to be located in the heart, see Solmsen, 1961, p. 195. Solmsen points out that even after this demonstration by dissection that the *hegemonikon* must be situated in the brain, Chrysippus sought doggedly to defend the Stoic dogma by an appeal to Praxagoras, an authority of about half a century earlier.

78 Galen, *De anatomicis administrationibus* 9, 5 (II.731K.).

79 ibid., 9, 3 (II.719K.).

80 Galen, *De usu partium* 9, 6 (III.708K.).

81 For a discussion of the *Torcular Herophili* see Finlayson, 1893, p. 336.

82 Galen, *De pulsuum usu* 2 (V.155K.).

83 By M. Simon, 1906, vol. II, p. xxxvi. See also Sigerist, 1924, p. 201, who follows Simon in maintaining 'ihre Kenntnisse fast ausschliesslich an Tierleichen gewonnen wurden. Das die

Alexandriner systematisch menschliche Leichen zergliedert hätten, ist eine uralte fable convenue, die wir Abendländer begierig aufgennomen haben.'

84 With Dobson, 1925, p. 20.

85 Chapter 6, p. 174.

86 See the detailed account in Galen, *De placitis Hippocratis et Platonis* I, 6, 13 to 7, 15 (= V.187K.) = Steckerl, 1958, Frag. 11 = de Lacy, vol. I, 1978 pp. 80–5.

87 *De placitis Hippocratis et Platonis* I, 6, 13 to 7, 15.

88 Solmsen, 1961, p. 180.

89 ibid., p. 185.

90 Rufus, *De corporis humani partium appellationibus* 71–4 (p. 184, 13 Daremberg-Ruelle).

91 Galen, *De usu partium* 10,12 (III.813K.).

92 Galen, ibid. and *De symptomatum causis* 1, 2 (VII.89K.).

93 See Chalcidius, *In Timaeum* 246 (p. 279 Wrobel = *D.K.*24A10): *multa et praeclara in lucem (protulit)*.

94 Aëtius, VII 48 (*Corpus Medicorum Graecorum* VIII, 2, pp. 302–3).

95 Chalcidius in the passage cited in n. 93, after citing Herophilus along with Alcmaeon of Croton and Callisthenes, Aristotle's pupil, adds (p. 280 Wrobel): 'oculi porro ipsius continentiam in quattuor membranis seu tunicis notauerunt disparili soliditate.' Since in the Hippocratic *Corpus* only two (see Ps. Galen, *Introductio* 11 XIV.712K.) or three coats are recognised (see *De locis in homine* II, 104 Kühlewein = VI.280L.) and Aristotle's account of the eye at *Historia animalium* 491b18ff. is sketchy and patently not based upon any detailed anatomical investigation, it is not unreasonable to conclude with Oppermann, 1925, pp. 14–32 that it was Herophilus who first distinguished *four* tunics of the eye.

96 Pseudo Rufus, *De anatomia hominis partium* 12 (p. 171 Daremberg-Ruelle).

97 Rufus, *De corporis humani partium appellationibus* 153 (p. 154, 9 Daremberg-Ruelle).

98 p. 191.

99 Callimachus in Hymn III, 53 likens the eye of the Cyclops to a 'shield of four bullhides' (*sakos tetraboeion*) instead of using the traditional Homeric simile 'shield of seven bullhides' (*sakos heptaboeion*). Oppermann (1925 pp.14ff) has persuasively argued that the modification introduced here by Callimachus stems from his interest in Herophilus' pioneering work upon the anatomy of the eye.

100 See, for example, Magnus, 1901, p. 211.

101 There is a slightly variant text in Oribasius. See *Collectiones medicae* III, 24 (Raeder, 1928-33, p. 36.)

102 Fraser, 1972, vol. II, p. 510, n. 92.

103 ibid.

104 M. Simon, 1906, vol. II, pp. xxxvii–viii.

105 Allbutt, 1921, pp. 313–14.

106 Galen, *De placitis Hippocratis et Platonis* 6, 5 (V.543K.).

107 Galen, *De venarum arteriarumque dissectione* 1, 1 (II.780K.). He

gave it this name, we learn elsewhere from Galen, *De locis affectis* 6, 3 (VIII.396K.), because of its length.

108 Galen, *De usu partium* 4, 19 (III.335K.) and *De semine* 2, 6 (IV.646K.)

109 See Aselli, 1627.

110 *De generatione animalium* 717a34-6; and 787b24-6.

111 Galen, *De semine* 1, 16 (IV.582K.).

112 See Longrigg, 1985a, p. 282.

113 See Jaeger, 1938a, pp. 193-201, who argues that the four subsequent 'proofs' in this fragment supporting this theory that the blood is the origin of the semen were also derived from Herophilus. See too von Staden's recent analysis (1989, p. 292) which supports Jaeger's standpoint.

114 Galen, *De anatomicis administrationibus* 12, 8 (Duckworth's translation from Hunain's Arabic version of the lost original) and *De semine* 1, 16 (IV.582K.)

115 Galen, *De usu partium* 14, 11 (II, p. 321 Helmreich; IV.190K.).

116 Galen, *De semine* 2, 1 (IV.597K.). See *De semine* 1, 16 (IV.582K.) for the description of the male vessels as varicose.

117 Galen, *De uteri dissectione* 3 (II.890K.)

118 M. Simon, 1906, vol. II, p. xxxvi.

119 See Fraser, 1972, vol. II p. 511 n. 94.

120 It is possible that this mistake was due to the false inferences based on the dissection of elderly women in whom these vessels are not easily identified.

121 Galen, *De semine* 2, 1 (IV.596-8K.)

122 Galen, *De placitis Hippocratis et Platonis* 1, 10 (V.206K.).

123 Galen, *De anatomicis administrationibus* 7, 11 (II.624K.).

124 Galen, *De dignoscendis pulsibus* 4, 3 (VIII.950K.) and *De plenitudine* 11 (VII.573K.). As was seen in Chapter 6, p. 174, Galen also attributes this distinction to Praxagoras' father Nicarchus and Diocles of Carystus.

125 Galen, *De usu partium* 6, 10 (III.445K.).

126 Galen, *De pulsuum differentiis* 4, 10 (VIII.747K.).

127 *De corporis humani partium appellationibus* 203 (p. 162 Daremberg-Ruelle).

128 In citing this text C. R. S. Harris (1973, p. 179) unfortunately miscopies and reads ἀρτηρίαν instead of the received ἀρτηριώδη (ἀρτηρίαν is clearly incorrect and, indeed, illogical within this context). Furley and Wilkie (1984, p. 25) seem to have been subsequently misled by Harris' error.

129 See, for example, L. G. Wilson, 1959, p. 296 n. 18 and Scarborough, 1976, p. 31.

130 C. R. S. Harris, 1973, p. 180. See too Gossen, 1912, p. 1106; Dobson, 1925, p. 21; Phillips, 1973, p. 143 and, more cautiously, Fraser, 1972, vol. I, p. 352.

131 For example by Dobson, 1925, p. 21.

132 For Praxagoras' view on this matter see Galen's explicit statement at *De plenitudine* 11 (VII.573K.) = Steckerl, 1958, Frag. 85.

133 For the suggestion that Herophilus may have held that the arteries contained both blood and *pneuma* in anticipation of Galen's own view see von Staden, 1989, pp. 266ff.
134 See Longrigg, 1985b, pp. 149–50.
135 Unfortunately, the account of Herophilus' doctrine of the pulse which Galen promises at *De praesagitione ex pulsibus* 2, 3 (IX.279K.) was either not written or has failed to survive. But other Galenic treatises have survived which provide useful information for doctrines of pulsation in general and those of Herophilus in particular. For a full listing of the treatises see Fraser, 1972, vol. II, p. 514 n. 101.
136 Galen, *De pulsuum differentiis* 4, 2 (VIII.702K.).
137 ibid. (VIII.703K.).
138 Galen, *De tremore* 1 (VII.584K.).
139 Galen, *De pulsuum differentiis* 2, 6 (VIII.592K.).
140 Galen, *Synopsis librorum suorum de pulsibus* 12 (IX.463K.). But see von Staden, 1989, pp. 278ff., who warns against the dangers of exaggerating Aristoxenus' influence here.
141 Galen, *Synopsis librorum suorum de pulsibus* 14 (IX.471K.).
142 Ps. Galen, *Definitiones medicae* 220 (XIX.409K.). See Pigeaud, 1978, pp. 258–67.
143 Galen, *De pulsuum differentiis* 1, 28 (VIII.556K.).
144 Galen, *Synopsis de pulsibus* 8 (IX.453K.).
145 *De pulsibus* 11 ed. Schöne.
146 See Galen, *De anatomicis administrationibus* 10, 7; 11, 1 and 14, 5 (Duckworth's translation from Hunain's Arabic version).
147 For these and other terminological innovations by Herophilus see Dobson, 1925, pp. 24–5; Fraser, 1972, vol. I, pp. 354–5, and von Staden, 1989, *passim*.
148 Galen, *De pulsuum usu* 5 (V.166K.) and *De placitis* 1, 10 (V.206K.).
149 I see no good reason to follow Müller (1874) and emend the manuscript reading here.
150 With Lonie, 1973, Pt ii, p. 152. See too Lonie's discussion of the question whether the author of *De corde* had previously recognised the ventricular valves as such (1973, Pt i, pp. 11–14).
151 By L. G. Wilson, 1959, p. 297.
152 With Lonie, 1973, Pt ii, p. 139 n. 43.
153 Lonie, 1973, Pt ii, p. 138.
154 By Majno, 1975, p. 332.
155 Lonie, 1973, Pt ii, p. 139 n. 42.
156 *Pneumatica* I, 28. The pump (Figure 7) is also described by Philo of Byzantium, Appendix, 1, 2 (Carra de Vaux) and by Vitruvius X, 7. There is a convenient translation and illustration printed in Cohen and Drabkin, 1958, pp. 329–31.
157 Majno, 1975, p. 332.
158 Galen, *De placitis* 6, 6 (V.549K.). This analogy is a fairly common one and is used, for example, by Aristotle (*De resp.* 480a20), the author of *De corde* 8 and elsewhere in Galen (e.g. at *De pulsuum differentiis* 4, 2 (VIII.703K.).

159 Galen, *De placitis* 6, 7 (V.562K.).

160 See, for example, Wellmann, 1907, p. 340; Allbutt, 1921, pp. 305-6; Dobson, 1925, p. 19 and Singer, 1925, p. 33.

161 For this analogy see Plato, *Timaeus*, 77c; Aristotle, *De partibus animalium* 668a13ff.; *Historia animalium* 515a21ff.; [Hippocrates] *De corde* 7 and Galen, *De naturalibus facultatibus* 3, 14 (II.211K.). See, generally, Lonie, 1964, p. 426 n. 2.

162 Ibn al-Nafis is a rare example of a writer in Arabic contradicting Galen. His work, however, went virtually unrecognised and the Latin West had to wait another three centuries for Servetus' rediscovery of the lesser circulation (see Chéhadé, 1955).

163 See C. R. S. Harris, 1973, p. 93, who refers to the experiments of the Swedish pathologist Fahraeus (1958-9, vol. I, pp. 151-3). Fahraeus discovered that although the larger arteries emerging from the heart revealed negative pressure after death, upon severance their arterial pressure rose to zero because some air had been drawn into them.

164 Galen, *De venae sectione* 3 (XI.154K.). See too *Anonymus Londinensis* XXVI, 103J.

165 Galen, *An in arteriis natura sanguis contineatur* 6 (IV.724K.). See Furley and Wilkie, 1984, p. 37.

166 Galen, *De placitis* 7, 8 (V.646K.) and ibid. 7, 3 (V.602K.) (translated above, p. 211).

167 See Galen, *De atra bile* 5 (V.125K.) and Fuchs, 1894a, Frag. 20, p. 550.

168 Galen, *De placitis* 7, 3 (V.602-4K.).

169 For the use of this word see especially Theophrastus, *Historia plantarum* 1. 2. 6; 3. 17. 5.

170 See, for example, Wellmann in Susemihl, 1891, vol. I, p. 803 n. 139 and his own work, 1907, pp. 343-4; Neuberger, 1906, p. 267; Singer, 1925, p. 32; Verbeke, 1945, p. 184 and, most recently, Phillips, 1973, p. 148 and footnote 410.

171 Solmsen, 1961, p. 188.

172 With C. R. S. Harris, 1973, p. 232.

173 Wellmann, however, has maintained (1907, p. 334) that through his Peripatetic connections Erasistratus was first introduced to the physical theory of Democritus, which he modified and adapted as the basis for his own physiology. This particular misconception has been more persuasive than it really merits and has subsequently been uncritically accepted by several scholars (e.g. by Dobson 1926-7, p. 825 (21); Singer and Underwood, 1962, p. 49; and Phillips, 1973, p. 146).

174 Diels, 1893b, pp. 101-27.

175 Hero I, 24, 20 Schmidt = Simplicius, *In physica* 693.10ff. = Strato, Frag. 65b Wehrli, 1950, p. 23.

176 Wellmann is not alone, however, in rejecting Diels' thesis. In particular the latter's view that the Preface to Hero's *Pneumatica* is patently influenced by Strato has been attacked by Schmekel (1938, vol. I, pp. 110ff.), who maintains that Hero was an Atomist and, therefore, closer to Asclepiades than to Strato, and by M. Gatzemeier (1970, pp. 94-7), who questions the accuracy of Simplicius'

testimony and contends that Hero and Erasistratus were not influenced by Strato's theory at all. Gatzemeier's arguments have been attacked in their turn by Furley (1985, pp. 594-609; see too Furley and Wilkie, 1984, pp. 35ff.), who concludes that it is likely that Erasistratus was influenced by Strato, but maintains that the pneumatic theory described here in the *Pneumatica* should not be accepted unreservedly as 'precisely that which was worked out by Strato and that this is also the theory of Erasistratus'. Furley himself finds Epicurean elements in Hero's pneumatic theory and believes that Hero is more likely to have been the borrower than Strato. Furley is right to tread cautiously here. Yet the possibility that Hellenistic philosophy may itself have been influenced by developments within the Lyceum or Museum should not be discounted. As Solmsen cogently reminds us (1961, p. 182), '[the Epicurean] system too was by no means immune to the influence of contemporary physiological thoughts and trends.'

177 For Strato's corpuscular theory, generally, see Wehrli, 1950, pp. 53-4; Diels, 1893b, pp. 101-27; and Gottschalk, 1965, p. 146.

178 See Wehrli's commentary upon Frag. 108 (1950, p. 71), and Solmsen, 1961, p. 183.

179 Wellmann, however, maintains, again in opposition to Diels, that Erasistratus' doctrine of *horror vacui* was derived not from Strato but from Chrysippus, who, he believes, had in his turn derived the theory, from Philistion of Locri, the author (?) of the theory of respiration by 'circular thrust' (*periōsis*) adopted by Plato in the *Timaeus* 79a-e (1900, p. 377 n. 1).

180 On this experiment see von Staden, 1975, pp. 179ff.

181 Ps.-Galen, *In Hippocratis librum de alimento commentarius* 2, 7 (XV.247K.).

182 Ps.-Galen, *Definitiones medicae* 99 (XIX.372K.) and *De naturalibus facultatibus* 2, 8 (II.119-20K.).

183 Galen, *De placitis* 6, 6 (V.550K.). Lonie (1964, p. 440 n. 45) raises the interesting question 'who first ascribed the important function of hematosis to the liver which is taken for granted by the Pneumatic School and by Galen?' This theory that the blood is the agent of nutrition and is manufactured in the liver became the generally accepted doctrine of European medicine until the seventeenth century. Excluding Aristotle, Diocles and Praxagoras, Lonie considers Herophilus a 'possible candidate', but his final choice devolves on Erasistratus. There is, however, as Lonie has accepted, evidence which strongly suggests that this highly influential theory should now be regarded as a discovery not of the third but of the *fifth* century BC (see Longrigg, 1985a, p. 285 n. 21).

184 Galen, *De usu partium* 4, 13 (III.304K.).

185 Galen, *De usu partium* 7, 8 (III.538K.); *De naturalibus facultatibus* 2, 6 (II.96K.) and *Anonymus Londinensis* XXI, 82J.

186 Ps. Galen, *Introductio seu medicus* 9 (XIV.695-9K.).

187 Galen, *De naturalibus facultatibus* 2, 3 (II.87K.).

188 Galen, *De usu partium* 7, 8 (III.537-9K.).

189 Galen, *De venae sectione adversus Erasistrateos* 8 (XI.239K.).
190 ibid. (XI.237K.).
191 Von Staden correctly points out (1989, p. 124) that for all their clinical interests the primary concentration of Herophilus and Erasistratus lay in theoretical medicine. W. D. Smith (1982, p. 409) also stresses that Erasistratus' dietetic medicine is a clear development from the classical period.
192 See above, p. 204.
193 Above, n. 61.
194 Galen, *De compositione medicamentorum* 6, 8 (XII.966K.).
195 Galen, *De atra bile* 5 (V.123K.).
196 Caelius Aurelianus, *De morbis chronicis* IV, 4, 65.
197 Ps. Galen, *Introductio seu medicus* 13 (XIV.751K.).
198 See Wellmann, in Susemihl 1891, pp. 811ff. and now von Staden, 1989, Part 2.
199 *De corporis humani partium appellationibus* 9 (p. 134 Daremberg-Ruelle).
200 See Edelstein, 1967, p. 250. This viewpoint has subsequently been accepted by Lloyd, 1973, p. 86.
201 Book 1, Chapter 2 (II.220K.).
202 With Kudlien, 1969, pp. 78ff. and C. R. S. Harris, 1973, p. 234.
203 The rising popularity of the Alexandrian Empiricists' theory of scientific method which denied the scientific value and clinical relevance of dissection may possibly have been an additional factor. See von Staden, 1975, pp. 186–93 and 1982, p. 86.

Appendix

1 See Simplicius *In phys.* 150. 24; Aristotle, *Physics* 187a20ff. (*D.K.*12A9) and [Plutarch] *Strom.* 2 (*D.K.*12A10).
2 See, for example, Cornford, 1952, p. 341.
3 See Cherniss (1935), who questions the reliability of Aristotle's evidence and McDiarmid (1953), who, following Cherniss' lead, queries that of Theophrastus.
4 For more balanced views of Aristotle and Theophrastus as historians of philosophy see Guthrie, 1957, pp. 35ff. and Kahn, 1960, pp. 17ff.
5 See, for example, McDiarmid, 1953, p. 85.
6 At *Physics* 188a20ff., for example, Aristotle himself makes it clear that he has reformulated the doctrine of Parmenides' *Way of Opinion* and expressed it in terms of the opposites, hot and cold. For a similar doxographical reformulation see Hippolytus, *Ref.* I, 7, 3 (*D.K.*13A7).
7 Solmsen, for instance, confidently declares 'in Anaximander hot and cold, moist and dry stuff are the component parts of our world – nothing less.' (1960, p. 342). See too Fränkel, 1962, pp. 342ff.; Kahn, 1960, pp. 119ff., and Guthrie 1962, pp. 78ff.
8 Hölscher, for example, declares 'die gegensätzlichen Quälitaten

Heiss und Kalt können als solche nicht anaximandrisch sein' (1953, p. 266).

9 Kahn, 1960, p. 40.
10 Lloyd, 1964, pp. 96ff.
11 Kirk and Raven, 1957, p. 133.
12 *Pace* both Gigon, 1935, p. 99 and Reinhardt, 1916, p. 223 who both anachronistically find the four element theory implicit in it.
13 Kirk, 1954, p. 154.
14 Kahn, 1960, p. 159.
15 Kirk, 1954, p. 344 and 1951, pp. 35ff. See too Heidel, 1906, pp. 333ff.
16 See Fragments 4, 8, 12, 15, 16.
17 Kahn, 1960, p. 127.
18 This fragment is quoted in Chapter 5, p. 107.
19 See Chapter 5, p. 107.
20 Chapter 1.
21 For Diogenes' relationship to Empedocles see Longrigg, 1985a, pp. 277ff. and 1985c, pp. 100ff.
22 See Simplicius, *In phys.* 151. 28ff. (*D.K.*64B2).
23 See Frags 96, 98 and Aëtius, V 22, 1 (*D.K.*31A78).
24 Plutarch, *De primo frigido* 7, 947f (*D.K.*13B1).
25 Sextus, *Adv. math.* VII, 135 (*D.K.*68B9).
26 See Theophrastus' account of the views of Democritus at *De sens.* 63 (*D.K.*68A135). Theophrastus does, however, maintain that Plato differs from the Atomist in that he does not deprive τὰ αἰσθητα of their independent reality, *De sens.* 61. But this standpoint is extremely difficult to reconcile with the *Theaetetus* and Theophrastus himself acknowledges in the next chapter that Plato does account for τὰ αἰσθητα as affections of sensation.
27 The Stoics also identified each element with a single quality (Diogenes Laërtius, VII, 137 (*S.V.F.* II. 580). See, too, Plutarch, *De Stoicorum repugnantiis* 43, 1053f and *De primo frigido* 9, 948d and 17, 952c (*S.V.F.* II. 429); Galen, *De simplicium medicamentorum temperamentis et facultatibus* 2, 20 (XI.510K. and *S.V.F.* II. 431); Seneca, *Quaestiones naturales* II, 10. 4 and *Epistulae* 31. 5; Clement, *Protrepticus* 1, 5, 1; and Cicero, *De natura deorum* II, 26. Zeno may have been influenced by his older contemporary at Athens, Diocles of Carystus, who almost certainly adopted Philistion's distribution of qualities to elements (see p. 162). In that case, we would then have yet another instance of the highly influential role played by the 'Sicilian' medical tradition in the development of Greek philosophy.
28 See Littré (1839, vol. I, p. 384); Zeller, who finds the influence of Aristotle in this reference to the elements (1856-81, vol. II, 2 (1862) p. 334 n. 5), and Grensemann (1968a, pp. 53-95).
29 See further vols I, p. 220 and IX, pp. 163-5.
30 Sticker, for example, believes it to be 'ein Jugendwerk des Hippokrates' (1923, p. 14), while Willerding (1914, p. 73) followed by Deichgräber *et al.* (1935, p. 27 n. 4) holds that it was written at the end of the fifth century. Diels (1899, p. 17 n. 3) however, who is

followed by Wellmann (1901, p. 90) in his belief that our author has influenced Diocles (NB for the revised dating of Diocles see Chapter 6, pp. 162ff.), argues for a date within the first half of the fourth century.

31 While scholars of the last century in general were of the opinion that the date of the *De victu* was around 400 BC (see, for example, Fredrich, 1899, pp. 81ff.), some later scholars, notably Jaeger (1939–45, vol. III, 1946, pp. 36ff.) and Kirk (1954, pp. 21ff.), have argued for a date around the middle of the fourth century. Kirk even believes that Peripatetic influences can be detected in this work. More recently, however, Joly (1967, pp. xiv–xvi; 1984, pp. 44ff.) has advocated a return to the traditional dating of this treatise to the end of the fifth or the beginning of the fourth century BC. (See the latter reference for a fuller discussion of this matter than can be presented here.)

32 *Historia animalium*, 512b12ff.

33 Most scholars place the work at the very end of the fifth century. See Fredrich, 1899, pp. 45ff.; Deichgräber, 1933, pp. 111ff.; Heinimann, 1945, pp. 158ff; and, most recently, Jouanna, 1975, pp. 59ff. Bourgey, however, goes for an earlier date and places it in the second half of this century (1953, pp. 31ff.). Only Link, it appears, has argued that the treatise is post-Aristotelian (1814/15, pp. 238ff.).

Bibliography

The bibliography aims to provide details of all the books and articles cited in the text. I have also cited certain other works which, though not explicitly mentioned in my discussion, are relevant to the issues raised there. I have only been able to make perfunctory reference to works published from 1990 onwards.

Abel, K. 1958. 'Die Lehre vom Blutkreislauf im Corpus Hippocraticum', *Hermes*, 86, pp. 192–219 (repr. with a 'retractatio' in Flashar, 1971, pp. 121–64).

Allbutt, T. C. 1921. *Greek Medicine in Rome*, London (repr. New York, 1970).

Allen, R. E. and Furley, D. J. (eds). 1970 and 1975. *Studies in Presocratic Philosophy*, 2 vols, London.

Arnim, H. von. 1903–24. *Stoicorum Veterum Fragmenta*, Leipzig.

Aselli, G. 1627. *De lactibus siue lacteis uenis quarto uasorum mesaraicorum genere nouo inuento Gasparis Asellii Cremonensis anatomici Ticinensis disseratio*, Milan.

Baldry, H. C. 1932. 'Embryological analogies in early Greek cosmology', *Classical Quarterly*, 26, pp. 27–34.

Bardong, K. 1954. 'Praxagoras', Pauly-Wissowa, *Real-Encyclopädie der klassischen Altertumswissenschaft*, 22, 2, Stuttgart, cols 1735–43.

Barnes, J. 1982. *The Presocratic Philosophers*, 2 vols (revised edn), London.

Baumann, E. D. 1925. 'Die heilige Krankheit', *Janus*, 29, pp. 7–32.

—— 1937. 'Praxagoras of Kos', *Janus*, 41, pp. 167–85.

Beloch, K. J. 1904. *Griechische Geschichte*, 4 vols in 8, Strassburg, Berlin and Leipzig (2nd edn 1927).

Bernhard, O. 1928. 'Über Malariabekämpfung im klassischen Altertum', in *Neuburger's Festschrift*, Vienna, pp. 44–6.

Bidez, J. and Leboucq, G. 1944. 'Une anatomie antique du coeur humain', *Revue des études grecques*, 57, pp. 7–40.

Booth, N. B. 1960. 'Empedocles' account of breathing', *Journal of Hellenic Studies*, 80, pp. 10–15.

Bourgey, L. 1953. *Observation et expérience chez les médecins de la collection hippocratique*, Paris.

Bourgey, L. and Jouanna, J. (eds). 1975. *La collection hippocratique et son rôle dans l'histoire de la médecine: colloque de Strasbourg*, Leiden.

Breasted, J. H. 1930. *The Edwin Smith Surgical Papyrus*, 2 vols, Chicago.

Brisson, L. 1987. *Platon, lettres*, Paris.

Bruins, E. M. 1951. 'La chimie du Timée', *Revue de métaphysique et morale*, 56, pp. 269-82.

Burnet, J. 1930. *Early Greek Philosophy* (4th edn), London.

Capelle, W. 1931. 'Straton von Lampsakos', 13, Pauly-Wissowa, *Real-Encyclopädie der klassischen Altertumswissenschaft*, 4, 1, Stuttgart, cols 278-315.

Capriglione, J. C. 1983. *Prassagora di Cos*, Naples.

Cardini, M. Timpanaro. 1957. 'Respirazione e la clessidra', *Parola del Passato*, 12, pp. 250-70.

Chéhadé, A.-K. 1955. *Ibn al-Nafis et la découverte de la circulation pulmonaire*, Damascus.

Cherniss, H. 1935. *Aristotle's Criticism of Presocratic Philosophy*, Baltimore.

Clarke, E. 1963a. 'Apoplexy in the Hippocratic writings', *Bulletin of the History of Medicine*, 37, pp. 301-14.

—— 1963b. 'Aristotelian concepts of the form and function of the brain', *Bulletin of the History of Medicine*, 37, pp. 1-14.

Clarke, E. and Stannard, J. 1963. 'Aristotle on the anatomy of the brain', *Journal of the History of Medicine*, 18, pp. 130-48.

Cochrane, C. N. 1929. *Thucydides and the Science of History*, London.

Cohen, M. R. and Drabkin, I. E. 1958. *A Source Book in Greek Science*, Cambridge, Ma.

Cornford, F. M. 1937. *Plato's Cosmology* (repr. 1948), London.

—— 1952. *Principium Sapientiae*, Cambridge.

Crawfurd, R. 1919. 'Forerunners of Harvey in antiquity', Harveian Oration (repr. in the *British Medical Journal*, 2 (1919), pp. 551-6).

Crombie, I. M. 1963. *An Examination of Plato's Doctrines*, 2 vols, London.

Daremberg, C. V. 1865. *La médecine dans Homère*, Paris.

Daremberg, C. and Ruelle, C. E. 1879. *Oeuvres de Rufus d'Ephèse*, Paris (repr. Amsterdam, 1963).

Dawson, W. R. 1953. 'Egypt's place in medical history', in *Science, Medicine and History: Essays in Honour of Charles Singer*, 2 vols, Oxford.

Deichgräber, K. 1930. *Die griechische Empirikerschule: Sammlung und Darstellung der Lehre*, Berlin.

—— 1933. *Die Epidemien und das Corpus Hippocraticum*, Berlin.

—— 1973. *Pseud-Hippokrates, Über die Nahrung. Text, Kommentar und Würdigung einer stoisch-heraklitisierenden Schrift aus der Zeit um Christi Geburt (Abhandlungen des geistes- und sozialwissenschaftlichen Klasse*, Jahrgang 1973, Nr 3), Darmstadt.

Deichgräber, K., Schubring, K. and Schwyzer, E. 1935. *Über Entstehung und Aufbau des menschlichen Körpers*, Leipzig and Berlin.

Delatte, A. 1922. *Essai sur la politique Pythagoricienne*, Liège.

Derenne, E. 1930. *Les procès d'impiété intentés aux philosophes à Athènes au V' et au IV' siècles avant J. C.*, Liège.

GREEK RATIONAL MEDICINE

Diels, H. 1879. *Doxographi Graeci*, Berlin.
—— 1893a. *Anonymi Londinensis ex Aristotelis Iatricis Menoniis et aliis Medicis Eclogae*, Berlin.
—— 1893b. 'Ueber das physikalische System des Straton', *Sitzungsberichte der Preussischen Akademie der Wissenschaften zu Berlin*, 1, pp. 101-27.
—— 1899. *Elementum*, Leipzig.
Diels, H. and Kranz, W. 1956. *Die Fragmente der Vorsokratiker* (8th edn), 3 vols, Berlin.
Diepgen, P. 1937. 'Die Frauenheilkunde in der alten Welt', *Handbuch der Gynäkologie*, Bnd. 12, Teil 1, Munich.
—— 1949. *Geschichte der Medizin*, Berlin.
Dietz, F. R. 1834. *Scholia in Hippocratem et Galenum*, 2 vols, Königsberg.
Diller, H. 1932. "Ὄψις ἀδήλων τὰ φαινόμενα', *Hermes*, 67, pp. 14-42 (repr. in his *Kleine Schriften zur antiken Literatur*, Munich, 1971, pp. 119-43).
—— 1934. *Wanderarzt und Aitiologe (Philologus Suppl. Bd. 26, 3)*, Leipzig.
—— 1936. 'Eine stoisch-pneumatische Schrift im Corpus Hippocraticum', *Sudhoffs Archiv für die Geschichte der Medizin*, 29, pp. 178-95 (repr. in his *Kleine Schriften zur antike Medizin*, ed. G. Baader and H. Grensemann (Ars Medica, II, 3 Berlin/New York, 1973).
—— 1941. 'Die philosophiegeschichtliche Stellung des Diogenes von Apollonia', *Hermes*, 76, pp. 359-81.
—— 1952. 'Hippokratische Medizin und attische Philosophie', *Hermes*, 80, pp. 385-409.
—— 1959. 'Stand und Aufgaben der Hippokratesforschung', *Jahrbuch der Akademie der Wissenschaften und der Literatur*, Mainz, pp. 271-87 (repr. in Flashar, 1971, pp. 29-51).
—— 1962. *Hippokrates Schriften: Die Anfänge der abendländischen Medizin*, Hamburg.
—— 1973. *Kleine Schriften zur antiken Medizin*, Berlin.
—— 1975. 'Das Selbstverständnis der griechischen Medizin in der Zeit des Hippokrates', in Bourgey and Jouanna, 1975, pp. 77-93.
Dobson, J. F. 1925. 'Herophilus', *Proceedings of the Royal Society of Medicine*, 18, Pts i and ii, pp. 19-32.
—— 1926-7. 'Erasistratus', *Proceedings of the Royal Society of Medicine*, 20, pp. 825-32.
Dodds, E. R. 1951. *The Greeks and the Irrational*, Berkeley.
Drachmann, A. G. 1948. *Ktesibios, Philon and Heron*, Copenhagen.
—— 1967. *Grosse Griechische Erfinder*, Zurich.
Ducatillon, J. 1977. *Polémiques dans la collection hippocratique*, Paris.
Duminil, M.-P. 1983. *Le sang, les vaisseaux, le coeur dans la collection hippocratique*, Paris.
During, I. and Owen, G. E. L. 1960. *Aristotle and Plato in the Mid-Fourth Century*, Göteborg.
Ebbell, B. 1937. *The Papyrus Ebers*, Copenhagen.
Ebstein, E. 1931. 'Klassische Krankengeschichten: II. Der Mumps bei Hippokrates', *Kinderärtzliche Praxis*, 2, pp. 140-1.

Edelstein, E. J. and Edelstein, L. 1945. *Asclepius*, 2 vols, Baltimore.

Edelstein, L. 1931. *Περὶ ἀέρων und die Sammlung der hippokratischen Schriften*, Berlin.

—— 1932. 'Die Geschichte der Sektion in der Antike', in *Quellen und Studien zur Geschichte der Naturwissenschaften und der Medizin*, Bnd. III, Hft. 2, Berlin, pp. 50–106 (repr. in *Ancient Medicine*, ed. O. and C. L. Temkin, Baltimore, 1967, pp. 247–301 as 'The history of anatomy in antiquity').

—— 1935. 'Hippokrates', Pauly-Wissowa, *Real-Encyclopädie der klassischen Altertumswissenschaft*, Nachträge 6, Stuttgart, cols 1290–345.

—— 1937. 'Greek medicine in its relation to religion and magic', *Bulletin of the History of Medicine*, 5, pp. 201–46.

—— 1939. 'The genuine works of Hippocrates', *Bulletin of the History of Medicine*, 7, pp. 236–48.

—— 1940. 'Review of *Diokles von Karystos*', *American Journal of Philology*, 61, pp. 483–9 (repr. in *Ancient Medicine*, ed. O. and C. L. Temkin, Baltimore, 1967, pp. 145–52).

—— 1952a. 'The relation of ancient philosophy to medicine', *Bulletin of the History of Medicine*, 26, pp. 299–316 (repr. in *Ancient Medicine*, ed. O. and C. L. Temkin, Baltimore, 1967, pp. 349–66).

—— 1952b. 'Recent trends in the interpretation of ancient science', *Journal of the History of Ideas*, 13, pp. 573–604.

—— 1966. *Plato's Seventh Letter*, Leiden.

—— 1967. *Ancient Medicine. Selected Papers of Ludwig Edelstein*, ed. O. and C. L. Temkin, Baltimore.

Eijk, Ph. J. van der. 1990. 'The "theology" of the Hippocratic treatise on the sacred disease', *Apeiron*, 23, pp. 87–119.

—— 1991. ' "Airs, Waters, Places" and "On the Sacred Disease": two different religiosities?', *Hermes*, 119, Hft. 2, pp. 168–76.

Fahraeus, R. 1958–9. 'L'air dans les artères', *Proceedings of the Fifteenth International Congress for the History of Medicine, Madrid, 1957*, 2 vols, Madrid, 1, pp. 151–3.

Farrington, B. 1961. *Greek Science* (revised edn, Penguin), London.

Festugière, A. J. 1948. *Hippocrate: l'ancienne médicine*, Paris.

Finlayson, J. 1893. 'Herophilus and Erasistratus: a bibliographical demonstration', *Glasgow Medical Journal*, 39, pp. 321–52.

Flashar, H. (ed.). 1971. *Antike Medizin*, Darmstadt.

Fränkel, H. 1925. 'Xenophanesstudien I and II', *Hermes*, 60, pp. 174–92 (repr. in Fränkel, 1960, pp. 335–49).

—— 1960. *Wege und Formen frühgriechischen Denkens* (2nd edn), ed. F. Tietze, Munich.

—— 1962. *Dichtung und Philosophie des frühen Griechentums* (2nd edn), Munich.

—— 1974. 'Xenophanes's empiricism and his critique of knowledge (B34)', in Mourelatos, 1974, pp. 118–31.

—— 1975. *Early Greek Poetry and Philosophy*, Oxford (trans. M. Hadas and J. Willis of *Dichtung und Philosophie* (2nd edn), Munich, 1962).

Fraser, P. M. 1969. 'The career of Erasistratus of Ceos', *Rendiconti del Istituto Lombardo*, 103, pp. 518–37.

—— 1972. *Ptolemaic Alexandria*, 3 vols, Oxford.

Frazer, R. M. 1972. 'Pandora's diseases, *Erga*, 102-104', *Greek, Roman and Byzantine Studies*, 13, pp. 235-8.

Fredrich, C. 1899. *Hippokratische Untersuchungen (Philologische Untersuchungen 15)*, Berlin.

French, R. K. 1978. 'The thorax in history', *Thorax*, 33, pp. 10-18, 153-66, 295-306, 439-56, 555-64, 714-27.

Fritz, H. von. 1971. *Grundprobleme der Geschichte der antiken Wissenschaft*, Berlin and New York.

Fuchs, R. 1892. *Erasistratea*, Diss., Leipzig.

—— 1894a. 'Anecdota medica graeca', *Rheinisches Museum*, 49, pp. 532-58.

—— 1894b. 'De Erasistrato capita selecta', *Hermes*, 29, pp. 171-203.

—— 1897. 'Lebte Erasistratos in Alexandreia?', *Rheinisches Museum*, 52, pp. 377-90.

Furley, D. J. 1957. 'Empedocles and the clepsydra', *Journal of Hellenic Studies*, 77, pp. 31-4 (repr. in Allen and Furley, 1975, vol. II, pp. 265-74).

Furley, D. J. and Wilkie, J. S. 1972. 'An Arabic translation solves some problems in Galen', *Classical Review*, 22, pp. 164-7.

—— 1984. *Galen on Respiration and the Arteries*, Princeton.

—— 1985. 'Strato's theory of the void', in *Aristoteles Werk und Wirkung*, vol. I, ed. J. Wiesner, Berlin and New York, pp. 594-609 (repr. in *Cosmic Problems*, Cambridge, 1989, 13, pp. 149-60).

Garofalo, I. 1988. *Erasistrati Fragmenta*, Pisa.

Gask, G. E. 1939-40. 'Early medical schools I-III', *Annals of Medical History*, 1 (1939), pp. 128-57 and 2 (1940), pp. 15-21, 383-92.

Gatzemeier, M. 1970. *Die Naturphilosophie des Straton von Lampsakos*, Meisenheim.

Ghalioungui, P. 1968. 'The relation of Pharaonic to Greek and later medicine', *Bulletin of the Cleveland Medical Library*, 15.3, pp. 96-107.

—— 1973. *The House of Life: Per Ankh. Magic and Medical Science in Ancient Egypt*, Amsterdam.

Gigon, O. 1935. *Untersuchungen zu Heraklit*, Leipzig.

Gomperz, H. 1943. 'Problems and methods of early Greek science', *Journal of the History of Ideas*, 4, pp. 161-76.

Gomperz, T. 1910. *Die Apologie der Heilkunst* (2nd edn), Leipzig.

Gossen, H. 1912. 'Herophilos', Pauly-Wissowa, *Real-Encyclopädie der klassischen Altertumswissenschaft*, 8, 1, Stuttgart, cols 1104-10.

Gottschalk, H. B. 1965. 'Strato of Lampsacus, some texts', *Proceedings of the Leeds Philosophical and Literary Society*, 11, Pt 6, pp. 95-182.

Grapow, H., von Deines, H. and Westendorf, W. 1954-62. *Grundriss der Medizin in der alten Ägypter*, 7 vols in 9, Berlin.

Green, P. 1990. *Alexander to Actium: The Historical Evolution of the Hellenistic Age*, London.

Greenhill, W. A. 1843. 'Professor Marx's Herophilus', *British and Foreign Medical Review*, 15, pp. 106-14.

—— 1873a. 'Erasistratus', *Dictionary of Greek and Roman Biography*, 2, London, pp. 42-4.

—— 1873b. 'Herophilus', *Dictionary of Greek and Roman Biography*, 2, London, pp. 438-9.

Grensemann, H. 1968a. 'Der Arzt Polybos als Verfasser hippokratischer Schriften', *Abhandlungen der Akademie der Wissenschaften und der Literatur im Mainz*, 2 *(Geistes- u. soz. wiss. Kl.*, 1968), pp. 53-95, Mainz.

—— 1968b. *Die hippokratische Schrift 'Über die heilige Krankheit'* (Ars Medica, Abt. ii, Bd. i) Berlin.

Griffiths, A. 1987. 'Democedes of Croton: a Greek doctor at the court of Darius', in *Achaemenid History, II: The Greek Sources*, ed. H. Sancisi-Weerdenburg and A. Kuhrt, Leiden, pp. 37-51.

Grmek, M. 1980. *Hippocratica* (Actes du colloque hippocratique de Paris, 4-9 Septembre 1978), Paris.

—— 1989. *Diseases in the Ancient Greek World*, Baltimore and London.

Guthrie, W. K. C. 1957. 'Aristotle as a historian of philosophy', *Journal of Hellenic Studies*, 77, pp. 35-41.

—— 1962. *A History of Greek Philosophy*, vol. I, Cambridge.

—— 1965. *A History of Greek Philosophy*, vol. II, Cambridge.

—— 1969. *A History of Greek Philosophy*, vol. III, Cambridge.

—— 1975. *A History of Greek Philosophy*, vol. IV, Cambridge.

—— 1978. *A History of Greek Philosophy*, vol. V, Cambridge.

—— 1981. *A History of Greek Philosophy*, vol. VI, Cambridge.

Hahm, D. E. 1977. *The Origins of Stoic Cosmology*, Columbus, Ohio.

Halliday, W. R. 1910-11. *Annual of the British School at Athens*, 17, pp. 95-102.

Harris, C. R. S. 1973. *The Heart and the Vascular System in Ancient Greek Medicine*, Oxford.

Harris, J. R. 1971. *The Legacy of Egypt* (2nd edn), Oxford.

Heiberg, I. L. 1894. *Simplicii in Aristotelis De Caelo Commentaria (Commentaria in Aristotelem Graeca VII)*, Berlin.

Heidel, W. A. 1906. 'Qualitative change in presocratic philosophy', *Archiv für Geschichte der Philosophie*, 19, pp. 333-79.

—— 1910. 'Περὶ φύσεως: a study of the conception of nature among the Presocratics', *Proceedings of the American Academy of Arts and Sciences*, 45, pp. 77-133.

—— 1933. *The Heroic Age of Science*, Baltimore.

—— 1940. 'The Pythagoreans and Greek mathematics', *American Journal of Philology*, 61, pp. 1-33.

—— 1941. *Hippocratic Medicine: Its Spirit and Method*, New York.

Heinimann, F. 1945. *Nomos und Physis*, Basel.

—— 1955. 'Diokles von Karystos und der prophylaktische Brief an König Antigonus', *Museum Helveticum*, 12, pp. 158-72.

—— 1961. 'Eine vorplatonische Theorie der τέχνη', *Museum Helveticum*, 18, pp. 105-30.

Helmreich, G. 1893. *Scripta Minora III*, Leipzig.

Hershbell, J. P. 1974. 'Empedoclean influences on the Timaeus', *Phoenix*, 28, pp. 145-66.

Herzog, R. 1899. *Koische Forschungen und Funde*, Leipzig.

—— 1931. 'Die Wunderheilungen von Epidauros', *Philologus Supplementband*, 22, Hft. 3, Leipzig.

Hett, W. S. 1957. *Aristotle On the Soul, Parva Naturalia, On Breath* (Loeb Classical Library), Cambridge, Ma.

Hölscher, U. 1953. 'Anaximander und die Anfänge der Philosophie', *Hermes*, 81, pp. 257-77, 385-418.

Horine, E. F. 1941. 'An epitome of ancient pulse lore', *Bulletin of the History of Medicine*, 10, pp. 209-49.

Hurlbutt, F. R. 1939. '*Peri kardiēs*: a treatise from the Hippocratic Corpus', *Bulletin of the History of Medicine*, 7, pp. 1104-13.

Huxley, T. H. 1880. 'On certain errors respecting the structure of the heart attributed to Aristotle', *Nature*, 21, pp. 1-5.

Ideler, I. L. 1834-6. *Aristotelis Meteorologica Libri IV*, vol. I, Leipzig.

Ilberg, J. 1927. *Sorani Gynaeciorum Libri iv. De signis fracturarum. De fasciis. Vita Hippocratis secundum Soranum . . . (Corpus Medicorum Graecorum*, iv), Leipzig and Berlin.

Iverson, E. 1939. 'Papyrus Carlsberg no. VIII: with some remarks on the Egyptian origin of some popular birth prognoses', *Historiskfilologiske Meddelelser udgivet af det Kgl. Danske Videnskabernes Selskab*, 26.5, pp. 1-31.

—— 1953. 'Wounds in the head in Egyptian and Greek medicine', *Studia orientalia Ioanni Pedersen Septuagenario*, Copenhagen, pp. 163-71.

Jaeger, W. W. 1913. 'Das Pneuma im Lykeion', *Hermes*, 48, pp. 29-74 (repr. in *Scripta Minora*, Rome, 1960, pp. 57-102).

—— 1934. *Aristotle: Fundamentals of the History of his Development*, Oxford.

—— 1938a. *Diokles von Karystos, die griechische Medizin und die Schule des Aristoteles*, Berlin.

—— 1938b. 'Vergessene Fragmente des Peripatetikers Diokles von Karystos nebst zwei Anhaengen zur Chronologie der dogmatischen Aerzteschule', *Abhandlungen der Preussischen Akademie der Wissenschaften*, Phil-hist. Klasse, no. 3, pp. 1-46 (repr. in *Scripta Minora* II, Rome, 1960, pp. 185-241).

—— 1939-45. *Paideia: The Ideals of Greek Culture* (Eng. trans. by G. Highet), 3 vols, Oxford.

—— 1940. 'Diocles of Carystus: a new pupil of Aristotle', *Philosophical Review*, 49, pp. 393-414 (repr. in *Scripta Minora* II, Rome, 1960, pp. 243-65).

—— 1947. *The Theology of the Early Greek Philosophers*, Oxford.

—— 1957. 'Aristotle's use of medicine as a model of method in his ethics', *Journal of Hellenic Studies*, 77, pp. 54-61 (repr. in *Scripta Minora* II, Rome, 1960, pp. 491-509).

Joachim, H. H. 1922. *Aristotle on Coming-to-be and Passing-away*, Oxford.

Joly, R. 1960. *Recherches sur le traité pseudo-hippocratique Du régime*, Paris/Liège.

—— 1964. *Médecine grecque*, Paris.

—— 1966. *Le niveau de la science hippocratique*, Paris.

—— 1967. *Hippocrate: Du régime* (Budé edn, 6, 1), Paris.

—— 1970. *Hippocrate: De la génération. De la nature de l'enfant. Des maladies IV. Du foetus de huit mois* (Budé edn, 11), Paris.

—— 1972. *Hippocrate: Du régime des maladies aiguës etc.* (Budé edn, 6, 2), Paris.

—— (ed.). 1977. *Corpus Hippocraticum* (Actes du colloque hippocratique de Mons, 1975), Mons.

—— 1984. *Hippocrate: Du régime* (*Corpus Medicorum Graecorum* I 2, 4), Berlin.

Jones, W. H. S. 1923-31. *Hippocrates* (Loeb Classical Library), London and Cambridge, Ma.

—— 1945. ' "Hippocrates" and the Corpus Hippocraticum', *Proceedings of the British Academy*, 31, pp. 103-25.

—— 1946. *Philosophy and Medicine in Ancient Greece*, Baltimore.

—— 1947. *The Medical Writings of the Anonymus Londinensis*, Cambridge.

Jones, W. H. S. and Withington, E. T. 1948-53. *Hippocrates* (Loeb Classical Library) 4 vols, London and Cambridge, Ma.

Jouanna, J. 1961. 'Présence d'Empédocle dans la collection hippocratique', *Bulletin de l'association Guillaume Budé*, pp. 452-63.

—— 1965. 'Rapports entre Mélissos de Samos et Diogène d'Apollonie à la lumière du traité hippocratique', *Revue des études anciennes*, 67, pp. 306-23.

—— 1966. 'La théorie de l'intelligence et de l'âme dans le traité hippocratique *Du régime*: ses rapports avec Empédocle et le *Timée* de Platon', *Revue des études grecques*, 79, pp. 15-19.

—— 1975. *Hippocrate: La nature de l'homme* (*Corpus Medicorum Graecorum* I 1, 3), Berlin.

—— 1988. *Hippocrate: Des vents. De l'art*, Paris.

—— 1990. *Hippocrate: L'ancienne médicine*, Paris.

Kahlenberg, W. 1955. 'Die zeitliche Reihenfolge der Schriften περὶ γονῆς περὶ φύσιος παιδίου und περὶ νούσων 4 und ihre Zusammengehörigkeit', *Hermes* 83, pp. 252-6.

Kahn, C. H. 1960. *Anaximander and the Origins of Greek Cosmology*, New York.

Kalbfleisch, K. 1943. 'Die verkannten Venenklappen', *Rheinisches Museum*, 92, pp. 383-4.

Karsten, S. 1830. *Xenophanes Colophonii carminum reliquiae*, Amsterdam.

—— 1838. *Empedoclis Agrigentini carminum reliquiae*, Amsterdam.

King, H. 1983. 'Bound to bleed: Artemis and Greek women', Chapter 18 in *Images of Women in Antiquity*, ed. A. Cameron and A. Kuhrt, Beckenham, pp. 109-41.

Kirk, G. S. 1951. 'Natural change in Heraclitus', *Mind*, 60 n.s. 237, pp. 35-42.

—— 1954. *Heraclitus: The Cosmic Fragments*, Cambridge.

Kirk G. S. and Raven, J. E. 1957. *The Presocratic Philosophers*, Cambridge (2nd edn, M. Schofield, Cambridge, 1983).

Kôrbler, J. 1973. *Geschichte der Krebskrankheit*, Vienna.

Kotrc, R. F. 1977. 'A new fragment of Erasistratus' 'Η ΤΩΝ

'ΥΓΕΙΝΩΝ ΠΡΑΓΜΑΤΕΙΑ', *Rheinisches Museum*, 120, pp. 159-61.

Krug, A. 1985. *Heilkunst und Heilkult*, Munich.

Kucharski, P. 1964. 'Anaxagore et les idées biologiques de son siècle', *Revue philosophique de la France et de l'étranger*, 154, pp. 137-66.

Kudlien, F. 1962. 'Poseidonios und die Arzteschule der Pneumatiker', *Hermes*, 90, pp. 419-29.

—— 1963. 'Probleme um Diokles von Karystos', *Sudhoffs Archiv für Geschichte der Medizin und Naturwissenschaften*, 47, pp. 456-64 (repr. in Flashar, 1971, pp. 192-201).

—— 1964. 'Herophilus und der Beginn der medizinischen Skepsis', *Gesnerus*, 21, pp. 1-13 (repr. in Flashar, 1971, pp. 280-95).

—— 1967. *Der Beginn des medizinischen Denkens bei den Griechen*, Zurich and Stuttgart.

—— 1968a. 'Pneumatische Arzte', Pauly-Wissowa, *Real-Encyclopädie der klassischen Altertumswissenschaft*, Supp. Bd. 11, Stuttgart, col. 1101.

—— 1968b. 'Anatomie', in Pauly-Wissowa, *Real-Encyclopädie der klassischen Altertumswissenschaft*, Supp. Bd. 11, Stuttgart, cols 38-48.

——1968c. 'Early Greek primitive medicine', *Clio Modica*, 3, pp. 305-36.

—— 1969. 'Antike Anatomie und menschlicher Leichnam', *Hermes*, 97, pp. 78-94.

—— 1981. 'A new testimony for Erasistratus?', *Clio Medica*, 15, pp. 137-47.

Kühn, C. G. 1821-33. *Claudii Galeni Opera Omnia*, 20 vols in 22, Leipzig.

Kühn, J.-H. 1956. *System- und Methodenprobleme im Corpus Hippocraticum*, Hermes Einzelschriften, 11, Wiesbaden.

Kühn, J.-H. and Fleischer, U. 1986-9. *Index Hippocraticus*, Göttingen.

Lacy, P. de. 1978-84. *Galen: On the Doctrines of Hippocrates and Plato*, (*Corpus Medicorum Graecorum*, V 4, 1, 2), 3 vols, Berlin.

Langholf, V. 1986. 'Kallimachos, Komödie und hippokratische Frage', *Medizinhistorisches Journal*, Bord., 21, Hft. 1/2, pp. 3-30.

Lasserre, F. and Mudry, P. (eds). 1983. *Formes de pensée dans la collection hippocratique*, Geneva.

Last, H. 1924. 'Empedokles and his klepsydra again', *Classical Quarterly*, 18, pp. 169-73.

Lefebvre, G. 1956. *Essai sur la médecine Egyptienne de l'époque pharaonique*, Paris.

Leitner, H. 1973. *Bibliography to the Ancient Medical Authors*, Bern, Stuttgart and Vienna.

Le Page Renouf, P. 1873. 'Note on the Medical Papyrus of Berlin', *Zeitschrift für ägyptische Sprache und Alterthumskunde*, 11, pp. 123-5.

Lesky, E. 1951. *Die Zeugungs- und Vererbungslehren der Antike*, Wiesbaden.

Lichtenthaeler, C. 1948. *La médecine hippocratique*, 1: *méthode expérimental et méthode hippocratique*, Lausanne.

—— 1965. *Thucydide et Hippocrate vus par un historien médecin*, Geneva.

BIBLIOGRAPHY

—— 1979. 'οὔτε γὰρ ἰατροὶ ἤρκουν τὸ πρῶτον θεραπεύοντες ἀγνοίᾳ', *Hermes*, Bnd. 107, Hft. 3, pp. 270–86.

Link, H. F. 1814/15. *Über die Theorien in den Hippokratischen Schriften nebst Bemerkungen über die Echtheit dieser Schriften*, Abhndl. Kgl. Akad., Berlin.

Littré, E. 1839–61. *Oeuvres complètes d'Hippocrate*, 10 vols, Paris.

Lloyd, G. E. R. 1963. 'Who is attacked in *On Ancient Medicine?*', *Phronesis*, 8, pp. 108–26.

—— 1964. 'Hot and cold, dry and wet in Greek philosophy', *Journal of Hellenic Studies*, 84, pp. 92–106 (repr. in Allen and Furley, 1970, vol. I, pp. 255–80).

—— 1966. *Polarity and Analogy*, Cambridge.

—— 1968a. *Aristotle: The Growth and Structure of his Thought*, Cambridge.

—— 1968b. 'Plato as a natural scientist', *Journal of Hellenic Studies*, 88, pp. 78–92.

—— 1973. *Greek Science after Aristotle*, London.

—— 1975a. 'A note on Erasistratus of Ceos', *Journal of Hellenic Studies*, 95, pp. 172–5.

—— 1975b. 'Alcmaeon and the early history of dissection', *Sudhoffs Archiv für Geschichte der Medizin und Naturwissenschaften*, 59, pp. 113–47.

—— 1975c. 'The Hippocratic question', *Classical Quarterly*, N. S. 25, pp. 171–92.

—— 1975d. 'Aspects of the interrelations of medicine, magic and philosophy in ancient Greece', *Apeiron*, 9, pp. 1–16.

—— 1975e. 'The role of medicine in the development of early Greek science', *Lampas*, 8, pp. 327–33.

—— 1979. *Magic, Reason and Experience*, Cambridge.

—— 1983. *Science, Folklore and Ideology*, Cambridge.

—— 1985. *Science and Morality in Greco-Roman Antiquity*, Inaugural Lecture, Cambridge.

—— 1987. *The Revolutions of Wisdom*, Berkeley and Los Angeles.

—— 1990. *Demystifying Mentalities*, Cambridge.

—— 1990. 'Plato and Archytas in the Seventh Letter', *Phronesis*, 35, pp. 159–74.

Longrigg, J. 1963. 'Philosophy and medicine: some early interactions', *Harvard Studies in Classical Philology*, 67, pp. 147–75.

—— 1964a. 'A note on Anaximenes Fragment 2', *Phronesis*, 9, pp. 1–4.

—— 1964b. 'Galen on Empedocles (Fragment 67)' *Philologus*, Bnd. 108, Hft. 3/4, pp. 297–300.

—— 1965. 'Empedocles's fiery fish', *Journal of the Warburg and Courtauld Institutes*, 28, pp. 314–15.

—— 1966. 'The sun and the planets', *Apeiron*, 1, pp. 19–31.

—— 1971. 'Erasistratus', *Dictionary of Scientific Biography*, 4, New York, pp. 382–6.

—— 1972. 'Herophilus', *Dictionary of Scientific Biography*, 6, New York, pp. 316–19.

—— 1973. 'Darwinism and Presocratic philosophy', *Durham University Journal*, 65, pp. 307-15.
—— 1974. 'Empedocles' fertile fish (Fragment B74)', *Journal of Hellenic Studies*, 94, pp. 173-4.
—— 1975a. 'Praxagoras', *Dictionary of Scientific Biography*, 11, New York, pp. 127-8.
—— 1975b. 'Thales', *Dictionary of Scientific Biography*, 13, New York, pp. 295-8.
—— 1975c. 'Elementary physics in the Lyceum and Stoa', *Isis*, 66, pp. 211-29.
—— 1976. 'The "roots" of all things', *Isis*, 67, pp. 420-38.
—— 1980. 'The great plague of Athens', *History of Science*, 18, pp. 209-25.
—— 1981. 'Superlative achievement and comparative neglect: Alexandrian medical science and modern historical research', *History of Science*, 19, pp. 155-200.
—— 1983. '[Hippocrates] *Ancient Medicine* and its intellectual context', in Lasserre and Mudry, 1983, pp. 249-56.
—— 1985a. 'A seminal "debate" in the fifth century B.C.?', in *Aristotle on Nature and Living Things: Philosophical and Historical Studies presented to D. M. Balme*, ed. A. Gotthelf, Pittsburgh and Bristol, pp. 277-87.
—— 1985b. 'Herophilus and the arterial vein', *Liverpool Classical Monthly*, 10.10, pp. 149-50.
—— 1985c. 'Elements and after: a study in Presocratic physics of the second half of the fifth century', *Apeiron*, 19, pp. 93-115.
—— 1988. 'Anatomy in Alexandria in the third century B.C.', *British Journal for the History of Science*, 21, pp. 455-88.
—— 1989. 'Presocratic philosophy and Hippocratic medicine', *History of Science*, 27, pp. 1-39.
—— 1992 'Epidemics, ideas and classical Athenian society', Chapter 2 in *Epidemics and Ideas: Essays on the Historical Perception of Pestilence*, ed. T. Ranger and P. Slack, Cambridge, pp. 21-44.
—— 1993. 'Empedocles and the plague of Selinus: a cock and bull story?', *Tria Lustra: A Festschrift in Honour of John Pinsent*, 1992, pp. 37-42.
Lonie, I. M. 1964. 'Erasistratus, the Erasistrateans, and Aristotle', *Bulletin of the History of Medicine*, 38, pp. 426-43.
—— 1973. 'The paradoxical text "On the Heart" ', *Medical History*, 17, pp. 1-15, 136-53.
—— 1981. *The Hippocratic Treatises 'On Generation', 'On the Nature of the Child', 'Diseases' IV (Ars Medica, II. 7)*, Berlin.
McDiarmid, J. B. 1953. 'Theophrastus on the presocratic causes', *Harvard Studies in Classical Philology*, 61, pp. 85-156 (repr. in Allen and Furley, 1970, vol. I, pp. 178-238).
Magnus, H. 1901. *Die Augenheilkunde der Alten*, Breslau.
Majno. G. 1975. *The Healing Hand: Man and Wound in the Ancient World*, Cambridge, Ma.

Maloney, G. and Savoie, R. 1982. *Cinq cent ans de bibliographie hippocratique 1473-1982*, Quebec.

Manetti, D. 1989. 'Alcmaeon', *Corpus dei Papiri Filosofici Greci e Latini*, 1, pp. 149-51.

—— 1990. 'Doxographical deformation of medical tradition in the report of the *Anonymus Londinensis* on Philolaus', *Zeitschrift für Papyrologie und Epigraphik*, 83, pp. 219-23.

Mani, N. 1959-67. *Die historischen Grundlagen der Leberforschung*, 2 vols, Basel.

Mansfeld, J. 1971. *The Pseudo-Hippocratic Tract περὶ ἑβδομάδων Chaps 1-11 and Greek Philosophy*, Assen.

—— 1975. 'Alcmaeon: "physikos" or physician?', in *Kephalaion*, ed. J. Mansfeld and L. M. de Rijk, Assen, pp. 26-38.

—— 1980. 'Theoretical and empirical attitudes in early Greek medicine', in Grmek, 1980, pp. 371-91.

Manuli, P. and Vegetti, M. 1977. *Cuore, Sangue e Cervello*, Milan.

Marx, F. 1915. *Auli Cornelii Celsi quae supersunt*, (*Corpus Medicorum Latinorum*), 1, Leipzig and Berlin.

Marx, K. F. H. 1838. *Herophilus, ein Beitrag zur Geschichte der Medizin*, Karlsruhe and Baden.

—— 1840. *De Herophili celeberrimi medici vita scriptis atque in medicina meritis*, Göttingen.

May, M. T. 1958. 'Galen on human dissection', *Journal of the History of Medicine*, 13, pp. 409-10.

Mesk, J. 1913. 'Antiochus und Stratonike', *Rheinisches Museum*, 68, pp. 366-94.

Michler, M. 1968. *Die hellenistische Chirurgie, I. Die alexandrinischen Chirurgen*, Wiesbaden.

Mikalson, J. D. 1984. 'Religion and the plague in Athens, 431-423 BC', *Greek, Roman and Byzantine Studies*, 10 (Studies presented to Sterling Dow on his 80th birthday), Durham, NC, pp. 217-25.

Miller, H. W. 1948. 'A medical theory of cognition', *Transactions of the American Philological Association*, 79, pp. 168-83.

—— 1952. 'Dynamis and physis in *On Ancient Medicine*', *Transactions of the American Philological Association*, 83, pp. 184-97.

—— 1953. 'The concept of the divine in *De morbo sacro*', *Transactions of the American Philological Association*, 84, pp. 1-15.

—— 1955. '*Technē* and discovery in *On Ancient Medicine*', *Transactions of the American Philological Association*, 86, pp. 51-62.

—— 1957. 'The flux of the body in Plato's *Timaeus*', *Transactions of the American Philological Association*, 88, pp. 103-11.

—— 1960. 'The concept of dynamis in *De victu*', *Transactions of the American Philological Association*, 90, pp. 147-64.

—— 1962. 'The aetiology of disease in Plato's *Timaeus*', *Transactions of the American Philological Association*, 93, pp. 175-87.

Moon, R. O. 1923. *Hippocrates and his Successors in Relation to the Philosophy of their Time* (Fitzpatrick Lectures), London.

Morrow, G. R. 1969. 'Qualitative change in Aristotle's *Physics*', in

Naturphilosophie bei Aristoteles und Theophrast, Heidelberg, pp. 154-67.

Mourelatos, A. P. D. (ed.). 1974. *The Presocratics*, New York.

Mudry, P. 1982. *La préface du 'De medicina' de Celse* (Bibliotheca Helvetica Romana 19), Lausanne.

Mugler, C. 1963. *Les origines de la science grecque*, Paris.

Müllach, F. G. A. 1881. *Fragment Philosophorum Graecorum*, vol. III, Paris.

Müller, I. 1874. *Claudii Galeni De Placitis et Platonis Libri Novem*, Leipzig.

Müri, W. 1953. 'Melancholie und schwarze Galle', *Museum Helveticum*, 10, pp. 21-38.

Nelson, A. H. 1909. *Die hippokratische Schrift Περὶ φυσῶν Text und Studien*, Diss., Uppsala.

Nestle, W. 1942. *Vom Mythos zum Logos*, Stuttgart.

Neuberger, M. 1906. *Die Geschichte der Medizin*, Stuttgart.

Nörenberg, H.-W. 1968. *Das Göttliche und die Natur in der Schrift über die heilige Krankheit*, Diss., Bonn.

Nutton, V. 1979. *Galen: On Prognosis (Corpus Medicorum Graecorum, V, 8, 1)*, Berlin.

—— 1981. *Galen: Problems and Prospects*, London.

—— 1988. *From Democedes to Harvey*, London.

—— 1992. 'Healers in the medical market place: towards a social history of Graeco-Roman medicine', *Medicine in Society*, Cambridge, pp. 15-58.

O'Brien, D. 1969. *Empedocles' Cosmic Cycle*, Cambridge.

—— 1970. 'The effect of a simile: Empedocles' theories of seeing and breathing', *Journal of Hellenic Studies*, 90, pp. 140-79.

Ogle, W. 1882. *Aristotle on the Parts of Animals*, London.

Olivieri, A. 1919. 'Alcmeone di Crotone', *Memorie della reale Accademia di Archeologia, Lettere e Belle Arti* (Società Reale di Napoli) 4, pp. 15-41.

Onians, R. B. 1951. *The Origins of European Thought*, Cambridge.

Oppermann, H. 1925. 'Herophilos bei Kallimachos', *Hermes*, 60, pp. 14-32.

Parker, R. C. T. 1983. *Miasma: Pollution and Purification in Early Greek Religion*, Oxford.

Parry, A. 1969. 'The language of Thucydides' description of the plague', *Bulletin of the Institute of Classical Studies*, 16, pp. 106-18.

Peck, A. L. 1926. 'Anaxagoras and the parts', *Classical Quarterly*, 20, pp. 57-71.

Phillips, E. D. 1973. *Greek Medicine*, London.

Pigeaud, J. M. 1978. 'Du rhythme dans le corps: quelques notes sur l'interprétation du pouls par le méthode Hérophile', *Bulletin de l'Association Guillaume Budé*, 3, pp. 258-67.

Pinault, J. R. 1983. *Biographical Fiction in the Lives of Hippocrates*, Diss., University of Pennsylvania.

—— 1986. 'How Hippocrates cured the plague', *Journal of the History of Medicine and the Allied Sciences*, 41, pp. 52-75.

BIBLIOGRAPHY

—— 1992. *Hippocratic Lives and Legends*, Leiden, New York and Cologne.

Pinoff, J. 1847. 'Herophilos: ein Beitrag zur Geschichte der Geburts-hilfe', *Janus*, 2, pp. 739-43.

Pohlenz, M. 1917. 'Zu den hippokratischen Briefen', *Hermes*, 52, pp. 348-53.

—— 1938. *Hippokrates und die Begründung der wissenschaftlichen Medizin*, Berlin.

—— 1953. 'Nomos und Physis', *Hermes*, 81, pp. 418-38.

Popper, K. R. 1952. 'The nature of philosophical problems and their roots in science', *British Journal for the Philosophy of Science*, 3, pp. 124-56 (repr. in his *Conjectures and Refutations* (5th edn), London, 1974, pp. 66-96.

—— 1966. *The Open Society and its Enemies* (5th edn), vol. I, London.

Potter, P. 1976. 'Herophilus of Chalcedon', *Bulletin of the History of Medicine*, 50, pp. 45-60.

—— 1988. *Hippocrates*, vols V and VI (Loeb Classical Library), Cambridge, Ma. and London.

Prag, A. J. N. 1990. 'Reconstructing King Philip II: the "nice" version', *American Journal of Archaeology*, 94, pp. 237-47.

Prag, A. J. N., Musgrave, J. H. and Neave, R. A. H. 1984. 'The skull from Tomb II at Vergina: King Philip II of Macedon', *Journal of Hellenic Studies*, 104, pp. 60-78.

Raeder, J. 1928-33. *Oribasii collectionum medicarum reliquiae* (*Corpus Medicorum Graecorum* VI, 1, 1-VI 2, 2), Leipzig and Berlin (repr. Amsterdam, 1964).

Rechenauer, G. 1991. *Thukydides und die hippokratische Medizin*, Hildesheim, Zurich and New York.

Regenbogen, O. 1931. 'Eine Forschungsmethode antiker Naturwissen-schaft', *Quellen und Studien zur Geschichte der Mathematik, Astronomie und Physik*, Bnd, 1, 2 (1930), Berlin, pp. 131-82 (repr. in his *Kleine Schriften*, Munich, 1961, pp. 141-94).

Reinhardt, K. 1916. *Parmenides und die Geschichte der griechischen Philosophie*, Bonn.

Rivaud, A. 1925. *Platon: 'Timée', 'Critias'*, vol. 10 in *Platon: oeuvres complètes*, Paris.

Rose, V. 1863. *Aristoteles Pseudepigraphus*, Leipzig.

Ross, W. D. 1924. *Aristotle's Metaphysics*, Oxford.

Rüsche, F. 1930. *Blut, Leben und Seele*, Paderborn.

Sallares, R. 1991. *The Ecology of the Ancient Greek World*, London.

Sambursky, S. 1956. *The Physical World of the Greeks*, London.

—— 1962. *The Physical World of Late Antiquity*, London.

Sandison, A. T. 1959. 'The first recorded case of inflammatory mastitis: Queen Atossa of Persia and the physician Democedes', *Medical History*, 3, pp. 317-22.

Sarton, G. 1952, 1959. *A History of Science*, vols I and II, Cambridge, Ma.

Saunders, J. B. de C. M. 1963. *The Transition from Ancient Egyptian to Greek Medicine*, Lawrence, Kansas.

Scarborough, J. 1970. 'Thucydides, Greek medicine, and the plague at Athens', *Episteme*, 4, pp. 77-90.
—— 1976. 'Celsus on human vivisection at Ptolemaic Alexandria', *Clio Medica*, 11, pp. 25-38.
Schmekel, E. 1938. *Die positive Philosophie in ihrer geschichtlichen Entwicklung*, Bnd. 1, Berlin.
Schmitt, C. B. 1985. 'Aristotle among the physicians', Chapter 1 in *The Medical Renaissance of the Sixteenth Century*, ed. A. Wear, R. K. French and I. M. Lonie, Cambridge.
Schöne, H. 1907. 'Markellinos' Pulslehre: ein griechisches Anekdoton', *Festschrift zur 49 Versammlung deutscher Philologen und Schulmänner in Basel im Jahre 1907*, Basel, pp. 448-72.
Schöner, E. 1964. *Das Viererschema in der antiken Humoralpathologie* (*Sudhoffs Archiv für Geschichte der Medizin und der Naturwissenschaften*, 4), Wiesbaden.
Schumacher, J. 1940. *Antike Medizin: Die Naturphilosophischen Grundlagen der Medizin in der griechischen Antike*, Berlin.
—— 1965. *Die Anfänge abendländischer Medizin in der griechischen Antike*, Stuttgart.
Semeria, A. 1986. 'Per un censimento degli *Asklepieia* della Grecia continentale e delle isole', *Annali Scuola Normale Superiore di Pisa*, 16, pp. 931-58.
Senn, G. 1929. 'Über Herkunft und Stil der Beschreibungen von Experimenten im Corpus Hippocraticum', *Archiv für Geschichte der Medizin*, 22, pp. 217-89.
Sherwin-White, S. M. 1978. *Ancient Cos, Hypomnemata*, Hft. 51, Göttingen.
Sigerist, H. E. 1924. 'Die Geburt der abendländischen Medizin', *Essays on the History of Medicine: Presented to Karl Sudhoff*, ed. Charles Singer and H. E. Sigerist, London and Zurich, pp. 185-205.
—— 1951-1961. *A History of Medicine*, 2 vols, Oxford.
Simon, B. 1978. *Mind and Madness in Ancient Greece*, Ithaca and London.
Simon, M. 1906. *Sieben Bücher Anatomie des Galen*, 2 vols, Leipzig.
Singer, C. 1925. *The Evolution of Anatomy*, London.
Singer, C. and Underwood, E. A. 1962. *A Short History of Medicine* (2nd edn), London.
Smith, G. Elliott. 1914. 'Egyptian mummies', *Journal of Egyptian Archaeology*, 10, pp. 189-96.
Smith, W. D. 1979. *The Hippocratic Tradition*, Ithaca and London.
—— 1982. 'Erasistratus's dietetic medicine', *Bulletin of the History of Medicine*, 56, pp. 398-409.
—— 1990. *Hippocrates: Pseudepigraphic Writings*, Leiden.
Solmsen, F. S. 1950. 'Tissues and the soul', *Philosophical Review*, 59, pp. 435-68.
—— 1957. 'The vital heat, the inborn *pneuma* and the *aether*', *Journal of Hellenic Studies*, 77, pp. 119-23.
—— 1960. *Aristotle's System of the Physical World*, Ithaca and New York.
—— 1961. 'Greek philosophy and the discovery of the nerves', *Museum*

Helveticum, 18, pp. 150-67, 169-97 (repr. in *Kleine Schriften*, Hildesheim, 1968, pp. 536-82 and in Flashar, 1971, pp. 202-79).

—— 1965. 'Love and Strife in Empedocles' cosmology', *Phronesis*, 10, pp. 109-48.

Spencer, W. G. 1935-8. *Celsus: De Medicina*, 3 vols (Loeb Classical Library), London.

Sprengel, K. 1792. *Versuch einer pragmatischen Geschichte der Arznei-kunde*, Halle (4th edn, Leipzig, 1846).

Staden, H. von. 1975. 'Experiment and experience in Hellenistic medicine', *Bulletin of the Institute of Classical Studies*, 22, pp. 178-99.

—— 1982. 'Hairesis and heresy: the case of the *haireseis iatrikai*', in *Jewish and Christian Self-Definition, III: Self-Definition in the Graeco-Roman World*, ed. B. F. Meyer and E. P. Sanders, London, pp. 76-100, 199-206.

—— 1989. *Herophilus: The Art of Medicine in Early Alexandria*, Cambridge.

Steckerl, F. 1958. *The Fragments of Praxagoras of Cos and his School* (*Philosophia Antiqua*, 8), Leiden.

Stella, L. A. 1939. 'L'importanza di Alcmeone nella storia del pensiero greco', *Memorie della Reale Accademia Nazionali dei Lincei*, ser. 6, vol. 8, fasc. 4, pp. 233-87.

Steuer, R. O. 1948. *whdw: Aetiological Principle of Pyaemia in Ancient Egyptian Medicine*, Baltimore (*Supplement to the Bulletin of the History of Medicine*, no. 10).

Steuer, R. O. and Saunders, J. B. de C. M. 1959. *Ancient Egyptian and Cnidian Medicine*, Berkeley and Los Angeles.

Sticker, G. 1923. *Hippokrates, der Volkskrankheiten erstes und drittes Buch*, Leipzig.

Stückelberger, A. 1984. *Vestigia Democritea: Die Rezeption der Lehre von den Atomen in der antiken Naturwissenschaft und Medizin, Schweizer-ische Beiträge zur Altertumswissenschaft*, Hft. 17, Basel.

Susemihl, F. 1891. *Geschichte der griechischen Literatur in der Alexan-drinerzeit*, 2 vols, Leipzig.

Tannery, P. 1887. *Pour l'histoire de la science hellène*, Paris.

Taylor, A. E. 1928. *A Commentary on Plato's Timaeus*, Oxford.

Temkin, O. 1933. 'Views on epilepsy in the Hippocratic period', *Bulletin of the History of Medicine*, 1, pp. 41-4.

—— 1945. *The Falling Sickness: A History of Epilepsy from the Greeks to the Beginnings of Modern Neurology*, Baltimore.

—— 1953. 'Greek medicine as science and craft', *Isis*, 44, pp. 213-25.

—— 1956a. *Soranus, Gynecology: Translation with an Introduction*, Baltimore.

—— 1956b. 'On the interrelationship of the history and the philosophy of medicine', *Bulletin of the History of Medicine*, 30, pp. 241-51.

—— 1985. 'Hippocrates as the physician of Democritus', *Gesnerus*, 42, pp. 455-64.

Theiler, W. 1925. *Zur Geschichte der teleologischen Naturbetrachtung bis auf Aristoteles*, Zurich and Leipzig.

Thivel, A. 1981. *Cnide et Cos?*, Paris.

Thompson, R. Campbell. 1903-4. *The Devils and Evil Spirits in Babylonia*, London.
Torraca, L. 1965. 'Diocle di Carysto, il "Corpus Hippocraticum" ed Aristotele', *Sophia*, 33, pp. 105-15.
Tuke, Sir J. B. 1910-11. 'Hippocrates', *Encyclopaedia Britannica* (11th edn), vol. 13, Cambridge, pp. 517-19.
Unger, F. C. 1923a. *Liber Hippocraticus de corde editus cum prolegomenis et commentario*, Diss., Utrecht.
—— 1923b. 'Liber Hippocraticus ΠΕΡΙ ΚΑΡΔΙΗΣ', *Mnemosyne*, 51, pp. 1-101.
Vallance, J. T. 1990. *The Lost Theory of Asclepiades of Bithynia*, Oxford.
Verbeke, G. 1945. *L'évolution de la doctrine du pneuma*, Paris and Louvain.
Verdenius, W. J. 1962. 'Science grecque et science moderne', *Revue philosophique*, 87, pp. 319-36.
Villaret, O. 1911. *Hippocratis De natura hominis liber ad codicum fidem recensitus*, Diss., Göttingen and Berlin.
Vitrac, B. 1989. *Médecine et philosophie au temps d'Hippocrate*, Paris.
Vlastos, G. 1947. 'Equality and justice in early Greek cosmologies', *Classical Philology*, 42, pp. 156-78 (repr. in Allen and Furley, 1970, pp. 56-91).
—— 1950. 'The physical theory of Anaxagoras', *Philosophical Review*, 59, pp. 31-57.
—— 1952. 'Theology and philosophy in early Greek thought', *Philosophical Quarterly*, 2, pp. 97-123 (repr. in Allen and Furley, 1970, pp. 92-129).
—— 1953. 'Isonomia', *American Journal of Philology*, 74, pp. 337-66.
—— 1975. *Plato's Universe*, Oxford.
Wachtler, J. 1896. *De Alcmaeone Crotoniata*, Diss., Leipzig.
Wasserstein, A. 1972. 'Le rôle des hypothèses dans la médecine grecque', *Revue philosophique*, 162, pp. 3-14.
Waszink, J. H. 1947. *Tertullian De Anima: Edition with Introduction and Commentary*, Amsterdam.
Waterlow, S. 1982. *Nature, Change and Agency in Aristotle's Physics*, Oxford.
Wehrli, F. 1950. *Straton von Lampsakos: Die Schule des Aristoteles*, Hft. 5, Basel.
Weidauer, K. 1954. *Thukydides und die Hippokratischen Schriften*, Heidelberg.
Wellmann, M. 1888. 'Zur Geschichte der Medicin im Alterthume', *Hermes*, 23, pp. 556-66.
—— 1900. 'Zur Geschichte der Medizin im Alterthum', *Hermes*, 35, pp. 349-84.
—— 1901. *Fragmentsammlung der griechischen Ärzte Bd. 1 Die Fragmente der Sikelischen Ärzte*, Berlin.
—— 1903. 'Diokles', Pauly-Wissowa, *Real-Encyclopädie der klassischen Altertumswissenschaft*, 5, 1, Stuttgart, cols 802-12.

—— 1907. 'Erasistratos', Pauly-Wissowa, *Real-Encyclopädie der klassischen Altertumswissenschaft*, 6, 1, Stuttgart, cols 333-50.

—— 1922. 'Der Verfasser des *Anonymus Londinensis*', *Hermes*, 57, pp. 396-430.

—— 1929a. 'Spuren Demokrits von Abdera im Corpus Hippocraticum', *Archeion*, 11, pp. 297-330.

—— 1929b. 'Die Schrift Περὶ ἱρῆς νούσου des *Corpus Hippocraticum*', *Sudhoffs Archiv für Geschichte der Medizin und Naturwissenschaften*, 22, pp. 290-312.

—— 1930. 'Die pseudohippokratische Schrift Περὶ ἀρκαίης ἰατρικῆς', *Sudhoffs Archiv für Geschichte der Medizin und Naturwissenschaften*, 23, pp. 299-305.

Wenkebach E. and Pfaff, P. 1956. *Galeni in Hippocratis Epidemiarum librum VI commentaria*, I-VIII, Berlin (*Corpus Medicorum Graecorum*, V 10, 2, 2).

Wightman, W. P. D. 1971. *The Emergence of Scientific Medicine*, Edinburgh.

Wilamowitz-Moellendorff, U. von. 1901. 'Die hippokratische Schrift περὶ ἱρῆς νούσου', *Sitzungsberichte der königlich preussischen Akademie der Wissenschaften*, Berlin, pp. 2-23.

—— 1902. *Griechisches Lesebuch*, vol. II, Berlin.

Willerding, G. K. F. 1914. *Studia Hippocratica*, Diss., Göttingen.

Wilson, J. V. Kinnier and Reynolds, E. H. 1990. 'Translation and analysis of a cuneiform text forming part of a Babylonian treatise on epilepsy', *Medical History*, 34, pp. 185-98.

Wilson, L. G. 1959. 'Erasistratus, Galen and the pneuma', *Bulletin of the History of Medicine*, 33, pp. 293-314.

Withington, E. T. 1921. 'The Asclepiadae and the priests of Asclepius', in *Studies in the History and Method of Science*, ed. C. Singer, vol. II, Oxford.

Wright, M. R. 1981. *Empedocles: The Extant Fragments*, New Haven and London.

Zafiropulo, J. 1953. *Empédocle d'Agrigente*, Paris.

Zeller, E. 1856-81. *Die Philosophie der Griechen* (2nd edn), Tübingen.

—— 1920-. *Die Philosophie der Griechen*, I, 1 (7th edn, 1923) and I, 2 (6th edn, 1920) edited and enlarged by W. Nestle, Leipzig.

Zeller, E. and Mondolfo, R. 1932-. *La filosofia dei Greci nel suo sviluppo storico*, Florence.

Index locorum

Aelian *Nat. an.* (IX 33) 20; (XII
16) 240 n32; (XII 18-20) 94, 96,
240 n25
[Aeschylus] *P. V.* (442-68) 102,
240 n52; (446-83) 23; (478-506)
102, 240 n52; (853ff.) 250 n58
Aëtius *Plac.* (I 3, 4) 233 n53; (I 3,
5) 65; (I 3, 8) 231 n3; (I 3, 20)
231 n20; (I 7, 13) 231 n18; (II
11, 5) 221; (II 13, 10) 231 n15;
(II 14, 3-4) 231 n14; (II 20, 1)
231 n13; (II 22, 1) 231 n14; (II
24, 2) 231 n13; (II 25, 1) 231
n13; (II 29, 1) 231 n13; (III 16,
3) 236 n73, 243 n56; (IV 4, 6)
56; (IV 5, 1) 56; (IV 5, 4) 251
n77; (IV 5, 6-8) 170, 247 n68;
(IV 5, 7) 171, 238 n103, 247
n70; (IV 9, 15) 239 n11; (IV 22,
1) 237 n84; (V 3, 3) 61, 243 n64;
(V 3, 6) 54, 240 n28; (V 4, 1) 54;
(V 5, 1) 54; (V 5, 3) 54; (V 7, 3)
55; (V 14, 1) 57; (V 14, 2) 57,
245 n27; (V 15, 4) 237 n88; (V
16, 1) 56; (V 16, 3) 56, 61; (V
17, 3) 56, 61; (V 22, 1) 73, 76,
236 n71, 237 n78, 240 n26; (V
24, 1) 57, 62; (V 24, 2) 57, 237
n84; (V 24, 3) 78; (V 24, 33) 57;
(V 25, 2) 57; (V 25, 3) 57, 236
n63; (V 25, 4) 237 n84; (V 26, 4)
237 n78; (V 27, 1) 73, 237 n84;
(V 28) 239 n11; (V 30, 1) 52; (V
30, 2) 247 n82; (VII 48) 252 n94

Alcaeus (4) 30
Alcmaeon (*D.K.*24A1) 48;
(*D.K.*24A2) 234 n17; (*D.K.*24A3)
49; (*D.K.*24A5) 53, 57;
(*D.K.*24A10) 58, 252 n93;
(*D.K.*24A13) 54, 56, 61, 62, 243
n64; (*D.K.*24A14) 54, 61;
(*D.K.*24A16) 61; (*D.K.*24A17)
56, 61, 234 n33; (*D.K.*24A18) 57;
(*D.K.*24B1) 51, 234 n20;
(*D.K.*24B3) 57; (*D.K.*24B4) 52
Alexander Aphrodisiensis *In
metaph.* (26, 21) 235 n44
Anaxagoras (*D.K.*59A30) 231 n2;
(*D.K.*59A45) 235 n51;
(*D.K.*59A47) 242 n37;
(*D.K.*59A92) 57, 239 n11;
(*D.K.*59A103) 57; (*D.K.*59A107)
55, 242 n41; (*D.K.*59A108) 55,
56; (*D.K.*59A110) 56;
(*D.K.*59B10) 235 n50
Anaximander (*D.K.*12A9) 220, 257
n1; (*D.K.*12A10) 221, 257 n1;
(*D.K.*12A11) 231 n17;
(*D.K.*12A15) 231 n16;
(*D.K.*12AA17a) 221;
(*D.K.*12A21) 231 n13;
(*D.K.*12A22) 231 n13;
(*D.K.*12A23) 31; (*D.K.*12A28)
31; (*D.K.*12B1) 234 n22;
(*D.K.*12B2) 231 n17
Anaximenes (*D.K.*13A7) 231 n14,
231 n19, 257 n6; (*D.K.*13A10)
231 n18, 231 n19; (*D.K.*13A14)

231 n14, 231 n15; (*D.K.*13A15)
231 n14; (*D.K.*13A17) 31, 46;
(*D.K.*13A21) 30; (*D.K.*13B1) 258
n24; (*D.K.*13B2) 233 n53
Anecdota medica 3 (541 Fuchs)
248 n94; 4 (542 Fuchs) 248 n95;
20 (550 Fuchs) 248 n93
Anon. Lond. (V 35–VII 40) 239
n20; (XI 13) 66; (XI 14) 242
n23; (XI 22) 235 n46; (XVIII 8)
237 n88; (XVIII 41) 244 n76;
(XIX 9) 226; (XX 25) 106, 110,
140, 234 n24, 241 n11, 247 n80;
(XX 47) 247 n83; (XXI 5–XXIX
32) 32, 183; (XXI 82) 256 n185;
(XXVI 31) 202; (XXVI 103) 255
n164; (XXVIII 28) 202;
(XXVIII 47) 201; (XXXIII 30)
215
Archilochus *Frag.* 74, 3 (Diehl)
31; *Frag.* 96 (Diehl) 92
Archimedes *Sphaer. et cyl.* II (iii,
84 Heib.) 242 n28
Archytas (*D.K.*47A1) 242 n27;
(*D.K.*47A14) 242 n28;
(*D.K.*47B1) 242 n29; (*D.K.*47B2)
242 n40; (*D.K.*47B3) 242 n30
Aristophanes *Epit. hist. anim.* (I
78) 56, 247 n76; *Pax* (376) 231
n8; (1253) 10; *Plutus* (659ff.) 19;
Nubes (187ff.) 240 n42; (227ff.)
77; (367ff.) 30
Aristotle *Anal. Post.* (71b19–25)
245 n11; *Anal. Prior.* (46a7ff.)
245 n11; *De anima* (404a9) 236
n62; (405a19) 231 n18;
(405b1ff.) 235 n47, n56; (405b5)
76; (405b24) 237 n88; (411a7)
231 n18; (416a9–10) 245 n21;
(416b28) 237 n89; *De caelo*
(299a2) 245 n11; (302b5) 245 n7;
(305b20) 151; (305b30–307b20)
152; (306a1) 126; (306a10) 245
n11; (306a23) 152; (311a15) 245
n14; *De generatione animalium*
(717a34–6) 253 n110; (721a30)
95; (721b6–724b31) 69; (722b10)
54; (723a23) 54; (726b1–11) 238
n105; (732b31) 237 n89;

(733a34) 237 n89; (735b32) 238
n105; (736a14) 238 n106;
(737a11–12) 245 n22; (74013) 55
(740a33) 56, 247 n76; (744a27)
169; (746a15) 244 n3; (746a19)
56, 172, 247 n76; (747a18) 245
n22; (747a29) 57; (747a34) 57,
75; (752b25) 61; (763b30) 55,
242 n41; (764a6) 54, 240 n33;
(764a34) 247 n63; (777a7) 74,
237 n83, 246 n35; (779a8) 247
n63; (787b24–6) 253 n110; *De
gen. et corr.* (315a11) 241 n9;
(315b30) 152; (323b18) 245 n18;
(323b29) 245 n18; (324a5) 245
n18; (324b26) 235 n48; (329a25)
154; (329b18) 155; (329b30) 155;
(329b32–330a26) 245 n15;
(331a3–6) 155; (331a24) 157;
(331b2) 157; (333a35) 244 n71;
(334b34) 245 n16; *De iuventute*
(470a19) 237 n89; (480a28–b6)
158; *De long. et brev. vitae*
(464b32) 150; *De motu
animalium* (703a13) 248 n89;
De partibus animalium
(640a18) 243 n58; (640b36) 249
n42; (642a31) 245 n24; (644b22–
645a36) 159; (645a26) 59;
(650a3) 237 n89; (650b3) 174;
(651a33) 245 n23; (653a8) 150;
(653a22–4) 245 n23; (656b3) 247
n85; (656b19) 174; (665a30) 169;
(666a6) 247 n60; (666a19) 247
n63; (666b1) 169; (666b22–3)
247 n64; (666b23–33) 247 n72;
(668a13) 255 n161; (668b33) 245
n24; (668b34) 237 n93; (676b30)
169; (688a22–5) 247 n87; *De
progressu animalium* (708b4)
245 n26, 247 n59; *De
respiratione* (471b19ff.) 245
n26, 247 n59; (471b30) 236 n62;
(472b12) 244 n67; (473a4) 245
n21; (473a15) 74; (474b12) 245
n21; (475b15) 245 n24; (475b17)
237 n93; (477b24) 245 n23;
(478a16–17) 245 n21; (478a28)
245 n24; (480a20) 254 n158;

(480b24ff.) 244 n82; (480b24) 3, 151; *De sensu* (436a19) 151; (436a18) 227 n2; (436a19) 244 n82; (437b23) 72; (438a4) 72; *De somno* (461b11 & b17) 247 n85; *Ethica nichomachea* (1154b7) 239 n11; *Historia animalium* (491b18) 252 n95; (493a8) 247 n58; (494b19) 169; (494b21-4) 161; (495a10) 251 n76; (495b8) 167; (496a4) 168, 247 n60; (497a32) 162, 244 n3; (509b23) 244 n3; (510a30) 244 n3; (511a13) 244 n3; (511b13) 168; (511b30) 54, 75, 79, 136, 239 n21; (513a27-30) 168, 247 n64; (513a30) 169, 247 n60; (515a21) 255 n161; (519a25) 245 n26, 247 n59; (525a8) 244 n3; (565a13) 244 n3; (566a15) 244 n3; *Metaphysics* (982b12) 231 n7; (984a3) 235 n44; (983b17) 231 n11, 231 n12, 235 n47; (984a3) 235 n56; (985a18) 242 n37; (986a2) 242 n32; (986a22) 49; (986a27) 234 n13; (986a29) 50; (989a19) 245 n9; (989b29) 28; (1000a5-9) 245 n11; (1000b20-1001a34) 245 n11; (1060a27-36) 245 n11; 1075b13-14) 245 n11; *Meteorologica* (365b6) 30; (382a3) 245 n16; *Physica* (187a20) 257 n1; (188a20) 257 n6; (198b17) 242 n39; (203b13) 231 n16; (224a21-226b17) 157; *Poetica* (1447b16-20) 70

[Aristotle] *Problemata* (937a11) 236 n73, 243 n56

Arrian *Anab.* (6, 11, 1) 249 n17

Athenaeus (II 59ff.) 241 n15; (II 59a) 246 n44

Augustine, St *De civ. dei* (VIII 2) 231 n19

Caelius Aurelianus *De morbis chronicis*: (I 5) 236 n71, 244 n79; (IV 4, 65) 257 n196

Callimachus *Hymn to Artemis* (53) 252 n99

Carlsberg Papyrus (VIII 4) 228 n11

Celsus *De medicina*, Proem: (4) 6; (6) 26, 47; (7) 82; (8) 149, 227 n4, 236 n59; (13-26) 227 n6, 248 n3; (15) 250 n47; (23) 177, 181, 188; (26) 250 n59; (40-2) 251 n72; (46) 104; (47) ii, 177; (74-5) 190; (III 4) 240 n36; (III 26) 41

Censorinus *De die natali* (5, 2) 54, 55, 61, 243 n62; (5, 3) 62; (5, 4) 54, 55; (6, 1) 55, 56; (6, 3) 56; (6, 4) 55, 61; (9,2) 238 n101

Chalcidius *In Timaeum* (246 {27 Wrobel}) 252 n93; (246 {28 Wrobel}) 252 n95

Cicero *De finibus* (V 87) 114, 242 n31; *De natura deorum* (II 26) 258 n27; *De oratore* (III 34) 242 n35; *Tusc. disp.* (I 10) 114, 242 n31

Clemens Alexandrinus *Paedagogus* (I 6, 48) 54, 79; *Protrepticus* (I 5, 1) 258 n27; *Stromateis* (VI 16) 233 n54

Critias (*D.K.*88A23) 76; (*D.K.*88BB25) 102

Curtius Rufus (Quintus) (9, 5, 22-9, 6) 249 n16, n17

Democritus (*D.K.*68A10) 67; (*D.K.*33) 67; (*D.K.*105) 56; (*D.K.*135) 57, 68, 258 n26; (*D.K.*140) 68; (*D.K.*141) 54, 68, 240 n28; (*D.K.*142) 54, 68; (*D.K.*143) 54, 240 n33; (*D.K.*144) 56; (*D.K.*145) 55; (*D.K.*149) 57; (*D.K.*151) 240 n32; (*D.K.*153-5) 240-5; (*D.K.*68B9) 258 n25; (*D.K.*148) 55; (*D.K.*159) 67; (*D.K.*191) 244 n79; (*D.K.*234) 67

Diocles of Carystus (Wellmann Frag. 2) 245 n31; (5) 245 n30, 246 n52; (7) 245 n32, 247 n77; (8) 247 n78; (9) 247 n78; (14) 245 n34; (15) 245 n33, 248 n100; (22) 246 n35; (26) 246 n52; (27)

247 n75; (29) 245 n27; (30) 247
n82; (40) 247 n84; (43) 247 n84;
(51) 247 n84; (51) 248 n94; (55)
248 n95; (57) 174, 248 n90, 248
n93; (59) 247 n84; (63) 247 n84;
(125) 246 n44; (141) 247 n79;
(175) 246, n36, n37
Diodorus Siculus (I 25) 228 n8;
(I 182) 229 n18; (XII 45, 2) 232
n34; (XII 58) 232 n35, n52;
(XIV 70, 4) 232 n36; (Frag.
XXX 43) 230 n43
Diogenes of Apollonia
(D.K.64A19) 56, 57, 77, 78, 238
n101, 243 n54; (D.K.A20) 238
n103; (D.K.A24) 54, 79;
(D.K.A25) 56, 247 n76;
(D.K.A26) 238 n101; (D.K.A27)
54, 55; (D.K.A28) 237 n88;
(D.K.A29) 57, 78; (D.K.A29a)
238 n101; (D.K.B2) 86, 87, 258
n22; (D.K.B4) 234 n42;
(D.K.B5) 32, 77, 224; (D.K.B6)
54, 75, 79, 136; (D.K.B8) 232
n24; (D.K.B9) 238 n101
Diogenes Laërtius (V 25) 149,
150, 234 n18; (V 37) 249 n10; (V
88) 248 n12; (VII 137) 258 n27;
(VIII 25) 242 n46; (VIII 59) 236
n67; (VIII 62) 69; (VIII 77) 69;
(VIII 79) 242 n2; (VIII 83) 48,
51, 233 n7, 234 n20; (VIII 8, 86)
241 n6, n14; (IX 24) 239 n4; (IX
42) 236 n60; (X 13) 236 n58

Empedocles (D.K.31A1) 69;
(D.K.31A2) 69; (D.K.31A3) 105;
(D.K.31A4) 235 n47;
(D.K.31A70) 237 n78;
(D.K.31A74) 73, 237 n84;
(D.K.31A77) 73, 237 n83, n84,
244 n71; (D.K.31A78) 73, 76,
234 n23, 236 n71, 237 n78, 240
n26, 258 n23; (D.K.31A79) 56,
73; (D.K.31A80) 246 n37;
(D.K.31A81) 73; (D.K.31A82)
57; (D.K.31A83) 246 n36;
(D.K.31A84) 55; (D.K.31A85)
57, 73, 237 n84; (D.K.31A86) 56,

57, 234 n23, 235 n48, 236 n71,
236 n72, 237 n76, 237 n79;
(D.K.31A87) 235 n48;
(D.K.31A92) 72; (D.K.31A95)
239 n11; (D.K.31A98) 236 n71,
244 n79; (D.K.31B2) 165;
(D.K.31B6) 79, 231 n20, 232
n23; (D.K.31B17, 22) 235 n49;
(D.K.31B21) 107, 223, 231 n21,
233 n22, 236 n72; (D.K.31B23)
27, 232 n22; (D.K.31B34) 243
n55; (D.K.31B37) 244 n71;
(D.K.31B61) 73, 237 n83;
(D.K.31B63) 54; (D.K.31B65) 54
222, 241 n10; (D.K.31B67) 222,
241 n10; (D.K.31B68) 74, 237
n83, 246 n35; (D.K.31B70) 237
n97; (D.K.31B75) 222, 241 n10;
(D.K.31B81) 237 n83, 246 n35;
(D.K.31B84) 72; (D.K.31B85)
237 n79; (D.K.31B90) 222, 241
n10; (D.K.31B92) 76;
(D.K.31B96) 71, 131, 237 n74,
258 n23; (D.K.31B97) 243 n58;
(D.K.31B98) 71, 73, 132, 234
n23, 236 n71, 258 n23;
(D.K.31B100) 108, 165;
(D.K.31B104) 222, 241 n10;
(D.K.31B105) 56, 76, 134, 165,
234 n30; (D.K.31B109) 237 n79;
(D.K.31B111) 27, 69, 70, 236
n67; (D.K.31B112) 69;
(D.K.31B150) 75
Euripides Supplices (201-13) 102,
241 n54; (Frag. 910 Nauck) 231
n2
Eusebius Chron. (p. 200 Karst.)
240 n25

Galen An in art. sang. nat. cont.
6 (IV 724K.) 255 n165; 8 (IV
731K.) 201; De anatom. admin.
1, 2 (II 220K.) 219, 257 n201; 2,
1 (II 280K.) 244 n2; 2, 1 (II
282K.) 245 n27; 6, 8 (II 570K.)
196; 7, 10 (II 621K.) 247 n67; 7,
11 (II 624K.) 253 n123; 9, 3 (II
719K.) 251 n79; 9, 5 (II 731K.)
251 n78; 10, 7 (Duckworth)

254 n146; 11, 1 (Duckworth)
254 n146; 12, 8 (Duckworth)
253 n114; 14, 5 (Duckworth)
254 n146; *De atra bile* 5 (V
123-5K.) 255 n167, 257 n195;
De dignoscendis pulsibus 4
(VIII 947K.) 201; 4, 3 (VIII
950K.) 253 n124; *De elem. sec.
Hipp.* 1, 9 (I 487K., 54, 18
Helmr.) 234 n17; *De locis
affectis* 5, 3 (VIII 311K.) 210; 6,
3 (VIII 396K.) 252 n107; *De
methodo medendi* 1, 1 (X 5K.)
104; 7, 3 (X 462K.) 245 n32, 247
n77; *De naturalibus
facultatibus* 1, 7 (II 71K.) 183;
2, 3 (II 87K.) 256 n187; 2, 6 (II
96K.) 256 n185; 2, 8 (II
110K.=181 Helmr.) 247 n78; 2,
8 (II 119-20K.) 256 n182; 2, 9
(II 141K.) 248 n99; 3, 15 (II
211K.) 255 n161; *De ordine
librorum suorum* 2 (XIX
55K.=Scr. Min. p.84 Müller)
189; *De placitis Hippocratis et
Platonis* 1, 6, 13-17, 15 (V
187K.) 252 n86, n87; 1, 10 (V
206K.) 253 n122, 254 n148; 2, 8
(V 283K.) 238 n100; 6, 5 (V
543K.) 252 n106; 6, 6 (V 548-
50K.) 205, 254 n158, 256 n183;
6, 7 (V 562K.) 255 n159; 7, 3 (V
602K.) 211, 255 n166, n168; 7, 3
(V 604K.) 189; 7, 8 (V 646K.)
255 n166; 8, 5 (V 685K.) 250
n47; 8, 8 (V 711K.) 244 n67; *De
plenitudine* 11 (VII 573K.) 248
n92, 253 n124, 253 n132; *De
praesagitione ex pulsibus* 2, 3
(IX 279K.) 254 n135; *De
pulsuum differentiis* 1, 28 (VIII
556K.) 254 n143; 2, 6 (VIII
592K.) 254 n139; 4, 2 (VIII
702K.) 254 n136; 4, 2 (VIII
703K.) 254 n137, 254 n158; 4,
10 (VIII 747K.) 253 n126; *De
pulsuum usu* 2 (V 155K.) 251
n82; 5 (V 166K.) 254 n148; *De
semine* 1, 5 (IV 531K.) 238
n106; 1 & 2 *passim* (IV,

512-651K.) 238 n109; 1, 16 (IV
582K.) 253 n111, 253 n114, 253
n116; 2, 1 (IV 596-8K.) 199, 253
n116, n121; 2, 6 (IV 646K.) 253
n108; *De simpl. med. temp. fac.*
2, 20 (XI 510K.) 258 n27; *De
symptomatum causis* 1, 2 (VII
89K.) 252 n92; *De tremore* 1,
(VII 584K.) 254 n138; *De usu
partium* 4, 13 (III 304K.) 256
n184; 4, 19 (III 335K.) 253
n108; 6, 10 (III 445K.) 253
n125; 7, 8 (III 538K.) 256 n185;
7, 8 (III 537-9K.) 256 n188; 8,
11 (III 665-7K.) 251 n75, n77;
9, 6 (III 708K.) 251 n80; 10, 12
(III 813K.) 252 n91, n92; 14, 11
(IV-190K.=II 321 Helmr.) 253
n115; *De usu respirationis* 1, 1
(IV 471K.) 237 n89, n92, 241
n11, 245 n33, 248 n100; *De
uteri dissectione* 5 (II 895K.)
191, 199; 10 (II 905K.) 246 n52;
De venae sectione 3 (XI 154K.)
255 n164; 5 (XI 221K.) 183;
8 (XI 237-9K.) 257 n189, n190;
*De venarum arteriarumque
dissectione* 1 (II 780K.) 252
n107; 9 (II 817K.) 247 n65; *In
Hippocratis Epidemiarum
libros* 2 (XVII 1006K.) 238
n101;
*In Hippocratis librum de
alimento* 2, 7 (XV 247K.) 256
n181; *On medical experience*
22, 3 (trans. Walz.) 238 n101;
Synopsis de pulsibus 8 (IX
453K.) 254 n144; 14 (IX 471K.)
254 n141
*Pseudo-Galen Definitiones
medicae* 99 (XIX 372K.) 237
n83, 256 n182; 220 (XIX 409K.)
204, 254 n142: *De humoribus*
(XIX 495K.) 238 n101;
Introductio seu medicus 1 (XIV
683K.) 248 n3; 4 (XIV 683K.)
241 n5; 9 (XIV 695-9K.) 256
n186; 11 (XIV 712K.) 252 n95;
13 (XIV 751K.) 257 n197

Gregor. Naz. (Schol. in) (XXXVI 911 Migne) 235 n50

Hearst Papyrus (85) 9
Heraclitus (*D.K.*22B36) 233 n54; (*D.K.*22B96) 249 n39; (*D.K.*22B117) 233 n54, 238 n102; (*D.K.*22B118) 233 n54, 238 n102, 244 n79; (*D.K.*22B126) 222
Hero *Pneumatica* (I 28) 254 n156; (I 24, 20) 255 n175
Herodotus (I 105) 34, 39; (II 84) 227 n2; (II 86) 250 n53, n56; (III 1, 129) 227 n2; (III 125) 47; (IV 202) 34; (VI 75) 34; (VI 84) 34; (VII 99) 232 n27, n28
Hesiod *Erga* (100-4) 13; (496-7) 12

Hippocratic Corpus *De aere, aquis, locis* (3) 38; (14. 5) 236 n66; (22) 38; *De carnibus* (2 & 6) 237 n89; *De corde* (6) 237 n89; (7) 255 n161; *De decenti habitu* (6) 230 n1; *De fistulis* (7) 228 n9; *De flatibus* (6, 19) 232 n30; (14) 244 n79; *De genitura* (2) 40; (3) 236 n66; (6-8) 95; (8-11) 236 n66; *De haemorrhoidibus* (7) 228 n9; *De internis affectionibus* (26, 31, 51) 228 n9; *De locis in homine* (II 104) 252 n95; *De morbis* (II 21) 41; *De morbis mulierum* (I 23, 63, 75, 78) 228 n9; (I 37, 74, 75, 78) 228 n10; (II 126, 181, 203) 228 n10; *De morbo sacro* (1) 35, 36, 232 n39; (2) 36, 236 n66; (3) 36, 239 n21; (7) 37; (18) 36; *De natura hominis* (1) 85, 87, 90; (1-6) 226; (2) 86; (4) 90; (9, 14) 33; (9, 44) 232 n30; (11) 226; (12) 237 n89; *De natura muliebri* (7, 32-4, 109) 228 n10; (97) 228 n9; *De natura pueri* (6-8) 97; (14) 237 n97; (20) 94; (31) 95; *De sterilibus* (=*De morbis mulierum* III 214) 229 n11; *De superfetatione* (33, 35)

228 n9; *De ulceribus* (14, 17-18) 228 n9; *De vetere medicina* (1) 83, 100, 223; (2) 23, 83, 85; (3) 103, 229 n16; (9) 101; (12) 83; (14) 85; (15-16) 84; (20) 70, 84, 239 n1; *De victu* (I) 98; (I 4) 225; (IV 87, 89, 90) 230 n1; *De virginum morbis* 43, 244 n79; *Epidemiarum* (II 6, 9, 29) 228 n9; (III Case 10) 240 n40; (III Case 16) 99; (V 69) 228 n9; (VI 7) 232 n30; (VII 66) 228 n9; *Epistulae* (10) 236 n61; (17) 236 n60
Hippolytus *Refutationes* (I 6, 1) 231 n17; (I 7, 1) 231 n19; (I 7, 3) 257 n6; (I 7, 4) 231 n14, 258 n6; (I 16) 54, 235 n47
Hippon (*D.K.*38A3) 54, 235 n47; (*D.K.*38A4) 54, 235 n44; (*D.K.*38A6) 235 n44; (*D.K.*38A7) 235 n56; (*D.K.*38A10) 237 n88; (*D.K.*38A11) 66, 235 n46; (*D.K.*38A12) 54, 243 n62; (*D.K.*38A13) 54; (*D.K.*38A14) 55; (*D.K.*38A15) 55, 56; (*D.K.*38A17) 56
Hipponax (Fragment 51 Diehl = 73 West) 92
Homer *Iliad* (I 46-52) 12, 231 n10; (IV 487) 235 n45; (V 99) 14; (V 305) 14; (V 447) 15; (XI 829) 229 n22; (XIII 43) 231 n9; (XVI 514) 15; (XX 56-8) 29; (XXI 198-9) 29; (XXIV 793) 71; *Odyssey* (III 444) 237 n97; (IV 220-32) 10, 228 n2; (V 394) 15; (VI 201) 235 n45; (IX 201) 235 n45; (IX 411) 12; (XI 171-3) 14; (XIX 455-8) 15

Iamblichus *D. comm. math. sc.* (11 p. 44, 10 Fest.) 242 n30; *I. G.* (II² 4960a) 230 n26; (IV² 1, nos 121-2, 70-3, 113-19) 21; *V. Pyth.* (104) 50, 233 n6; (267) 49, 233 n9
Iohannes Alexandrinus *Comm.*

in [Hipp.] *De nat. pueri* (Dietz) 251 n69

Jerome, St (131 Helm.) 249 n25

Leucippus (*D.K.*67A34) 57; (*D.K.*67A35) 54

Macrobius *In Somnium Scipionis* (I 14, 19) 238 n100
Marcellinus *De pulsibus* (11) 254 n145
Marmor Parium (Fr. Gr. Hist. II B239) B19 (309/8) 248 n14)
Maximus (Valerius) (V 7) 182)
Melissus (*D.K.*30A1) 239 n4; (*D.K.*30A3) 239 n3; (*D.K.*30B7) 88, 89; (*D.K.*30B8) 88
Moschion (Frag. 6, 30-3 Nauck) 249 n40

Oribasius (ed. Raeder) (III 24) 252 n101; (III 78) 246 n36; (III 156) 234 n33; (III 168) 247 n79; (V 300) 105
Ovid *Metamorphoses* (XV 622) 17

Parmenides (*D.K.*28A46) 237 n87; (*D.K.*28B1, 30) 234, n39; (*D.K.*28B8, 53) 234 n40
Pausanias (I 34, 4) 16
Philistion Frag. 2 (Wellmann) 108; 3 (Welman) 241 n14; 6 (Welman) 237 n89
Philolaus (*D.K.*44A27) 237 n88, 244 n76; (*D.K.*44B2) 114
Philoponus *In de anima* (9, 19) 76; (88) 233 n6; (92, 2) 237 n88; (178, 6) 237 n75, n77
Pindar *Pythian* (III 46-54) 18
Plato *Apology* (18b) 240 n42; *Gorgias* (507c6) 242 n33; *Laws* X (888e-890b) 115, 121; (889b) 120; *Meno* (76c) 72; *Phaedo* (110b5) 243 n49: *Philebus* (28d) 116; *Protagoras* (311b) 21; *Republic* (405a) 229 n16; (500c9) 242 n33; *Epist.* 2 (314d) 108; *Epist.* 7 (324a) 109; (326b) 113; *Sophist* (265c) 116; *Theaetetus* (155d) 231 n6;

Timaeus (30d) 121; (31b-32c) 117; (32c-33a) 141; (42e-43a) 128; (44c) 117; (47b-c) 242 n33; (47e) 118; (48b) 117; (48d) 117; (50e) 119; (51a) 119; (51e) 118; (52b) 119; (53b) 121, 122; (53c) 122; (53d) 122; (54a) 126; (55d) 124; (56c-57c) 126; (56d) 126; (56e) 127; (57a) 243 n52, 245 n18; (57c6-d7) 241 n17; (57d) 117; (58c5) 241 n17; (59d) 243 n59; (61e) 225; (68b) 244 n68; (80d) 110, 244 n73; (80d-e) 141; (81b-d) 244 n70; (81e) 109, 247 n81; (81e-86a) 146; (82b) 110, 111, 142; (82d) 132; (82e-83a) 111; (84c) 110, 144; (84d) 247 n83; (85b) 244 n77; (86a) 142; (86b) 147; (87a3-4) 145; (90c-d) 242 n33; (91a) 241 n19; (91b) 131

Pliny the Elder *Nat. Hist.* (VII 37, 124) 249 n15; (VII 56, 196) 229 n17; (VII 123) 182; (XXV 23, 58) 229 n24; (XXVI 10) 164, 245 n30, 246 n48, n52; (XXIX 1) 229 n17; (XXIX 1, 5) 105; (XXIX 2) 21, 33; (XXIX 5) 182; (XXX 98) 230 n43; (XXXVI 53) 164, 246 n47; (XXXVI 69, 202) 70

Plutarch *De amore prol.* (3 p. 495e) 55; *De prim. frig.* (7 p. 947f) 258 n24; (9 p. 948d) 258 n27; (17 p. 952c) 258 n27; (19, 4 p. 953e) 236 n73, 243 n56; *De Stoic. repugnantiis* (43, 1053f) 258 n27; *Pericles* (26) 239 n3; *Quaestiones conviviales* (IV 4, 3 p. 669a) 249 n39; (V 8, 2 p. 683e) 75; (VII 1 p. 699b) 241 n19; *Quaestiones naturales* (2 p. 912c) 237 n83; (20, 2 p. 917a) 76

Ps. Plutarch *Stromateis* (2) 221, 257 n1
Pollux *Onomasticon* (ii 222s, i 155, 8 Bethe) 237 n97
Porphyry *De Styge ap. Stob. Ecl.*

(I 49, 53) 56; *In Ptol. Harm.* (p. 56 Düring) 114; (p. 92 Düring) 242 n40

Praxagoras (Frag. 21 Steckerl) 248 n99; (Frag. 32 Steckerl) 248 n100; (Frag. 70 Steckerl) 248 n94; (Frag. 74 Steckerl) 248 n95; (Frag. 75 Steckerl) 248 n93; (Frag. 85 Steckerl) 253 n132

Pythagoras (*D.K.*17.1) 233 n9; (*D.K.*58B15) 231 n3

Pythagorean School (*D.K.*58B1a) 242 n46

Rufus *De corporis humani partium appellationibus* (9) 257 n199; (71-4) 252 n90; (153) 193, 252 n97; (203) 200, 253 n127; (229) 237 n97; *In Oribas* (III 156=*C.M.G.* VI 2. 2, 136) 56

Pseudo-Rufus *De anatomia hominis partium* (9) 195; (12) 252 n96; (74) 251 n77

Seneca *Epistulae* (31, 5) 258 n27; *Quaestiones naturales* (II, 10, 4) 258 n27; (III, 14) 231 n12

Sextus *Adversus mathematicos* (VII 49) 102, 240 n46, n47; (VII 110) 240 n46; (VII 135) 258 n25; (VIII 326) 240 n46; (IX 54) 241 n55; *Pyrrhoniae hypotyposes* (II, 18) 240 n46

Simplicus *In de anima* (68. 5) 237 n74, n77; *In de caelo* (665.25) 245 n10; *In physica* (23. 22) 235 n44; (24. 13) 220, 234 n22; (32. 3) 71, 73, 234 n23, 236 n71; (150. 24) 220, 257 n1; (151. 28) 86, 258 n22; (152. 18) 234 n42; (152. 22) 77; (153. 12) 235 n43; (153. 13) 54; (159. 13) 107; (300. 19) 71; (371. 33) 73, 75; (460. 4) 235 n51; (460. 28) 235 n54; (693. 10) 255 n175

Sotades (Frag. 1 Powell) 250 n58

Edwin Smith Surgical Papyrus (Case 18) 9; (Case 21) 9

Sophocles *Antigone* (361) 23;

(332-71) 102, 241 n53; *Oedipus Rex* (1182, 1248, 1357, 1403, 1496) 250 n58; *Trachiniae* (1054) 247 n58

Soranus *Gynaecia* (I 14, 2) 247 n75; (I 21) 246 n37; (I 57) 56, 73

Pseudo-Soranus *Quaestiones medicae* (61) 246 n35

Stobaeus *Ecl. phys.* (I 8, 2) 102; *Florilegium* (III 1, 210) 244 n79; (III 5, 7) 238 n102, 244 n79; (III 5, 8) 238 n102; (IV 1, 139) 114, 242 n30

Strabo *Geographia* (VIII 6, 15) 23; (XIV 2, 19) 21

Strato (Frag. 68b Wehrli) 255 n175; (Frag. 108 Wehrli) 256 n178

Stoics *S.V.F.* (II 429) 258 n27; (II 431) 258 n27; (II 580) 258 n27; (II 897) 234 n31

Suda, the *s.v.* Acron 241 n3; *Empedocles* 69; *Hippocrates* 249 n18

Tertullianus *De anima* (5) 238 n100; (10) 250 n60; (25) 250 n61

Thales: (*D.K.*11A12) 231 n11, n12, 235 n47; (*D.K.*11A14) 231 n12; (*D.K.*11A15) 30, 231 n12; (*D.K.*11A22) 231 n18

Theophrastus *De lapidibus* (5) 163, 164; *De sensibus* (1-2) 57; (3) 237 n87; (7) 57, 72, 236 n72, 237 n79; (9) 239 n11; (10) 56, 234 n23, 236 n71, 239 n11; (11) 243 n63; (14) 243 n54; (16) 239 n11; (23) 237 n76; (25-6) 53, 57; (26) 60; (27-37) 57; (29) 239 n11; (39) 78; (39-48) 56, 57; (41) 79; (43) 77, 238 n101; (44) 78; (49-58) 57; (59) 57, 72, 236 n72; (60-83) 57; (61) 258 n26; (63) 258 n26

Thucydides (II 47) 23, 25, 229 n23; (II 52) 185

Vindicianus Fragmentum *De*

semine (ex cod. Bruxellensi ed. Wellmann) (1) 54, 79; (2) 245 n31; (3) 75; (41) 247 n69; (44) 171

Vitruvius (X, 7) 254 n157

Xenophanes (*D.K.*21B18) 102
(*D.K.*21B34) 102

General index

absorption (*anadosis*) 201
Academy 22, 151
Achilles 12, 17
Acron 105
Aelian 20, 94-6
Aelius Aristides 25
Aeneas 14
aēr 221, 224 (*see* air and *pneuma*)
Aesculapius 22
Aëtius of Amida 193
Agamemnon 11
air 37, 64, 68, 71, 76-80, 86-8, 90,
    93, 105-6, 109, 111, 115, 118-19,
    124-8, 136-7, 140-5, 151, 155,
    157-9, 201-2, 207, 221, 223,
    225-6 (*see aēr* and *pneuma*)
Ajax 43
Alcaeus of Lesbos 30
Alcmaeon 47-64, 67-8, 78-9, 90,
    100-1, 103, 128, 134; excision of
    the eye 58ff.; physiological
    theories *see esp.* 54-7, 60-3;
    theory of health 52; theory of
    knowledge 51, 101, 103
Alexander the Great 149, 178, 180
Alexander Philalethes 183
Alexander Polyhistor 122
Alexandria 2, 59, 176, 178-87
    passim, 190-1, 205, 219
amathia 145
ampelos Chironia (white bryony)
    17
Amphiaraus 16
amphiblēstroedēs (retiform) 193

ampullae 198
Amyntas II 149
Anarieis 38
Anatomai (*Dissections*) 149,
    161-2
anatomy: advances in animal
    anatomy in Lyceum 161; of the
    brain 191, 211-12; development
    of human anatomy at
    Alexandria 186; of the eye 193-
    5; of the heart 205-7; influence
    of Diocles on anatomy in
    Lyceum 172; knowledge of
    human anatomy in Lyceum
    169, 170; of the nervous system
    191, 212; of the vascular system
    199ff.
Anaxagoras: adoption of
    pangenesis theory 95; belief
    that female contributes nothing
    to generation 119; concept of
    Mind criticised by Plato 116;
    conception of role of opposites
    222; influence of physiological
    interests upon his physics 65ff;
    influence upon *De genitura*,
    De natura pueri, De morbis IV
    97; influence upon *De victu* I
    98; physiological theories 54-7
Anaximander: belief in divinity
    of *archē* 31; explanation of
    earthquakes 30; explanation of
    thunder and lightning and
    eclipses 31; influence upon

287

Alcmaeon's theory of health 90, 100; role of opposites in Anaximander 52, 220-1; view of cosmos as a balance between opposed forces 52

Anaximenes: belief in divinity of *archē* 31; explanation of earthquakes 30; explanation of thunder and lightning and eclipses 31; implicitly rejects belief that Zeus sends rain 46

Antioch: cucumbers of 163; date of foundation of 163-4; Erasistratus' employment at 182; practice of human vivisection at (?) 181-2

Antiochus I: illness allegedly diagnosed by Erasistratus 182

antiperistasis 140 (*see periōsis*, circular thrust)

aorta 135, 167-8, 170, 175

Apeiron: of Anaximander 220-1

Aphrodite 14, 34, 39, 41

Apollo 11-12, 14, 15, 17, 20, 30, 33, 45

apophyseis mastoeideis 198 (*see* Fallopian tubes)

apoplexy 41-2, 175

arachnoid 193, 195

Archelaus: influence upon *De victu* I 98

Archigenes 189

Archilochus 31, 92

Archytas 113-14, 118

Ares 45

Arginusae 185

Aristophanes 10, 18, 30, 77-8

Aristotle 3, 29-31, 48-51, 59, 61-2, 64, 69-70, 72-4, 76, 79-80, 95, 98, 108, 119, 126, 140, 146, 149-64, 167-75, 185-6, 191-2, 197, 214, 220-2, 225-6

Aristoxenus of Tarentum 203

Arsinoe II 187

Artemis 12, 14-18, 42-3

arteria venalis (*artēria phlebōdēs*, the pulmonary vein) 200

arteries: aorta 135, 166-8, 170, 175; carotid 199; as channels

containing *pneuma* 174-5, 188, 192, 200-2, 210-11; distinguished from veins 174-5, 199-200; ovarian 199; pulmonary (= vein resembling an artery, *phleps artēriōdēs*, *vena arterialis*) 200, 202, 207-8, 210, 216; pulsation of (*see* pulse)

arthritis 39

Asclepeion at Cos 22-5

Asclepiads 23-4, 105, 149, 180

Asclepius 15, 17-18, 20-1, 23-5, 149; cult of 3, 10, 23-4

Aselli, Gasparo 197

asthma 38

Athena 14, 16, 43

Athens 177-8, 181; plague at 185

Atlas 30

atomic theory 66-8; influence upon Hippocratic *Corpus* 93

Atomists: physiological theories 54-7; Plato's agreement with 224; Plato's correction of 121; pluralist reaction to Parmenides 63, 66; postulate random and aimless motion 120

attonitus 41 (*see sideratio*)

Babylon 6, 15

Bacchae 43

Bacchius 204

barbary ape 219

Barce 34

Bassanio 60

beestings (*colostrum*) 74

bellows 206, 208

Berenice 180

bile 44, 109, 111, 143-5, 173; black 53, 90, 92; yellow 53, 90-2

birth: prognoses 11; multiple 96

blood: circulation of attributed to Erasistratus 208; composition of blood according to Empedocles 71, 112; composition of blood according to Plato 112, 141;

distribution of conceived as an irrigation system 135-6, 208, 255 n161; formed by action of innate heat 73-4, 141, 173-5, 215; formed in the liver (*haematopoiēsis, hematōsis* 73, 75, 98, 112 (*see* liver); lesser or pulmonary circulation of 210; as material of the semen 197 (haematogenous theory of *see* seed) 197; as nourishment 74-5, 79, 110, 134-5, 140-1, 174, 201; as one of the four humours 53, 90-2; as seat of the intellect 76, 134, 165

blood vessels: 'blood-flowing'(?) veins attributed to Alcmaeon 57, 62; description of by Aristotle 168, 170; description of by Diogenes 79; description of by Plato 65-6, 129, 170; description in *Nature of Man* 226, 258 n32 (*see* arteries, veins)

bone: formation of, according to Empedocles 71; formation of, according to Plato 131, 143

brain: Aristotle's belief in greater fluidity of human brain 169; *calamus scriptorius* or *calamus Herophili* 191, 205; as central organ of sensation and seat of the intellect 56, 58, 60-2, 78-9, 93, 128, 134-5, 147, 171, 212; cerebellum (*epenkranis and parenkephalis*) 191, 211-12; cerebrum (*enkephalos*) 189, 191, 211; chorioid membranes 191, 195; description of by Diocles(?) 171; description of by Herophilus 191; description of by Erasistratus 211-12; *dura mater* 212; marrow as substance of 131, 133, 135, 145; mental disturbances due to afflictions of 36-7, 44; nerves originate from 192, 212-13; psychic-*pneuma* originates from 213; ventricles 191, 212

Calchas 12
Callicles 115
Callimachus 108
Callisthenes 59
Canopic jars 187
castration 40
catheter: S-shaped 218
Centaurion 17
cerebellum *see* brain
cerebrum *see* brain
Chalcidius 58-60
chamber-pot sieve 30
Chartres 154
Chiron, the Centaur 17-18
chorion 194-5
chorioid plexus 193, 205
Chryses 11
Chrysippus, Stoic philosopher 61
Chrysippus the Younger 180-1
chyle 215
chyle-vessels 197
Cicero 114
circular thrust 140 (*see* antiperistasis, periōsis)
Cleidemus 97
Clement of Alexandria 79
Cleombrotus of Ceos 182
Cleomenes, King of Sparta, suicide of 34
Clepsydra: domestic utensil for lifting water 108; water-clock 204, 218
Cnidians 105
Cnidus 2, 33, 105, 180
Coans 105, 181
colostrum 74 (*see* beestings)
coprotherapy 9
cornea 193-4
Coronis 12, 17, 18
corpse 2, 184-6; mummified 186-7
Cos 2, 20-1, 23-4, 33, 105, 175, 177-81
cotyledons 56
Critias 76, 102
critical days 98
Critobulus 180
Croton 47-8
Ctesibius 208-9

cube (hexahedron) of earth 121-7
(see solids, regular)
Curtius Rufus (Q.) 180

Darwin, Charles 68
Delian problem 113
delusions 1, 42-3
Demaratus 34
Demetrius of Phaleron 179
Demiurge or Divine Craftsman in
Timaeus 116-18, 121-2, 128,
130-2, 136-7
Democedes 47
Democritus 66-9, 93-7, 224
demons 6-7, 9-10, 42
De sanitate et morbo 150
diaphragm 42, 129-30, 167, 196
diarrhoea 144
didymoi: term applied to ovaries
198; term applied to testicles
197
digestion: conceived of as
concoction 215; conceived of as
putrefaction see putrefaction,
sēpsis; effected by innate heat
see innate heat; effected by
pyramids of fire 136; effected
by peristaltic action of gastric
muscles 215
Diocles of Carystos 61, 80, 145,
149, 158, 161-4, 166, 170-5
Diogenes of Apollonia 32, 37, 60,
63-4, 66, 68-9, 75-80, 86-9, 93,
98, 113, 128, 134-6, 223-4
Diomedes 14
Dionysius II 108-9
Dionysus 15, 43
disease 13, 32-4, 38-9, 52-3, 66,
81, 106, 109-11, 128, 142-5, 150,
173, 175, 188, 216-17
dissection: animal 61-2, 135, 149,
161, 168-72, 179, 184, 189, 191,
196, 199, 211-12, 217-19;
human 59, 135, 169, 184-91,
196-200, 203, 210-13, 217-19
Dissections see Anatomai
Divine Craftsman see Demiurge
dodecahedron 243 n49

Dogmatic sect 4, 178, 186, 188,
190
dropsy 218
drugs 8, 69, 146, 218
duodenal process (dōdekadaktylos
ekphysis) 197
dura mater 189, 191, 212
dysentery 38, 144

earth 64, 71, 86-8, 90, 106-7, 109,
115, 117-19, 124-8, 131-2, 136,
142, 151, 155, 157-8, 221-6
eczema 144
Edwin Smith Surgical Papyrus
10, 92
Egyptian medical papyri 8, 10
Egyptian medicine 2, 6, 8-11, 15,
26, 186
eidōlon 68
Eileithyia 16
Eleatic elenchus 63 (see
parmenidean elenchus);
impasse 65-6; logic 65
embalming (mummification) 187
embryo: aborted 169; initial
development of 55; mode of
nourishment of 56, 61, 63, 172,
196; negative contribution to
by mother 119; sexual-
differentiation of 68, 73; twins
95-6
embryotome (embryosphaktēs)
218
Empedocles 27, 32, 43, 49, 51, 53,
54-7, 61, 64-5, 68-77, 79-80, 84,
88-9, 91-2, 95, 98, 101, 104-8,
110, 112-13, 116, 120, 128,
131-4, 137, 141, 151, 162, 165,
170, 173, 175, 197, 222-3
Empiricists 4, 105, 180, 190
Enareis 34 (see Anarieis)
enkephalos see brain
Enlightenment (Greek) 3, 33
Ennosigaios 30 (see Poseidon)
enteriōnē 212-14
entypōsis 68
epenkranis see brain
Epicrates 109
Epidaurus 20-1, 23-4

epididymis 198
epilepsy 1, 7-8, 34-8, 41-2, 44, 93,
    144-5, 175
Epimetheus 13
Erasistrateans 206-7, 218
Erasistratus 61-2, 80, 136, 175,
    181-3, 188-9, 199-203, 205-8,
    210-18
Eudoxus of Cnidus 108
eunuchs 40; baldness of 95
Euripides 102
Eustachian tubes 58
experimentation 81
eye: Alcmaeon's excision of 58-
    60; Empedocles' description of
    71-2; Herophilus' description
    of 193-5

Fallopian tubes 198-9
Fallopio 177, 189
Faustus, Dr 149
fever 38, 142, 173, 217
fibrin 110-11, 143
fire 63-4, 71-2, 86-8, 90, 106-7,
    109, 115, 117-20, 124-8, 131-2,
    136-7, 140-2, 148, 151, 157-8,
    165, 221-6
fire-engine 209
fish-trap (weel) 136-7
flap-valve 208
foetus 170, 191, 195, 218
force-pump 208-9
Forms (Platonic theory of) 118-20
Four Element Theory 32, 53, 64,
    70-2, 74, 88, 91-2, 105-7, 109,
    112-14, 117-28, 130, 132, 134,
    142-3, 146, 151-2, 154-8, 162,
    173, 223, 226

Galatia 163-4
Galen 2, 17, 51, 80, 98, 104, 140,
    149, 161, 164, 170, 174, 180,
    182-3, 188-93, 196-7, 199-201,
    203, 205, 207-8, 210-14, 216,
    218-19
Galileo 153
gall-bladder 169, 216
geometrical theory of matter 130,
    153

glandular assistants 198 (*see
    parastatai adenoeideis*)
Glaucus 15
Golden Age, degeneration from
    102
Gorgias 76
gynaecology 3, 10, 198-9

haemorrhoids 38
Harvey, William 207-8, 210
health 52-3, 67, 70-1, 76-7, 88,
    90-1, 100, 110-11, 142-3, 150,
    203
hearing, theory of 58, 78-9
Hearst Papyrus 9
heart: auricles 170-1, 199;
    biscuspid valve 207; cavities
    (chambers) of *see generally* 135,
    168-71, 206; as central organ of
    sensation and seat of the
    intellect 60-1, 162, 165, 170,
    174-5; as centre of vascular
    system 129, 165-6, 170;
    conception of heart as a pump
    207-8; description of: by
    Aristotle 167-70; description of
    by Diocles (?) 171; description
    of by Erasistratus 205-10;
    description of by Plato ('knot
    of veins') 135, 165-6, 170, 225;
    description of in *De carnibus*
    166-8; description of in *De
    corde* 166; description of in *De
    nutrimento* 166; as seat of
    spirited element of the soul
    129; semi-lunar or sigmoid
    valve 206-7; tricuspid valve
    206-7; valves 199, 205, 207;
    ventricles 170-1, 174, 200, 210,
    216
Hecate 45
Helen of Troy 10
Helios 15
hellebore, black (Christmas rose)
    16
Hephaestus 71
Hera 16, 43
Heraclitus 46, 53, 97, 184, 222
Herakles 43

Hermes, 13
Hero of Alexandria 208, 214
Herodotus, 33-4, 39, 47, 187
Herophilus 16, 59, 61, 175, 180-1, 183, 186-8, 190-205, 211-12, 214, 218
Hesiod 12-14, 17, 38, 52, 105
Hiero, tyrant of Syracuse 18
Hippocrates of Chios 113
Hippocrates of Cos 3, 21-5, 67, 105, 148, 162, 164
Hippocrates, son of Dracon 180
Hippocratic: *Corpus* (treatises/ writings) 2, 11, 14, 24, 26, 33-4, 40-1, 43, 47, 53, 62, 68, 85, 90, 92-3, 97-8, 100, 144-6, 166, 168, 182, 225; Egyptian influences on Hippocratic medicine/ doctors 10, 228 n9, 10; medicine/doctors 22-5, 33, 99, 145, 162; treatises, individual *see* Index locorum
Hippon 54-7, 63-4, 66, 76, 79, 86, 134
Hipponax 92
Hippys of Rhegium 20
Homer/Homeric poems 11, 15, 24, 33, 37, 52 (for *Iliad* and *Odyssey, see* Index locorum)
Homeric theology 31, 35, 38, 101, 103
horror vacui 210, 215-16 (*see* Strato and Erasistratus)
humoral theory 203, 218
humours: aqueous and vitreous 193-4
humours, the four (blood, phlegm, black and yellow bile) 53, 89-92, 173, 178, 183, 186, 226

iamata 20-3
Ibn al-Nafis 210
icosahedron of water 121-7 (*see* solids, regular)
Idea of Progress 102
Imhotep 21
impotence 2, 38-40
incest 187

incommensurability between side and diagonal of a square 123
innate heat 73-4, 79-80, 98, 107-8, 110, 135-7, 140-1, 148, 158, 166, 173-5, 215
intellect, seat of 56, 134, 147, 192
intellectual immaturity of children 77
Ionian dialect 2
Ionian Rationalism/Rationalists 2, 33-4, 90, 99, 184
iris 193, 195
Ishtar, hand of 8 (*see* epilepsy)
isomoiria 53
isonomia 85

Kepler, J. 153
Keraunobrontēs 30 (see Zeus, thunder and lightning)
Kypris (Love) 71

lacteals (chyle vessels) 197
Laodamia 12
Iēnos, wine-press (*see torcular Herophili*) 191
lens 194-5
Leptines 182
Leucippus 66, 68
Leto 12, 15
lightning (and thunder) 1, 30-1, 41
Lilu, Lilu-la'bi, Lilitu 7-8
liver 73, 98, 112, 130, 135, 169, 191, 196-7, 215-16, 218; haematopoieic function of (*hematōsis*) 75, 197, 256 n183
Logistici *see* Dogmatists
Love (motor causes) 64-5, 72
lumen 192
lungs 129-30, 135-6, 141, 165-6, 170, 202, 206-7, 210; congestion in 144
Lyceum 150, 161-2, 164, 171-2, 175, 178-80, 183-4, 186, 214

Machaeon 149
madness 1, 16, 34, 43-4
magic 44
Magna Graecia 113
mania 145

Marduk 6
marrow 40, 110-11, 130-5, 141, 143, 147, 212-13 (*see myelos*, *medulla*)
materia medica 17
medicine: Babylonian 6; Egyptian 2, 6, 8-11; Hippocratic 2; religious 15ff.
medulla 213 (*see* marrow)
Melampus (melampodium) 16-17
Melissus 49, 63, 85, 87-9, 226
Meno (Peripatetic) 48, 150, 183
menstruation (*menses*) 42, 94, 162
Merchant of Venice 60
Mesopotamia 9, 11, 26
metabolism 215
Methodist sect 69, 190
Methone, siege of 180
Metrodorus, third husband of Pythias and teacher of Erasistratus 181
Miletus 28-9
Milesian philosophers 30-1, 37, 85, 220-1
Miqtu 7-8 (*see* epilepsy)
Modus tollens 40
monarchia 85
Monists, monism 63-4, 85, 87
Moschion 184
motor causes 64-5 (*see* Love)
Multan, siege of 180
Museum 22, 178-80
myelos 213 (*see* marrow, *medulla*)

nama 143
Natural philosophers (Milesian/ Ionian) 1, 26, 28, 30, 32-3, 37, 46, 48, 101, 103
Naucratis 28
Neoplatonism 154
nerve-like process 199
nerves: motor 193, 211-12; optic 60, 193; sensory 193, 211-12
nervous system: discovery of 61, 173, 191-2, 211-14; starting point of 213
Nestis 71
neuron 192
Nicarchus 174

Niobe 12
nutrition, nutriment, nourishment 65, 73-5, 79, 98, 110-12, 134-5, 140-3, 147-8, 201-2, 216

observation, clinical in *Epidemics* 99
octahedron of air 121-7 (*see* solids, regular)
Odysseus 12, 14-15, 43
Okeanos 29
Olympian gods 32
opposites 49-50, 77, 82, 84, 105-7, 146, 154-8, 162, 172, 220, 226
Orestes 43
osteology 219
ovaries 198-9

Paeon 15
pain 85-8, 91
Panacea 19
Pandora 13
Pangenesis theory 68, 95, 97
parastatai adenoeideis ('glandular assistants') 198
parastatai kirsoeideis ('varix-like assistants') 198
parenchyma 216-17
parenkephalis see brain
Parmenides 49, 63, 73, 85
Parmenidean *elenchus* 64
Paul of Aegina 17
Pausanias 69, 105
pepsis (concoction) 74
perception, physiological psychology of 57
periōsis 140 (*see* antiperistasis, circular thrust)
Peripatetic 150, 163, 175, 179, 225-6
peristalsis 215
pharoid process 205
Philadephus *see* Ptolemy
Philinus, pupil of Herophilus 180
Philip II 180
Philistion of Locri 53, 61, 73-4, 80, 105-10, 113, 137, 140, 142, 144, 158, 162, 172-3, 223-5

Philitas 180
Philolaus 114, 144
phlebotomy 25, 183, 217-18
phlegm 37, 44, 53, 90, 92-3, 109, 111, 143-5, 173, 175 (see humours)
phrenetica passio 171
Phrontis 12
Pindar 18
placebo effect 5
plague, Athenian 3, 15, 18, 23, 33-4, 105, 185; -demon 6-7; at Rome 17; at Syracuse 34; at Troy 11, 30
plethōra 216-17
pleurisy 144
Pluralists (pluralism) 63-4, 87, 89
Plutus, god of wealth 18-19
Plutus (comedy by Aristophanes) 18-19
pneuma 62, 68, 80, 98, 144, 162, 167-9, 171, 173-5, 192-3, 200-2, 206-8, 210-17
Polybus, son-in-law of Hippocrates, author(?) of *De natura hominis* 226
Polyneices 185
pore-theory 64, 108, 110, 137, 166
portal fissure 196
Poseidon 29-30, 44
Praxagoras 61-2, 149, 167, 174-5, 180-1, 191-2, 199-201, 203, 214
Priscianus, Theodor 171
Proclus, Neoplatonist 152
progression: arithmetical 118; geometrical 117-18; harmonic 118
Prometheus 13, 23
pros to kenoumenon akolouthia 215 (see *horror vacui*)
Protarchus 116
psoriasis 144
psychology (tripartite in *Timaeus*) 129, 147, 166
psychic disorders/ psychopathology 145, 147
Ptolemy: Philadelphus 2, 178-81, 217, 219; Sōtēr 2, 178-9, 187, 217, 219

public health engineering 69
pulse, pulsation: classification of 203-4; diagnostic importance of 166, 203-4; measured by clepsydra 204; restricted to arteries 203
putrefaction 43, 73-6, 112, 162, 175 (see *sēpsis*)
pyramid (tetrahedron) of fire 125-7, 141, 148, 224-5 (see solids, regular)
Pyrrhonian scepticism 186
Pythias, daughter of Aristotle 181
Pythagoras 48-51
Pythagorean numerology: in *De carnibus* 98; in *De hebdomadis* 98; in *De natura pueri* 98
Pythagoreans: Brotherhood of 48-9, 118; description of mathematical progressions 118; identification of four elements with regular solids 122; influence upon exact sciences 27; religious way of life 27

Receptacle ('Nurse of all Becoming', Space) 118-20
Renaissance 177, 200
reproduction 54, 68, 95-6, 205; organs of 197-9
respiration: blockage of causes disease 109, 144-5; cools innate heat 73-4, 79, 98, 108, 110, 135, 162, 165-6, 175; restores soul atoms 68; role in digestion 140-1; through pores in the skin 108, 110, 137, 140, 162, 166 (see circular thrust)
retina 193-4
Rhoxane, wife of Alexander the Great 180
Rhexenor 12

'Sacred disease' see epilepsy
Sakikku, 'All Disease' 7
Santorio of Capo d'Istria 215
Scythians 34, 40; impotence of 38-9
seed 54, 97, 131, 141;

haematogenous theory of 197
(*see* sperm, semen)
Seleucus 181-2
semen 39, 54, 61, 63-4, 75-6, 79-
80, 94-5, 97-8, 131, 134-5, 158,
197-8
seminal ducts: Fallopian tubes
198; *vasa deferentia* 198
seminal vesicles (*vesiculae
seminales*) 198
sensation: organs of 128; theories
of 51, 53, 57-8, 64, 68, 78-9,
173, 192
sēpsis 73-4 (*see also* putrefaction)
ser'anu-vessels 8
Servetus, Michael 210
sex-differentiation 54, 63, 68, 73,
97
'Sicilian' tradition 74, 80, 98,
104-6, 109, 113, 130, 133-5,
141-2, 145, 147-8, 159, 162, 166,
172-3, 175, 224-5
sideratio 41 (*see attonitus*)
sleep 57, 62-3, 68, 73, 78
Smyrna, lettuce of 163
Socrates 114, 116
solids, regular 121-7, 141, 148
Sophists 115
Sōtêr *see* Ptolemy
Sotion 49
soul: Aristotle on 173-4, 192;
composed of air 77; composed
of atoms 67-8; composed of
blood 76, 134; microcosm of
world-soul 115; Plato on 128-
30, 132-3, 145, 147; transmitted
with semen 76, 135
Space *see* Receptacle
sperm (*sperma*) 40, 65, 94, 96-7
spermatic duct 198 (*see* seminal
duct)
spermatic veins described by
Diogenes 79
Speusippus 108
spleen 130
Stagira 149
sterility: of mules 57, 63-4; of
women 13, 38, 43
stoicheia 117

Stoics 61, 80, 170, 225; physics of
112
Strato of Lampsacus 179, 214-15
Stratonice, stepson's passion for
182
stupidity (*amathia*), disorder of
the soul according to Plato 145
styloid process 205
Suda, the 69
sunanastomōses 210, 216
supernatural causation 37-8,
40-1, 44-6, 100
taboo 184, 186-7, 190, 217
teleology 116-17, 121, 128-30,
132, 135, 147-8, 161, 171
testes, testicles 40, 197-8 (*see
didymoi*)
tetanus (opisthotonos) 144-5
Thales 30, 63, 85-6
Theaetetus, theoretical
construction of regular solids
121
Theophrastus 16, 48, 51, 53, 68,
76-8, 163-4, 179, 220-1
thorax 129
Thrasymachus 115
Thucydides 15, 18, 23, 33-4, 185
thunder and lightning 1, 30-1
(*see Keraunobrontēs*)
thunderbolt 31, 41
Timaeus 118-19, 126-8, 130,
135-6, 141
Timaeus, the 58, 61, 80, 109, 111-
14, 116-18, 120, 128, 131, 133,
135, 140-1, 144-5, 151-3, 166
tissues, formation of 130-4 (*see
also* bone, marrow)
torcular Herophili 205
triangles 130-1, 134; right-angled
isosceles 122, 124; right-angled
scalene 123-4
Tricca (see Asclepius) 23
tripartite psychology 166
triplokia tōn angeiōn 216
trophē 201
twins, born from single
intercourse 95-6

uterus 96, 198

varix-like assistants (*parastatai kirsoeideis*) 198
Varro 21
vascular system 166, 191, 197, 199, 205, 216 (*see also* blood vessels)
vasa deferentia 198
veins: ovarian 199; portal 197; pulmonary (= 'artery resembling a vein', *artēria phlebōdēs, arteria venalis*) 199-200, 202, 206; spermatic 79; subclavian 199; 'varicose' 39, 198; *vena cava* (hollow vein) 135, 166-7, 170, 199, 207, 216
vena arterialis 200 (*see phleps artēriōdēs*, the pulmonary artery)
vena cava 135, 166-7, 199, 216
ventricles: of brain 171, 211; of heart 169-71, 174, 200, 216

Vesalius 170, 177, 189; *De humani corporis fabrica* 177
Vindicianus 75, 162, 171, 198
vision theories: of Democritus 68 of Diogenes 78; of Empedocles 72
vivisection: animal 188-9, 210, 217; human 2, 181, 184-5, 188-90, 217, 219 (*see also* 59, 61, 179, 212)

water 64-5, 71-2, 86-8, 90, 106-7, 109, 115, 118-19, 124-8, 131-2, 136, 142, 151, 155-8, 222-3, 225-6
womb 11, 42, 56, 95-7, 161, 218

Xenophanes of Colophon 51, 101, 103

Zeno of Elea 63
Zeno, disciple of Herophilus 204
Zeus 12-13, 15-16, 18, 29-31, 46